THE KAISER

This is a collection of innovative essays examining the role of Wilhelm II in Imperial Germany, focusing in particular on the later years of the monarch's reign. The essays highlight the Kaiser's relationship with statesmen and rulers, at home and abroad; his role in international relations; the erosion of his power during the First World War; and his ultimate downfall in 1918.

The book demonstrates the extent to which Wilhelm II was able to exercise 'personal rule', largely unopposed by the responsible government, and supported in his decision-making by his influential entourage. But it also shows that there was no lack of contemporary critics of Wilhelm and *Wilhelminismus*. The essays are based on the latest research and on a wide range of archival sources, and provide an up-to-date evaluation of the role and importance of this controversial monarch. They have been written to honour the innovative work of John Röhl, Wilhelm II's most famous biographer, on his sixty-fifth birthday.

ANNIKA MOMBAUER is Lecturer in European History, The Open University. Her previous publications include *Helmuth von Moltke and the Origins of the First World War* (Cambridge 2001), and *The Origins of the First World War. Controversies and Consensus* (Longman 2002).

WILHELM DEIST was Honorary Professor in the History Department, Albert-Ludwigs-Universität Freiburg, Germany. His many books include *The Wehrmacht and German Rearmament* (Macmillan 1981) and *Militär, Staat und Gesellschaft* (Oldenbourg 1991).

THE KAISER

*New Research on Wilhelm II's role
in Imperial Germany*

EDITED BY

ANNIKA MOMBAUER AND WILHELM DEIST

CAMBRIDGE
UNIVERSITY PRESS

PUBLISHED BY THE PRESS SYNDICATE OF THE UNIVERSITY OF CAMBRIDGE
The Pitt Building, Trumpington Street, Cambridge, United Kingdom

CAMBRIDGE UNIVERSITY PRESS
The Edinburgh Building, Cambridge, CB2 2RU, UK
40 West 20th Street, New York, NY 10011–4211, USA
477 Williamstown Road, Port Melbourne, VIC 3207, Australia
Ruiz de Alarcón 13, 28014 Madrid, Spain
Dock House, The Waterfront, Cape Town 8001, South Africa

http://www.cambridge.org

First published 2003

Printed in the United Kingdom at the University Press, Cambridge

Typeface Adobe Garamond 10/12.5 pt.   *System* LATEX 2ε   [TB]

A catalogue record for this book is available from the British Library

Library of Congress Cataloguing in Publication data
The Kaiser : new research on Wilhelm II's role in imperial Germany / edited by
Annika Mombauer and Wilhelm Deist.
p.   cm.
Includes bibliographical references and index.
ISBN 0 521 82408 7
1. William II, German Emperor, 1859–1941.   2. Germany – Kings and rulers – Biography.
3. Germany – Politics and government – 1888–1918.   4. Germany – Military policy.
5. Germany – Foreign relations – 1888–1918.   I. Mombauer, Annika.   II. Deist, Wilhelm.
DD229.K33   2003
940.08′4′092 – dc21   2003051523

ISBN 0 521 82408 7

Dedicated to John C. G. Röhl
on the occasion of his sixty-fifth birthday
31 May 2003

Contents

Notes on contributors

HOLGER AFFLERBACH is DADD Professor of German History at Emory University, Atlanta. He has spent several years at German, Italian, and Austrian universities, as well as in spring 2001 as Visiting Fellow at the University of Sussex in Great Britain. Among his book publications are the political biography of the Prussian War Minister and Chief of General Staff *Erich von Falkenhayn*, Munich 1994, second edition 1996; his study of the Triple Alliance, entitled '*Der Dreibund'. Europäische Grossmacht- und Allianzpolitik vor dem Ersten Weltkrieg*, Vienna 2002; and his book on the history of the Atlantic published under the title *Das entfesselte Meer*, Munich 2002; an edition of the diaries and letters of two generals of the First World War under the title *Kaiser Wilhelm II. als Oberster Kriegsherr während des Ersten Weltkrieges – Quellen aus der militärischen Umgebung des Kaisers* is in preparation.

VOLKER R. BERGHAHN is Seth Low Professor of History at Columbia University. His research interests are in modern German and European history. His publications include *Der Tirpitz-Plan. Genesis und Verfall einer innenpolitischen Krisenstrategie unter Wilhelm II*, Düsseldorf 1971; *Germany and the Approach of War in 1914*, London 1973, 2nd edn 1993; *Militarism. The History of an International Debate. 1861–1979*, Leamington Spa 1981; co-edited with Wilhelm Deist, *Rüstung im Zeichen wilhelminischer Weltpolitik. Grundlegende Dokumente 1890–1914*, Düsseldorf 1988; co-authored with Paul J. Friedrich, *Otto A. Friedrich. Ein politischer Unternehmer*, Frankfurt 1993; *Imperial Germany 1871–1914. Economy, Society, Culture and Politics*, Oxford 1994; *America and the Intellectual Cold Wars in Europe*, Princeton 2001; and *Europa im Zeitalter der beiden Weltkriege*, Frankfurt 2002.

WILHELM DEIST was Emeritus Professor at the University of Freiburg, Germany, and chaired the *Arbeitskreis Militärgeschichte* until 2002. His numerous publications include *Flottenpolitik und Flottenpropaganda. Das*

Nachrichtenbüro des Reichsmarineamtes, 1897–1914, Stuttgart 1976; *The German Military in the Age of Total War*, Leamington Spa 1985; 'The Rearmament of the Wehrmacht', in Militärgeschichtliches Forschungsamt (ed.), *Germany and the Second World War*, vol. I, *The Build-up of German Aggression*, Oxford 1990, pp. 373–540; 'Die Reichswehr und der Krieg der Zukunft', *Militärgeschichtliche Mitteilungen* 1 (1989); *Militär, Staat und Gesellschaft. Studien zur preußisch-deutschen Militärgeschichte*, Munich 1991; 'The German Army, the Authoritarian Nation-state and Total War', in John Horne (ed.), *State, Society and Mobilization in Europe during the First World War*, Cambridge 1997. Wilhelm Deist died in June 2003 just before this volume was finished.

MICHAEL EPKENHANS is director of the Otto-von-Bismarck Stiftung in Friedrichsruh, and teaches history at the University of Hamburg. His publications include *Die wilhelminische Flottenrüstung 1908–1914. Weltmachtstreben, industrieller Fortschritt, soziale Integration*, Munich 1991; 'Die kaiserliche Marine im Ersten Weltkrieg: Weltmacht oder Untergang?', in Wolfgang Michalka (ed.), *Der Erste Weltkrieg*, Munich 1994; and 'Military-Industrial Relations in Imperial Germany', *War in History*, forthcoming. He is currently working on a biography of Admiral von Tirpitz and on an edition of the private papers of Vice Admiral Hopman.

RAGNHILD FIEBIG-VON HASE, now retired, studied at Cologne University, and taught at the Institute of Anglo-American History, Cologne University, and the Department for Political Science at Tübingen University. Her publications include *Lateinamerika als Konfliktherd der deutsch-amerikanischen Beziehungen, 1890–1903. Vom Beginn der Panamerikapolitik bis zur Venezuelakrise von 1902/03*, Schriftenreihe der Historischen Kommission bei der Bayerischen Akademie der Wissenschaften 27, Göttingen, 1986; with Ursula Lehmkuhl (eds.), *Enemy Images in American History*, Providence, RI and Oxford 1997; and with Jürgen Heideking (eds.), *Zwei Wege in die Moderne. Aspekte der deutsch-amerikanischen Beziehungen, 1900–1918*, Trier 1998.

ISABEL V. HULL teaches History at Cornell University. Her publications include *The Entourage of Kaiser Wilhelm II, 1888–1918*, Cambridge 1982; *German Nationalism and the European Response, 1890–1945*, co-edited with Carole Fink and MacGregor Knox, Norman, OK 1985; and *Sexuality, State and Civil Society in Germany, 1700–1815*, Ithaca, NY 1996, as well as numerous articles (*Central European History, Journal of Contemporary*

History) and chapters in edited volumes. She is currently writing a book entitled *Military Culture and 'Final Solutions' in Imperial Germany*.

KATHARINE A. LERMAN is Senior Lecturer in Modern European History at London Metropolitan University. Her research interests are in Bismarckian and Wilhelmine Germany, in imperial German high politics and decision-making, and the history of Berlin. Her publications include *Bernhard von Bülow and the Governance of Germany 1900–1909*, Cambridge 1990; 'Bismarck's Heir: Chancellor Bernhard von Bülow and the National Idea 1890–1918', in J. Breuilly (ed.), *The State of Germany*, London 1992; 'Kaiser Wilhelm II: Last Emperor of Imperial Germany', in P. Catterall and R. Vinen (eds.), *Europe 1870–1914*, Oxford 1994; 'Bismarckian Germany and the Structure of the German Empire' and 'Wilhelmine Germany', in M. Fulbrook (ed.), *German History since 1800*, London 1997. Her forthcoming book on Bismarck will be published as part of Pearson's Profiles in Power series.

RODERICK R. McLEAN taught history at Northampton University College, the University of Edinburgh, and the University of Glasgow, before entering the Civil Service. His publications include (with Matthew Seligmann) *Germany from Reich to Republic, 1871–1918: Politics, Hierarchy and Elites*, London 2000; *Royalty and Diplomacy in Europe, 1890–1914*, Cambridge 2001; 'Kaiser Wilhelm II and his Hessian Cousins: Intra-state Relations in the German Empire and International Dynastic Politics, 1890–1918', in *German History* 19, 1 (2001), pp. 28–53; 'Kaiser Wilhelm II and the British Royal Family: Anglo-German Dynastic Relations in their Political Context, 1890–1914', in *History* (forthcoming). He has also contributed to the *New Dictionary of National Biography*, forthcoming, Oxford.

ANNIKA MOMBAUER is a lecturer in European history at The Open University. She completed her doctorate with John Röhl in 1998. Her publications include *Helmuth von Moltke and the Origins of the First World War*, Cambridge 2001 and *The Origins of the First World War: Controversies and Consensus*, London, 2002, as well as articles and essays, including 'The German General Staff and the July Crisis of 1914', *War in History*, 4 (1999), pp. 417–46; 'Helmuth von Moltke and the Battle of the Marne', in M. Seligmann and M. Hughes (eds.); *The First World War. Personalities in Conflict*, Barnsley 2000.

HARTMUT POGGE VON STRANDMANN teaches nineteenth- and twentieth-century European History at the University of Oxford and is Official Fellow and Praelector at University College, Oxford. He has published several articles on Rathenau and has edited *Walther Rathenau. Industrialist, Banker, Intellectual, and Politician. Notes and Diaries 1907–1922*, Oxford 1967, repr. 1988. His more recent publications include *The European Revolutions from 1848–1849. From Reform to Reaction* (together with R. J. W. Evans), Oxford 2001; 'The Role of British and German Historians in Mobilizing Public Opinion in 1914', in Benedikt Stuchtey and Peter Wende (eds.), *British and German Historiography 1750–1950. Traditions, Perceptions, and Transfers*, Oxford 2000; and 'Nationalisierungsdruck und königliche Namensänderung in England. Das Ende der Großfamilie europäischer Dynastien', in Gerhard A. Ritter und Peter Wende (eds.), *Rivalität und Partnerschaft. Studien zu den deutsch-britischen Beziehungen im 19. und 20. Jahrhundert*, Festschrift für Anthony J. Nicholls, Paderborn 1999.

MATTHEW SELIGMANN is a Senior Lecturer in modern world history at University College Northampton. He is author of *Rivalry in Southern Africa, 1893–99*, London 1998; co-author of *Germany from Reich to Republic, 1870–1918*, London 2000; co-editor of *Leadership in Conflict 1914–1918*, Barnsley 2000; co-author of *Does Peace Lead to War? Peace Settlements and Conflict in the Modern Age*, Stroud 2002; and author of scholarly articles in *The English Historical Review, German History, Imago Mundi, Imperial War Museum Review*, and *Journal of Strategic Studies*. He is currently working on British intelligence assessments of Germany before the First World War.

BERND SÖSEMANN teaches at the Freie Universität Berlin, where he is also Director of the Institute for the History of Communications and Applied Cultural Sciences. His publications include the scholarly edition *Theodor Wolff. Tagebücher 1914–1918. Der Erste Weltkrieg und die Entstehung der Weimarer Republik in Tagebüchern, Leitartikeln und Briefen des Chefredakteurs am 'Berliner Tageblatt' und Mitbegründer der 'Deutschen Demokratischen Partei'*, 2 vols., Boppard-am-Rhein 1984; *Theodor Wolff. Ein Leben für die Zeitung*, Düsseldorf 2000; and most recently *Der Nationalsozialismus und die deutsche Gesellschaft*, Stuttgart 2002; and *Kommunikation und Medien in Preußen vom 16. bis zum 19. Jahrhundert*, Stuttgart 2002, as well as numerous articles and chapters in essay collections.

JONATHAN STEINBERG is Walter H. Annenberg Professor of Modern European History at Pennsylvania University, and an expert in the history of the German and Austrian Empires, Nazi Germany, Fascist Italy, and Modern Jewish history. He recently moved to Pennsylvania after more than thirty years at Cambridge University. He has written on twentieth-century Germany, Italy, Austria, and Switzerland and has also prepared the official report on the Deutsche Bank's gold transactions in the Second World War. His publications include *Yesterday's Deterrent. Tirpitz and the Birth of the German Battle Fleet*, London 1965; 'The Copenhagen Complex', *Journal of Contemporary History*, 1/3 (July 1966); 'Diplomatie als Wille und Vorstellung: Die Berliner Mission Lord Haldanes im Februar 1912', in H. Schottelius and W. Deist (eds.), *Marine und Marinepolitik im Kaiserlichen Deutschland 1871–1914*, Düsseldorf 1972; *Why Switzerland*, 2nd edn, Cambridge 1996; *All or Nothing: The Axis and the Holocaust, 1941–1943*, London and New York, 1990, 2nd edn 2002; *Deutsche, Italiener und Juden. Der italienische Widerstand gegen den Holocaust*, Göttingen 1994, 1997; *Tutto o Niente. L'Asse e gli Ebrei nei territori occupati 1941–1943*, Milan 1997.

MATTHEW STIBBE teaches European history at Sheffield Hallam University. He completed his doctorate with John Röhl in 1997, and his research interests are in late nineteenth- and twentieth-century German history. His publications include *German Anglophobia in the First World War*, Cambridge 2001; 'Kaiser Wilhelm II. The Hohenzollerns at War', in M. Seligmann and M. Hughes (eds.), *The First World War. Personalities in Conflict*, Barnsley 2000; and articles in historical journals. He is now working on a history of women in Nazi Germany, due to be published by Arnold in 2003.

Acknowledgements

The editors would like to thank their editor at Cambridge University Press, William Davies, for his enthusiastic support of this volume, and Diana Göbel for her help in proof-reading the manuscript.

Even a *Festschrift* is subject to strict word limits, and the editors regret that it was unfortunately not possible to approach everyone who would have liked to add a contribution to this volume as a way of congratulating John Röhl on the occasion of his sixty-fifth birthday.

A. M. and W. D.
May 2003

Postscript

Sadly, Wilhelm Deist did not live to see the completion of this volume. Until the end, he worked tirelessly on this and other projects, and despite his severe illness, he was determined to contribute to the making of this *Festschrift* for his friend John Röhl. Wilhelm Deist's death in June 2003 is a great loss to his family, friends, and colleagues, but also to German history. It has been a privilege and a pleasure working with him, and I am extremely grateful to him for his enthusiastic support of this volume over the last two years.

Annika Mombauer
July 2003

Abbreviations

AA	Auswärtiges Amt
AA-PA	Auswärtiges Amt, Politische Abteilung
AEG	Allgemeine Elektrizitäts-Gesellschaft
BA	Bundesarchiv
BA-MA	Bundesarchiv-Militärarchiv
BD	*British Documents on the Origins of the War*
DDF	*Documents Diplomatiques Français*
EK	*Eulenburgs Politische Korrespondenz*
FO	Foreign Office
FRUS	*Papers Relating to the Foreign Relations of the United States*
GLA	General-Landesarchiv
GP	*Die Große Politik der Europäischen Kabinette 1871–1914*
GStA	Geheimes Staatsarchiv
HHSA	Haus-, Hof- und Staatsarchiv
HP	Holstein Papers
HSA	Hauptstaatsarchiv
IWM	Imperial War Museum
LC	Library of Congress
MGM	*Militärgeschichtliche Mitteilungen*
N, NL	Nachlass
NA	National Archives
NAZ	*Norddeutsche Allgemeine Zeitung*
NFMG	Notes from Foreign Missions, Germany
NPZ	*Neue Preussische Kreuz-Zeitung*
OHL	Oberste Heeresleitung
PA	Politisches Archiv
PAAA	Politisches Archiv des Auswärtigen Amtes
PRO	Public Record Office
RA	Royal Archives
SA	Staatsarchiv
SPD	Sozialdemokratische Partei Deutschlands
VStNA	Vereinigte Staaten von Nord-Amerika

Introduction

Annika Mombauer and Wilhelm Deist

In March 1960 Gerhard Ritter noted in the preface to the second volume of his work *Staatskunst und Kriegshandwerk* that during his studies of the Wilhelmine era he had become aware of 'much darker shadows' than his generation and that of his academic teachers had considered possible.[1] Following more than forty years of intensive research, this dark vision has noticeably expanded and has been put into even sharper relief – and as such is in stark contrast with accounts of the Kaiserreich which focus on developments in the economy, in industry and technology, the sciences and culture. The shadows apply to aspects of the Reich's constitutional law, and to its political structures and their consequences which, according to Wolfgang Mommsen, have resulted in a 'relatively high immobility of the . . . system'.[2]

A significant factor of that system, however – Wilhelm II as German Kaiser – embodied anything but immobility. His incessant activity necessarily had to lead to tensions whose general and specific effects within the system, and within society as a whole, have by no means yet been analysed to a sufficient degree by historians. The following volume presents a further step in that direction. Based to a large extent on new archival sources, the essays in this collection illuminate different aspects of Wilhelm II's 'personal rule', both in domestic and foreign policy, focusing particularly on the time after the turn of the century when the monarch was increasingly confronted by national and international limitations to his desire to rule Germany personally.

John Röhl, the historian to whom this volume is dedicated, has been striving for decades to understand and explain the Kaiser's role, making extensive use of the indispensable tools of the trade: written contemporary

[1] Gerhard Ritter, *Staatskunst und Kriegshandwerk. Das Problem des 'Militarismus' in Deutschland*, vol. II, *Die Hauptmächte Europas und das wilhelminische Reich (1890–1914)*, Munich 1960, p. 8.
[2] Wolfgang J. Mommsen, 'Die latente Krise des Wilhelminischen Reiches', in his *Der autoritäre Nationalstaat. Verfassung, Gesellschaft und Kultur im deutschen Kaiserreich*, Frankfurt 1990, p. 291.

evidence and their judicious interpretation. In the second volume of his impressively wide-ranging biography of Wilhelm II, he has described the monarch's intentions by the term 'personal monarchy'. Quite apart from the irrational idea that a rapidly developing industrial nation like Germany, with her complex economic and social structures, could be ruled by a quasi-absolutist monarchical regime, any such attempt was already bound to fail because of the Kaiser's personality, as John Röhl has already clearly demonstrated in his many publications on the subject.

However, despite such shortcomings of personality, it cannot be denied that, in the first decade of his rule, Wilhelm II managed to approach his goal in regard to important decisions. In his disputes with Chancellor Bismarck in the spring of 1890 a decisive role was played by the cabinet order of 8 September 1852, according to which Prussian ministers were only allowed to report to the monarch in the presence of the Prussian Minister President. Only if this were adhered to – claimed Bismarck – could he accept responsibility for governmental policy, and he demanded that the same should apply to the State Secretaries of the Reich *vis-à-vis* the Chancellor. With Wilhelm's decisive refusal to go along with this suggestion (favouring instead a so-called *Immediatsystem* in which his subordinates reported only to him), his 'personal regime' was ushered in, while at the same time the Prussian state ministry as an advising and decision-making institution was stripped of its political power, as would be demonstrated during the 1890s.

Wilhelm consciously combined this *Immediatsystem* in Prussia's and the Reich's civilian executive with a military equivalent, based on his extra-constitutional right to command the army (*Kommandogewalt*), a decision that had grave consequences not only for personnel policy, but also for the political culture and structure of the Reich. On the one hand, Wilhelm II thus managed to secure his power over the military and civilian leadership and effectively exercised his own personnel policy with the help of his cabinets. On the other hand, this very leadership found itself in a position of dependency on the monarch which far exceeded the loyalty that was normally accorded a head of state. The result was Byzantinism in the Kaiser's immediate and wider surroundings, a fact which finally, albeit to a lesser extent, also began to affect the country's middle classes, and that was repeatedly criticized by contemporaries. The effects of this system on the Berlin administration are highlighted by Katharine Lerman's contribution to this volume. But the Kaiser's public addresses, his desire for public celebration and recognition, and his sometimes ridiculous self-display, already began to ring hollow before the war, and aside from the sycophants and courtiers, there was increasing public criticism, as Bernd Sösemann's study of the media's perception of public celebrations in the pre-war years demonstrates.

For the statesmen and government officials who had to work within this *Immediatsystem*, a further consequence was the fact that each concentrated solely on the task they had been given, thus losing sight of the overall picture. As a consequence, for example, Schlieffen was able to develop his operational plan without the need to consider political or economic realities or possibilities, while at the same time Tirpitz developed his own plan for a battle fleet. Yet there never was any attempt to co-ordinate both initiatives, least of all subjugate them to a general strategic concept, and neither Schlieffen nor Tirpitz considered it important to discuss his plan with the other. The navy played a particularly important role in the Kaiser's scheme, and here he felt in his element when it came to decision-making, as Michael Epkenhans outlines. But the Kaiser also considered himself a military man, and often attempted to circumvent responsible politicians and diplomats with the help of his military entourage. An example of this was the way he sought to instrumentalize military attachés, as Matthew Seligmann's study of British attachés demonstrates.

According to his own conviction, only the Kaiser had responsibility for co-ordinating the political actions of the Reich's executive, and yet he failed totally in this role. Detrimentally, the Reich did not possess – particularly due to the monarch's claims to personal rule – any other co-ordinating body that could have taken over this task. The Kaiser's infamous order of 1 August 1914 to send 'his troops' east is another perfect example of the ill-effects of his personal rule. The episode demonstrates both how he understood his role as supreme warlord of the army (whose right it was to give such orders), and the fact that he was completely unaware of the army's strategic plans (which at that time no longer included a contingency plan for a deployment in the east). Unaware of the details of German war planning, and even having been deliberately kept in the dark about some of its details, he nonetheless reserved for himself the right to give such orders.

Personnel decisions, like the search for a suitable successor to Chancellor Bethmann Hollweg during the war, are another example of the way Wilhelm II exercised power. As Holger Afflerbach's analysis of the Kaiser's role as supreme warlord during the war illustrates, the process of elimination until one had arrived at a candidate that Wilhelm did not object to (even if only on the basis of a proposed candidate's short frame!) stood in no relation to the significance of appointing the fifth successor to Bismarck.

It is this which John Röhl has aptly termed the Kaiser's 'negative personal rule'.[3]

Such examples demonstrate that Wilhelm II's will to rule, as epitomized in the idea of 'personal monarchy', resulted in a ruling structure of an essentially polycratic nature which made it impossible to speak generally of a unified government. Even Bülow's concept of 'Weltpolitik' became an illusion, as is demonstrated by Annika Mombauer's account of the Kaiser's role in the events surrounding the China expedition of 1900, and by Roderick McLean's discussion of the events and results of the Björkö agreement. Wilhelm's often ridiculous behaviour in relation to other monarchs and rulers emerges from these accounts, and particularly starkly from Ragnhild Fiebig-von Hase's investigation of the relationship between Wilhelm II and Roosevelt in the pre-war years.

Finally, the First World War became the nemesis for this system of government. Although Wilhelm II remained the indispensable tip of the pyramid of power, in terms of his actual power only the realm of personnel decisions remained, while the Kaiser increasingly lost his symbolic, unifying power. At the very end, in November 1918, as Isabel Hull outlines, Wilhelm managed to avoid being instrumentalized by the officer corps of his army (normally the actual guarantor of the Hohenzollern monarchy) by refusing to sacrifice himself for the greater good of Germany by seeking death in the battlefield by way of a 'death ride'. Nor was he willing to abdicate, even if this might have been a way of preserving the Prussian monarchy. Wilhelm's role during the First World War is further illuminated by Matthew Stibbe's account of the Kaiser's part in the decision for unlimited submarine warfare, while Hartmut Pogge von Strandmann highlights some of the criticisms of the Kaiser that were voiced after the war in his study of Walther Rathenau's critical position *vis-à-vis* the monarch.

During the forty years that John Röhl has studied the Kaiser, his choice of subject was at times very much out of favour with many critics and colleagues, but it is now once again in vogue. It is to no small extent due to John Röhl's efforts that it is becoming increasingly difficult to write the history of Wilhelmine Germany without the Kaiser. In that context, Jonathan Steinberg's *Laudatio* evaluates John Röhl's contribution to our knowledge of Imperial Germany, while Volker Berghahn's contribution provides an overview of recent historiographical debates and points the way forward for further studies of Wilhelmine Germany.

---

[3] John C. G. Röhl, *Kaiser, Hof und Staat*, Munich, 4th edn 1995, p. 126.

Perhaps the most important task of any biographer of Wilhelm II is to explain how the German Empire ended up in the catastrophe that would spell its downfall: the First World War. In his many publications, John Röhl has already outlined the Kaiser's crucial role in influencing German decision-making. In many ways, his forthcoming third volume, focusing in much more detail on the Kaiser in those significant pre-war years, is the most important, and the one most eagerly awaited by other historians of Wilhelmine Germany.

To congratulate John Röhl on the occasion of his sixty-fifth birthday, a number of his friends and former students undertook to examine aspects of Wilhelm II's rule in those crucial later years, and the following contributions demonstrate across a wide range of topics how important it is to write the history of Wilhelmine Germany with due consideration for the country's last monarch. The editors and authors of this volume are looking forward with high expectations to further results of John Röhl's impressive biography and wish him the necessary strength to complete this important work. They hope that their own contributions to the study of Wilhelm II in this volume may have added to it in a small way.

Reflections on John Röhl: a Laudatio

Jonathan Steinberg

My ancient *Dr Smith's Smaller Latin–English Dictionary* defines a *Laudatio* as 'a praising commendation, a eulogy or a panegyric', and that is what I intend to write in the next few pages. This pleasant task has its difficulties. I have no distance, either temporal or personal, from the subject. I propose to comment on the work of a distinguished colleague, who is a direct contemporary (we started graduate study together) and a friend. I am also quite unashamedly an admirer. What John Röhl has accomplished demands that 'praising commendation' which Dr Smith suggested. His is an unusual career, which indeed deserves to be heartily commended.

The electronic catalogue at the University of Pennsylvania's Van Pelt Library lists eleven titles under John Röhl's name. All of them deal with the political history of the German Empire from 1888 to 1918. John Röhl has spent his entire career and his very considerable intellectual energies on 'Germany after Bismarck', as he called his first book. Thirty years of history have been the subject of nearly forty years of research and writing. The ratio of life to subject must be unusual, though not unique. In American history, crowded with practitioners as it is, careers spent on the Civil War, Jacksonian Democracy, the New Deal or the Second World War occur frequently and there the ratio of life to subject is even more dramatic. On the other hand, the scale of events like the American Civil War or the New Deal and the number of participants compensate for the brevity of the period; breadth makes up for length.

The Röhl case is different. To say that John Röhl has concentrated on thirty years of German history understates the peculiar character of his enterprise. In effect, he has worked exclusively on Kaiser Wilhelm II and his part in German history. In his first book he looked at the way government worked in the early years of the Kaiser's reign. The first seventy pages of *Germany without Bismarck* offer as sharp and lucid an analysis of the ramshackle structures that Bismarck bequeathed to his successor as can be found anywhere.[1] It is elegantly and lucidly written and retains a vividness that the older among us can only wish for in our own works. Take a typical passage, chosen literally at random:

> As Bismarck grew older, the Government's dilemma presented itself with increasing clarity. Bismarck's autocracy was intolerable and his pedantic insistence on formal distinctions seriously hindered efficient government. There was a widespread feeling that the Government must accustom itself to take decisions collectively, as other governments did. And yet Bismarck's autocracy was necessary to hold the conglomerate departments together.[2]

The Bismarckian legacy has rarely been so neatly summarized. The Kaiser inherited the problem, and, with the interlude of the Weimar Republic, so did Hitler. The legacy of the 'genius-statesman' led to the atrophy of those collective habits of consultation which marked the evolution of other European bureaucracies. The scramble for the attention of the 'All-Highest' in the Kaiser's day was simply a transformation of those traditions of absolutism which Bismarck had himself inherited and which reached back to the time when the young Friedrich II in 1740 abolished the Tabakskollegium of his father and put an abrupt end to consultative procedures. Interminable committee meetings, mountains of minutes, and ponderous decision-making no doubt are bad things but they prevent worse ones, as the catastrophes of Prusso-German history only too vividly illustrate. If every petty bureaucrat 'works toward the Führer', as Ian Kershaw has taught us to think, a Hobbesian war of all agents within government against all other agents must result. Radical solutions, dramatic initiatives, and hare-brained schemes help to grab attention in the competition for 'All-Highest' decision. Contradictory forces push the government out from steady policies and produce uncertain lurches and unstable execution of those policies that survive. Lord Haldane reported to London in 1912 that above a certain level in German government there was 'chaos, absolute chaos'.

    In this sense Röhl's work has always been 'structural' and never entirely 'personalistic' as his critics of the 1970s complained. I recall, but cannot locate, a German review of one of John's books, which began 'der personalistische Ansatz John Röhls ist unhaltbar' (John Röhl's personalistic approach is untenable). Like many such lapidary judgements, time has undone it. During the 1960s and 1970s it sounded plausible, if sharply

---

[1] John C. G. Röhl, *Germany without Bismarck. The Crisis of Government in the Second Reich, 1890–1900*, London 1967.
[2] Ibid., p. 25.

formulated. Historiography occupied itself with 'forces and factors' and
not with human agents. It seemed odd even at the time that the twentieth century, which had been overshadowed by larger-than-life human
beings – Hitler, Stalin, Mussolini, Mao, Roosevelt, Churchill, De Gaulle –
should have spawned a generation of historians who rejected biography as
a tool. Perhaps the one had caused the other. In addition, a kind of diluted
Marxism mixed with prejudices about 'history from above' went with the
new plate-glass universities and their radical student activism to create an
attitude which led its holders to condemn the personal, the biographical,
and the political as reactionary by definition. 'History from above' meant
'politics from above'. Radicals rebelled against such structures in the political sphere and restored the presence of subaltern and forgotten groups
in their writing. The intellectual Right took a certain sardonic delight in
asserting the 'primacy of politics' as if they had discovered the ultimate
weapon in the battle of the books.

By the 1990s those lines of battle began to blur. The collapse of the communist bloc certainly accelerated the discrediting of all 'systematic' theories
of social and historical causation, especially those which relied on imper-
sonal factors like class and other socio-economic categories. Purely socio-
economic arguments faltered in the presence of the murder of the Jews.
Structuralists had a hard time finding socio-economic causes for the policy.
Even Nazi bureaucrats themselves, especially those in the economic ministries, despaired of a regime which murdered vital artisans in the occupied
Soviet Union because they were Jewish. How could economic rationality
be used to explain the way the SS in 1944 exterminated the Jewish diamond
cutters in an SS-owned diamond business?[3] Something was going on that
purely analytic categories could not explain. As Jane Caplan shrewdly ob-
serves in her introduction to Tim Mason's *Nazism, Fascism and the Working
Class*, even Mason, the most brilliant of the British Marxist historians of
Germany, could not find an inner rationality in the murder of the Jews:

> He admitted that he was psychologically incapable of dealing with the record
> of inhumanity and suffering generated by Nazi anti-Semitism, and subjecting it
> to the kind of critical analysis that he believed was the only path to historical
> comprehension.[4]

[3] Christian Gerlach, *Kalkulierte Morde: die deutsche Wirtschafts- und Vernichtungspolitik in Weissrussland 1941 bis 1944*, Hamburg 2000, p. 292 and Walter Naasner, *Neue Machtzentren in der deutschen Kriegswirtschaft, 1942–1945: die Wirtschaftsorganisation der SS, das Amt des Generalbevollmächtigten für den Arbeitseinsatz und das Reichsministerium für Bewaffnung und Munition, Reichsministerium für Rüstung und Kriegsproduktion im nationalsozialistischen Wirtschaftssystem*, Boppard am Rhein 1994, p. 367.
[4] Tim Mason, *Nazism, Fascism and the Working Class*, edited by Jane Caplan, Cambridge 1995, p. 22.

In the 1990s, biography emerged again as a major tool of historical analysis. In the twelve years since 1990 Ian Kershaw has produced his impressive two-volume study of Hitler,[5] Paul Preston his great biography of Franco,[6] Ulrich Herbert a study of Werner Best of the SS,[7] Joachim Fest a new biography of Albert Speer,[8] and in 2002 a brilliant new biography of Mussolini by Richard Bosworth was published.[9] Most of these historians started out as 'structural' historians, as Bosworth himself admits. They were scholars for whom analysis of forces and factors took precedence over the purely biographical. Nor has this been confined to historical writing. In philosophy, too, the biographical has begun to displace the purely analytical approach to the work. As Danny Postel wrote in a recent article in *The Chronicle of Higher Education*, the American equivalent of *The Times Higher Education Supplement*:

The past two decades have seen a veritable explosion in biographical studies of philosophers. Since 1982, more than 30 biographies of philosophers have appeared. Of those, 20 have been published in the past decade, a dozen just since 1999. And more are in the works. Some see the trend as principally a reflection of currents in the publishing world, while others say it is a direct result of conceptual shifts in philosophy and in intellectual life more generally. But as the books keep coming, sceptics remain unpersuaded that this biographical 'turn' is of any philosophical importance.[10]

John Röhl anticipated this 'biographical turn' almost by default. He found his subject in the 1960s and has not left it for four decades. When it was unfashionable, he did it; now that it has become fashionable, he still does it. The German edition of Röhl's huge new biography of Kaiser Wilhelm II appeared in 1993[11] and the English version in 1998.[12] Both versions run to nearly 1,000 pages with notes and bibliography and end on 15 June 1888, when Wilhelm's father, the ill-fated Friedrich III, died and Wilhelm became, as Röhl writes, 'German Kaiser and King of Prussia, Summus Episcopus and Supreme War Lord'.[13] His first act was to order the

---

[5] Ian Kershaw, *Hitler, 1889–1936: Hubris*, New York 1998; Ian Kershaw, *Hitler, 1936–45: Nemesis*, New York 2000.

[6] Paul Preston, *Franco: A Biography*, London 1993.

[7] Ulrich Herbert, *Best: biographische Studien über Radikalismus, Weltanschauung und Vernunft, 1903–1989*, Bonn 1996.

[8] Joachim C. Fest, *Speer: eine Biographie*, Berlin 1999.

[9] Richard J. B. Bosworth, *Mussolini*, London 2002.

[10] Danny Postel, 'The Life and the Mind', *The Chronicle of Higher Education*, 7 June 2002, p. A.16.

[11] John C. G. Röhl, *Wilhelm II, Die Jugend des Kaisers, 1859–1888*, Munich 1993.

[12] John C. G. Röhl, *Young Wilhelm: The Kaiser's Early Life, 1859–1888*, translated by Jeremy Gaines and Rebecca Wallach, Cambridge, UK and New York, 1998.

[13] Ibid., p. 824.

Charlottenburg guard to surround the palace to prevent his mother, the Empress Friedrich, from getting her and her husband's private papers out of the new Kaiser's control. It was an ominous opening to a fateful reign and the book ends with a prophecy from Friedrich von Holstein, the grey eminence of the German foreign office, who noted in his diary a month earlier:

Today the Kaiserin is reaping what she formerly sowed with her ostentatious contempt for everything that is German. But the people who are now gratuitously insulting the Kaiserin will get their own back under Wilhelm II; he will show them what a monarch is. That is the nemesis of world history.[14]

When I compare the grand new biography *Young Wilhelm* of 1998 with *Germany without Bismarck* of 1967, there is a subtle but marked shift of emphasis. The early book used the personalities to understand the structures of rule. The latest work aims

to set the characters on the stage and let them speak for themselves, which, in their abundant letters and diaries, the Victorians and Wilhelminians did with quite extraordinary clarity, colour and persuasive power – though of course without knowing their future, which is our past.[15]

Its central theme, Röhl writes, is the 'bitter conflict' between parents and child; in other words the biography tells a story and lets the reader get to know the personalities involved. Its impetus seems to me to lie much less than it once did in conventional historical matters – to what extent had Bismarck's constitutional arrangements failed even before he fell from power in 1890 – than in bringing to life the historical characters. In the preface to the German edition, Röhl quoted a maxim of Heraclitus, 'the soul of another person is a distant continent that cannot be visited or explored' and expressed the hope that he had 'managed to narrow the gap between ourselves and that "distant continent"'.[16]

In this last phrase we get close to what for me remains the enigma at the core of John Röhl's work: what has kept him fascinated and engaged in writing the same story over and over again? Is the Kaiser really that interesting? The quality of the prose in the latest work suggests quite unequivocally that for John Röhl he is. The thirty years between first and latest books have not dimmed his literary skills.

If any historian can be said to have an archival 'green thumb', John Röhl is the one. In the four decades of his research Röhl has collected tens of

---

[14] Friedrich von Holstein, *The Holstein Papers*, edited by Norman Rich and M. H. Fisher, Cambridge 1955–63, vol. II: *Diaries*, p. 377.
[15] Röhl, *Young Wilhelm*, p. xiii.   [16] Ibid.

thousands of documents and has got as complete an array of evidence as can be imagined. The prefaces to both German and English editions of the biography describe the rich archival sources which he has used and the bibliography lists the many personal collections and diaries on which the account rests. Because he has so much testimony he can weave primary sources seamlessly into the narrative. We hear the people of the time in their own tones of voice.

I imagine this grand enterprise building on its success. As he found more archives, he realized that more might yet be found and by the time he found the new sources, he became aware of yet more. What began as a choice became an artistic compulsion. Here was a story – dramatic, tragic, and historically important – which could be told in depth and from many angles. The sheer wealth of his material offered John Röhl an opportunity that few historians come near to achieving. He could tell the whole story.

His success can be measured by the sales of the German edition of the first volume of the biography, which have topped 20,000. The second volume *Wilhelm II. Der Aufbau der Persönlichen Monarchie 1888–1900* was published in 2001. At 1,437 pages it is 40 per cent longer but covers less than half the years. We can study Kaiser Wilhelm and his world in a vividness and detail that has few parallels in modern historiography. Röhl combines professional research with literary skill. Hence this is biography mediated by historical exactness. If historians naturally divide by temperament into storytellers and model-builders, John Röhl is a storyteller *par excellence* but, as so often in history, the consequences are unexpected. By telling the Kaiser's story in such detail, he creates a reality which becomes itself a new kind of model. John offers us an indirect structural analysis by telling us how monarchical power, personal intrigue, and human foibles merged at 'All-Highest' levels in late nineteenth- and twentieth-century Germany and how decisions were or were not made. To the German reading public he has given back the Kaiser; to students of Germany he has given the incomparable gift of living reality to think about. Both groups of readers have reason to praise John Röhl and his great achievement.

CHAPTER I

Wilhelm II and 'his' navy, 1888–1918

Michael Epkenhans

I

The uniform that the German Kaiser probably most loved was that of a British Admiral of the Fleet. Already as a child, when he had visited naval dockyards in Britain and Nelson's flagship *Victory* with his parents, he had been fascinated by the Royal Navy and both its great history and its achievements in making Britain the world's most powerful state and the supreme naval power in the nineteenth century. In order to emphasize his affection for the Royal Navy as well as the navy in general, one of his first acts after his appointment to the Royal Navy's highest rank was to have a picture painted showing him in this uniform and to present it to his grandmother, Queen Victoria. His pride and his vanity were so great that time and again he wore this uniform when he officially received the British ambassador to the court of Berlin.[1] Pride and vanity were, however, only one aspect of Wilhelm's strange 'love' of the Royal Navy. More importantly, following his appointment, the German Kaiser now even felt entitled to interfere with British naval matters, and, as John Röhl has described in great detail in his biography of Wilhelm II, did in fact do so whenever possible, however trivial the matter was in the end.[2]

Although German naval officers regarded this behaviour of their own 'supreme warlord' with deep contempt,[3] generally speaking, the latter's passion for the navy, which he had obviously 'inherited' from his mother and which had steadily grown during his visits to England as a child, was indeed a blessing for the nation's 'junior service'. For, when Wilhelm was a child, naval power did not seem very important in Germany. Both a

---

[1] Cf. Holger H. Herwig, *Das Elitekorps des Kaisers. Die Marineoffiziere im Wilhelminischen Deutschland*, Hamburg 1977, p. 34.
[2] See John C. G. Röhl, *Wilhelm II. Der Aufbau der Persönlichen Monarchie 1888–1900*, Munich 2001, pp. 127–35, 184–90.
[3] Cf. the diary of Captain Hopman, 4 May 1914, Bundesarchiv-Militärarchiv, henceforth abbreviated as BA-MA, Hopman papers N 326/10.

long-lasting tradition as a land power and the geographical situation in the centre of Europe, as well as the lack of important overseas interests, were responsible for the neglect of sea power.[4] After the unification of Germany in 1870/71, Imperial Germany was initially slow to build up a fleet. With regard to later interpretations of Germany's maritime ambitions, it is, of course, necessary to keep in mind that this fleet only ever aspired to second-class naval strength.[5] It is significant enough that it was commanded by army generals, Generals Stosch and Caprivi, until 1889. The small size of the navy and the operations plans, which were primarily aimed at defending the coast, at protecting commerce, and at supporting the army in case of war, as well as the poor state of the shipbuilding industry, further underscore the fact that sea power was not yet an aim in itself.

However, under Bismarck's chancellorship, it was very unlikely that the navy would ever play a more decisive role in political and military planning. In Bismarck's opinion, the precarious position of Germany in the centre of Europe required both a self-confident, though cautious, policy towards its neighbours and a powerful army to support it if need be. The validity of the doctrine that Germany's fate was to be decided on land and not on the high seas can best be illustrated by Bismarck's famous answer to a German explorer of the dark continent who tried to convince the Chancellor of the advantages of larger possessions in Africa: 'Your map of Africa is very nice', he answered, 'but my map of Africa lies here in Europe. Here lies Russia, and – pointing to the left – here lies France, and we are right in the middle; this is my map of Africa.'[6] Accordingly, the army was greatly increased twice within a few years, while the navy still lived from hand to mouth. In this respect, it is also significant that even General Caprivi, who had been Chief of the Admiralty until 1889, did not give naval development highest priority when he was appointed Chancellor after Bismarck's dismissal in 1890.[7]

---

[4] For a detailed survey of Germany's naval build-up see Volker R. Berghahn, *Der Tirpitz-Plan. Genesis und Verfall einer innenpolitischen Krisenstrategie unter Wilhelm II.*, Düsseldorf 1971. For a short description of German naval history in the nineteenth century see Wolfgang Petter, 'Deutsche Flottenrüstung von Wallenstein bis Tirpitz', in 'Deutsche Marinegeschichte der Neuzeit', in Militärgeschichtliches Forschungsamt (ed.), *Deutsche Militärgeschichte 1648–1939*, vol. v (repr.), Herrsching 1983, pp. 81–273; Werner Rahn, 'Die Kaiserliche Marine', in Karl-Volker Neugebauer (ed.), *Grundzüge der deutschen Militärgeschichte*, vol. 1, Freiburg 1993, pp. 225–31, and Ivo N. Lambi, *The Navy and German Power Politics, 1862–1914*, Boston, London, and Sydney 1984, *passim*.

[5] Cf. Lambi, *Navy*, pp. 3–30.

[6] Bismarck in a conversation with Eugen Wolff, 5 December 1888, quoted in Willy Andreas (ed.), *Bismarck – Gespräche*, vol. II: *Von der Reichsgründung bis zur Entlassung*, Birsfelden-Basel (no year), p. 525.

[7] Cf. Lambi, *Navy*, pp. 57–90.

II

Against this background the accession of Wilhelm II to the throne in 1888 did indeed mark the end of both a long era of land power thinking, and of the relative decline of the navy.[8] In contrast to his predecessors Wilhelm was the first member of the imperial family who was both really interested in naval affairs and willing to acknowledge the need for a powerful navy. As early as 1884, when he was still a young prince whose succession to one of the most important thrones in Europe still seemed a matter of the distant future, he had tried to convince Germany's 'Iron Chancellor' of the need to strengthen the country's naval forces. However, his suggestions for the enlargement of the navy, often accompanied by carefully designed drawings of battleships in action, were put aside by Bismarck, without being seriously considered.[9] And yet, only four years later, as a result of the early death of his father, Kaiser Friedrich III, Wilhelm II was in a position to redirect the course of German foreign as well as naval policy, and his first public speeches and decisions made clear that he was determined to exercise his powers in this respect.

In his first order to the armed forces upon ascending the throne on 15 June 1888, as well as in his opening speech to the Reichstag on 25 June 1888, Wilhelm II was the first Kaiser even to mention the navy, which, in the course of his reign, was to benefit greatly from this Imperial favour. In 1888, the victorious German army consisted of 19,294 officers and 468,409 non-commissioned officers and men in peacetime,[10] whereas the navy's total strength amounted to only 15,480 men, including 534 executive officers at the same time. The fleet itself consisted of 18 armour-clads and 8 large and 10 small cruising vessels.[11] Twenty-five years later, in 1913, when Wilhelm II celebrated his silver jubilee, the navy's strength had risen to 2,196 officers and 59,991 non-commissioned officers and men.[12] Moreover, the *Novelle* (amendment to the naval law) of 1912 had stipulated that the fleet was to consist of 61 capital ships, 40 small cruisers, 144 torpedo boats, and 72 submarines. In comparison to 1888, this was indeed a powerful military

---

[8] On the role of the Kaiser cf. ibid., pp. 3–39.

[9] Cf. Paul Heinsius, 'Bismarck legte Wilhelms Denkschrift zu den Privatakten. Wilhelm II. und seine Flottenskizzen', in Volker Plagemann (ed.), *Übersee. Seefahrt und Seemacht im deutschen Kaiserreich*, Munich 1988, pp. 207–8.

[10] Reichsarchiv (ed.), *Der Weltkrieg. Kriegsrüstung und Kriegswirtschaft*, Supplement vol. no. 1, Berlin 1930, p. 460.

[11] See Holger H. Herwig, *'Luxury' Fleet. The Imperial German Navy 1888–1918*, Atlantic Highlands, NJ (repr.) 1987, p. 15.

[12] See *Nauticus*, 16 (1914), pp. 27–8.

instrument, capable of both offensive and defensive warfare, though the army, for reasons which will be explained further below, was again to receive the lion's share of Germany's defence budget.

III

Doubtless this astonishing progress in Germany's naval build-up within one generation was in many respects the result of the Kaiser's passion for his 'mechanical toy', as Grand Admiral Tirpitz, many years later, in 1913, sarcastically put it to a close confidant.[13] But what were Wilhelm II's political aims, how did he try to achieve them, and, especially, which role did he assign to the navy in general and, above all, to himself in particular? These are difficult questions, for it seems that Wilhelm II, notwithstanding his often bellicose rhetoric or his great enthusiasm for naval affairs throughout his reign, had neither a precise, consistent idea of what he wanted, nor of how he was to achieve it. Moreover, in spite of his claim that he was both the Kaiser who re-established the decisive role of the monarch after Bismarck's 'dictatorship' as well as the nation's supreme warlord, again and again he also proved unable to co-ordinate the policy of 'his' government as well as of the different organizations of 'his' navy.[14]

In the early years of his reign Wilhelm II still seems to have favoured a mainly continental policy, for his main aim was to achieve 'some kind of Napoleonic supremacy in a peaceful manner', as he told one of his closest friends, Count Eulenburg, in 1892.[15] Against the background of a rapidly changing world, Wilhelm II soon came to regard a fundamental change in German foreign policy as a necessity. A number of crises in the Far East and in the Pacific Ocean had made him feel that 'without being a world power one was nothing but a poor appearance (*jämmerliche Figur*)'.[16] As a result he now openly began to demand specific islands and territories for Germany. As early as 1894 the British Ambassador to the imperial court, for

---

[13] Cf. the diary of Captain Hopman, entry of 4 January 1913, BA-MA, Hopman papers N 326/10.

[14] On this difficult and controversial subject see the instructive summaries by Isabel V. Hull, 'Persönliches Regiment', in John C. G. Röhl (ed.), *Der Ort Kaiser Wilhelms II. in der deutschen Geschichte*, Munich 1991, pp. 3–23; Wilhelm Deist, 'Kaiser Wilhelm II. als Oberster Kriegsherr', in ibid., pp. 25–42; John C. G. Röhl, 'Der "Königsmechanismus" im Kaiserreich', in his *Kaiser, Hof und Staat. Wilhelm II. und die deutsche Politik*, Munich 1987, pp. 116–40; Holger Afflerbach, 'Wilhelm II as Supreme Warlord in the First World War', *War in History*, 5 (1998), pp. 427–49 (now included in revised form in this volume, pp. 195–216).

[15] Wilhelm II to Count Eulenburg, July 1892, cited in Peter Winzen, 'Zur Genesis von Weltmachtkonzept und Weltpolitik', in Röhl, *Der Ort Kaiser Wilhelms II.*, p. 205; Röhl, *Wilhelm II.*, pp. 417–20.

[16] Wilhelm II to Count Eulenburg, 30 July 1893, cited in Röhl, *Wilhelm II.*, pp. 417–20.

example, reported that 'the Kaiser is known to be keenly in favour of the development and expansion of the German colonies'.[17] In early 1896, the Kaiser used the Transvaal crisis as a catalyst to announce his future policy. On 18 January 1896, at the ceremony commemorating the twenty-fifth anniversary of the founding of the German Empire, he proudly declared that the 'German Empire has become a world empire now'.[18] Against the background of many setbacks in the previous months, this statement was a somewhat bold attempt to show that he and 'his' country were no longer willing to accept that Germany was still inferior to Great Britain, whose 'place in the sun' excelled Germany's own many times.[19]

The driving motives behind the Kaiser's decision to change this situation by embarking on a new offensive course, which resulted in a far-reaching u-turn of German foreign policy in the mid-1890s, were, generally speaking, a mixture of personal aspirations, and both traditional power political and Social Darwinist convictions.[20] First, because of the nation's newly gained political, military, and economic strength, Wilhelm II regarded the acquisition of world-power status as a continuation of his grandfather's policy. While Wilhelm I had united Germany and had made it a Great Power with an almost hegemonic status on the continent, he wanted to transform it into one of the most powerful nations of the world. Second, in Wilhelm's eyes, becoming a world power of equal status was now a 'dire' necessity, for a new reapportioning of the world seemed imminent: 'Old empires pass away and new ones are in the process of being formed', he told an astonished audience in October 1899.[21] When he talked about 'dying empires', he did, however, not only mean the Spanish, Portuguese, Chinese and Ottoman Empires, but also the British Empire. To emphasize his concept of 'world policy' as well as his country's future position in the world, he exclaimed at the launching of the battleship *Wittelsbach* at Stettin that in his eyes world-power status meant that 'in distant areas [beyond the ocean], no important decision should be taken without Germany and the German Kaiser'.[22] This was, indeed, an ambitious aim, but what exactly

[17] Gosselin to Kimberley, 25 November 1894, cited ibid., pp. 206–7.   [18] Cited ibid., p. 1027.

[19] For a detailed description of the reorientation of Germany's foreign policy in the mid-1890s see Konrad Canis, *Von Bismarck zur Weltpolitik. Deutsche Außenpolitik 1890 bis 1902*, Berlin 1997, pp. 115–222.

[20] Cf. Röhl, *Wilhelm II.*, pp. 1028–72 and *passim*.

[21] See his speech in Hamburg, 18 October 1899, quoted in Ernst Johann (ed.), *Reden des Kaisers. Ansprachen, Predigten und Trinksprüche Wilhelms II.*, 2nd edn, Munich 1977, p. 83; cf. also Herwig, *'Luxury' Fleet*, p. 19.

[22] See the speech of Wilhelm II in Wilhelmshaven, 3 July 1900, quoted in Johann, *Reden des Kaisers*, p. 81.

it entailed remained rather vague throughout his reign. Only a few days after the Kaiser's speech at Stettin and more than four years after his public declaration of world policy at Berlin, Field Marshal Count Waldersee, formerly one of the Kaiser's closest friends and advisers, noted in his diary: 'We are supposed to pursue *Weltpolitik*. If I only knew what that is supposed to be; for the time being it is nothing but a slogan.'[23] Many years later the British Foreign Secretary, Sir Edward Grey, shared this opinion. To him as well as to many contemporaries, Wilhelm's behaviour still made it almost impossible to establish what he and the German Empire really wanted. Accordingly he rightly sighed: 'The German Kaiser is ageing me; he is like a battleship with steam up and screws going, but with no rudder, and he will run into something some day and cause a catastrophe.'[24] In spite of this vagueness of his ideas, which was one of the main characteristics of the Kaiser's personality, it seems justified to maintain that – as will be illustrated below – his most important aim was to follow Britain's example: while the latter had dominated the world in the eighteenth and nineteenth centuries, Germany, which he regarded as 'a young empire', was to take its place in the twentieth century.[25] Unfortunately, from his point of view, he still lacked the means which would enable him 'to speak a different language' in the future.[26]

Subsequently, in his eyes 'more ships' were the best and indeed the only solution to this problem. As he told his American friend Poultney Bigelow in 1894, having 'devoured' the 'Bible' of all naval enthusiasts at the turn of the century, the books of Captain Alfred T. Mahan on *The Influence of Sea-Power upon History*, Wilhelm II was soon deeply convinced of the interrelationship between naval power and world power which, in turn, was the prerequisite for power and national prestige, economic wealth and social stability. The Sino-Japanese War of 1894–5, which he closely observed, and the obviously impending collapse of the Chinese Empire and its ensuing division among the Great Powers both confirmed this conviction and were a new spur to his ambitions: 'We dare not lose out in this business', he wrote to Chancellor Prince Hohenlohe in November 1894, 'nor allow

[23] Heinrich O. Meisner (ed.), *Denkwürdigkeiten des Generalfeldmarschall Alfred Grafen Waldersee*, vol. II: 1888–1900, Stuttgart and Berlin 1922–3, p. 449, 13 July 1900.

[24] Cited (no date) in Jonathan Steinberg. 'Diplomatie als Wille und Vorstellung: Die Berliner Mission Lord Haldanes im Februar 1912', in Herbert Schottelius and Wilhelm Deist (eds.), *Marine und Marinepolitik im kaiserlichen Deutschland*, Düsseldorf 1972, p. 269.

[25] On the Kaiser's notion of 'Weltpolitik' cf. Röhl, *Wilhelm II.*, pp. 1027–72.

[26] Wilhelm II to the French ambassador, the Marquis de Noailles, on 28 October 1899, cited in Volker Berghahn, 'Des Kaisers Flotte und die Revolutionierung des Mächtesystems vor 1914', in Röhl, *Der Ort Kaiser Wilhelms II.*, p. 177; Lambi, *Navy*, p. 155.

ourselves to be surprised by events. We too need a firm base in China, where our trading turnover amounts to 400 million annually.'[27] It came as no surprise that, only a few weeks later, in early 1895, in two lengthy speeches before both members of the Reichstag and 500 officers in the Prussian Royal Military Academy, he further developed this idea of a new energetic foreign policy based on a powerful navy: 'Only he who dominates the sea can effectively reach his enemy and maintain, undisturbed by him, the freedom of military operations.'[28] In late 1896, when a British fleet demonstration in the Persian Gulf seemed imminent, he regarded this as a warning that some day, 'à la Transvaal, England would take away our colonies, which we are entirely incapable of preventing'.[29] Subsequently he wrote to Hohenlohe: 'It now again becomes evident how foolish it was ten years ago to launch a colonial policy without possessing a fleet, and to develop this policy without keeping equal pace in the development of the fleet. We now have the liability of a large colonial possession which has become the Achilles' heel of Germany.'[30] In 1897, last but not least, when Britain had terminated her commercial treaty with Germany, he regarded this step as another example of British egotism. In a conversation with the Württemberg minister in Berlin, Varnbüler, he summarized his notion of the interrelationship between states and the power they could exercise by pointing out:

In the face of such egotism nothing prevails but the actual might that stands behind one's claim. All skill of diplomacy is of no avail if it cannot threaten and induce fright through this threatening. And this automatically (*von selbst*) leads to the ceterum censeo of the strengthening of the German fleet – not only for the direct protection of German transoceanic trade – although it is also essential for that – but also much more effectively for the concentrated action of an armoured battle fleet which, protected by the North-Baltic Sea canal and leaning on Heligoland – whose strategic value is still not recognized – can at any moment break out of this strong position against the English Channel and threaten the English coastal cities, when the English naval power was occupied in the Mediterranean against the French or in the East Asian waters against the Russian fleet, perhaps simultaneously.[31]

These almost desperate statements reveal that it would take the Kaiser many years to fulfil his dream of enlarging the navy. Only in 1889 he had been successful in convincing the Reichstag to approve the construction of four more battleships. In the early 1890s, however, the Reichstag began

---

[27] Wilhelm II to Prince Hohenlohe, 17 November 1894, cited in Jonathan Steinberg, *Yesterday's Deterrent. Tirpitz and the Birth of the German Battle Fleet*, London 1965, p. 74.
[28] Cited in Lambi, *Navy*, p. 34.   [29] Cited in ibid., p. 35.   [30] Ibid.
[31] Varnbüler's report to Prime Minister Mittnacht, 5 November 1897, cited in ibid.

to become 'obstinate' in this respect, for the imperial government was neither able to describe the political aims these vessels were supposed to help achieve, nor could it put forward a coherent strategic maritime concept or a convincing building programme. Accordingly, the Kaiser's ideas to enlarge the navy were denounced as nothing but 'limitless fleet plans' which no one was willing to approve.[32] In 1895, for example, the Kaiser demanded thirty-six cruisers, the Reichstag, however, approved only four; the following year, all demands for new cruisers were rejected outright in spite of the Transvaal crisis, and in 1897, the Secretary of State of the Imperial Navy Office, Vice Admiral Hollmann, again proved unable to avoid serious cuts in an already piecemeal budget.[33]

At first sight, this failure is indeed astonishing, for Wilhelm II had done whatever possible to realize his aim after he had acceded to the throne. First, in his role as supreme warlord of the navy, he had dismissed the Chief of the Admiralty, General von Caprivi, and, for the first time in German naval history, had handed over command to a naval officer, Vice Admiral Count Monts. In 1889, Wilhelm had begun to change the navy's basic organization. In March he established a naval cabinet to strengthen his influence on all matters dealing with naval personnel, the Kaiser's naval correspondence, and the transmission of imperial orders to other responsible authorities. A few days later, the imperial Admiralty, which had been headed by Bismarck's arch-rival, General von Stosch for many years, was broken up into the High Command, responsible for the deployment of ships, military tactics, and strategy and the Imperial Navy Office as the centre of administrative control.

Second, following his claim of establishing a personal regime, Wilhelm almost continuously interfered directly with all matters dealing with naval policy. In this respect his 'fleet tables' and drawings of naval vessels soon became almost notorious. Moreover, in 1890, he appointed Vice Admiral Friedrich Hollmann Secretary of the Imperial Navy Office. In his opinion Hollmann seemed both fully loyal and highly capable of carrying out his plan of enlarging the navy, for he shared the aims of his imperial 'friend'. Last but not least, wherever and whenever possible, the Kaiser increasingly applied pressure, both directly and indirectly, upon all decision-makers within government and society to further his cause to the point that they

---

[32] For details see Steinberg, *Yesterday's Deterrent*, pp. 17–124; Berghahn, *Tirpitz-Plan*, pp. 23–107; Wilhelm Deist, *Flottenpolitik und Flottenpropaganda. Das Nachrichtenbureau des Reichsmarineamtes 1897–1914*, Stuttgart 1976, pp. 19–69; Hans Hallmann, *Der Weg zum deutschen Schlachtflottenbau*, Stuttgart 1933, pp. 48–101.
[33] Cf. Lambi, *Navy*, pp. 137–8.

began either to fear for the future of the army, the traditional backbone of Germany's defence, or even to doubt Wilhelm's state of mind. His reports to selected members of the Reichstag and the Prussian Royal Military Academy in 1895, mentioned above, were striking examples of his willingness to use all means in this respect. Therefore, the 'grey eminence' in the foreign office, Friedrich von Holstein, was right when he claimed in a letter to Count Eulenburg in 1897 'that today the value of a person for His Majesty depends on his willingness or usefulness to cooperate directly or indirectly in increasing our supply of ships'.[34] A few weeks later he wrote to the German ambassador in London: 'With the Kaiser the navy question now takes precedence over everything . . . The Kaiser wants a fleet like England's – with twenty-eight first-class battleships – and wants to direct his entire domestic policy to that end, i.e. to fight.'[35] Soon Wilhelm II was even willing to 'undertake a great period of conflict, change the Imperial constitution' to 'build countless cruisers', as Hohenlohe sarcastically wrote in his diary on 20 March 1897.[36]

So why did the Kaiser fail for so many years to implement the policy he deemed necessary? The most important reason besides the lack of clear political vision was that he simply wanted 'more ships' without putting forward either a consistent building plan or a strategic concept for the military use of the vessels he demanded from the Reichstag. It is true that, due to technical developments, the building policy of all naval powers had undergone a serious crisis in the 1870s and 1880s. Five great mid-nineteenth-century revolutions in naval technology – the introduction of steam, the screw propeller, shell guns, rifled ordnance, and armour – had fundamentally changed the parameters of naval power and naval strategy.[37] Contrary to the Nelsonian era, in which wooden battleships rigged with sails had been both the backbone of fleets and the guarantor of naval supremacy, a 'new – mainly French – school', the so-called *jeune école*, maintained that their time was over. Even weaker naval powers now seemed capable of successfully challenging the world's leading sea power, Great Britain, by adopting a *guerre de course* strategy which mainly relied on fast cruisers and highly sophisticated torpedo boats.

In naval circles this controversy about strategy had been raging for many years without arriving at any convincing solution. In many respects the Kaiser had been affected by this debate. To some extent the ideas of the

---

[34] Holstein to Count Eulenburg, 17 February 1897, cited in ibid., pp. 33–4.
[35] Holstein to Count Hatzfeldt, 14 April 1897, cited in ibid., p. 34.   [36] Ibid.
[37] For an excellent recent survey see now Rolf Hobson, *Imperialism at Sea. Naval Strategic Thought, the Ideology of Sea Power, and the Tirpitz Plan, 1875–1914*, Boston and Leiden 2002, pp. 24–57.

jeune école had been congruent with his own views of naval strategy. In this concept cruisers were assigned an important role, for, unlike battleships, whose speed and range were limited, they were capable both of showing the flag in distant areas and of destroying the enemies' commerce in wartime. Unfortunately his preference for cruisers hardly seemed to make sense. Due to Germany's peculiar geographical position as well as the lack of a sufficient number of foreign stations, cruiser warfare was simply unsuitable for the German navy. Accordingly the members of the Reichstag were in fact right in demanding a reunion of strategy with construction as a prerequisite of approving more money to finance Germany's defence needs. For several years the Kaiser was unable to comply with these demands, for his naval advisers were deeply divided over all questions of construction and strategy. For example, when the Kaiser visited Kiel in 1891, a lively discussion about the future of the navy took place, which was characterized more by angry, bombastic gestures than by sober appreciation of the navy's problems.[38] This situation dragged on for several years. Even as late as 1895–6, when the High Command, under the influence of Tirpitz, its energetic, determined, and modern young Chief of Staff, had finally developed a long-term building plan for a battle fleet, the Imperial Navy Office, backed by the Kaiser, again asked for cruisers, thus once more giving an example of incompetent planning.[39]

IV

Against this background a more detailed explanation is required of the Kaiser's eventual success in changing Germany's course in 1897–8. In this context, several important aspects and developments which are closely interrelated deserve attention.

First, generally speaking, neither the Kaiser's naval passion nor his threats of a *coup d'état* can sufficiently explain the shift in German politics as well as in military thinking in the 1890s.[40] It seems unlikely that Wilhelm II would have been successful, if the importance of enlarging the navy had not been realized by a steadily increasing number of people. Like the Kaiser, many contemporaries were proud of their political, economic, and military achievements since unification and they felt that Imperial Germany was a vigorous young nation which, bursting at the seams in many ways, had to become more imperialist in order to preserve them and, above all, its

---

[38] Steinberg, *Yesterday's Deterrent*, p. 68.   [39] Ibid., pp. 31–124; Lambi, *Navy*, pp. 84–6, 114–16.
[40] Cf. Berghahn, 'Des Kaisers Flotte und die Revolutionierung des Mächtesystems vor 1914', pp. 173–88.

status in the concert of the Great Powers.[41] Looking back in the 1920s, one of Germany's leading liberal historians, Friedrich Meinecke, described this public perception quite rightly:

Given how the world looked at that time, a nation like Germany, in its narrow and, due to its expansion, increasingly narrowing existence, had necessarily (*mit elementarer Notwendigkeit*) to come to the conclusion that the creation of a larger colonial empire was indispensable to secure its future.[42]

The Kaiser and his 'young men' seemed apt to fulfil this 'desire' for world-power status. The demand for equal entitlement (*Gleichberechtigung*) and a larger 'place in the sun', which Bülow had postulated in his famous first speech in the Reichstag in December 1897 (in which he successfully justified the occupation of Kiaochow), appealed to them just as much as Tirpitz's claim that a powerful navy would greatly enhance Germany's alliance value (*Bündnisfähigkeit*)[43] and thus strengthen the nation's position in the emerging new world-power system. Though the final aims of the Kaiser's new men, namely to replace the 'Pax Britannica' by a 'Pax Germanica' either through a cold or, if necessary, even a hot war against the supreme world and sea power,[44] were probably unknown, the 'risk theory' and many public statements left no doubt that this new course in German foreign policy was directed against Great Britain. When Tirpitz assured the Kaiser in 1899 that after completion of the High Seas Fleet Britain would lose 'every inclination to attack us, and as a result concede to Your Majesty such a measure of naval influence and enable Your Majesty to carry out a great overseas policy',[45] he did in fact describe an aim that many contemporaries were willing to accept, at least to some extent, for, since the mid-1890s, they had the impression that Britain was the main stumbling block on Germany's way to national greatness.

Second, sea power or, as Tirpitz more often put it, naval presence (*Seegeltung*) was allegedly also a prerequisite for the protection of the German colonies, as well as of economic wealth, industrial progress, and commerce. Without a strong navy, Tirpitz argued (for many people quite convincingly), Germany, whose industrial production and commerce had increased

[41] See Canis, *Von Bismarck zur Weltpolitik*, pp. 223–395.
[42] Cited in ibid., p. 225. See also Sönke Neitzel, *Weltmacht oder Untergang. Die Weltreichslehre im Zeitalter des Imperialismus*, Paderborn 2000, pp. 81–209.
[43] Alfred von Tirpitz, *Erinnerungen*, Leipzig 1919, p. 51.
[44] See Berghahn, *Tirpitz-Plan*, pp. 173–201; for Bülow see Peter Winzen, *Bülows Weltmachtkonzept. Untersuchungen zur Frühphase seiner Außenpolitik 1897–1901*, Boppard 1977, pp. 61–127.
[45] Tirpitz's report (*Immediatvortrag*) to the Kaiser, 28 September 1899, quoted in Volker R. Berghahn and Wilhelm Deist (eds.), *Rüstung im Zeichen der wilhelminischen Weltpolitik. Grundlegende Dokumente 1890–1914*, Düsseldorf 1988, p. 161.

immensely since unification, would be unable to preserve her steadily rising 'sea-interests'. As a consequence, according to Tirpitz, Germany would inevitably decline to the status of a pre-industrial 'poor farming country'.[46]

Third, sea power also had important domestic political implications.[47] In contrast to the modernity of its industrial system, the German political and social order was pre-modern in many respects. The influence of parliament was restricted through the strong position of the Kaiser and his government within the constitution. The military, the bureaucracy, and the diplomatic service were still parts of the traditional monarchical prerogative over which the Reichstag had almost no influence. Moreover, in spite of their decreasing economic importance in a quickly industrializing country, the old agrarian elites still exerted more political influence on the development of the state and society than seemed justified, with regard to their small number and their general decline, as well as, above all, to the democratic ideas of the nineteenth century.

Fourth, after all other measures had failed in the past, the government also hoped that the acquisition of sea power and the envisaged great success of world politics through the plan carefully designed by Tirpitz, would safeguard the overall expansion of German industry, foreign trade, colonies and the navy, and, most importantly, thus offer a permanent solution to the 'social problem' which threatened the existing political and social order at home.

Fifth, and probably most importantly, it is an open question whether the Kaiser would ever have achieved his aim in spite of a gradual improvement of circumstances, if he had not had two men at his disposal: Bernhard von Bülow who, as newly appointed Secretary of State for Foreign Affairs and designated Chancellor, was fully willing to implement 'world policy', and Rear Admiral Alfred Tirpitz, who systematically dealt with the political, military, strategic, and economic aspects of becoming a sea power.[48] Appointed Secretary of State of the Imperial Navy Office in 1897, it was he, not the Kaiser, who eventually developed a convincing concept of a naval build-up in the mid-1890s and who thus helped to end a decade of incompetent naval planning, of uncertainties about both naval construction and naval strategy, and of a lack of precise aims. In many respects, the concept he developed was congruent with Mahan's ideas, though, because of Tirpitz's own experience in the High Command, it is unlikely that he

---

[46] Tirpitz, *Erinnerungen*, p. 167.   [47] See Berghahn, *Tirpitz-Plan*, pp. 145–57.

[48] On the 'Tirpitz-Plan' see the detailed analysis by Berghahn, *Tirpitz-Plan, passim,* and for the period 1908 until 1914 Michael Epkenhans, *Die wilhelminische Flottenrüstung 1908–1914. Weltmachtstreben, industrieller Fortschritt, soziale Integration,* Munich 1991.

simply adopted them.[49] Like Mahan, Tirpitz was convinced that only a battle fleet could defeat the enemy's fleet in order to gain command of the sea, and thus attain sea supremacy.[50] Germany's fate, Tirpitz alleged, was to be decided in the vital theatre of war, the North Sea, and there only ships-of-the-line could secure victory in a traditional and decisive naval battle. Accordingly, the fleet he suggested to build step by step in twenty years' time was to be a remarkable force. Nevertheless it would still be inferior to the Royal Navy, but Tirpitz was convinced that Britain could not outbuild Germany because of financial restraints and lack of personnel, and that, therefore, the margin of inferiority between the Imperial Navy and its future enemy would not exceed one third. With high-quality ships, superior tactics, and better trained crews, Tirpitz considered victory over the Royal Navy in the 'wet triangle around Heligoland' a possibility. An integral part of this optimistic view, however, was the assumption that the latter would only be able to bring about half of its strength into action due to its overseas commitments.[51]

V

In 1897–8 and throughout the following decade until the outbreak of the First World War, the Kaiser, by and large, fully supported this grandiose scheme developed and implemented by Tirpitz and Bülow, the men, it is true, that he had selected. Even though the two of them were the main architects of both German foreign and naval policy during these years, Wilhelm II tried repeatedly to direct the course of the Empire as the following examples will show. In theory he could exert his influence as head of state in at least three ways, which were closely interrelated.

First, according to Article 15 of the Bismarckian constitution, the Kaiser appointed the Chancellor who, in turn, was only responsible to him, not to the Reichstag. Even though the Chancellor eventually needed a majority in parliament to run the country successfully, this ancient royal prerogative secured that the Kaiser would choose a man who had his confidence. In 1890, 1894, 1900, and 1909 Wilhelm II exercised his royal prerogative, when he appointed a new Chancellor. Although the political reality of a modern and highly complex industrial society soon revealed the limitations of this

---

[49] Tirpitz, *Erinnerungen*, p. 47.
[50] See Lambi, *Navy*, pp. 62–8; Hobson, *Imperialism at Sea*, pp. 178–295.
[51] See Berghahn, *Tirpitz-Plan*, pp. 184–201; Paul M. Kennedy, 'Maritime Strategieprobleme der deutsch-englischen Flottenrivalität', in Herbert Schottelius and Wilhelm Deist (eds.), *Marine und Marinepolitik im kaiserlichen Deutschland 1871–1914*, 2nd edn, Düsseldorf 1981, pp. 181–210.

idea of personal rule, Bülow, designated Chancellor since 1897 and appointed in 1900 and, again, Bethmann Hollweg, appointed in 1909, were supposed to govern according to Wilhelm's guidelines.

Similarly, according to his own conception of a personal regime, the Kaiser tried to direct the course of both German naval policy and strategy. Although the first steps in this direction had already been taken at the beginning of his reign in 1888–9, he continued to strengthen his position by dissolving the High Command in 1899. The impact of this change was far-reaching. As Ivo Lambi has rightly summarized, from 1899, when he thus finally personally became Commander-in-Chief of the navy, 'a single erratic man had in his hands the final decisions of the Prussian and Imperial government, of the administration and command of both the army and the navy, and the coordination of this highly complex and unwieldy machinery'.[52] The Chief of the Naval Cabinet, the Secretary of State of the Imperial Navy Office, the Chief of the Admiralty Staff as well as a number of chiefs of different naval agencies were now not only directly responsible to him, but also had the right of direct access. Although the Secretary of the Imperial Navy Office was, at least according to the constitution, the Chancellor's subordinate, he could be by-passed and decisions could be made without his input which, in the worst case, seriously impeded the smooth working of the machinery of government and which could thus prove detrimental to both domestic and foreign policy. Normally, the three most important naval officers reported to the Kaiser on Tuesdays or Saturdays respectively, unless they were ordered to report immediately, if something strange or important had occurred to the Kaiser. The topics they had to report on covered all questions of naval personnel, naval policy, and operational planning, however important or, often enough, trivial they might be. For example, during the reports of the Chief of the Naval Cabinet the Kaiser personally decided about promotions and new appointments; he also carefully read the annual reports of commanding officers about the qualification of each executive officer; moreover he even decided whether executive officers were allowed to marry, and he tried to arbitrate issues of dispute between the different agencies of the navy. All questions regarding naval policy in general, as well as naval planning, naval construction, and civil–naval relations were discussed when the Secretary of the Imperial Navy Office reported to the Kaiser. The Chief of the Admiralty Staff in turn discussed all aspects of operational planning

[52] Lambi, *Navy*, p. 167. It is true that Tirpitz thus tried to enhance his own position as Secretary of State of the Imperial Navy Office; nevertheless the Kaiser also hoped that the break-up of the High Command would strengthen his influence in naval affairs.

with the Kaiser. In order to emphasize further his authority as Commander-in-Chief the Kaiser regularly visited the navy's bases on the North Sea and Baltic coasts, embarked on its vessels for shorter or longer cruises, and, last but not least, took part in its annual manoeuvres, using this opportunity to give 'advice' on naval strategy and tactics.

Unfortunately, however, Wilhelm II proved unable to meet the requirements of this powerful position. It is true that as long as Wilhelm II, Bülow, and Tirpitz more or less fully agreed about the course of German domestic and foreign policy, there was no need to decide controversial issues of principal importance. This, however, changed when Germany's international position began to deteriorate in 1905–6. Bülow eventually realized that some steps had to be taken to adjust Germany's domestic and foreign policy to the existing situation. For a number of reasons, this adjustment never materialized. On the contrary, somewhat ironically, the only and most important decision Wilhelm II did take was to dismiss Bülow in 1909. This dismissal was, however, less the result of far-reaching political differences than of a lack of confidence in the Chancellor as a result of the latter's behaviour during the '*Daily Telegraph* affair'.[53]

Nevertheless, Bülow's dismissal coincided with a serious crisis in domestic and foreign policy, caused to a great extent by Germany's embarkation on an offensive world and naval policy a decade earlier. According to his claim that he was the final arbiter, this situation would have required a thorough analysis of the existing situation as well as clear decisions about the country's future course by the Kaiser. At first sight, some political observers in fact regarded the appointment of the new Chancellor, former Home Secretary Theobald von Bethmann Hollweg who was totally inexperienced in foreign policy, as an indication that Wilhelm II was now obviously willing to be his own Foreign Secretary.[54] Their apprehensions were not justified, for the governmental machinery soon gave the impression of what many historians today call 'polycratic chaos'. Many contemporaries shared this opinion. For example, back in Great Britain after his visit to Berlin in February 1912, where he had tried to negotiate a last-minute agreement to avoid another *Novelle*, Lord Haldane remembered that he had experienced nothing but chaos at the top of the German government.[55] In his eyes, the Kaiser, Tirpitz,

[53] See now Peter Winzen, *Das Kaiserreich am Abgrund. Die Daily-Telegraph-Affäre und das Hale Interview von 1908*, Stuttgart 2002, pp. 19–91.

[54] See the letter of the designated Secretary for Foreign Affairs Kiderlen-Wächter to Kypke, 15 July 1909, in Ernst Jäckh (ed.), *Kiderlen-Wächter. Der Staatsmann und der Mensch. Briefwechsel und Nachlaß*, Stuttgart 1924, vol. II, p. 32.

[55] See Klaus Hildebrand, *Das vergangene Reich. Deutsche Außenpolitik von Bismarck bis Hitler*, Stuttgart 1995, p. 275.

and the Chancellor seemed to disagree in almost every respect with regard to German foreign and naval policy towards Great Britain. As Tirpitz bitterly recalled in November 1912, since Bülow had 'deserted' him in 1908 for fear of a dramatic deterioration both of Anglo-German relations and of the financial situation of the Empire,[56] the unity among Germany's leading 'world politicians' no longer existed. Instead, there was heavy infighting between the new Chancellor, Bethmann Hollweg, the Secretaries for Foreign Affairs, Kiderlen-Wächter, and of the Treasury, Wermuth, on the one hand and Tirpitz on the other. Repeatedly reminded by Tirpitz that a failure of the envisaged naval build-up would mean a 'historic fiasco', Wilhelm II continued to support the Secretary of the Imperial Navy Office, instead of initiating a thorough re-evaluation of German world policy. Subsequently, the Chancellor's attempts at improving Anglo-German relations appeared half-hearted, for it was obvious to the British government that the support he received from the Kaiser was at best luke-warm.

In 1911 and again in 1912, following the débâcle of the second Moroccan Crisis, Bethmann Hollweg, with the support of the Chief of the Great General Staff who was deeply concerned about the Empire's security on the continent, argued that a new *Novelle* would again impede an improvement of Anglo-German relations and that, moreover, a strengthening of the army was more important than new battleships. The Kaiser had great difficulty in taking a final decision about the reorientation of Germany's foreign and military policy which the Chancellor had in his mind. As the Empress, to whom Tirpitz had appealed in despair,[57] told Chancellor Bethmann Hollweg in February 1912, her husband was allegedly on the verge of a nervous breakdown.[58] It is not surprising that Tirpitz as well as even the Empress considered Wilhelm's often abrupt changes not only as an indication of increasing nervousness, but also as a proof that 'at the bottom of his heart the Kaiser regarded our bad relations with England as detestable'.[59]

---

[56] Undated memorandum by Tirpitz, November 1912, BA-MA Tirpitz papers N 253/9.

[57] Cf. the diary entry of Captain Hopman, 28 February 1912: 'Tirpitz tells me that the Empress has written to the Chancellor that he should eventually put his foot down (*durchgreifen*) in the interest of the Kaiser, who was melting away (*zergehen*) with unrest and excitement.' BA-MA Hopman papers N 326/9.

[58] Cf. the diary entry of Captain Hopman, 12 March 1912. When Tirpitz told Hopman about the details of this intervention of the Empress with the Chancellor, he wrote: 'The whole story is unbelievable, but it is unfortunately true. We can now start to have doubts about Wilhelm II's state of mind. He is certainly a pathological case.' BA-MA Hopman papers N 329/9.

[59] Diary entry of Captain Hopman, 9 September 1912, ibid. On 26 March 1912 the Empress had told Tirpitz: 'At heart, he [the Kaiser] is enthusiastic about England and everything which is English (*er schwärme ja innerlich doch für England und englische Verhältnisse*), it is in his blood. She, however, has taken care that her sons would think differently.' Ibid.

Wilhelm II changed his opinion several times and, from Tirpitz's point of view, became increasingly 'unreliable'.[60] Moreover, the Kaiser not only shied away from important decisions in times of crisis. Often, he was also simply too lazy or much more interested in trivial matters like hunting to give more important decisions proper attention. For example, in 1913, after Tirpitz had travelled all the way from the Black Forest to East Prussia for his annual detailed report on naval affairs, the Kaiser immediately left the room only minutes after the Secretary of State had begun reporting, because a servant had informed him that a big stag had been sighted, instead of discussing Germany's future naval policy with Tirpitz.[61] On 29 July 1914, when war was imminent, the Chief of the Admiralty Staff could not give a report on his proposals for a war against Russia and France, because the Kaiser was too tired.[62]

Similarly, the organization of the navy remained 'chaotic' in spite of the Kaiser's position as Commander-in-Chief. During their visit to Kiel, British officers were, no doubt, impressed by the strength of the Imperial Navy. Fortunately, from their point of view, its 'administration appeared to be too decentralized to be entirely successful'.[63] By and large this judgement was correct. Moreover, contrary to Tirpitz's hopes when he had urged the Kaiser to dissolve the powerful High Command in his own interest, decentralization did not put an end to heavy infighting between the navy's different agencies about strategy and tactics, and Tirpitz's building policy. Commanding admirals continued to accuse each other of interfering within their own respective spheres. For example, the 'front' almost continuously complained about both the lack of personnel, inferior weapons, and, moreover, a neglect of fighting efficiency. In return, the Imperial Navy Office accused the 'front' of not appreciating the enormous political and financial difficulties involved in carrying out the envisaged naval build-up. Rather than paying due attention to these rivalries and tensions, which increased greatly when Tirpitz's arch-enemy, Admiral Holtzendorff, became Commander-in-Chief of the High Seas Fleet in 1909, and trying to find a satisfactory solution to these problems, Wilhelm II often simply reacted erratically. In 1912, for example, having read a report by the 'front' about allegedly inferior material, he immediately wrote an irate letter to Tirpitz

---

[60] For details see Epkenhans, *Flottenrüstung*, pp. 93–137, 325–99.

[61] Cf. the diary entry of the Chief of the Naval Cabinet, Admiral von Müller, 27 September 1913, BA-MA Müller papers N 153/4.

[62] Cf. the diary of the Chief of the Naval Cabinet, Admiral von Müller, 29 July 1914, BA-MA Müller papers N 153/5.

[63] Cited in Arthur J. Marder, *The Anatomy of British Sea Power. A History of British Naval Policy in the Pre-Dreadnought Era, 1880–1905*, London 1964 (repr.), p. 478, n. 17.

accusing him of neglecting his duties, instead of investigating the matter carefully.[64] Deeply hurt, as often before as well as later, Tirpitz seriously considered resigning from office as a result of this affront. However, the Secretary of State of the Imperial Navy Office was not only a victim of the Kaiser's erratic behaviour. Often, he also cleverly used the Kaiser to silence internal critics. For example, when a former friend of his and a successful teacher at the naval academy, Captain Curt von Maltzahn, requested permission to publish a book whose main ideas seemed most objectionable to Tirpitz's own theories about naval strategy, the latter secured an imperial order prohibiting its publication.[65] Once again, Wilhelm II proved unable to reconcile conflicting opinions or, at least, to allow their free exchange in the interest of a rational development of the navy and of naval strategy.

In the eyes of the Kaiser another means of personally promoting German world policy and the build-up of a powerful navy were his many speeches, which he enjoyed giving whenever and wherever possible throughout his reign. In this respect he distinctly differed from his predecessors or the monarchs of neighbouring countries, who regarded this as either incompatible with their traditional monarchical role or with the constitution. In Wilhelm's opinion, however, public speeches were also a means of emphasizing that it was he who really ruled the country. As a result, by picking up issues he considered important, he often tried to direct the course of public debate or to anticipate governmental decisions, as for example in 1899 and 1911, when he – prematurely – demanded another *Novelle*.[66]

To some extent, at least initially, his speeches seem to have helped to make both world policy and the navy more 'popular'. Whether he spoke at the launching of a new battleship,[67] the opening of a new bridge,[68] or the unveiling of a statue,[69] he used these opportunities to elaborate on the need for a powerful navy. However, unable and probably also unwilling to give

---

[64] See Epkenhans, *Flottenrüstung*, pp. 323–4.   [65] See Lambi, *Navy*, pp. 164–6.

[66] There is still no detailed analysis of the impact of the Kaiser's speeches. For a short survey see Bernd Sösemann, '"Pardon wird nicht gegeben; Gefangene nicht gemacht." Zeugnisse und Wirkungen einer rhetorischen Mobilmachung', in Deutsches Historisches Museum (ed.), *Der letzte Kaiser. Wilhelm II. im Exil*, Berlin, Gütersloh and Munich 1991, pp. 79–94.

[67] Most infamous are his speeches at the launching of the battleship *Karl der Große* in Hamburg in 1899, when he coined the phrase 'dire need', and at the launching of the battleship *Wittelsbach*, see above, note 22.

[68] In 1897 Wilhelm II opened the new bridge over the River Rhine at Cologne. In this speech he claimed that the 'trident belongs in our fist'. Johann, *Reden des Kaisers*, p. 71.

[69] In 1905 he unveiled a statue of his father, Kaiser Friedrich III, at Bremen, in 1913 a statue of the French Admiral de Coligny at Wilhelmshaven. He used both occasions to justify the build-up of a powerful battle fleet. Schulthess, *Europäischer Geschichtskalender*, 46 (1905), pp. 67–9, and 53 (1912), p. 218.

careful judgements, these speeches very often also had a disastrous impact. On the domestic front, they were often a means for polarizing instead of integrating the populace. In Great Britain, Germany's 'main enemy'[70] since 1897, the Kaiser's speeches were soon regarded with great concern. In 1904, for example, Wilhelm II proudly displayed almost the whole German Fleet before his uncle King Edward VII during the latter's visit to Kiel yacht week. At the state banquet after the naval review he referred in glowing terms to the greatness of his fleet. His Majesty the King of England 'has been greeted by the thunder of the guns of the German Fleet', which, though 'the youngest in point of creation among the Navies of the world, is an expression of the renewal in strength of the sea power of the German Empire as reconstructed by the great Kaiser William I'.[71] The King and his naval advisers were, of course, impressed, but unfortunately not in the way the Kaiser had expected them to be. Instead of admiring him for his achievements, they regarded this display of naval strength as a threat that Britain had to meet. Only a few days later, on 1 July 1904, *The Times* wrote:

No phantom as to German aggression haunts us; but the consciousness we feel that it is our duty to watch the progress of German naval power, and to consider the possible purposes for which it might be used, will certainly not be lessened by what we have seen at Kiel or by any such assurances as we have heard there.[72]

Even naval officers were soon disgusted when they had to listen to speeches which often were a mixture of both bellicose and mystical rhetoric.[73] Against this background it is hardly astonishing that Tirpitz openly criticized the Kaiser in his memoirs. 'Instead of keeping one's mouth shut and building ships', Wilhelm II enjoyed presenting himself as well as his navy as often as possible to the public.[74]

   Direct interferences in foreign affairs and naval policy were eventually both the most important and most dangerous ways in which Wilhelm II meddled in government. These interferences ranged from direct letters to neighbouring monarchs and their ministers to imperial orders to the Chancellor, ambassadors, or the Secretary of State of the Imperial Navy Office. At the turn of 1907–8, for example, after the announcement of

[70] In his famous report to the Kaiser on 15 June 1897, Tirpitz put forward a memorandum in which this idea was laid down as the guiding principle: 'For Germany at the present time the most dangerous enemy at sea is England. It is also the enemy against which we most urgently require a certain measure of naval force as a political power factor.' Cited in Lambi, *Navy*, p. 141.
[71] Cited in Marder, *Anatomy*, p. 477.   [72] Ibid., p. 478.
[73] See the diary entry of Captain Hopman, 18 November 1912, BA-MA Hopman papers N 326/9.
[74] Cf. Tirpitz, *Erinnerungen*, p. 133; Alfred von Tirpitz, *Politische Dokumente*, vol. 1: *Der Aufbau der deutschen Weltmacht*, Stuttgart and Berlin 1924, p. 16, fn.

another *Novelle* which accelerated naval ship-building at an alarming rate
from the British point of view, Anglo-German relations quickly deterio-
rated because of the so-called fleet question. Accordingly, there was a great
public stir in Great Britain in the spring of 1908. In order to calm the waves,
Wilhelm II, remembering his position as Admiral of the Fleet, and, moreover, without informing either the Chancellor or the Secretary of State of
the Imperial Navy Office, wrote directly to the First Lord of the Admiralty,
Lord Tweedmouth, in February, claiming again that 'the German Naval
Bill is not aimed at England and is not a '"Challenge to British Supremacy
of the Sea", which will remain unchallenged to [*sic*] generations to come'.[75]
This was indeed 'a new departure',[76] as King Edward VII sarcastically described this direct intervention in British domestic politics. The commotion
caused by this letter to a member of the cabinet was, however, by no means a
'lesson' to the Kaiser. On the contrary, during a private visit of his cousin,
King Edward VII, to Kronberg in August 1908, the Kaiser met with a high-
ranking foreign office official, Sir Charles Hardinge, to discuss the matter
again. The outcome of this meeting was disastrous. When Hardinge, who
had at first asked him: 'Can't you put a stop to your building? Or build
less ships?', in the course of a dramatic conversation, in which Wilhelm II
denied that the navy was directed against Great Britain, appealed to him:
'You must stop or build more slowly', Wilhelm finally answered in his usual
un-diplomatic manner: 'Then we shall fight for it is a question of national
honour and dignity.'[77] The result of this intransigent attitude, which, it is
true, still found the principal backing of Bülow and Tirpitz at that time,
was that Britain began to outbuild the High Seas Fleet by doubling the
building-rate of capital ships in 1909.

In 1912, to give another example, Wilhelm directly interfered with foreign
policy at the height of the domestic crisis about the new navy law. Excited
about the reactions of the British government to the details of the *Novelle*,
he sent a telegram to Chancellor Bethmann Hollweg, telling him to publish
the *Novelle* immediately. If the Chancellor refused to follow his orders, he
would, as he told him, 'give orders to the [Prussian] Minister of War and
the Secretary of the Imperial Navy Office to publish the new army and
navy laws themselves. My patience as well as that of the German people is

[75] Wilhelm II to Lord Tweedmouth, 16 February 1908, quoted in Johannes Lepsius, Albrecht
Mendelssohn Bartholdy, and Friedrich Thimme (eds.), *Die Große Politik der Europäischen Kabinette 1871–1914*, Berlin 1925, vol. xxiv, pp. 32–5.

[76] Edward VII to Wilhelm II, 22 February 1908, ibid., p. 36.

[77] Wilhelm II to Bülow, 13 August 1908, ibid., pp. 126–9.

over.'[78] At the same time he sent a telegram to the German Ambassador in London, ordering him to tell the British government that he would consider a withdrawal of British naval vessels from the Mediterranean to the North Sea as a 'threat of war' and answer by increasing the building-rate from two to three capital ships a year or even 'mobilizing' his armed forces.[79] Only by threatening to resign immediately was Bethmann Hollweg able to avert any serious damage to Anglo-German relations and to continue negotiating with the British government. Nevertheless, the impact of these erratic interventions was far-reaching. While on the one hand Bethmann Hollweg's room for diplomatic manoeuvres to improve Anglo-German relations had thus become narrower still, Tirpitz and his fellow officers regarded the Kaiser's wavering attitude once more as an indication of his inability to take a strong line over the naval question in spite of his promises or his bellicose rhetoric.[80]

Similarly disturbing were the Kaiser's erratic interventions in naval policy and strategy. Never fully convinced of Tirpitz's Mahanian-like strategic concept and its emphasis on battleships which were supposed to gain command of the sea after a decisive battle in the 'wet triangle' off Heligoland, Wilhelm II often tried to use his authority as Commander-in-Chief to change the former's carefully designed building-plan by demanding more cruisers, fast battleships, or even a strange merger of a torpedo boat and a battleship as in 1912, instead of proper battleships and battlecruisers. In 1904, for example, he even went so far as to publish an anonymous article on armoured cruisers in the *Marine-Rundschau*, only to be publicly rebuffed by two younger naval officers at Tirpitz's (!) request.[81] Though Wilhelm's ideas were very similar to those harboured by Tirpitz's most important adversary on the other side of the North Sea, Admiral John Fisher, who was also a fervent advocate of fast battleships,[82] the way he opened this discussion on new strategic options proved futile. Unfortunately, Wilhelm II simply did not realize that he thus imperilled the programme as well as its basic strategic implications which he had endorsed only a few years either. For the time being, he increasingly just made himself an object of mockery within the naval officer corps. In 1912, at the end of the annual 'Imperial manoeuvres', during which he had once again given a detailed 'critique' of

---

[78] Wilhelm II to Bethmann Hollweg, 5 March 1912, cited in *Die große Politik*, vol. XXXI, p. 155.
[79] Wilhelm II to Count Metternich, 5 March 1912, ibid., p. 156.
[80] Cf. the diary entries of Captain Hopman, 6/7 March 1912, BA-MA Hopman papers N 326/9.
[81] 'Einiges über Panzerkreuzer', written by L[ehmann], in *Marine-Rundschau*, 15 (1904), pp. 13–17. Cf. ibid., pp. 215–23, for the answers by lieutenant-captain (ret.), Ernst Count Reventlow, and lieutenant-captain Hopman. For details see Berghahn, *Tirpitz-Plan*, pp. 361–72.
[82] Nicholas A. Lambert, *Sir John Fisher's Naval Revolution*, Columbia and South Carolina 1999.

both strategic and tactical principles of naval warfare in the North Sea, the Chief of the Naval Cabinet recorded in his diary: 'My criticism of this critique is as follows: You need enormous courage (*Mordsstirn*) to tell so much unprofessional nonsense (*laienhaften Unsinn*) to so many professional naval officers (*Sachverständigen*).'[83] Against this background it was hardly astonishing that politicians as well as naval officers welcomed the Kaiser's increasing enthusiasm for archaeology with some relief. In April 1914, when the German Ambassador to the High Porte told the Chancellor that this 'mania for archaeology (*Ausgrabungsmanie*) was on the verge of insanity (*grenzt an Verrücktheit*)', the latter answered: 'Let him get on with it (*Lassen Sie ihn doch*), for as long as he is digging, he does not send telegrams and interfere with politics.'[84]

VI

The outbreak of war in August 1914, for which Bethmann Hollweg's risk policy was largely responsible, soon proved a great challenge to Wilhelm's concept as Commander-in-Chief of the navy. While he more or less completely left operations on the land-fronts to the Supreme High Command, he at least tried to direct naval operations himself. Unfortunately, he was never able to fulfil this task. Most important in this respect was his inability either to develop a convincing strategic concept against the Grand Fleet with his naval advisers or to give his admirals a free hand in naval operations in the North Sea, where the Royal Navy's distant blockade had trapped the Kaiser's splendid vessels.[85] Instead, not wanting to risk the High Sea Fleet, he almost continuously wavered with regard to all questions of naval operations as well as naval strategy. In some respects, it is true, in his reluctance to risk both the fleet in a decisive battle and a breach with the United States by embarking on unrestricted submarine warfare, Wilhelm proved more far-sighted than his admirals, especially Tirpitz, who simply wanted to save the navy's honour. Nevertheless, his inability effectively to 'lead' the navy soon caused serious discontent among all ranks, and chaos between the political and naval leadership. His attempts at restoring harmony through an All-Highest Order signed on 7 September 1915, demanding that the officers

[83] Müller, diary entry of 20 September 1912, BA-MA Müller papers N 159/4.
[84] Cf. the diary entry of Captain Hopman, 4 May 1914, BA-MA Hopman papers N 326/10.
[85] For an excellent summary of the strategic problems of German naval operations during the war see Werner Rahn, 'Strategische Probleme der deutschen Seekriegführung 1914–1918', in Wolfgang Michalka (ed.), *Der Erste Weltkrieg. Wirkung, Wahrnehmung, Analyse*, Munich 1997, pp. 341–65.

of the imperial navy 'loyally submit to his will as supreme warlord',[86] were of no avail. This inability to comply with his own claim of being the nation's supreme warlord and of implementing either a convincing policy or strategy was detrimental to his own authority. It was also detrimental to Germany's political culture in so far as both politicians and naval officers alike still clung to the idea that the Kaiser was the final arbiter in every respect, in spite of many complaints about Wilhelm's 'character failings'. In this light it is hardly surprising that young naval officers, supported by the Commander-in-Chief of the High Sea Fleet, Admiral Reinhard Scheer, tried to solve this unbearable situation by establishing a Supreme Navy Command in the autumn of 1918.[87]

From a military point of view, this streamlining of the navy's command structure came too late. However, by pushing the Kaiser aside, the new triumvirate of Scheer, Trotha, and Levetzow made clear that in their eyes Wilhelm II was hardly more than a 'shadow Emperor'.[88] Ironically, Grand Admiral Tirpitz, the real 'father of the German battle fleet', who, at the urgent request of Chancellor Bethmann Hollweg, had been forced to leave office in March 1916, had already gone much further. After earlier attempts to depose the Kaiser by declaring him insane had failed in the spring of 1915,[89] because Generals von Einem and von Kessel refused to support him, Tirpitz helped to establish the German Fatherland Party in 1917, whose programme eventually opened the gates for a more fundamental criticism of the monarchical idea in which Wilhelm II no longer played a role.[90]

In late October 1918, the wheel had finally turned full circle. When the Supreme High Command asked for an immediate truce in September 1918, because the army was neither able nor willing to withstand the Allied onslaught on the battlefields of the Western Front any more, the Supreme Navy Command regarded this as a favourable opportunity to prove the importance of a fleet for the future and to save the honour of the naval officer corps. Most importantly in this respect, the Kaiser, who was still 'nominally' Commander-in-Chief, as Captain Levetzow had put it when

---

[86] Cited in Alfred von Tirpitz, *Politische Dokumente*, vol. II: *Deutsche Ohnmachtspolitik im Weltkriege*, Hamburg and Berlin 1926, p. 420.

[87] Herwig, *'Luxury' Fleet*, p. 245.

[88] Cf. Afflerbach, 'Wilhelm II as Supreme War-Lord', pp. 427–49, who denies that Wilhelm II was a 'shadow Emperor', and, similarly, Deist, 'Kaiser Wilhelm II. als Oberster Kriegsherr', pp. 25–42.

[89] Cf. the entries in the diary of Captain Hopman of 22 and 27 March 1915, BA-MA Hopman papers N 326/13.

[90] Raffael Scheck, *Alfred von Tirpitz and German Right-Wing Politics, 1914–1930*, Atlantic Highlands, NJ 1998, pp. 65–81.

helping to establish the new command structure, was more or less left in the dark about the final objectives of this sortie. Completely misjudging the desire for peace among the rank-and-file of the High Sea Fleet, it proved the final blow to the Kaiser's dream of a powerful navy and, moreover, of establishing the German Empire as the new leading world power in the twentieth century. Instead, the navy mutinied and thus gave the final signal for a revolution which swept away the old order within days.

The 'Fleet Kaiser', whose work now lay in ruins, replied to Admiral Scheer's report about the naval mutinies before boarding the train which was to take him into Dutch exile: 'My dear admiral, the Navy has deserted me nicely . . . I no longer have a Navy.'[91] This statement was nothing but further evidence of the Kaiser's self-deception. As early as 6 October 1918, Vice Admiral Hopman, then Commander-in-Chief of all German Naval Forces in the Black Sea, had noted in his diary, when he had heard that the German government had asked for peace:

Everything has turned out as I have expected, not only during recent weeks, but for a long, long time before. World history is Judgement Day. Germany now will have to pay for her sins of the last three decades. Politically she had grown stiff through blind confidence, through the slavish subordination under the will of a fool who burst with vanity and over-estimation. No victory without fighting! Politically, we have not fought for 3 decades, but played only, played like children full of illusions and self-deceptions. This is why politically we remained children, did not become men and did not produce any men.[92]

It is striking that a naval officer who had once been proud of the navy and its Supreme Commander-in-Chief, the Kaiser, finally realized what the latter was unwilling to acknowledge. Seen against this background, the Kaiser and his navy were but two sides of the same coin: agents for Germany's attempt to gain world power status which was the main cause of the great catastrophe of the twentieth century. And yet, the majority of naval officers still obeyed the Kaiser's orders. When Vice Admiral von Reuter scuttled the formerly proud vessels of the High Sea Fleet at Scapa Flow in June 1919, he ironically followed an All-Highest Order of August 1914 'that in case of bad luck, an honourable sinking of my ships will preserve them from striking the flag'.[93] Thus Vice Admiral von Reuter tried to

[91] Cited in Herwig, *'Luxury' Fleet*, p. 252.

[92] Diary of Vice Admiral Hopman, 6 October 1918, cited in Winfried Baumgart (ed.), *Von Brest-Litovsk zur Deutschen Novemberrevolution. Aus den Aufzeichnungen von Alfons Paquet, Wilhelm Groener, Albert Hopman*, Göttingen 1971, p. 615.

[93] Cited in Andreas Krause, *Scapa Flow. Die Selbstversenkung der wilhelminischen Flotte*, Berlin 1999, p. 270.

preserve an *esprit de corps* which would soon prove disastrous again. In the interwar years, Germany's naval leadership, which was unwilling to give up the ideals of the Wilhelmine era and which never ceased to suffer from the revolution in November 1918 and the inglorious end of the High Sea Fleet, fully supported Hitler's grasp for world power from the start. Once again, the navy thus helped to pave the way for an aggressive policy which could only end in Germany's total destruction.

CHAPTER 2

Hollow-sounding jubilees: forms and effects of public self-display in Wilhelmine Germany

Bernd Sösemann

Contemporaries referred to Wilhelm II's time of government before 1914 as an 'age of festivities' and speeches.[1] In 1913, the *Sozialdemokratische Flugschriften* commented: 'The amount of official celebrations that the German Empire has had to endure over these last twenty-five years has been seemingly endless. They follow each other as uninterruptedly as film-reels do in a cinema . . . And each festivity is a "milestone", each is glorified by speeches . . .'[2] The Kaiser's appearances in public are revealing processes of public communication. Contemporaries counted among them 'national public holidays' (*Nationalfesttage*), 'state celebrations' (*Staatsfeste*), regional and local events, as well as a number of other public holidays and jubilees of very different natures. Addresses, speeches and toasts formed part of these, as did marches and parades, flags and standards, obelisks and memorials, illuminations, torch-lit processions and fireworks, church visits, poems, songs, and the *Hohenzollernfestspiele* in the new opera house (*Neues Königliches Operntheater*). The court ceremonial planned all details and accompanied the media from the first announcement of an event to the publications which were intended to record and secure its fame for the future.

As in most monarchies at the end of the nineteenth century, in the German Reich and in Prussia, the birthday of the ruler and his more famous ancestors, selected historical events, funerals, and the coronation formed the core of an increasingly secularized culture of celebration.[3] Laws and decrees stipulated whatever was necessary for this. For example, shortly after acceding to the throne, Wilhelm decreed that forthwith all schools should

---

Translated by Annika Mombauer.

[1] *Gloria industria alitur!* Dedicated to John, friend, critical editor of sources, and unbiased researcher, for 31 May 2003. This essay forms part of a larger study on 'Wilhelminism' and 'Prussianism' in the history of the German Kaiserreich.

[2] 'Dichtung und Wahrheit über 1813', *Sozialdemokratische Flugschriften* 19 (Berlin 1913), p. 1.

[3] Sabine Behrenbeck and Alexander Nützenadel (eds.), *Inszenierungen des Nationalstaats*, Cologne 2000.

commemorate the birthdays and anniversaries of the deaths of his two predecessors 'as patriotic days of remembrance'.[4] The Kaiser and his advisors
had interpretive power over an event – often, although not consistently,
they exercised this in agreement with the government. They attempted to
transform ideas and programmes and the results of history from a Prussian-
dynastic perspective into an immediately recognizable social reality. Thus
the *Neue Preußische (Kreuz-) Zeitung* commented on the occasion of the
celebration of 22 March 1897:

The character of national festivities, even when they are about the celebration of
a famous personality, a ruler or a statesman, is influenced by the feelings of large
sectors of the population to such an extent that the person to whom the celebration
is dedicated preferably appears as the embodiment of some national idea, an idea
to which large parts of the population are attached.[5]

Moreover, the Kaiser and his advisors gave validity to an official canon which
included legally fixed religious and secular holidays, ranging from Whitsun
to *Sedanstag*.[6] They documented the lifestyle and self-confidence of the
monarch, the 'grandeur' of the monarchy and the state, of court and society,
by distinguishing and accentuating the festivity and its programmatic aim
in as obvious and impressive a way as possible, using personnel, architecture,
ceremony, and symbolism to do so.[7]

Wilhelm himself offered a definition of such festivities, arguing that the
national holidays were 'particularly comforting in these fast-moving times

---

[4] Decree of 9 July 1888. Gerhard J. Bürgel, *Die Feier vaterländischer Gedenk- und Erinnerungstage in der Volksschule*, Cologne 1894, p. 5. At that time, days of celebration, in chronological order, were as follows: January: 18th, coronation of the King, and foundation of the Reich; 24th, birthday of Friedrich the Great; 27th, birthday of Wilhelm II; March; 9th, remembrance of the death of Wilhelm I, 10th, accession to power of Friedrich III; 16th, the funeral of Wilhelm I; 22nd, birthday of Wilhelm I; April: 1st, Bismarck's birthday; 30th, Roon's birthday; May: 10th, Peace of Frankfurt; June: 15th, death of Friedrich III and accession of Wilhelm II; July: 19th, remembrance of the death of Luise; September: 2nd, *Sedanstag*; 30th, Kaiserin Augusta's birthday; October: 14th, remembrance of Jena and Auerstedt; 18th, coronation of Wilhelm I and Friedrich III's birthday; 26th, Moltke's birthday; November: 21st, Viktoria's birthday (Kaiserin Friedrich).

[5] *Neue Preußische (Kreuz-) Zeitung (NPZ)*, 136, 22 March 1897: 'Der 22. März – ein preußischer Festtag'. Lieselotte E. Saurma-Jeltsch (ed.), *Karl der Große als vielberufener Vorfahr*, Sigmaringen 1994, pp. 9–21, refers in this context to an 'ideological complex'; a similar argument can be found in Elfie Rembold, *Die festliche Nation. Geschichtsinszenierungen und regionaler Nationalismus in Großbritannien vor dem Ersten Weltkrieg*, Berlin 2000, pp. 17–19.

[6] Cf. the section on 'Volksfeste' in the *Gothaischer Genealogischer Hofkalender*.

[7] Long reports on details can be found in the semi-official conservative local and regional press; shorter versions in *Norddeutsche Allgemeine Zeitung (NAZ)*, 22 March 1897: 'Unter den Linden'. On this point generally see Heinrich Popitz, *Phänomene der Macht. Autorität – Herrschaft – Gewalt – Technik*, Tübingen 1986.

Figure 1 Silver three mark and jubilee coin (1913) on the occasion of the centenary celebration for the wars of liberation/unification (Ø 33 millimetres, 15 grams). The legend on the front reads: 'The King called and all, all came. With God for King and Fatherland. 17. 3. 1813.'

which are so dominated by economic and political interests, for they force one to halt for a moment in the haste of the working life and to look at the past'.[8] Other contemporary commentators offered a more grandiose interpretation still: 'What is the task of the Jubilee of 1913? – To remind the German that this is about his very own business, his own pride, and his best effort. It was not just the wars of liberation in which this power unfolded, but it was completely contained within them; it was a strong punch into world history.'[9]

Extraordinary in character, clearly distinguished from everyday life and aimed at long-term effect, all spectacular public celebrations helped to form and solidify collective memories. Politics of mentality and culture, historical

---

[8] Decree (*Dankerlaß*) on the occasion of Friedrich the Great's 200th birthday and his own birthday, 29 January 1912, quoted from Schultheß, *Europäischer Geschichtskalender* 54 (Berlin 1913), p. 11.

[9] Edgar Ubisch, 'Der Freiheitskampf von 1813', in *Preußische Jahrbücher*, 151 (January–March 1913), p. 149. Cf. Elisabeth Fehrenbach, *Wandlungen des Kaisergedankens*, 1871–1918, Munich 1969.

ceremonial and art-forms, personal love of pomp and offers of integration culminated in these major events.[10]

State celebrations were thus able to contribute repeatedly and long-term to the visualization, legitimization, and authenticity of control and power, as long as the organizers used the media intelligently and adapted themselves to the particular possibilities and forms of public communication offered by them. Under these conditions various versions of a celebration, in writing, drawing and photography, theatre and festivals, sound, narratives and rumours, which could be repeated any number of times, continued to have an effect over and above the ephemeral public event.

From the perspective of communications history, it was not just public appearances of the monarch, his actions or speeches, that were centre-stage, but to almost the same degree the audience, and with that different forms and methods of conveying meaning and the varying contexts in which such meanings were understood. As Friedrich Naumann once noted, an Emperor's words have a stronger effect if he repeats something which has been said before: 'In such cases it is the Emperor who stamps his image onto the copper of an everyday opinion and thus turns it into a national coin . . . Given the nature of the German Empire it is very difficult to distinguish between a private point, publicized at the Kaiser's behest, and a direct imperial announcement.'[11]

Wilhelm II appeared in public more often than any of his predecessors. While his participation in the business of government was arbitrary and irregular, even sporadic, he displayed a disproportionately greater sense of

[10] A good overview can be found in Michael Maurer, 'Feste und Feiern als historischer Forschungsgegenstand', *Historische Zeitschrift*, 253 (1991), pp. 101–30; in addition see W. Gebhardt, 'Fest, Feier und Alltag. Über die gesellschaftliche Wirklichkeit des Menschen und ihre Deutung', DPhil dissertation, Tübingen 1986, and the essay collection of Uwe Schultz (ed.), *Das Fest. Eine Kulturgeschichte von der Antike bis zur Gegenwart*, Munich 1988; Dieter Düding Paul Friedemann, and Paul Münich (eds.), *Öffentliche Festkultur. Politische Feste in Deutschland von der Aufklärung bis zum Ersten Weltkrieg*, Reinbeck 1988; Manfred Hettling and Paul Nolte (eds.), *Bürgerliche Feste. Symbolische Formen politischen Handelns im 19. Jahrhundert*, Göttingen 1993; and the research by Volker Ackermann, *Nationale Totenfeiern in Deutschland: von Wilhelm I. bis Franz Josef Strauss; eine Studie zur politischen Semiotik*, Stuttgart 1990; Wolfgang Hardtwich, 'Nationsbildung und politische Mentalität. Denkmal und Fest im Kaiserreich', in his *Geschichtskultur und Wissenschaft*, Munich 1990, pp. 264–301. For the early history of celebrations in Prussia, and in particular the jubilee celebrations of the coronation of 1701, see now Bernd Sösemann, 'Zeremoniell und Inszenierung. Öffentlichkeit und dynastisch-höfische Selbstdarstellung in der preußischen Krönung und den Jubiläumsfeiern (1701–1851)', in: Bernd Sösemann (ed.), *Kommunikation und Medien in Preußen vom 16. bis zum 19. Jahrhundert* (Beiträge zur Kommunikationsgeschichte 12), Stuttgart 2002, pp. 85–135, and for the subject as a whole the bibliography in Bernd Sösemann (ed.), *Öffentliche Kommunikation in Brandenburg-Preußen. Eine Spezialbibliographie* (Beiträge zur Kommunikationsgeschichte 13), Stuttgart 2002.

[11] *Die Zukunft*, 34 (1896), pp. 337–45: 'Das Kaisertelegramm am Friedensfeste'; citations pp. 337 and 342.

responsibility when it came to invitations to holidays and celebrations, the suggestion of festivities, and his personal involvement in the planning of the programme and the stage-management of the event. Contemporaries who welcomed the Kaiser to such festivities often paid homage to him: 'Your Majesty explained yourself how important it is when the Kaiser and Kaiserin personally attend a festivity and thus uphold its national importance.'[12]

The files not only reveal with how much commitment and decisiveness Wilhelm exercised his 'personal rule'[13] in this respect. They also show how densely the Kaiser's diary was crammed with this kind of public engagement and what a huge effort was afforded to his domestic and foreign trips, and to the planning of a suitably majestic appearance even down to the small provincial towns. Given the knowledge of the complex demands placed upon a modern-day government, this is surprising. Little wonder that the former Minister of War Karl von Einem (Minister of War from 1903 to 1909) concluded in 1915: 'We have not had a functioning head of state for 25 years.'[14] Instead, the head of the German Reich worked as hard in the officers' mess and on the dance floor as he did on stage and exercise ground. In the latter years of the Kaiserreich, the value of such festivities was determined primarily by the Kaiser's opinion and his preferences, and much less by dynastic or class-representative concerns or general power-political necessities.

Therefore the politically disparate development of the latter years of the Kaiserreich will be investigated in terms of public reception within the media, and thus within the context of public life from a perspective, and with the help of documents, that have until now been neglected.[15] This

---

[12] Such reports can often be found in the collections of speeches edited by Johannes Penzler and Bugdan Krieger, *Die Reden Kaiser Wilhelms II.*, part 4, Leipzig 1913, p. 175.

[13] Because the public perception was that of 'personal rule', it is not necessary here to go into the details of the complexities around this term, which has repeatedly been explored by John Röhl with the help of contemporary sources.

[14] Cited in Wilhelm Deist (ed.), *Militär und Innenpolitik im Weltkrieg 1914–1918*, 2 vols., Düsseldorf 1970, no. 425, note 5); cf. also Wilhelm Deist, 'Kaiser Wilhelm II in the Context of His Military and Naval Entourage', in John Röhl and Nicolaus Sombart (eds.), *Kaiser Wilhelm II. New Interpretations*, Cambridge 1982, pp. 169–92. Chief of the General Staff Graf von Waldersee declared in his memoirs that by 1890 the Kaiser had not had 'the slightest inclination to work anymore'. Heinrich Otto Meisner (ed.), *Denkwürdigkeiten des Generalfeldmarschall Alfred Grafen Waldersee*, 3 vols., Stuttgart and Berlin 1922–3, vol. II: *1888–1900*, p. 152.

[15] This deficit is more than apparent. Journalism and communication studies rarely include more than an 'historical dimension' in the guise of whatever the current predominant theory might be. The *Jahrbuch für Kommunikationsgeschichte*, thus far in three volumes, is obviously determined to effect a change in this regard. Although parts of the historical sciences, as well as some literary studies scholars, have disovered the media as a topic for investigation, and publicist and audio-visual accounts as sources, they have not widely drawn any far-ranging convincing theoretical or methodological conclusions from them. Even recent overviews of the history of the past century depict decisions,

includes subjects which were dealt with in literary or theatrical ways, as well as public celebrations and union, church or party congresses, newspapers and (specialized) journals, official commemorative publications, competitions, flyers, memorials, uniforms and flags, coins and medals.

An addition to the traditional media of picture stories and illustrated journals, caricatures and posters was the latest medium of film.[16] Wilhelm II used it in connection with the celebrations in honour of Queen Luise by authorizing and supporting the first film on Luise.[17] The countless, usually spontaneous speeches of the Kaiser,[18] often delivered to ambivalent or even disastrous effect, are as much to be considered as the symbol-laden staging of his appearances at manoeuvres and the naming of ships, unveilings of memorials or blessing of flags, opening of buildings or exhibitions,[19] parliaments, and factories, welcoming of deputations or organizations.

In each case the presentation and the medium are of central importance, as are the conditions for communication and the forms of delivery and reception. What will be examined is a meaningful sub-section of reality, namely the space of public communication. For the audience, for people from all groups, classes and walks of life, this space was filled with questions and answers, with truth and lies – be that the content of rumours or that of confirmed information, be that insights, realizations, signs, or symbols.

An analysis of the changes which occurred in the self-image of the monarchy, in the general political style, and in public perception in the latter years of the Kaiserreich is made easier by the fact that Wilhelminism itself was closely bound up with the public. Wilhelm II liked to demonstrate his

---

events, and developments as if the media had not yet been invented or – if they are mentioned – as if they had been without influence. Cf. Bernd Sösemann, 'Einführende Bemerkungen zur Erforschung der Geschichte der Medien und der öffentlichen Kommunikation in Preußen', in Bernd Sösemann (ed.), *Kommunikation und Medien in Preußen*, pp. 9–21. An older publication concentrates solely on the attitude of the press during the abdication question: Adolf Stutzenberger, *Die Abdankung Kaiser Wilhelms II. Die Entstehung und Entwicklung der Kaiserfrage und die Haltung der Presse*, Berlin 1937. Cf. also the thematically broader study by Friedrich Zipfel, 'Kritik der Öffentlichkeit an der Person und an der Monarchie Wilhelms II. bis 1914', Diss. phil., Berlin 1952.

[16] Ulrike Oppelt, *Film und Propaganda im Ersten Weltkrieg. Propaganda als Medienrealität im Aktualitäten- und Dokumentarfilm* (Beiträge zur Kommunikationsgeschichte 10), Stuttgart 2002, pp. 65–79.

[17] The film elevated the Queen to a 'mother of the fatherland' and placed her in the tradition of the 'Protestant madonna'. For details cf. Axel Marquardt and Heinz Rathsack (eds.), *Preußen. Versuch einer Ausstellung*, Berlin 1981, vol. IV, p. 237.

[18] 'For the rest of the world', commented Ludwig Thoma in *März*, 'that wants to get to know Wilhelm II, can do so in detail and at length by reading the speeches . . .' *März*, 3 (16 February 1909), pp. 248–50: 'Die Krügerdepesche'; this citation p. 250.

[19] The centenary celebrations in Breslau in 1902 led to a confrontation when Gerhart Hauptmann's 'Festspiel' was considered such a provocation by the court that the Crown Prince resigned from the position of patron of the exhibition; the public performance of the play had to be stopped on 18 June. Schultheß, *Europäischer Geschichtskalender* 43 (20 May 1902).

'closeness to the people' (*Volksnähe*) and a certain joviality during his public appearances. The monarch sought his success primarily in staged events (which, though largely based on protocol, were planned also by him), that is to say in the circle of those 'people who crowded around each royal appearance and shouted vivat'.[20] This tendency was more pronounced following the 'Hun-speech', the first climax in a whole series of negative experiences with imperial self-representation.[21] For the rhetorical slip made by the Kaiser when seeing off the troops bound for the war against the Boxers on 27 July 1900, by no means a singular or isolated mistake, led in the autumn of that year to a serious loss of popularity for the monarchy. This was despite extensive attempts at calming the situation which were embarked upon immediately following the speech.[22]

In the Reichstag, within the political parties and the public, the Kaiser's reputation had suffered to such an extent that what still remained of the already corroded 'royalist capital'[23] now threatened to dissolve further even in conservative and generally monarchist circles. A decade earlier, *Die Zukunft* had asked: 'How can it be that his [Wilhelm's] words, intended to evoke a new mood for celebration, nonetheless had such a negative effect on the sensibility of even the most reliable monarchists? This effect is produced by the tone, not by the meaning of the words – and once more on this occasion it was the tone that caused the anxiety.'[24]

The Kaiser's discourse, at best intended to be 'popularizing', had failed not only due to the monarch's weak self-control, his failure to follow individual and collective ministerial advice, and his lack of tact, but primarily because of an insufficient sensitivity *vis-à-vis* the media and because of the strategy of conflict which he directed most pointedly at journalists. Wilhelm II wanted to be 'modern' and to have a public effect. He did

---

[20] Walther Rathenau, *Der Kaiser. Eine Betrachtung*, Berlin 1912, p. 8. Nor was this propensity confined to any particular class, as Walther Rathenau commented: 'Not only the so-called "better" circles, but also simple, little folk take great interest in the fate of the Kaiser's court . . .' Ibid. See also *Intelligenzblatt (Kreise Teltow-Beeskow-Storkow)* 11, 26 January 1899: 'Zum 27. Januar'. The local and regional press was dominated by an uncritical, panegyrical tenor: 'It is not in wars and battles that H.M. seeks honour and fame, no, the gun at ease, the powder dry, the sharpened sword in hand is how today Germany's Kaiser stands, Germany's people stand, a faithful friend to its friends, a dreaded enemy to its enemies, a refuge for peace through its power and strength.' *Grunewald-Echo* (Berlin), 5 (31 January 1909): 'Die einzige Kaisergeburtstagsfeier'.

[21] For details, and for the correct version of the text, cf. Bernd Sösemann, 'Die sogenannte Hunnenrede Wilhelms II.', *Historische Zeitschrift*, 222 (1976), pp. 324–58. See also Annika Mombauer's contribution to this volume, pp. 91–118.

[22] Bernd Sösemann, 'Der Verfall des Kaisergedankens im Ersten Weltkrieg', in John C. G. Röhl (ed.), *Der Ort Kaiser Wilhelms II. in der deutschen Geschichte*, Munich 1991, pp. 145–70.

[23] A term used by Friedrich von Holstein, letter to Philipp Eulenburg, 1 January 1895. John Röhl (ed.), *Philipp Eulenburgs Politische Korrespondenz*, 3 vols., Boppard 1978, vol. 11, p. 1071.

[24] *Die Zukunft*, 18 (13 March 1897), p. 489: 'Sankt Wilhelm'.

Figure 2 Wilhelm II in festive robes, much in demand as a journalistic object in the 'new medium'. A caricature by Thomas Theodor Heine (1867–1948) in *Simplicissimus*, 9 June 1913: 'Im großen Festjahr'. The caption reads: 'Before glory the Gods have placed sweat! Today I covered the one hundred thousandth metre of film!'

possess the gift of approaching people and succeeded when he appealed directly to his audience,[25] but he lacked a deeper understanding of the media and the 'press market'.

His advisors did not even succeed in convincing him to study a slim file of press-cuttings on a regular basis.[26] Thus Wilhelm II did not develop a deeper understanding of contemporary discourse or even a modest sensitivity for the changes taking place in society and mentality. This is also why his sporadic and amateurish attempts to instrumentalize individual publications or editors had to fail. The study of which this essay forms a part begins its analysis of festivities and public celebrations, particularly within the media, in 1896–7 with the twenty-five year jubilee of the founding of the Reich, at a time when Bernhard von Bülow was influential in the background,[27] and continues until October 1913, with the unveiling of the *Völkerschlachtdenkmal* in Leipzig.[28] In total, this study takes account of a large number of public events of importance for the politics of the media, of culture and society. These include the commemoration of the King's coronation of 1701 and of the founding of the Reich in 1871, as well as countless birthdays and remembrance days.[29]

The publication of the *Daily Telegraph* Interview of 28 October 1908 is, from the point of view of the history of communications, the key event

[25] His most frequently chosen topic for this was an appeal against 'enemies of the Reich'. 'Especially today there are powers within the Volk which want to rob the people of this idealism. Help me to preserve the ideal assets of the people which enthused our Volk in 1813 and which also had their effect in 1870.' Wilhelm II's speech to a deputation of Berlin students, on the occasion of the twenty-fifth anniversary of the founding of the German Reich (18 January 1896), Penzler and Krieger, *Reden*, III, p. 8.

[26] Röhl, *Eulenburgs Korrespondenz*, no. 276; Eulenburg's letter to Wilhelm II, 1 January 1890, vol. 1, p. 402. In relation to his neglect of political business, Eley refers to a 'model of absenteeism'. Geoff Eley, *Wilhelminismus, Nationalismus, Faschismus. Zur historischen Kontinuität in Deutschland*, Münster 1991, p. 72; cf. also Isabel V. Hull, *The Entourage of Kaiser Wilhelm II, 1888–1918*, Cambridge 1982, pp. 31–44.

[27] The influence of this smooth and sycophantic courtier can be seen earlier than just immediately prior to his taking over the Chancellorship on 18 October 1900.

[28] These turning points correspond to the different phases referred to in John C. G. Röhl, 'Kaiser Wilhelm II., Großherzog Friedrich I. und der "Königsmechanismus" im Kaiserreich', *Historische Zeitschrift*, 236 (1983), p. 554.

[29] They included: King's coronation (1701); founding of the Reich (1871); birthday of Friedrich the Great (1712); birthday Wilhelm II (1859); East-Prussian *Landtag* (1813); founding of Friedrich-Wilhelm-University (1813); Wilhelm I's death (1888); accession of Friedrich III (1888); birthday of Queen Luise (1776); 'Iron Cross' (1813); address 'To My People' (1813); Academy of Sciences (1700); birthday of Wilhelm I (1797); Schiller celebrations/ parades; Peace of Frankfurt (1871); Johanniter-Orden-Celebration; Tannenberg (15 July 1410); Mansfeld Mining (1200); death of Friedrich III and accession of Wilhelm II (1888); victory celebration (1871); *Turnplatz Hasenheide* (1811); *Großer Kurfürst*; 'Begegnung in Tilsit' (1807); anniversary of Queen Luise's death (1810); centenary celebration (1813); Sedan (1870); Jena and Auerstedt (1806); Wilhelm I's coronation (1861); birthday of Friedrich III (1831); *Völkerschlacht*, Leipzig (1813); birthday of Helmuth von Moltke (1800); social legislation (1881); *Siegesallee* (1886); millennium celebrations.

Figure 3 'Ich bin Ich' ('I am myself'). The Swiss illustrated journal *Der Nebelspalter*
commented in 1904 on Wilhelm's tendency to instrumentalize Prussian history by
celebrating his grandfather ('Wilhelm the Great') and Friedrich the Great, whose famous
dictum 'I am the first servant of my state' the journal used as its motivation for this
cartoon, together with Louis XIV's 'L'état c'est moi.'

for the investigation of the politics of public relations with regard to state
celebrations. In the 'six-some' of communications politics (Kaiser, Chancellor, Parliament, Media, Journalists, Public/Recipients), the balance changed
dramatically following the Eulenburg scandal and the *Daily Telegraph* affair.
Although Wilhelm II did restrict his public speeches and conversations for
a while following this crisis, he did not really stop delivering contentious

addresses.[30] Since the autumn of 1908, since this 'November-Revolution',[31] it is possible repeatedly to demonstrate a latent readiness for protest in society.[32] Since Bülow's fall, an increasingly self-confident parliament had had a chance to practise its inter-fractional desire to shape policies, and this meant that in times of crisis, this readiness for protest could even be increased.

The *Gottesfriede* ('divine peace')[33] that the Kaiser and his people had agreed in November 1908 had lasted barely two years when the next big scandal occurred in Königsberg. With this event Wilhelm had, in the opinion of his critics, returned to his true self and was bound to suffer the inevitable consequences.[34] Democrats, Liberals, and Socialists in Germany and Austria-Hungary all criticized this renewed breach of the domestic peace and regarded it as a 'call for war' of a late-comer against constitution and parliamentarianism which would at best have been worthy of a Tsar.[35] In public gatherings the SPD protested vehemently against 'the absolutism proclaimed in the Kaiser's speech' and against the 'irresponsible

---

[30] Elisabeth Fehrenbach is wrong when she states that Wilhelm's Königsberg 'expectation' speech was the last speech that was critically received. Elisabeth Fehrenbach, *Wandlungen des deutschen Kaisergedankens 1871–1918*, Munich 1969, p. 133. It was followed by a number of other contentious speeches, including Marienburg/East Prussia on 29 August 1910, Hamburg on 20 June and 27 August 1911, Königsberg on 5 February 1913, Berlin on 9 February and 15 June 1913, Bremen on 15 June 1913, Kehlheim on 25 August 1913, and again in Berlin and Hamburg on 22 March and 23 May 1914 respectively.

[31] Maximilian Harden's phrase in an interview, *Leipziger Tageblatt*, 29 August 1910: 'Maximilian Harden über die Kaiserrede', which was immediately sent to the Chancellor at Hohenfinow.

[32] It is therefore possible to speak of an 'inter-fractional policy *in statu nascendi*'. After 1912, and particularly in January 1913, following the anti-conservative direction of the Centrum and the parties' more self-confident treatment of the army bills (acceptance by the Social Democrats and rejection by the Conservatives) that policy received a much clearer political outline than ever before.

[33] *Kölnische Zeitung*, 30 August 1910: 'Schluß der Debatte'.

[34] For this speech (*Festmahl* in Königsberg), see *Der Morgen* (Vienna), 32, 29 August 1910: 'Die Königsfanfare' (Leader); *Ostdeutsche Rundschau*, 28 August 1910: 'Die neue Kaiserrede'; *Hannoverscher Courier*, 28 August 1910. In his speech of 25 August, the Kaiser had drawn conclusions regarding the lessons to be learnt from Queen Luise's example. 'She teaches us that . . . us men should cultivate all martial virtues; . . . For only in our armaments lies our peace. And what are our women supposed to learn from the Queen? They should learn that the main task of the German woman is not in the area of assemblies and associations, not in achieving alleged rights in which they could be equal to men, but in quiet work at home and in the family. They are supposed to educate the young generation, particularly to obedience and to be respectful of age . . . Regarding Myself as an instrument of the Lord, without regard for current opinions of the day, I go my way, which is dedicated solely to the well-being and peaceful development of our Fatherland.'

[35] *Illustriertes Wiener Extrablatt*, 27 August 1910: 'Der Gottesgnadenkaiser': 'This speech is among his worst excesses (*gehört zu seinen schärfsten Entgleisungen*)', and *Neues Wiener Journal*, 27 August 1910: 'Also sprach Kaiser Wilhelm . . .', *Neue Freie Presse* (Vienna) 16527, 27 August 1910. However, there were also calming commentaries: 'The Kaiser only speaks aggressively, but he acts tamely', *Die Zeit* (Vienna) 30 August 1910: 'Der Weinprediger', and similarly: *Wiener Allgemeine Zeitung*, 27 August 1910; *Neues Wiener Tageblatt*, 238, 31 August 1910: 'Die Königsberger Kaiserrede'; *Fremden-Blatt* (Vienna) 238, 31 August 1910.

powerbroker (*Drahtzieher*)'.[36] They claimed that all of Germany was of the impression that 'the clique which holds the Kaiser in its hands' could lead the world towards catastrophe, war, or *coup d'état*.[37]

Thomas Nipperdey's interpretation of the last two and a half years before the war 'as a stable, not acute crisis'[38] is at best true for the *Grosse Politik* and for the parliamentary affairs in the Reich. Within the media and the public, including middle-class national-liberal circles, the impression was rather that of an increasing inability to arrive at convincing and stable long-term crisis management, even where urgent domestic policy topics were concerned. The number of demonstrations and strikes, and their vehemence, size, and thematic concerns (for example against the price increases for meat) increased. Despite economic prosperity, the costs for armaments were becoming a growing burden; the policy of the agrarians was increasingly regarded as demagogic, reactionary, and egotistical; in South Germany the anti-Prussian mood grew, as did the polemic in the media against Prussianism; in the entire country the aversion increased against populist-demagogic groupings such as the old-established Pan-German League (1891–4), as well as the newly founded 'German Army League' (1912) and the 'Prussian League' (1913). At the same time there was a popular loathing of the 'militarization' of politics and society (evidence of which seemed to be provided by the Zabern affair).

The focal point of the Kaiser's popular activities shifted after 1910 towards festivities which were more restricted by ceremony. The Chancellor lost influence *vis-à-vis* the monarch and parliament. The Reichstag and the media increased their importance for public discourse despite the fact that initiatives for legislation to change the constitution had failed. Under such conditions, increased domestic pressure had to result, especially when in addition a nationalist right wing protest developed among the public, as happened later in the Moroccan Crisis.[39]

While the ceremony of festivities and the rituals of public holidays protected the Reichstag from direct degradation of parliament and its members, or the Social Democrats from drastic attacks by the Kaiser, it did

---

[36] *Arbeiter-Zeitung* (Vienna) 27 August 1910: 'Er hat die Sprache wiedergefunden.'

[37] *Badischer Landesbote*, 215, 16 September 1910: Theodor Butz, 'Eine taktische Frage' (reader's letter). The Auswärtiges Amt presented this article to the Chancellor, together with a report by the German consul in Moscow (31 August 1910) which refers to the newspaper *Golos Moskwy*, which enquired anxiously whether German policy could still be trusted and who was responsible for it, if it was headed by a 'mystic'.

[38] Thomas Nipperdey, *Deutsche Geschichte 1866–1918*, vol. II: *Machtstaat vor der Demokratie*, Munich 1992, p. 755.

[39] Bernd Sösemann, *Theodor Wolff. Ein Leben mit der Zeitung*, 2nd edn, Munich 2001, pp. 122–31.

not protect the monarch's opponents completely from his spontaneous outbursts or exaggerated displays of overbearing views of divine right and absolute power to rule within the perceived sanctuary of the Brandenburg Landtag. Following the *Daily Telegraph* scandal, the politics of communication and reception had changed. This was a significant, broad shift, and provided a new basis for the final years of the Kaiserreich. No subject and hardly a politically interested person remained untouched by it, because the shock it caused in public and parliamentary life, as well as in the media and party-political scene, was given more attention and was more strongly registered, analysed, interpreted, and reacted to than ever before.

If Nipperdey considers the majority of voters to have been hardly touched by the crisis and if he concludes noticeably vaguely that the Kaiser's self-esteem had 'of course . . . suffered a blow since then',[40] then he exaggerates the importance of the external factor that the public unrest and the revolutionary upsurge among radical Socialists calmed down after a while.

The disturbance had at times taken on revolutionary traits in public discourse and was able to continue in less spectacular, but politically no less important ways. The politicization of the public, the parliamentarization of government work, the self-confidence of the oppositional powers, and the importance and scope for influence of the media had, however, not come about just at that point. They had merely increased and grown, so that in contrast with the time before the 'November storms' of 1908, any criticism or defence of the monarch, of the person or deeds of the Kaiser or the Hohenzollerns, of the social and constitutional situation of the Reich or Prussia had to be more fundamental.[41] In addition, the repertoire of convincing excuses had decreased, and their recipients, both at home and abroad, were increasingly less inclined to disregard 'spontaneities', 'clumsiness', and discrepancies between the spoken word and the government's official version of an imperial speech.[42] The Kaiser's word had to

---

[40] Nipperdey, *Geschichte*, vol. II, p. 737; see also Thomas Nipperdey, 'Organisierter Kapitalismus, Verbände und die Krise des Kaiserreichs', in *Geschichte und Gesellschaft*, 5 (1979), pp. 418–33.

[41] On the occasion of the centenary of the wars of liberation, Theodor Wolff recorded his criticism by casting back his eyes to Friedrich III: 'The civil rights which had been promised to them [the German patriots of 1813] were not granted; yesterday's celebrated heroes of liberation were put in chains as demagogues, the parasites returned to the places drenched in the people's blood, and a nation just united was once more divided into casts and classes, into well- and ill-meaning camps . . . Would we have seen this happen if fate had given him [Friedrich III] more time? – we do not know. But perhaps he would have kept his promise.' *Berliner Tageblatt*, 125, 10 March 1913: T. W. 'An mein Volk'.

[42] Following the 'Hun-Speech' officials started to deny the 'public character' of a speech in cases of conflict with the press over the correct wording of an address by the Kaiser. 'Fridericus-Rex-speech'; Döberitz, 29 May 1903, in Penzler and Krieger (eds.), *Reden*, vol. III, pp. 159f.

Figure 4 The loquacious Wilhelm II and his eldest son Wilhelm, Crown Prince of Prussia and of the German Reich (1882–1951). A caricature by Thomas Theodor Heine in *Simplicissimus* (summer 1898): 'An anecdote from Greek history based on an antique vase. Alexander the Great was the son of King Philipp of Macedonia. Philipp raised his state to a high level of perfection, not least by the excellent speeches and addresses which he liked to give frequently to his troops, military leaders, and his people. After a particularly inspiring speech, King Philipp found his son in tears and he said: 'My son, why are you crying?' 'Oh, royal lord and father', answered Alexander, 'I fear that if you go on ruling for much longer, you will leave nothing for me to say.'

lose its impact if discussions arose in the press over the different versions of a speech or the meaning of a word, for 'nothing is worse', as the *Berliner Tageblatt* commented, 'than if the other, perhaps exaggerated and vulnerable interpretation [of a speech] has become firmly stuck in the heads [of the public]. And as is known, the subsequent semi-officious or officious corrections do not enjoy a high regard among our people.'[43]

At the same time, excuses such as lack of experience or likeable shortcomings which were explicably 'human' were hardly able to have calming or apologetic effects any longer. This was because neither had time helped to 'heal' them, nor had the negative experiences of the past led the political advisors and others in positions of responsibility to manage such situations with more imagination and determination. Following the turn of the century the unease with which the abundant public celebrations were received turned into ever more strongly voiced public criticism. 'We won't join in the celebration!', the *Vorwärts* declared in 1913:

We stand uninvolved on the sideline and shrug our shoulders when a frothing wild water of celebratory speeches, articles and hurrahs pours over the country. We know how much despicable hypocrisy is voiced in this noisy carry-on, and we know how convinced monarchists talk about the carrier of the crown when they are in private – if all the lèses-majesté were known that are uttered in these circles, the prosecutors would have to introduce night shifts.[44]

But the disapproval of parties and editors, even those of conservative leanings, only heightened Wilhelm's triumphant displays and the increasingly inappropriate desire to impress of a statesman who was visibly failing to mature. In this context the *Berliner Tageblatt* commented:

The first and most painful [realization] that we have to emphasise is that we cannot write without restraint: the Kaiser and *his* people, or the German people and *their* Kaiser. There are many among us who are lacking the feeling that the personal bond between a master and his people should be a matter of course. And although doubtless a large majority of the German people is still currently monarchically inclined it cannot be denied that this relationship has shifted to the detriment of the *Kaisertum* since the death of Kaiser Wilhelm I.[45]

On the other hand the 'simple' subject did not seem to tire of celebrating his Kaiser whenever the opportunity arose, and appeared to follow his self-confident and exaggerated accounts with equal enthusiasm even when

---

[43] *Berliner Tageblatt*, 251, 18 May 1905; for similar views see *Freisinnige Zeitung*, 226, 15 May 1905 (evening edn), *Deutsche Tageszeitung*, 228 and 234, 16 and 19 May 1905 (evening edn).
[44] *Vorwärts*, 149, 16 June 1913: 'Wir und Wilhelm'.
[45] *Berliner Tageblatt*, 298, 15 June 1913: Wilhelm Ostwald, 'Der Kaiser und das Volk'.

they modelled themselves on the images of leaders and politics of bygone
eras. But even among these recipients changes were taking place. In addition, national celebrations were increasingly losing their political profile in
favour of public entertainment. Even the *Norddeutsche Allgemeine*, on the
occasion of the jubilee of the Kaiser's accession to the throne in 1913, only
published sixteen articles by academics on legislation and the navy, technical matters or the economy, industry, and sport, but without offering a
historical or political commentary on the event itself anywhere in the paper.
Die Gartenlaube restricted itself to a double-page reproduction of a drawing
depicting part of the formal dinner in the Kaiser's *Schloss*.[46] The preparation
of the celebrations in the media decreased, too, and became more one-sided,
restricting itself to conventional historical paintings or eulogies in which
even the weakest of Prussian kings were glorified and in which Prussia's path
to national unity was related uncritically as an inevitable development.[47]
The Wilhelmine state was depicted under the motto 'Ein Volk, Ein Kaiser,
Ein Reich!' as the culmination and completion of German history. Leaders
and commentaries were dedicated almost entirely to conjuring up political
and social unity, economic and military strength, and to declaring the desire
to support the path of the German Reich towards *Weltmacht* also by way
of journalism. Only occasionally a reflection of reality is visible at the mar-
gins where the fact was not glossed over that there existed in Germany not
only differences of opinion, but profound controversies over constitutional,
confessional, economic, party-political, and ethnic questions which could
lead to a 'new Jena', 'this time however a domestic Jena (*ein inneres Jena*)'.[48]

   Festivities and celebrations are not fixed entities, they are not autonomous and do not contain a purpose within themselves. For Wilhelm II,
they were not only removed from everyday political life in a peculiar way,
but for the biggest group in society they were even in obvious contrast to it.
They were intended to provide a 'free space' away from 'party quarrels',[49] in
which harmony and the propaganda-based image of history had to prevail.
This protective zone was intended to deflect from politics and the economy and at least on the celebration day itself to prevent conflicting interests

[46] *Die Gartenlaube*, no. 27 (1913), pp. 570f.
[47] The *Kreuz-Zeitung* was not alone in spreading this view, but it did so particularly often and celebrated
    the 'world historical importance' of events immoderately and exaggeratedly: 'There are basic truths
    in history about which there is no disagreement. Among those is foremost the one that everything
    big or important that has happened in Prussia and Germany since the days of the Reformation was
    particularly the work of the house of Hohenzollern . . .' *NPZ*, 16, 10 January 1901 (evening edn):
    'Die Hohenzollern in demokratischer Beleuchtung'.
[48] *Vorwärts*, 69, 22 March 1897: 'Politische Übersicht'.
[49] *Intelligenzblatt*, 99, 26 August 1913: 'Die Fürstenfeier bei Kehlheim'.

and arguments. In the process of societal change and public discourse domestic policy debates developed their own dynamic. As the *Intelligenzblatt* commented, such public discourse was seen as 'a sign of strength and not of weakness. It is understandable that in times in which the vital interests of the whole seem secure, the quarrels and differences of interests of the parts come to the fore and seem temporarily to overshadow the unifying interest.'[50]

It was not just the public's 'loss of monarchical conviction' that was detectable in the Wilhelmine epoch. Lost in its 'political shape', 'social atmosphere' and rhetorical behaviour were 'natural authority' and role model function for the future.[51] In the 'democratic current' the monarchical aura suffered continually and to a degree that had not even been experienced during the revolution of 1848–9. The *Kreuz-Zeitung* commented in 1913: 'Never in the history of the German people, the most monarchical people in its conviction and character, its customs and habit, has the monarchical thought been so attacked, has the monarchy faced such a strong front of open and hidden opponents as in this most recent past.'[52]

Wilhelm II did not succeed in developing new, more sophisticated, and politically convincing forms of leadership-aesthetic, suitable for an industrial nation. Demonstrative visits to factories or an openly displayed interest in modern technology did not suffice to cancel out the impression of the staged and superficial. The Kaiser did not even manage to change the traditional ceremonial forms of state and court celebration, so that they could be accepted by a society that was less guided by league or party dignitaries, and increasingly by middle-class expectations, and by functionaries and the conditions of a differentiated press.[53] In the latter years of

---

[50] Ibid., 37, 21 January 1911: 'Vierzig Jahre deutscher Einheit'.

[51] The former Reichstag-member of the National-Liberal Party and travel companion of the Crown Prince, Friedrich Dernburg (1833–1911) had urged on the occasion of the Kaiser's fiftieth birthday that the 'reciprocal trust between Kaiser and Volk' had to be reproduced, because otherwise 'an element of national strength' would be lost. 'Zum 50. Geburtstag des Kaisers', *Berliner Tageblatt*, 47, 27 January 1909. Only two years later, on the occasion of the fourtieth anniversary of the founding of the Reich, negative visions of the future prevailed: 'Among the people one no longer thinks that things are about averting a catastrophe, but rather about delaying one if possible. Après nous le déluge . . .' *Bayerisches Vaterland*, 18 January 1911. Similar accounts can be found in *Deutsche Tageszeitung*, *Berliner Tageblatt* and *Germania*.

[52] *NPZ*, 275, 15 June 1913.

[53] 'We had to experience how a whole number of pseudo-patriots just in these days intended to conjure up the Prussian epoch of conflict of the sixties which had been happily overcome . . . Added to this were the utterly superfluous attempts at intimidation which had been instigated in as clumsy a way as possible by irresponsible, alleged confidants of the crown, like Freiherr v. Stumm . . . Thus politically the centenary celebrations began in a disharmonious way which only served too well to diminish the joy of the memorable jubilee days both with the government and the governed alike.' *Berliner Tageblatt*, 146, 21 March 1897: Arthur Levysohn, 'Politische Wochenschau'.

the Kaiserreich public celebrations were reduced to a self-congratulatory, backward-looking, and triumphant gesturing[54] and an intoxicated national monumental cult. As a result they were regarded, if not as completely anachronistic, then at least as a historicizing political myth[55] whose main parts were no longer considered to be appropriate. The *Fränkische Tagespost* expressed this unhappiness thus:

> Oh, no, the wishes of the present and the hopes for the future of the people are not attached to such displays of royal splendour and pompous expansion of power, which makes obvious to everyone the extent to which the *privileges* (*Vorrechte*) still connected with royalty, and the extent of the *denial of privileges of the people* (*Volksentrechtung*); to such displays which swallow *hundreds of thousands* which have *to be paid by the poorest of the poor*; to such displays which aim at giving an undeserving gloss to an *old and innerly rotten glory* in the eyes of the foolish and the young . . . We no longer rebel against the new German Reich, we accept it, although many millions of Germans remain excluded from it: but even within the given borders; how much is still lacking from a unity as we envisage it! . . . Of course, we too want to know that the ties which bind us Bavarians to the Reich are unbreakable. But this makes the demand all the more urgent that this Reich not be placed under the thumb of Prussia and its Junker-class, that this Prussian coercion does not suffocate these progressive buds in other states, too, allowing to flower and grow only that which is spiritually congenial to its reactionary clique.[56]

Even in the case of the *Sedanstag* the constant evocation led first to a weakening of the message both journalistically and at the psychological level of reception, then to a partial re-interpretation[57] and finally even a devaluation of the event.[58]

---

[54] *Vorwärts*, 66, 20 March 1900. On the occasion of the twenty-fifth anniversary of Wilhelm's accession to the throne, *März* published an ironic, quotation-filled essay on the topic of the Byzantinism of obtrusive flatterers in publishing houses, editorial offices, and academic offices ('superiority of the Wilhelmine epoch over similar eras, such as the Medici or Augustus. And all that: through only one man'. *März* 25, 21 March 1913, pp. 397–402: Wilhelm Herzog, 'Wie sie Ihn umjubeln', here: p. 398).

[55] 'Myth is the most important medium of society's "imagination" . . . Tales of the past serve to create a consciousness of unity and uniqueness, i.e. identity. Knowledge about the past secures identity . . . Only at a next step is the decision made whether such further development assumes the character of circular insistence, resisting against the powers of change, or if on the contrary it strives for change, in opposition to the powers of insistence. In either case there is a narrative virulence at work, and stories exercise power to determine actions.' Dieter Harth and Jan Assmann (eds.), *Revolution und Mythos*, Frankfurt am Main 1992, pp. 9–35, 39–43; here: pp. 41f.; Rüdiger Voigt (ed.), *Politik der Symbole, Symbole der Politik*, Opladen 1989, pp. 9–14.

[56] *Fränkische Tagespost*, 198, 25 August 1913: 'Fürstentag zu Kehlheim'; see also 'Weckruf zur Preußenwahl', *Sozialdemokratische Flugschriften* 17, Berlin 1913, pp. 5–8: 'Preußen und das Reich' (original italics).

[57] Some papers undertook this re-interpretation gradually with the aim no longer to humiliate the French. 'We are not celebrating the defeat of the enemy (*des Erbfeindes*), we are celebrating the birth of German unity . . .' *Intelligenzblatt*, 104, 3 March 1910: 'Sedan'.

[58] 'May the Sedanstag lead our German people back to faith; for from faith alone does new life flow, all virtues spring from it. If the right faith becomes alive again, then duty and obedience, order and

When *Die Gartenlaube* published an historical overview and a portrait of Leibnitz on the occasion of the celebration of the Academy of Science,[59] it is true that it chose a less engaging and original approach than in comparable cases of the immediate past, but at least this approach does not reveal the same lack of imagination in subject matter, conventionality in style, and indifference in presentation than the reporting of numerous publications on the occasion of high-ranking celebrations. The *Berliner Tageblatt* commented: 'Memorial celebrations of the old Kaiser, who led us to peace through victorious wars, are more and more clearly turning into demonstrations for internal and external peace. The creation of the new *Nationalkokarde* [national emblem on uniforms] is a step on the way of closer amalgamation of the German peoples into one German people.'[60]

Although Wilhelm II did not appear prominently during the building and particularly the inauguration of the *Völkerschlachtdenkmal* in Leipzig in 1913 – although present, he did not give a speech for reasons of domestic policy and diplomacy[61] – the importance for the public of this state celebration should not be rated lower than that of the *Sedanstag* or the Kaiser's birthday. Thus the *Illustrirte Zeitung* published two extensive special editions, and the *Leipziger Neuesten Nachrichten* summarized its editions from 16–19 October into one special edition.[62] *Die Gartenlaube* boasted a large-scale illustration of the 'gigantic scaffolding' during the building of the memorial, without however emphasizing more than the technical aspects of it, while reporting the usual fare in its four-page highly illustrated spread on the 'Battle of Leipzig'.[63] This relative restraint was most obvious on the occasion of the inauguration of the *Völkerschlachtdenkmal*, which was criticized sharply not only by the SPD. *Der Morgen* judged the memorial to be 'a monster of unprecedented nature',

---

modesty will return; then love for King and Fatherland, respect for superiority and regard for the law will emerge again.' *NPZ*, 408, 31 August 1895: 'Sedan'.

[59] *Die Gartenlaube*, 6 (1900), pp. 196f.

[60] *Berliner Tageblatt*, 150, 23 March 1897: 'Das Wilhelmsfest. Kaiser, Fürsten und Volk' (cited in overview of press reports in the *Kreuz-Zeitung*).

[61] *Illustrirte Zeitung*, 3669, 23 October 1913, pp. 705–10: 'Das Leipziger Jahrhundertfest'; pp. 710–17: 'Die Leipziger Erinnerungs- und Festtage'; pp. 718–19: 'Die Eilbotenläufe der Deutschen Turnerschaft zur Weihe des Völkerschlachtdenkmals'; pp. 720–72: 'Die russische Gedächtniskirche in Leipzig'; pp. 725f.: 'Die Gedenkfeier der Völkerschlacht vor fünfzig Jahren'.

[62] *Illustrirte Zeitung* 3668, 16 October 1913, pp. 2–10: 'Die Schlacht bei Leipzig'; pp. 11f.: 'Das Denkmal' (poem by Freiherr Börries von Münchhausen); pp. 13f.: 'Die Völkerschlacht in der Karikatur'; pp. 686–8: 'Wie es Leipzigs Einwohnern während der Völkerschlacht erging'; *Leipziger Neueste Nachrichten*, no number, no date: 'Die Leipziger Jahrhundertfeier'; with a leader by the historian Karl Lamprecht, 'Zur Denkmal-Weihe'.

[63] *Die Gartenlaube*, 45 (1911), pp. 1067; 893–7.

A contradiction within itself, a symbol of thoughtlessness and of lying helpless-
ness. . . . The greatness of the memorial consists of roses the size of men, of toes
which weigh a ton, and of the puffed-up bodies of wrinkled acrobats rolling around.
Where in this bombastic fever of stone is there even a shred of the German spirit
and thankful belief in our fathers? One stands crushed by this raw materialism
which suffocates all but the last spark of soulful reflection; one stands hopelessly
in front of such advertised exaggeration of such infertile poverty of thought. This
tool of arbitrary power lacks inner proportion, which is why, despite its many-digit
figures, it appears like a toy, like the babble of epigones who want to be heroic but
are actually only childish.[64]

The editors of *Die Gartenlaube* celebrated the inauguration with a conspicuously short illustrated report about the 'real people's celebration' of the
'German Patriots' League', prefacing it with the statement that the event
had passed 'without any disharmony'.[65]
    Because of such critical receptions, these celebrations could have little
more than politically restorative power. Neither the Kaiser nor the court
were able to offer appropriate future-oriented ideals to 'public opinion',
which had become a recognized 'power factor of political progress', as the *Intelligenzblatt* had already foreseen in 1899.[66] All that 'Wilhelm the Sudden'
('Wilhelm der Plötzliche'), as South German humour mocked him, could
offer, was an exaggerated dynastic consciousness and a populist romanticized expressiveness in ever-changing variations. The 'Bayreutherization'
of state celebrations served a traditional national pedagogy. Even under
Wilhelm II it utilized the myths of a 'natural', purposeful and divinely willed
rise of Prussia and its 'German calling' of national unity, despite the fact
that this Kaiser, in the eyes of an increasing majority, had 'never achieved
anything useful'.[67] This imitative monarchical 'anti-world' unashamedly
demonstrated autocratic features in an increasingly parliamentarized constitutional state and thus tried to prevent change or reform programmes.
It managed, at least in the conservative and national liberal media, to
promote a favourable journalism consisting of a mostly undemanding eu-
logizing praise of the ruler.[68] However, the critical press, intellectuals, and

---

[64] *Der Morgen*, 7, 14 June 1913, p. 577: Robert Breuer, 'Das Leipziger Denkmal'.
[65] A fact that was important to the author (Carl Boysen, 'Das Leipziger Fest') because he closed by
    stating that the tie between the former allies had been torn, and the peoples no longer regarded each
    other 'in the same friendly matter', because 'politics (*die leidige Politik*) had split them apart during
    the course of the years.' *Die Gartenlaube*, 44 (1913), pp. 941f.
[66] *Intelligenzblatt*, 153, 30. XII. 1899: 'An der Jahrhundertwende'.
[67] Maximilian Harden, interview in the *Leipziger Tageblatt*, 29 August 1910: 'Maximilian Harden über
    die Kaiserrede'. See also note 34.
[68] Georg Barthel Roth, *Der deutsche Kaisergedanke. Ein ernstes Mahnwort an das deutsche Volk zum 27.
    Januar 1893*, Cologne 1893.

thoughtful contemporaries in the sciences, politics, and the economy missed ideals beyond the fleet and colonies, as well as a deeper enthusiasm directed at the major issue of imperfect national unity.[69] Friedrich Meinecke commented in the Kaiser's jubilee year: 'Our goals go beyond Fatherland and state, but our roots are well submerged within it . . . Thus we have entered, even in our inner development, a danger-zone whose outcome lies in the dark . . . Therefore we lack today the inclination to brag and boast.'[70]

The monarch's pathetic gesturing and the theatrical attitude had to have the ring of an anachronistic, banal, and hollow 'operetta regime' (in Holstein's worlds) amidst the sober prose and statistics of a society that was defined by technology and economy, matter-of-factness and efficiency.[71] Only parts of the audience condemned the Kaiser's speeches as careless diplomacy[72] and non-statesmanlike chattiness, as tactless and out of control, or even as the despicable 'unmanly childishness' of a dilettante on the throne who was damaging the German Reich both at home and abroad.[73] War veterans' associations approved of Wilhelm's departure from the 'old Prussian, measured' behaviour of his grandfather, from whom he wanted to distinguish himself on this point in public,[74] and also liked his approach

[69] *Berliner Tageblatt*, 292, 12 June 1910: 'Albert Traeger, Achtzig Jahre'.

[70] Friedrich Meinecke, 'Deutsche Jahrhundertfeier und Kaiserfeier' (speech at Freiburg University, 14 June 1913), in *Logos*, 4 (1913), pp. 161–75, here 161 and 175; Friedrich Meinecke, *Betrachtungen über Vergangenheit, Gegenwart und Zukunft des Deutschen Reichs von einem Süddeutschen*, Strasburg 1896, p. 38.

[71] In a piece on Friedrich the Great in the *Illustrirte Zeitung* the portrait of the most important German 'modern ruler' (p. 5) contained a careful, but distinctly drawn opposite picture. *Illustrirte Zeitung*, 138, no. 3577, 18 January 1912, pp. 2–5: J. v. Pflugk-Hartung, 'Friedrich der Große'. See also Paul Schulze-Berghof, *Die Nationalbühne und Volksfeier für Friedrich den Großen*, Berlin 1911, p. 4.

[72] 'The powder dry, the sword sharpened, the goal identified, the strength marshalled and the pessimists banned! My glass is raised to our people in arms!' Wilhelm II's 'powder speech' in Berlin on 26 October 1905, in Penzler and Krieger, *Reden*, vol. III, p. 279.

[73] On this point see Hildegard Freifrau von Spitzemberg, *Das Tagebuch der Baronin Spitzemberg*, ed. Rudolf Vierhaus, Göttingen, 2nd edn 1962, p. 489, or Marie Fürsting Radziwill, *Briefe vom deutschen Kaiserhof 1889–1915*, Berlin 1936, pp. 314f. Max Weber wrote to Friedrich Naumann on 14 December 1906: 'The measure of contempt which greets us, as a nation, abroad (Italy, America, everywhere! and rightly so! that's what is decisive), because we allow ourselves to accept this regime of this man, has become of late a factor of first class world political importance for us . . . [Politics that want to protect Wilhelm II's personal prestige] are today no longer politics which calculate on the basis of reality, be that at home or abroad. Because this prestige is gone . . .' *Max Weber Gesamtausgabe*, ed. Horst Baier *et al.*, Abt. II vol. v: Letters, p. 202.

[74] In addition, Wilhelm tried with his campaign to popularize the honouring of his grandfather (commemorative coins, construction of memorials, his naming as 'Wilhelm the Great' and particularly during the celebrations of his 100th birthday, 21–23 March 1897), which was not just supported by the *Kreuz-Zeitung*, to divert some of that glory onto his own time in office. Röhl, *Eulenburgs Korrespondenz*, no. 1301; letter from Monts to Holstein, 2 March 1897, p. 1795; Jakob Vogel, 'Zwischen protestantischem Herrscherideal und Mittelaltermystik. Wilhelm I. und die "Mythomotorik" des

to his God, the 'great Ally'.[75] They welcomed the exterior splendour of the celebration and the ever-present involvement in navy and colonial policy, because this was seen as a way in which the country could emerge from 'the shadow of the foundation of the Reich'.[76] In the celebrations of various clubs (singing, gymnastic, and war veterans), in university jubilee speeches and in the pamphlets accompanying state festivities, these images and ideas of the Kaiser[77] can be found particularly in those passages which try to propagate and legitimize a romanticized image of war which elevates death in battle, as well as trying to popularize national enthusiasm and willingness for sacrifice.[78] Such stylizations, like, for example, the Sedan-celebrations, did not explicitly rule out a great war, and called it either 'people's battle' (*Völkerschlacht*) or 'world war'. They grounded it historically along a traditional line which, although verbally conjuring up the 'ideas of 1813', was connected with completely new political ideas. These included the decadence of the Western 'civilizations', exaggerated beliefs in the chosen German nation, preparation for a 'war of beliefs' (*Glaubenskrieg*),[79] and ideologies which had until then been less well known: the slogan '*Ein Volk, ein Reich!*' and the idea that the Germans, as a 'world power', were faced with a 'racial war'.[80] There was criticism of this view of history and its official propaganda, and not only among the SPD, but also in the national-liberal *Bürgertum* who regarded the many celebrations,[81] the

Deutschen Kaiserreichs', in Gerd Krumeich and Hartmut Lehmann (eds.), '*Gott mit uns.' Nation, Religion und Geschichte im 19. und frühen 20. Jahrhundert*, Göttingen 2000, pp. 213–230.

75 'Fridericus-Rex-speech', Döberitz, 29 May 1903, in Penzler and Krieger, *Reden*, vol. III, p. 160.

76 Thomas Rohrkrämer, *Der Militarismus der 'kleinen Leute'. Die Kriegervereine im Deutschen Kaiserreich 1871–1914*, Munich 1990, pp. 20f.: thirty years after the wars of unification it was deemed time to end the 'current self-congratulatory saturatedness' and to depart for new goals.

77 An example here is Theodor Birt, *Preußen und der Befreiungskrieg. Gedenkworte am kaiserlichen Geburtstag gesprochen* (Marburger Akademische Reden 28), Marburg 1913: see also Wilhelm II's unveiling of the memorial on the Kyffhäuser, in Schultheß, *Europäischer Geschichtskalender*, 43 (1902), p. 84, 18 June 1902, and 'Dichtung und Wahrheit über 1813', *Sozialdemokratische Flugschriften* 19, (Berlin 1913), pp. 8–16.

78 On the subject of death in battle, see also Isabel Hull's contribution to this volume, pp. 235–58.

79 Werner Sombart, *Händler und Helden. Patriotische Besinnungen*, Munich 1915, p. 3.

80 An example of this is Karl Wahl, whose speech in Tübingen, 'The ideas of 1813', which was immediately published, demonstrated such racial-political views. *Die Ideen von 1813*, Tübingen 1913, p. 29; *Intelligenzblatt*, 10, 22 January 1901: 'Deutschland-Preußen 1701 und 1901'; ibid., 100 28 August 1913: 'Die Jahrhundertfeier in Kehlheim'.

81 Even the *Kreuz-Zeitung* concluded after seven years: 'Surely we have now celebrated enough', now it was necessary to become 'practical' and follow the celebrations up with deeds (Germany's development to a 'sea power'). *NPZ*, 29, 18 January 1896: 'Zum 18. Januar'), while *Die Zukunft* stated a year later: 'Seriously minded sons of Germany look forward with a strange anxiousness and almost shivering to the days of celebration which the beginning of spring brings us. Their unease not only stems from a feeling of having had one's fill which the many festivities of the last years must have aroused in any sober and hardworking person . . .' *Die Zukunft*, 18, 20 March 1897: 'Der große Kaiser', p. 34.

hollow-sounding pathos, the emotions against 'enemies of the Reich', the martial stereotypes and the anti-Polish excesses,[82] as well as the diversion attempts of an obtrusively practised tactics of *panem et circenses* at best as anachronistic and politically dangerous.

The *Berliner Tageblatt* commented in 1913:

The German Bürgertum is once again willing to make grave sacrifices for 'the glory of the Reich'. But one cannot deny the fact that even for the German Bürgertum there is a point beyond which it does not want to go. It has been treated as a quantité négligeable for twenty-five years; now it screams for reforms . . . The Kaiser is the living representative of German unity. May he become ever more conscious of the fact that this *unity* has its most secure roots in the *liberty* of the people.[83]

However, *Die Zukunft* had already voiced similar thoughts on the occasion of the Kaiser's birthday (and the twenty-fifth anniversary of German unification):

A people who are continually confronted with new sensations, who cannot calm down and develop a certain trust in a steady leadership, eventually loses the ability to be able to distinguish between what is important and unimportant. Unless one was telling lies one would have to admit that the Kaiser's birthday is not being celebrated in the mood for which one would hope and wish . . . Today, when everyone feels that the serious purpose of the celebration is more directed towards the present than the past, the image is unfortunately a different one: cheap generalizations are being shouted out . . . Black worries lie over the land and darken the joy of the glorious past; the enemies ask with scorn if the new Reich will ever experience a second jubilee . . .[84]

During the *Daily Telegraph* affair Harden had publicized his views regarding the Kaiser's weak leadership in such a sharp way, and had demanded an abdication so forcefully that the Prussian state minister Paul von Breitenbach in his role as head of the Reichs-Office for the administration of the Reichs-Railways immediately forbade the sale of *Die Zukunft* at railway stations.[85]

---

[82] For example, on 20 August 1910 in Poznan when Wilhelm II referred to it as a German province. For comments in the Polish press, see Schultheß, *Europäischer Geschichtskalender*, 51 (1910), pp. 336f., 23 August 1910. See also Jürgen Vietig, 'Die polnischen Grunwaldfeiern der Jahre 1902 und 1910', in Wolfgang H. Fritze (ed.), *Germania Slavica*, vol. IV, Berlin 1980, pp. 237–62; Wolfgang Wippermann, *Der Ordensstaat als Ideologie. Das Bild des Deutschen Ordens in der deutschen Geschichtsschreibung und Publizistik*, Berlin 1979, pp. 197–9.

[83] *Berliner Tageblatt*, 298, 15 June 1913: Paul Michaelis, 'Das Regierungsjubiläum des Kaisers'.

[84] *Die Zukunft*, 16, 18 January 1896: 'Das Deutsche Reich', p. 101.

[85] In the end, however, the Chancellor did not go as far as decreeing a general prohibition. For details see Peter Winzen, *Das Kaiserreich am Abgrund. Die Daily Telegraph Affäre und das Hale-Interview von 1908*, Stuttgart 2002, pp. 43, 260f.

The nation does not believe that the almost fifty-year-old will change,[86] will be able to practise reserve . . . The business of the Reich demands a political temperament, not a dramatic one. We don't want a Jupiter who sends lighting from the clouds . . . Wilhelm II has proven that he is utterly unable to conduct political business . . . The Kaiser is no monarch. The Reich is sovereign, not the Kaiser . . . We don't want to be insulted in our cultural feelings as educated Europeans day after day through speech and writing. We want to preserve state secrets . . . , to despise lies, charades (*Gaukelspiel*) and Byzantine pomp. [We want to] be able to have alliances again . . . And the old respect will return since it has been proven that the Germans still dare to have demands even against the Kaiser.[87]

Already by the turn of the century the public no longer regarded Wilhelm II as a personality who could have an integrative role within society and who could guarantee social cohesion consensually. Despite the fact that the anti-Socialist laws had not been renewed, the views of history and politics held by the SPD and those held by the Wilhelmine government were irreconcilably opposed.[88] The working classes removed themselves from state celebrations as much as possible and had in any case long begun to celebrate their own holidays and to develop their own traditions, myths, cults, and symbols.[89]

The state-organized festivities seemed increasingly deficient. Aside from the pomp, they mirrored an unsatisfactory backward-looking view which was dominated by Prussian interpretations of history.[90] In this way, new

[86] Cf. Wilhelm's view, following an intervention from Bülow, who claims to have asked the Kaiser in 1907 to exercise greater reserve in his public appearances. Wilhelm replied that 'he could not change himself and needed to stay the way he was. Everything else we want to leave to God's will . . .' Bernhard Fürst von Bülow, *Denkwürdigkeiten*, 4 vols., Berlin 1930, vol. 1, p. 601. *Der Morgen* also expressed this realization in 1909: 'It cannot be demanded that the personal character of a fifty-year old man can be changed fundamentally; it also cannot be expected, for it is an impossibility . . . The decisive nature of this moment is the fact that the Kaiser has to make the decision if he wants to continue in his high office in unison with the entire German people or according to the advice and whisperings of a small and until now powerful group. For every monarch there comes at one point the historic moment when he has to part with the powers that until that time had been seen to be his support, but that have actually become suppressing and a hindrance. For the Hohenzollern dynasty that moment has now come. If it wants to fulfil its mission, which the German people have given it, in a lively and powerful manner, then it must free itself from the influence of the class of courtiers and bureaucrats who refer to their former merits for Prussia, but who are strangers to the tasks of the present, if not hostile.' *Der Morgen*, 1909, pp. 92–4: Verus (Ps.), 'Zum fünfzigsten Geburtstag Wilhelms II.'

[87] *Die Zukunft*, 65, 21 November 1908–9, p. 304: 'Gegen den Kaiser'.

[88] Dieter Groh, *Emanzipation und Integration. Beiträge zur Sozial- und Politikgeschichte der deutschen Arbeiterbewegung und des Zweiten Reiches*, Konstanz 1999, pp. 307–23.

[89] Despite the inner opposition which he describes, Wolfgang J. Mommsen nonetheless attributes a high integrative power to the Kaiserreich. *Der autoritäre Nationalstaat*, Frankfurt am Main 1992, p. 38.

[90] See e.g. *NPZ*, 136, 22 March 1897: 'May *that Prussian spirit* . . . even in the changing times . . . *remain unchanged.*'

anti-Prussian views and prejudices were created or existing ones confirmed. In addition, Wilhelm gave support, not only abroad, to the misconception that the German Reich equalled Prussia[91] because it identified itself largely with the same traditions, and because it also glorified the military,[92] sought a militarization of public life, and had a longing for opportunities to prove itself in foreign policy and in wars and conflicts in an irresponsible fashion. In the programmes of public display this was documented with varying degrees of clarity, but it was nonetheless recognizable as a political concept,[93] whose main features consisted of an exaggerated view of the country's power and of increasingly narrowing national-conservative perspectives.[94] Most often these became more concrete in the attempts to legitimize a provocative patriotism with naval and world policy.[95] The prevailing messages could be reduced to the following core: all of Europe lived in continual crisis, a war was not impossible and a larger war, a 'world war', could actually be credited with a positive, progressive potency.[96]

As a result of the loss of the 'monarchical aura' during a worsening domestic political crisis, the level of attention for symbol-laden festivities and the journalistic commentary on such official celebrations increased. The planning and the programmes of state celebrations in Wilhelmine Germany, their order of events and their place in the media offered insights not only into the political profile and the personal inadequacy of the monarch, but also into the decreasing effectiveness of the 'Kaiser myth' and the increasing 'social will-power' of 'public opinion' in regard to the reception of official

[91] 'The new German Reich cannot be Roman, but it must also not be Prussian . . . The craze for world power would lead to dangerous enmity abroad while the rigid Prussiandom would do the same at home. Prussia certainly has done great things for Germany . . . The German Reich . . . must become German, be German, and remain German and must decisively break with all junk from a dead past.' *Die Zukunft*, 16, 18 January 1896, p. 108: 'Das Deutsche Reich'.

[92] Between 1891 and 1913 the numbers of members in the *Kriegervereine* in Prussia, Bavaria and in Württemberg increased threefold; in Baden, Hesse and Saxony they increased by more than double, and in the entire Reich from 1900 to 1913 they rose from 2,184 to 2,837 million. Rohkrämer, *Militarismus*, p. 271.

[93] On the topic of ceremonials see Miloš Vec, 'Das preußische Zeremonialrecht. Eine Zerfallsgeschichte', in Patrick Bahners and Gerd Roellecke (eds.), *Preußische Stile. Ein Staat als Kunstwerk*, Stuttgart 2001, pp. 101–13, here p. 101.

[94] 'Not only the so-called third Kaiserreich was destroyed at Sedan – this one fact alone would probably not have sufficed to give to that 2 September 1870 its inestimable historical meaning for all time – no . . . In the light of the irresistible flowing of national thought, here as there, and in the light of the power of the liberating thoughts of nationally minded politicians in Germany, the unnatural diplomatic system of the 'restored' Europe collapsed like a house of cards.' *Berliner Tageblatt*, 443, 1 September 1895: 'Sedan'.

[95] Gerhard Ritter, *Staatskunst und Kriegshandwerk*, vol. II, Munich 1960, pp. 126f.

[96] Cf. Manfred Messerschmidt, 'Reich und Nation im Bewußtsein der wilhelminischen Gesellschaft', in Herbert Schottelius and Wilhelm Deist (eds.), *Marine und Marinepolitik im kaiserlichen Deutschland 1871–1914*, Düsseldorf 1972, pp. 30–3.

events and collective memory.[97] In this way polarization and a negative general mood grew in a society which was displaying increasing political openness. The unease regarding Wilhelm's public appearances and the measures taken by the state leadership, detectable across the societal divides, promoted a radicalization not only of the left, but also a rethinking which extended into the political middle ground. The emphatic identification of the Kaiser with the state, practised over decades, and the covert, but latently effective identification of the history of Prussia, or rather of the Hohenzollern, with that of the German Reich in official celebrations, connected the public perception and fate of one person with that of the state. This ideology and societal development – taken further because of the Kaiser's strongly reduced and finally entirely lacking political and media presence during the war[98] – were among the prerequisites for the collapse of the monarchy and the revolutionary events of the autumn and winter of 1918–19.

[97] Friedrich Tönnies, *Kritik der öffentlichen Meinung*, Berlin 1922, pp. 91f.
[98] Deist, *Militär*, vol. II, no. 332, pp. 846f., note 5 (report from Major von Weiß for Ludendorff, 24 July 1917); see also Hans Delbrück's clear analysis in *Preussische Jahrbücher*, 174 (1918), p. 434; and in general Sösemann, *Verfall, passim* and particularly pp. 158–65.

CHAPTER 3

The Kaiser's elite? Wilhelm II and the Berlin administration, 1890–1914

Katharine A. Lerman

At the beginning of his reign Kaiser Wilhelm II did not have a great deal of confidence in the men who occupied the key positions in the Prussian government and imperial administration in Berlin. In January 1890, less than two months before his unceremonious dismissal of Imperial Germany's first Chancellor, he told the Grand Duke of Baden: 'These ministers are not my ministers, of course, they are the ministers of Prince Bismarck.'[1] Even so, he must have been gratified by the stance taken by the Prussian ministers and imperial state secretaries in the Chancellor crisis of March 1890 for only one of them, the Chancellor's son and Foreign Secretary, Herbert von Bismarck, chose to resign in a display of solidarity with his father. Three others – the Minister of War, Julius Verdy du Vernois, the Minister of Agriculture, Robert Lucius von Ballhausen, and the Minister of Finance, Adolf von Scholz – were to leave office later in the year for reasons unconnected with Bismarck's dismissal. The other Prussian ministers – Gustav von Gossler, Ernst Ludwig Herrfurth, Hermann von Schelling, Albert Maybach, and Hans Hermann von Berlepsch, who respectively headed the Ministries of Education, the Interior, Justice, Public Works, and Trade – remained at their posts for the time being under the new Chancellor, Leo von Caprivi. In the imperial administration, too, the transition to the 'New Course' was smoothly effected. Adolf Marschall von Bieberstein, notoriously dubbed the *ministre étranger aux affaires* because of his lack of diplomatic experience, took over from Herbert von Bismarck at the Foreign Office. Franz von Rottenburg, Bismarck's Chief of the Reich Chancellery, moved to the position of Under State Secretary in the Reich Office of the Interior, and Admiral Friedrich Hollmann was appointed State Secretary of the Reich Navy Office in April 1890. All the other state secretaries who had been Bismarck's

---

[1] W. P. Fuchs (ed.), *Grossherzog Friedrich von Baden und die Reichspolitik, 1871–1907*, 4 vols., vol. II, Stuttgart 1975, Kaiser Wilhelm II to Grossherzog Friedrich, 24 January 1890, p. 697, n. 3. See also Otto Pflanze, *Bismarck and the Development of Germany*, vol. III, *The Period of Fortification 1880–1898*, Princeton, NJ 1990, p. 367, note 55.

subordinates – Heinrich von Boetticher (who was also Vice-President of the Prussian State Ministry) at the Reich Office of the Interior, Otto von Oehlschläger at the Justice Office, Helmuth von Maltzahn-Gültz at the Treasury, Friedrich Schulz, the President of the Reich Railway Office, and Heinrich Stephan, the State Secretary of the Reich Post Office – were prepared to serve the new Chancellor.

These men, and most of their successors in Wilhelm II's government between Bismarck's fall and the outbreak of war in 1914, have largely been consigned to oblivion by recent historical scholarship.[2] When John Röhl re-opened the debate on 'who ruled in Berlin?' some forty years ago, he focused on Imperial Germany's power structure and decision-making processes in Berlin in the decade after Bismarck's dismissal through the lens of the Chancellor, ministers and state secretaries.[3] But his research led him down a tortuous path of political intrigues and constitutional struggles into a world of 'irresponsible advisors' and court institutions, none of which had a place in the imperial German constitution of 1871. His conclusion that Wilhelm II was the real victor of the political crisis which beset the 1890s triggered a lifelong quest to unmask the personality and power of Germany's last Kaiser and ensured that the extent of Wilhelm's personal and institutional power would be central to the subsequent historical debate.[4] Yet, even the critics of the 'personal rule' thesis failed to rescue Imperial Germany's highest public officials from relative obscurity. Whether they are seen as struggling to compete within an 'authoritarian polycracy',[5] 'responsible for

---

[2] Of the four Chancellors, only Bülow and Bethmann have been the subjects of recent studies. See Katharine A. Lerman, *The Chancellor as Courtier. Bernhard von Bülow and the Governance of Germany 1900–1909*, Cambridge 1990; Gerd Fesser, *Reichskanzler Fürst von Bülow. Eine Biographie*, Berlin 1991; Konrad Jarausch, *The Enigmatic Chancellor. Bethmann Hollweg and the Hubris of Imperial Germany*, New Haven 1973; Eberhard Vietsch, *Bethmann Hollweg: Staatsmann zwischen Macht und Ethos*, Boppard am Rhein 1969. For the role of Berlepsch, see Hans-Jörg von Berlepsch, *Neuer Kurs im Kaiserreich? Die Arbeiterpolitik des Freiherrn von Berlepsch 1890 bis 1906*, Bonn 1987; for Posadowsky, see Karl Erich Born, *Staat und Sozialpolitik seit Bismarcks Sturz*, Wiesbaden 1957. Even Tirpitz, in the absence of a biography, 'must remain a nonperson' (Ivo N. Lambi, *The Navy and German Power Politics 1862–1914*, London 1984, p. 437), though see now Raffael Scheck, *Alfred von Tirpitz and German Right-Wing Politics 1914–1930*, Boston 1998.

[3] See John C. G. Röhl, *Germany without Bismarck. The Crisis of Government in the Second Reich, 1890–1900*, London 1967.

[4] See especially John C. G. Röhl, *The Kaiser and his Court* (English translation), Cambridge 1994; *Young Wilhelm. The Kaiser's Early Life 1859–1888* (English translation), Cambridge 1998, and most recently *Wilhelm II. Der Aufbau der Persönlichen Monarchie 1888–1900*, Munich 2001. For the 'personal rule' debate, see John C. G. Röhl (ed.), *Kaiser Wilhelm II. New Interpretations*, Cambridge 1982; John C. G. Röhl (ed.), *Der Ort Kaiser Wilhelms II. in der deutschen Geschichte*, Munich 1991; Wolfgang J. Mommsen, 'Kaiser Wilhelm II and German Politics', *Journal of Contemporary History*, 25 (1990), pp. 289–316; Geoff Eley, 'The View from the Throne: The Personal Rule of Kaiser Wilhelm II', *Historical Journal*, 28 (1985).

[5] Hans-Ulrich Wehler, *Deutsche Gesellschaftsgeschichte*, 3 vols., vol. III: *1849–1918*, Munich 1995, p. 1004.

every significant decision in Prusso-German history during these decades',[6] or promoting modern, bourgeois policies supportive of industrial capitalism,[7] most of the Berlin administration, with the exception of the four Chancellors, have remained anonymous bureaucrats, all too often buffeted and even marginalized by other, more significant power factors.

The men who staffed the eight Prussian ministries and seven Reich offices in Berlin were, of course, not the kind of ambitious party politicians and aspiring statesmen who rose to prominence in the more democratic systems of France and Britain before the First World War.[8] Like their counterparts in Tsarist Russia and Austria-Hungary, they were, in the main, higher civil servants who had undergone a very rigorous and specific kind of formal training and then often spent many years working in the administration of Prussia or one of the lesser German states. Candidates for the higher civil service in Prussia had to spend at least three years studying law at university, four years as an apprentice or Referendar at a court or other official agency, and then take further exams to qualify as an Assessor; throughout these years they received no kind of financial remuneration from the state but rather, until 1911, had to pay a hefty deposit and demonstrate their independent means. As well as these obstacles which obviously discriminated in favour of the wealthy upper middle classes and landed nobility, there were other, less formalised mechanisms within the selection procedures to ensure that only men with the right social background and political disposition could progress to the higher echelons of state service. Catholics were under-represented (for a time, after the reshuffle of May 1901, there was only one Catholic minister left in the Prussian Ministry of State), and Poles and Jews were effectively excluded; Bismarck, for example, maintained that only a true Christian could be responsible for social policy in a German state.[9] Those groomed for high office were also inculcated over many years with a set of values which included discipline and

---

[6] Wolfgang J. Mommsen, *Imperial Germany 1867–1918. Politics, Society and Culture in an Authoritarian State,* London 1995, p. 52.

[7] See especially George Steinmetz, 'The Myth of an Autonomous State: Industrialists, Junkers and Social Policy in Imperial Germany', in Geoff Eley (ed.), *Society, Culture and the State in Germany 1870–1930,* Ann Arbor 1996, pp. 257–318. See also David Blackbourn and Geoff Eley, *The Peculiarities of German History. Bourgeois Society and Politics in Nineteenth Century Germany,* Oxford 1984.

[8] There were eight Prussian ministries, responsible for Agriculture, Education (also including ecclesiastical affairs and medicine), Finance, the Interior (mainly the Prussian internal administration), Justice, Public Works, Trade, and War; and seven Reich offices (eight from 1907): the Foreign Office, the Reich Office of the Interior, the Reich Justice Office, the Reich Navy Office, the Reich Treasury Office, the Reich Railway Office, the Reich Post Office and (from 1907) the Reich Colonial Office.

[9] GStA Berlin, Bosse Papers, 11, extract from *Westdeutsche Zeitung,* 9 July 1898.

obedience, a strong sense of duty and loyalty to the *corps*, and subservience and submission to a higher authority. In short, they were men who could work well within a hierarchy and they were trained to accept and execute orders rather than to think critically or strategically.

Some seventy men headed the key Berlin departments between 1890 and 1914[10] and, apart from several army officers, a few diplomats and, exceptionally, a couple of parliamentarians, the overwhelming majority of them were appointed from this highly restricted recruitment pool which had never set a premium on political talent.[11]

The Berlin administration prided itself on being 'above party' and independent of parliamentary majorities; professional civil servants allegedly ruled Germany in the interests of technical efficiency and the general welfare of the state rather than in the name of any particular social class or sectional interest. Thus ministers and state secretaries were appointed individually rather than collectively, and it was relatively seldom that there were ministerial reshuffles involving several departments, as happened in the summer of 1897 or, on a smaller scale, in May 1901 and June 1907. With each minister appointed at a specific time for a specific reason, the length of time each remained in office varied quite considerably. Some positions were not politically sensitive: there were only three State Secretaries of the Reich Post Office between 1875 and 1917, and Friedrich Schulz was President of the relatively minor Reich Railway Office for nineteen years (1890–1909). But longevity in office did not necessarily signify a politically uncontroversial career. Alfred von Tirpitz, the motor force behind the audacious naval armaments programme before the war, held sway at the Reich Navy Office, too, for nineteen years (1897–1916). By contrast, the Prussian Ministry of the Interior, charged with responsibility for the provincial administration, witnessed ten chiefs come and go between 1890 and 1914, only two of whom, Georg von Rheinbaben (1899–1901) and Theobald von Bethmann Hollweg (1905–7), moved on to more significant posts. The State Secretary-ship of the Foreign Office also had a reputation among diplomats as a 'poisoned chalice'. This was in part because the real German Foreign Minister

[10] This includes the Chancellors and Prussian minister-presidents, the Prussian ministers, state secretaries and Chancellery chiefs. Seventy-four individuals served as Chancellor, minister or state secretary between 1890 and 1914, a few of whom (Bethmann Hollweg, Posadowsky, Bosse, Podbielski, Rheinbaben, Delbrück, and Sydow) held more than one post during this period. A number of state secretaries were also simultaneously Prussian ministers without portfolio, a practice Bismarck had introduced to bolster the Chancellor's support in the Prussian Ministry of State and ensure that Prussian policy heeded Reich necessities.

[11] See especially John C. G. Röhl, 'Higher Civil Servants in Wilhelmine Germany 1890–1900', *Journal of Contemporary History*, 2, no. 3 (July 1967) and the revised version in Röhl, *Kaiser and his Court*, pp. 131–49.

was the Reich Chancellor who simultaneously held the office of Prussian Foreign Minister and also, except for an interlude between 1892 and 1894, was Prussian Minister-President. But it also doubtless reflected the fact that the Kaiser was most likely to interfere in the sphere of foreign policy.

The majority of the men who held high office between 1890 and 1914 had been born in the 1840s and 1850s, thus experiencing the German wars of unification in their youth or early adulthood. A significant minority, however, were older: some of the ministers in the early 1890s were nearing the end of their political careers and some, like Caprivi and the War Ministers Verdy, Hans von Kaltenborn-Stachau (1890–3) and Walther Bronsart von Schellendorf (1893–6), had had illustrious military careers before accepting political office. The oldest minister under Kaiser Wilhelm II was the third Chancellor, Chlodwig zu Hohenlohe-Schillingsfürst, who was born in 1819 and widely ridiculed for his passivity and senility by the time he made room for Bülow in October 1900, a few months before his eightieth birthday. Albert Maybach, the Minister of Public Works (1878–91), and Ludwig Schelling, the Minister of Justice (1889–94), also belonged to an earlier generation: Maybach had started on his bureaucratic career in 1845 and Schelling had worked for forty-nine years and eleven months in the state service before he retired at the age of seventy. Another minister, Johannes von Miquel, who was born in 1828, could never be accused of senility. A former banker, parliamentarian and co-founder of the National Association, he had bypassed the more traditional routes to the top and, as Prussian Finance Minister (1890–1901), was one of the dominant figures in the Berlin administration in the 1890s until he was ousted from his post at the age of seventy-three by the newly appointed Chancellor Bernhard von Bülow (1900–9).

Some men, however, achieved rapid promotion within the service and attained ministerial positions in their forties. Rheinbaben, a protégé of Miquel, was appointed Prussian Minister of the Interior in 1899 at the youthful age of forty-four; and Bethmann Hollweg was the same age when he was offered his first ministerial post in 1901. On this occasion he rejected the political conditions attached to the promotion (he became Prussian Minister of the Interior four years later), but he mused over being given 'position after position, effortlessly and indiscriminately'.[12] By 1914 two of Wilhelm's ministers, August Lentze, the Prussian Minister of Finance (1910–17), and Gottlieb von Jagow, the hapless Foreign Secretary (1913–16), had been born in the 1860s. Although the sight of Prussian troops parading

---

[12] Jarausch, *Enigmatic Chancellor*, p. 43.

through Berlin in 1866 may well have been a formative experience for the ten-year-old Bethmann,[13] it is highly unlikely that Jagow, born in Berlin in June 1863, could share this memory.

Most of the men who attained the highest positions in the administration were members of the nobility but by no means all came from the old Prussian landed aristocracy. Many had more humble bourgeois origins; they came from families which had traditionally served the state as bureaucrats and lawyers or they were the sons of professional men. Wilhelm von Heyden-Cadow, the very wealthy Minister of Agriculture (1890–4), came from a family which had originally been middle-class but had intermarried with the aristocracy; and many ministers and state secretaries, not least Miquel and Tirpitz, were only ennobled (and thus able to use the prefix *von*) in the course of their careers. Clemens Delbrück, the Minister of Trade (1905–9), State Secretary of the Interior (1909–16) and Vice-President of the Prussian State Ministry from 1914, was, like Miquel, the son of a doctor and was ennobled in 1916. Arnold Nieberding, the State Secretary of the Reich Justice Office (1893–1909), was the son of a grammar-school headmaster. Heinrich Stephan, the State Secretary of the Reich Post Office (1875–97), whose career was almost synonymous with the creation of a modern postal service in Germany, was the eighth son of a tailor who had started working for the Prussian postal service in 1848. Robert Bosse, the impecunious State Secretary of the Reich Justice Office (1891–2) and later Minister of Education (1892–9) who fathered a large family and whose diary recounts all the trials and tribulations which befell it, was the son of a distillery owner. He had refused to stand for election to the North German Confederation Reichstag in 1867 for financial reasons. 'If the law does not grant allowances, then people like me are excluded', he wrote in January 1867, 'and that is fine by me.'[14]

The majority of the men who staffed the highest offices in Berlin were also Prussian in origin although there were exceptions. Hohenlohe was a Bavarian Catholic (albeit hostile to ultramontanism) and the first Prussian Minister-President to come from another German state; the State Secretary of the Treasury, Hermann von Stengel (1903–8), was another Bavarian Catholic. Two Foreign Secretaries, Marschall and Alfred von Kiderlen-Wächter (1910–12), came from outside Prussia: the former was from Baden and the latter was a Swabian who had been born in Stuttgart. Hans von Hammerstein, appointed Minister of the Interior in 1901, was a Hanoverian whom Conservatives immediately criticized for his alleged lack of understanding for Prussian traditions.[15]

---

[13] Ibid., p. 18.   [14] GStA Berlin, Bosse Papers, diary, 5 January 1867.
[15] HSA Stuttgart, Varnbüler's Report, 8 May 1901.

Military experience was obviously the *sine qua non* of service as War Minister and all the incumbents were generals. Verdy (who came from an old Huguenot family which had settled in Brandenburg during the rule of the Great Elector), Kaltenborn and Bronsart had all emerged with glowing records from the Austro-Prussian war of 1866; Bronsart had additionally played a significant role at the storming of Düppel in the Danish war of 1864 and received the Iron Cross (First Class) for being Chief of the General Staff of the IX Army Corps during the Franco-Prussian war. Karl von Einem, too, had served as a young officer in the Franco-Prussian war.

Yet perhaps more significantly a substantial number of the men who headed the ministries and offices responsible for civil matters had also seen active service. Among the Chancellors, Caprivi was a former general, and Bülow had volunteered to fight in the Franco-Prussian war. Reinhold von Sydow, a lawyer's son who was State Secretary of the Treasury (1908–9) and then Minister of Trade (1909–18), also served as a nineteen-year-old volunteer in the Franco-Prussian war. Konrad von Studt, whom Wilhelm II rejected as Minister of the Interior in 1895 but later appointed Minister of Education (1899–1907), combined his training to be a higher civil servant with frequent periods of active service. He delayed his Assessor exams to take part in the occupation of the Russian border during the Polish uprising of 1863 and the Danish war of 1864. He also participated in the campaign of 1866 while he was a Gerichtsassessor, and his role in capturing Austrian guns at the battle of Königgrätz led to him being awarded the Red Eagle order. Wilhelm II later insisted, 'Of all my ministers, Minister Studt is the best. He does not worry about attacks in the press or attacks in parliament. He simply carries out my orders reliably, and does not care about anything else.'[16]

Another general who had served as an officer in the military campaigns of 1866 and 1870 and subsequently enjoyed a political career was Viktor von Podbielski, the State Secretary of the Reich Post Office (1897–1901) and then Minister of Agriculture (1901–6). He too became a favourite with Wilhelm II, regularly invited to his beer evenings and skat parties,[17] and his enforced dismissal in 1906 precipitated a major crisis between Wilhelm and Bülow.

The men who had served for many years in the Prussian army often saw their service in government as all of a piece with their military careers. Bronsart regarded himself as dispensable: if he were shot by a socialist,

---

[16] Robert Zedlitz-Trützschler, *Zwölf Jahre am deutschen Kaiserhof*, Berlin and Leipzig 1924, p. 162. See also Röhl, *Germany without Bismarck*, pp. 147, 267.
[17] HHSA Vienna, PA III, 156 (Varia), Szögyényi to Goluchowski, 6 May 1901.

he once declared, it would not be a tragedy as another could replace him immediately. Kaltenborn, who had had no experience of the Berlin administration before assuming office, remained first and foremost a soldier and despised the 'parliamentary economy' he found there, especially after the fiasco of the Army Bill in 1893. Sounded out for the War Ministry in 1889, he had made clear his lack of interest but he obeyed the Kaiser's order that he should replace Verdy in 1890.

Wilhelm II clearly liked to see generals in key posts, appreciating all those who ran their departments with a firm hand and closely supervised their subordinates. He expected military discipline from his ministers at times of crisis. 'When, with all my regiments in close ranks, I begin the attack will the "golden" Miquel regiment refuse to heed the signal "gallop"?' he wrote to the Finance Minister in 1894 in an effort to ensure the State Ministry's united representation of Caprivi's trade treaties.[18] He also expected his favourite Chancellor, Bülow, to ensure that 'the ministers stand to attention before him'.[19] His contempt for parliamentarians is equally well documented and, particularly after the opposition of many Conservative officials to the Canal Bill in the Prussian Landtag in 1899, it became much less customary for Prussian higher civil servants to have seats in parliament. Johann von Dallwitz, a Conservative member of the Prussian Landtag from 1893 and later Minister of the Interior (1910–14), was disciplined for opposing the Canal Bill and could only resume his career in the administration after he gave up his mandate.

Ministers who held office in the 1890s, such as Boetticher and the Ministers of the Interior, Herrfurth and Ernst von Köller (1894–5), could draw on their previous experience as Conservative members of the Prussian Lower House or German Reichstag; Miquel, of course, had had extensive parliamentary experience in a variety of forums (the Hanoverian second chamber, the Prussian Lower House, the Reichstag of the North German Confederation and the imperial Reichstag). After the turn of the century Friedrich Wilhelm von Loebell, who had been a Conservative member of the Reichstag and Prussian Lower House, gave up his parliamentary seat on being appointed Chief of the Reich Chancellery (1904–9), a position from which he was able to exert considerable political influence even though it only attained the status of an Under State Secretaryship in 1907; resigning shortly after Bülow in 1909 for health reasons, he left Berlin to become

---

[18] J. Alden Nichols, *Germany after Bismarck. The Caprivi Era 1890–1894*, Cambridge, MA 1958; New York edition, 1968, p. 306.
[19] BA Koblenz, Eulenburg Papers, 74, 'Ein Zwiegespräch', 29 August 1903, p. 37.

Oberpräsident of Brandenburg but spent most of his time on his estate before he was appointed State Secretary of the Interior in 1914.

The only parliamentarian appointed a minister under Bülow was Theodor Möller who headed the Ministry of Trade between 1901 and 1905. A prominent Rhine-Westphalian industrialist (he had set up his first factory making machines and steam boilers in 1863), he was a National Liberal member of the Reichstag from 1893 but was also prepared to give up his seat to become a minister. As the Baden Ambassador to Berlin commented barely five months after his appointment, his case revealed what difficulties could arise when men 'from outside' were given ministerial positions. The bureaucracy, always annoyed about any invasion of this kind, criticized him for talking too much and thereby creating numerous targets for attack; the Reich Treasury Office thought he launched too many inquiries and conferred too extensively with industrial experts; the trade department of the Foreign Office had always been of the opinion that he had been more useful to the government as a sympathetic deputy in the Reichstag.[20] Thus this experiment was not repeated before 1914.

The fact that many higher civil servants lacked parliamentary experience and skill was clearly a major handicap at a time when the Reichstag was increasingly becoming the focus of national public life. Those who took the Reichstag seriously and treated it with respect could thereby bolster their ministerial positions in such a way as to make it far more difficult for Wilhelm II to dismiss them. Both Marschall and Miquel had proven parliamentary skills; Posadowsky and Tirpitz, too, were adept at managing the majority parties in the Reichstag and it is doubtless no accident that both went on to have parliamentary careers in the Weimar Republic. A minister like Studt who had a stammer and spoke haltingly, searching for the right expression, had a much tougher time in parliament although he never shied away from a conflict. Heinrich von Tschirschky, the State Secretary of the Foreign Office (1906–7), became such a favourite with Wilhelm II that he appeared to rival Bülow, but his Berlin career foundered because he was a very poor speaker in the Reichstag.[21]

Bülow, a diplomat by training, and Tirpitz, an able professional with organizational, agitational, and technical skills who had begun his career as a naval cadet at the age of sixteen, were very ambitious to hold high office. But many Prussian higher civil servants, although concerned about

[20] GLA Karlsruhe, 34807, Jagemann's Report, 7 October 1901.
[21] Rudolf Vierhaus (ed.), *Das Tagebuch der Baronin Spitzemberg. Aufzeichnungen aus der Hofgesellschaft des Hohenzollernreiches*, Göttingen 1960, 21 April 1907, p. 472. See also Lerman, *Chancellor as Courtier*, p. 192.

issues of seniority, were more interested in how long they had to serve before they could receive their pensions rather than in climbing to the highest positions. Many professed a lack of interest in posts which carried political responsibility and a much higher public profile, and sudden elevation to leadership positions could induce a strong sense of anxiety and foreboding among those who had long experience of the Berlin bureaucracy. Unwilling to assume the heavy workload and increasingly aware of the pressures to which ministers were subjected, ministers and state secretaries were just as likely to respond to promotion with resignation as with enthusiasm, struggling to suppress their personal inclinations and, formally at least, bowing to the call of duty.

Bethmann Hollweg accepted only reluctantly the position of Prussian Minister of the Interior in 1905 and told a friend that he found 'this outwardly honourable position thoroughly repugnant'.[22] In 1909, on becoming Chancellor, he again only accepted with a heavy heart. 'Only a genius or a man driven by ambition and lust for power can covet this post. And I am neither. An ordinary man can only assume it when compelled by his sense of duty', he confided.[23] Caprivi, too, told the Reichstag in 1893:

The weight of the burden which I bear is so heavy that I shall bless the day when I am relieved of it. But I shall not take such a step, I shall remain at the helm, I shall carry out my bounden duty, adhering to the ancient Prussian traditions in which I have been trained. Not for myself, to be sure, but for Kaiser and Reich![24]

Ludwig Holle, a former official in the Ministry of Public Works, was a specialist in hydraulics who attracted the Kaiser's notice when he was involved in the project to build a canal across central Germany. He replaced Studt as Minister of Education in 1907 with a marked lack of enthusiasm, convinced that his health would not be equal to the demands of the office.[25] Rheinbaben had to be 'kicked upstairs' by the Kaiser in 1901, who made it clear to him that he could not remain Minister of the Interior if he turned down the Ministry of Finance.[26] Tschirschky would have preferred an embassy when he was appointed Oswald von Richthofen's successor as State Secretary of the Foreign Office in 1906. Richthofen had died of a heart attack induced by stress and overwork, in no small measure a corollary of the excessive reliance Bülow placed upon him. Kiderlen-Wächter was another Foreign Secretary who died suddenly from a stroke in December 1912

---

[22] Jarausch, *Enigmatic Chancellor*, p. 46   [23] Ibid., p. 66.

[24] Cited in Nichols, *Germany after Bismarck*, p. 249.

[25] HSA Stuttgart, Varnbüler's Report, 23 June 1907; Lerman, *Chancellor as Courtier*, pp. 175, 182.

[26] HSA Stuttgart, Varnbüler's Report, 8 May 1901. As Minister of the Interior and responsible for dealing with the Landräte, Rheinbaben had not been prepared to take on the Conservatives.

after dealing with the fall-out from the Second Moroccan Crisis; and the death of other ministers in office, including Holle in 1909, served as a warning to other candidates who pleaded that health or family reasons militated against their acceptance of high office. 'Nothing has helped me', Gottlieb von Jagow wrote to the former Chancellor Bülow in January 1913 on becoming the seventh State Secretary of the Foreign Office since the departure of the Bismarcks. 'I am appointed.'[27]

When key posts were offered to men with experience outside the bureaucracy, there were other objections too. When Stengel resigned as State Secretary of the Treasury in February 1908, convinced that at the age of seventy he was unable to continue the extensive work involved in a major Reich financial reform and distraught over the recent death of his son, the post was offered to a prominent Berlin banker who pointed out that the salary was very much less than his present position and that he could not leave the bank without the agreement of his partners. Since a second candidate, Franz Adickes, the Oberbürgermeister of Frankfurt, was disliked by the Kaiser, the position was eventually offered to Sydow, an Under State Secretary in the Reich Post Office. As Bülow acknowledged in the Ministry of State, Sydow had no experience at all of tax issues but possessed 'excellent qualities as a bureaucrat'.[28]

Civil service examinations and a lack of the requisite political and parliamentary skills may have represented significant hurdles for many potential ministers in Imperial Germany, but ultimately it was the Kaiser's favour which could make or break a political career. A crucial conclusion of Röhl's early research was that the Kaiser's most significant prerogative, which accounted for his victory over the internal administration in 1897, was his control of all personnel appointments. 'I always have a good look at my men beforehand', Wilhelm remarked in 1891,[29] and certainly in the 1890s he was much more likely to intervene directly in personnel matters than after the turn of the century when, for a variety of reasons, he was more likely to accept the recommendations of his Chancellors, Bülow and Bethmann Hollweg, both of whom usually worked in close consultation with Wilhelm's Civil Cabinet Chiefs, Hermann von Lucanus in the first twenty years of the reign and, from 1908, Rudolf von Valentini.

---

[27] Lamar Cecil, *The German Diplomatic Service 1871–1914*, Princeton, NJ 1976, p. 318.
[28] GStA Merseburg, Staatsministerium, 20 February 1908. Bülow told the State Ministry that Adickes had wanted longer to think about it because of his age, poor health, and illness in his family, and the fact that the Kaiser had not wanted to wait (Wilhelm's marginalia on Bülow's letter of 7 February 1908, BA Koblenz, Reichskanzlei, 1622 indicated his strong dislike of Adickes. See also Lerman, *Chancellor as Courtier*, p. 212.
[29] Röhl, *Germany without Bismarck*, p. 60.

The Kaiser's interventions, however, did not stop after 1900 and Wilhelm continued to guard his prerogative, needing to feel that he was personally involved in all appointments to 'his' government. This was significant not merely because Wilhelm often played a decisive role in the individual careers of civil servants, diplomats, and military men, advancing those he favoured and blocking the career prospects of men he disliked. More importantly, the system of government in which ministers and state secretaries collectively relied on the Kaiser's confidence and prided themselves on operating 'above the political parties' in the parliaments offered them very little leverage if they wished to challenge Wilhelm's authority. In the last analysis all the men who staffed the ministries and offices in Berlin knew that if they clashed with Wilhelm over an issue of power or principle, they risked immediate dismissal. So even at the government level, the system continued to encourage submission to a higher authority, the crown. The result was deference, flattery, and sycophancy rather than independence and initiative.

When Kaiser Wilhelm II did intervene in personnel matters, what kind of men did he choose for high office and is there any pattern discernible in his interventions? And what kind of relationship did the ministers and state secretaries have with the Kaiser? What can be said about their attitude to the monarchy and how far were they prepared to countenance political reform?

Christopher Clark has recently argued that at no time in his reign did Wilhelm really have a clear political vision or programme which he sought to implement through the installation of men with a particular political agenda. His appointees reflected 'the eclectic composition of his personal acquaintance, rather than a consistent preference for individuals with a specific political outlook', and imperial favouritism did not generally translate into effective power for Wilhelm himself.[30] It is certainly true that the Kaiser's favoured candidates could range politically from agrarian reactionaries to left-of-centre liberals, catering to the need to draw support from all the 'state-supporting' parties but not furthering the cohesion of the government or facilitating a coherent strategy. Moreover, if there is one guiding thread through all of Wilhelm's personnel choices, it is his preference for familiar faces, men he knew and felt comfortable with. Nevertheless the Kaiser did gravitate towards certain kinds of personalities, above all perhaps men who had 'a military aura wrapped around a courtier's soul';[31] and, while many of Wilhelm's appointments to the Berlin administration may not appear to have any overt political significance or obvious implications

---

[30] Christopher Clark, *Kaiser Wilhelm II*, Harlow 2000, especially pp. 59, 97, 105, 118.
[31] See Isabel V. Hull, *The Entourage of Kaiser Wilhelm II 1888–1918*, Cambridge 1982, especially pp. 22, 184–5.

for Wilhelm's ability and capacity to exercise power, this view needs to be qualified above all with respect to Bülow's appointment. For here it can be argued that the installation of a favourite did signify much more than the elevation of a friend. However imperfectly Wilhelm grasped the contours of the conspiracy hatched by Philipp zu Eulenburg and other 'irresponsible' advisors as early as 1893, the appointment of Bülow as State Secretary in the Foreign Office in 1897 and then as Chancellor in 1900 represented the realization of a long-term strategy to place the government of Germany on a new, ostensibly more stable footing.

Wilhelm II clearly had different kinds of relationships with his ministers and, indeed, different kinds of favourites, and it is important to distinguish between them. First and foremost there were individual men he knew and liked, those he wanted to see installed as ministers, sometimes regardless of their suitability for the post concerned. Hans von Hammerstein's appointment as Minister of the Interior in 1901 was a consequence of Wilhelm's frequent visits to Alsace-Lorraine where he got to know Hammerstein as Oberpräsident of Metz. Even Philipp Eulenburg thought that this was an unfortunate appointment and that Hammerstein would not be equal to his new role, a judgement which was confirmed when Hammerstein proved a highly inept performer in the parliaments.[32] Bülow attempted unsuccessfully to remove him in 1903, but Wilhelm was unyielding and it was only when Hammerstein died in office in 1905 that a more skilful replacement, Bethmann Hollweg, could be installed.[33]

Clemens Delbrück, appointed Minister of Trade in 1905, was another *persona grata* with the Kaiser, who knew him as Oberpräsident of West Prussia, as were the two Foreign Secretaries, Tschirschky and Wilhelm von Schön (1907–9). Tschirschky had regularly accompanied Wilhelm on his travels, developing an easy intimacy with him; similarly Wilhelm introduced Schön, then Minister in Copenhagen, as prospective ambassador to St Petersburg in a letter to the Tsar (in English) in 1905:

He was formerly a long time in Paris, is married to an elegant and most charming wife: he accompanied me on my journey to Tangiers and the Mediterranean this year and is a loyal, quiet, discreet man; a personal friend of mine having my fullest confidence since many years . . . He knows Italy well, speaks French, Italian, English like his mothertongue [*sic*], is most active and a good lawntennis player, in case you should need one.[34]

[32] John C. G. Röhl (ed.), *Philipp Eulenburgs Politische Korrespondenz*, 3 vols., Boppard am Rhein, 1976–83, vol. III, Eulenburg to Bülow, 14 May 1901, p. 2019.

[33] See Lerman, *Chancellor as Courtier*, pp. 113–14.

[34] Walter Goetz (ed.), *Briefe Wilhelms II. an den Zaren, 1894–1914*, Berlin 1920, Wilhelm II to Nicholas II, 26 September 1905, pp. 379–83.

In October 1906 the Kaiser enjoyed a lunch with Schön and his wife when they were in Berlin with the Russian Foreign Minister, Isvolsky, and his wife; this kind of contact undoubtedly encouraged Wilhelm to want Schön, 'a courtier and society man of the worst kind',[35] as Foreign Secretary the following year when it became clear that Tschirschky would have to go.[36]

Another Minister who was a great favourite with the Kaiser was Podbielski, the general placed in charge of the Reich Post Office in 1897 and then (to the relief of the Post Office, which regained a specialist[37]) appointed Minister of Agriculture in 1901. Podbielski, reputed to be a Junker militarist with extremely reactionary views (he wanted to see Prussia secede from the Reich), was one of the very few ministers whom Wilhelm continued to see regularly in social gatherings after Bülow's appointment as Chancellor. Podbielski was a very keen hunter and, like Studt, Bronsart, and Schön, he had also excelled at sport and gymnastics in his youth; indeed, after he left office he became a great promoter of sport, heading the German team which went to the Stockholm Olympic Games in 1912 and playing a key role in the creation of the first German stadium in Berlin-Grunewald in 1913. All this may have appealed to Wilhelm who notoriously forced the elderly members of his entourage to do gymnastic exercises on his yacht and once told a teachers' conference that all teachers 'must be proficient in gymnastic exercises and practise them every day'.[38] But there is little evidence that Podbielski's favoured position with the Kaiser gave him any undue leverage in the Prussian Ministry of State; certainly it mattered little that he played skat with the Kaiser when State Secretary of the Post Office and, even as Minister of Agriculture, he was often a lone voice of protest in the State Ministry and invariably in a minority. His relationship with the Kaiser only became a serious issue in 1906 when his political mistakes made him a liability to retain in office but Wilhelm ordered him to remain at his post. The Prussian Ministry of State unanimously insisted that he had to go and the episode significantly damaged Bülow's relationship with Wilhelm.

The Kaiser, however, could also intervene to appoint men who never subsequently could be regarded as personal favourites. He appointed virtually all the war ministers without consultation, confirming how difficult it was for civilian politicians to intrude at all into what the Kaiser perceived as

[35] Vierhaus, *Spitzemberg*, 9 October 1907, p. 475.
[36] GStA Merseburg, Hausarchiv, Adjutantenjournale, 28 October 1906; Lerman, *Chancellor as Courtier*, pp. 193–4.
[37] HSA Munich, Berlin 1073, Lerchenfeld's Report, 5 May 1901.
[38] Röhl, *Germany without Bismarck*, p. 29; Clark, *Wilhelm II*, p. 61.

his own personal sphere. Although Heinrich von Gossler (1896–1903) has been described by Röhl as 'a new type of Minister, sworn to obey Wilhelm II's commands',[39] men like Bronsart and Einem were far from willing to play the role of the Kaiser's stooges.

Tirpitz, too, was known to have the Kaiser's backing, but this was for political reasons, not because Wilhelm particularly liked Tirpitz; indeed Wilhelm found Tirpitz's predecessor, Hollmann, far more sympathetic and amenable, continuing to seek out his company long after he had dismissed him.[40] Similarly, Wilhelm knew Bethmann from visits to Hohenfinow but, although he respected him and although their personal relationship was immediately evident within the executive in 1905,[41] Wilhelm never really warmed to a man he regarded as formal and bureaucratic and even suspected of being a 'liberalizing parliamentarian' during the period of the Bülow Bloc.[42]

Not least, Wilhelm II was also responsible for the appointment of Posadowsky as State Secretary of the Treasury in 1893 and Posadowsky, like a number of other ministers who were conscious of the Chancellor's weakness, did capitalize on the monarch's support in the 1890s. But, especially once Bülow was in office, there was no evidence of any closeness between the two men; rather, observers noted a coolness in Wilhelm's attitude to Podsadowsky. In 1907, when this indefatigable and apparently irreplaceable higher civil servant was summarily dismissed because he had reservations about Bülow's Bloc policy, the Kaiser described him as 'a quite excellent departmental official but a bad politician'. Wilhelm's retrospective remarks about both Posadowsky and Miquel (whom he once called 'the greatest Finance Minister of the century' but later blamed for the economic slowdown after 1900[43]) indicate how Bülow had systematically undermined their positions by prejudicing the Kaiser against them.[44]

Wilhelm was also keen to appoint men who appeared to have qualities which he felt were lacking in the administration. In June 1890, after a visit to the Krupp works in Essen, he was so impressed that he wanted to appoint its general manager, Johann Jencke, as Finance Minister. Wilhelm had already secured Jencke's appointment to the advisory Council of State earlier

[39] Röhl, *Germany without Bismarck*, p. 199.   [40] Hull, *Entourage*, pp. 161–2.

[41] See GStA Merseburg, Staatsministerium, 17 October 1905 when Bethmann informed the other ministers that he had been summoned to Potsdam the next day.

[42] Vierhaus, *Spitzemberg*, 17 July 1909, p. 509.

[43] See Hans Herzfeld, *Johannes von Miquel*, 2 vols., Detmold 1938, vol. II, pp. 329ff.; see also Wilhelm's marginalia on Möller's *Immediatbericht* of 31 July 1901 in PA Bonn, AA, IA, Deutschland, 163 secr., vol. I.

[44] Lerman, *Chancellor as Courtier*, pp. 107–9, 176–80.

in the year, although the industrialist had courageously opposed Wilhelm's ideas on social welfare in that forum. Jencke declined the post in 1890 but Wilhelm immediately thought of him again the following year when the Minister of Public Works, Maybach, wanted to retire.[45] In 1901, when the position of Finance Minister fell vacant again, Wilhelm favoured the appointment of either the head of the Deutsche Bank, Georg von Siemens (whom he knew from his interest in the Anatolian Railway company), or the agrarian Conservative, Guido Henckel von Donnersmarck. These two men clearly did not share a similar outlook and had very different views about political and economic priorities.[46]

Wilhelm could also be persuaded to appoint men whom he did not know personally but felt a special kind of affinity with, for example, if they had also been members of the same Bonn student fraternity; or whose candidacy was presented to him in such a way as to attract his interest and flatter his self-image as a progressive man in tune with modern times. The best example of this is the appointment of Bernhard Dernburg in 1907 as prospective State Secretary of the new Colonial Office. Dernburg, the ambitious and dynamic director of the Darmstädter Bank, had left liberal political views and was of Jewish descent (something which the Kaiser, as in 1896 when he wanted to appoint Karl Bitter as Minister of Trade, was more prepared to overlook than some of his more antisemitic ministers[47]) and Wilhelm did not meet him prior to his appointment. Dernburg was seen as the kind of man who could spearhead a major reform of the colonial administration, and Loebell tellingly revealed that Bülow aroused Wilhelm's interest in his candidacy by informing him that the financier possessed his own automobile.[48]

Finally, of course, there was Bülow, whose appointment as Chancellor in 1900 elevated the Kaiser's personal favourite, 'the man with my *absolute confidence*',[49] to a position of unprecedented power under Wilhelm II and whose apparent betrayal of Wilhelm during the *Daily Telegraph* affair of 1908 ensured that the Kaiser's relationship with the Berlin administration would never be the same again.

[45] See Röhl, *Germany without Bismarck*, pp. 60f., 63, 77f. See also Nichols, *Germany after Bismarck*, p. 88.
[46] See HHSA Vienna, PA III, 156 (Varia), Szögyény to Goluchowski, 6 May 1901. For Siemens, see also John G. Williamson, *Karl Helfferich 1872–1924. Economist, Financier, Politician*, Princeton, NJ 1971, p. 78.
[47] Röhl, *Germany without Bismarck*, p. 148. See also Jarausch, *Enigmatic Chancellor*, pp. 28, 30, for evidence of Bethmann's antisemitism.
[48] BA Koblenz, Loebell Papers, 27, memoirs, p. 100.
[49] Röhl, *Eulenburg*, vol. III, Aufzeichnung Eulenburgs, 20 April 1897, p. 1817.

Bülow devoted an inordinate amount of time to cultivating his close friendship with the Kaiser and, most significantly, he used Wilhelm's confidence to secure his dominance over all the other ministers and state secretaries within the executive. The diaries of the Kaiser's adjutants indicate the sheer variety of contexts in which the two men liaised with each other, often on a daily basis. They met at the palace or in the Wilhelmstrasse, took walks in the Chancellery gardens or the Tiergarten, rode together on horseback or in motor cars. Wilhelm always had time to see Bülow whether in Berlin, Potsdam, Wilhelmshöhe or Homburg; in August 1908 Bülow interrupted his holiday in Norderney to go to Swinemünde and the two men spent over an hour walking along the beach. Bülow was sometimes the only guest the Kaiser invited to dinner (although sometimes his wife and mother-in-law went too) and on Bülow's birthday in May 1904 the Kaiser and Kaiserin spent the whole day and evening at the Bülows'. Wilhelm had no compunction about calling in unexpectedly to see Bülow at the office after his frequent trips to the dentist (though not when these lasted over three hours, as on 6 April 1906), or summoning him at 12.30 a.m. after a Court banquet (Bülow, who was fastidious about his health and rest only got away at 2 a.m.), or chatting to him at length with the Fürstenbergs in the car at Cassel station at 11 p.m. before seeing off his guests.[50]

The relaxed atmosphere and easy intercourse which Bülow was able to create (not without effort) in his dealings with Wilhelm brought a new degree of unity to the executive and facilitated an unprecedented degree of co-ordination between civilian and military authority in Imperial Germany. Because Wilhelm trusted his Chancellor implicitly, Bülow could be confident, for example in 1903, that he could use political arguments to persuade Wilhelm to modify the excessive demands of his Military Cabinet and to agree to the repeal of an important part of the Jesuit Law, a concession to the Catholic Centre Party which Wilhelm had been implacably opposed to in February 1900 before Bülow became Chancellor.[51]

Bülow appreciated that Wilhelm was too impatient to hear formal presentations or *Vorträge*, preferred newspaper clippings to long memoranda, liked to talk rather than to listen, and was generally far more amenable to influence and persuasion if these were cloaked in informality and social intimacy. What is equally evident, however, from surveying Wilhelm's relationship with Bülow and with lesser favourites is that the monarch had very little liking for traditional Prussian civil servants. Wilhelm regarded senior

---

[50] GStA Merseburg, Adjutantenjournale. See especially 26 November 1902, 3 May 1904, 19 August 1905, and 21 March 1906.
[51] GStA Merseburg, Staatsministerium, 8 January 1903 and 11 February 1903; cf. 5 February 1900.

bureaucrats without military experience as effete weaklings; like Bülow, he condemned hard-working civil servants as dull and unimaginative, lacking the skills of witty conversation and the broader horizons of foreign travel. His reluctance to accept Richthofen as Foreign Secretary in 1900 stemmed from his perception of him as colourless and uninspiring, qualities he could tolerate in higher civil servants who headed departments with which he had little contact, but not at the Foreign Office which he visited frequently.

Men like Bosse, Schönstedt, and Nieberding were thus never popular with the Kaiser and frequently felt slighted by the treatment meted out to them by their royal master. When Bosse was passed over 'yet again' in the Kaiser's birthday honours of January 1898 and did not receive the Grand Cross of the Red Eagle Order to which he felt entitled, he agonized over his best course of action, consulted with his colleagues, and prompted the Vice-President of the Prussian Ministry, Miquel, to take soundings from Lucanus.[52] 'It has worried me more than is right', he wrote in his diary. 'It seems all too reasonable to ask whether this lack of recognition is indeed an indication that the Kaiser no longer values my conduct of office, even if he will tolerate it formally for a while longer. For if that were the case, I must of course accept it and hand in my resignation.' After Lucanus assured Miquel that the omission was not a sign of the Kaiser's disfavour, Bosse resolved to remain in office until he received a broader hint. 'Now it's a matter of keeping quiet, remaining loyal [and] doing my duty.'[53]

In an (unheeded) letter of resignation in 1907, Nieberding similarly complained that in fifteen years of service he had never received any special honours from the Kaiser and that his department had consequently suffered a loss of prestige and status within the higher bureaucracy.[54] Even Rheinbaben, one of the ministers mentioned by Nieberding as a more favoured opponent, complained in 1907 when he was conspicuously passed over for the Vice-Presidency of the Prussian Ministry of State and the position was given to Bethmann, 'one of the younger State Ministers and 5–6 years junior to me in terms of service'. The Kaiser sent Lucanus to him expressly to request that he remain in office and, as Rheinbaben confirmed in a letter of resignation in August 1909, 'Although very painful for me personally to be passed over in this way, I of course regarded H.M.'s wish as an order and acted accordingly.' Rheinbaben was again denied the Vice-Presidency in 1909 when Bethmann became Chancellor, although he felt

[52] GStA Berlin, Bosse Papers, diary entries of 27 January 1898 and 30 January 1898.
[53] Ibid., 31 January 1898.
[54] BA Koblenz, Reichskanzlei, 1616, Nieberding to Loebell, 11 July 1907 and enclosed memorandum. See also Lerman, *Chancellor as Courtier*, pp. 185–6.

entitled to the position 'as by far the longest serving Prussian departmental chief, in accordance with existing practice in Prussia'. When Bethmann told him he had political objections to the transfer 'because our views would perhaps not be compatible on all points', Rheinbaben hastily submitted his resignation since 'After that I lack the fundamental precondition for any effective service.'[55]

As well as denying them outward signs of recognition, the Kaiser frequently insulted his ministers behind their backs. He called Caprivi a 'sensitive old fathead' and Boetticher 'a cowardly wet rag', despising most of the ministers he had to work with by 1896.[56] In 1909 the language he used about the departing Bülow to the South German ambassadors could not bear repetition and eight months later he told members of his military entourage that there had not been such a hypocritical and mendacious man since Cesare Borgia.[57]

He was contemptuous of any minister who felt that the Kaiser's confidence alone was insufficient to conduct the affairs of high office; he suspected Marschall of being a South German constitutionalist and particularly resented ministerial consultations with party leaders such as were necessary during the period of the Bülow Bloc.[58] On the other hand, Wilhelm remained almost touchingly loyal to ministers who stood by him in times of adversity. In 1901, despite Bülow's misgivings, he appointed the former Minister of the Interior, Köller, as State Secretary for Alsace-Lorraine; Köller had been at the centre of a major crisis in 1895 when the State Ministry had had to force his resignation against the Kaiser's will.[59] Wilhelm also remained very loyal to Bethmann after the Chancellor suppressed his own better judgement and defended the Kaiser during the public outcry over the Zabern affair in 1913.

Wilhelm clearly had much more direct contact with ministers and state secretaries before 1900 when he sought to be his own Chancellor, intervened regularly in departmental work and frequently called Crown Council meetings to discuss affairs of state. The ministers exploited the Chancellor's weakness to wage war against each other rather than asserting their

[55] GStA Merseburg, Zivilkabinett, 3698, Rheinbaben to Valentini, 23 August 1909.

[56] Röhl, *Germany without Bismarck*, pp. 86, 158.

[57] HSA Stuttgart, Weizsäcker Papers, Varnbüler to Weizsäcker, 14 July 1909; Robert Zedlitz-Trützschler, *Zwölf Jahre am deutschen Kaiserhof*, Stuttgart 1924, 4 March 1910, p. 237.

[58] See Röhl, *Germany without Bismarck*, pp. 150–1; Lerman, *Chancellor as Courtier*, p. 191. See also Alastair Thompson, *Left Liberals, the State and Popular Politics in Wilhelmine Germany*, Oxford 2000, pp. 167–70.

[59] HSA Munich, 1073, Lerchenfeld's Reports, 30 July 1901 and 7 August 1901; correspondence between Bülow and Holstein in PA Bonn, Auswärtiges Amt, IA, Deutschland, 122 no. 9, vol. 2. See also Röhl, *Germany without Bismarck*, pp. 142–6.

collective responsibility, and their disunity meant that Wilhelm, with some justification between 1897 and 1900, could claim to be the sole arbiter of Germany's fate, the only man to see the broader picture in contrast to the narrow vision and bureaucratic expertise of his officials.

After 1900, however, Wilhelm appeared relieved to leave political matters to Bülow, claiming he could now sleep peacefully at night, confident that everything would be all right.[60] Bülow's close identification with Wilhelm's will imposed a superficial harmony on the Prussian Ministry of State; ministers were conscious that most of the key decisions were taken outside the State Ministry, even without involving the relevant departments,[61] and that if they did not do the Chancellor's bidding, he would 'go to His Majesty' and force them to toe the line. The contact they had with Wilhelm personally thus became less and less frequent; Bülow restricted their access to the Kaiser through ensuring that there were few occasions when ministers needed to deliver *Vorträge* and that, if the ministers met the monarch socially, this was usually at the Chancellor's residence.[62] The diaries of the Kaiser's adjutants suggest that some ministers were only received formally by Wilhelm during Bülow's Chancellorship when they were appointed and when they resigned. Möller had to make a special request to the Kaiser to be granted a farewell audience before he left office in 1905.[63]

Bethmann as Chancellor was much less concerned than the jealous and watchful Bülow to regulate the ministers' contacts with Wilhelm and by 1910 the Kaiser was beginning to see more of his higher civil servants again, listening to their *Vorträge* as well as spending time with them socially, although some ministers still had to wait months for an opportunity to speak to Wilhelm.[64] How far ministers relished these new opportunities is questionable. Rheinbaben and Paul von Breitenbach, the Minister of Public Works (1906–18), lunched with Wilhelm in February 1910 at the palace, and the monarch, who was agitated about the delay of a pet project, 'grabbed Rheinbaben by the ear at the table and slapped Breitenbach several times on the shoulder in a not completely friendly way'. The court official who observed these events commented that it was not easy to behave oneself when invited to lunch and then treated badly by the host.[65]

---

[60] Röhl, *Eulenburg*, vol. III, Eulenburg to Bülow, 9 August 1903, p. 2096.

[61] See GStA Merseburg, Staatsministerium, 27 July 1904. The Ministers of Trade and Finance protested about being excluded from the final stage in the negotiation of a major trade treaty with Russia.

[62] See GStA Merseburg, Adjutantenjournale. Wilhelm saw most ministers (except Tirpitz and the Foreign Secretary) very infrequently; ministerial dinners at the Chancellor's palace took place on 12 November 1904 and 14 February 1906.

[63] GStA Merseburg, Zivilkabinett, 3697, Möller to Bülow, 14 October 1905.

[64] Zedlitz-Trützschler, *Zwölf Jahre*, 14 February 1910, p. 230 and 21 February 1910, p. 235.

[65] Ibid., 21 February 1910, p. 234.

At no time during Wilhelm II's long reign could the Berlin administration be confident that the Kaiser would not intervene directly in the affairs of government departments. Even in the 'honeymoon period' of Bülow's Chancellorship, Wilhelm's brief, approving marginalia on a petition from a Landtag deputy could precipitate a debate in the Ministry of State on the idea of creating a Ministry of Welfare;[66] and in April 1904 Wilhelm telegraphed the Foreign Office from Palermo because he had just been informed by the German Orient Society that the Finance Ministry had cut its annual subsidy for excavations in Syria to such an extent that archaeological work in Babylon would have to be halted.[67] Wilhelm claimed that this news would be greeted with jubilation in French, English, and American circles and that the consequences of dismissing the trained workforce would be incalculable.

As the German Orient Society is under my patronage and the excavations are carried out in accordance with my directives, as on top of this I contribute considerable sums from my private funds (*Privatschatulle*), I am highly astonished that the Finance Ministry did not consult with me beforehand and has not taken notice of my person in this important question. The officials in the Finance Ministry are not in a position to judge what kind of an influence the bureaucratic mania for cuts has on the fulfilment of our cultural mission abroad. In expressing my displeasure to the Finance Minister over this occurrence, I command that immediately an order be made out for a grant of 10,000 Marks from the Reich disposition fund and 20,000 Marks from the Prussian disposition fund.

Rheinbaben and Stengel immediately did as they were told and transferred the funds, although the former did write to Wilhelm the following day pointing out the extent of the state deficit and the fact that he, the Kaiser, had insisted on curbing expenditure in view of the big canal bill.[68]

Across a range of issues – the Polish question, the canal issue, the Jesuit Law, school legislation, even how much reliance should be placed on monopolies in the Reich finance reforms – the Kaiser's views had to be noted and heeded.[69] In civil emergencies such as miners' strikes or flood disasters, Wilhelm moved into centre-stage to oversee the government's strategy;[70] in crises which impinged on the military, as in the case of the colonial rebellions in German South-West and East Africa, the Kaiser was the only person constitutionally in a position to co-ordinate a coherent government response which took into account the views of the service chiefs.[71] Wilhelm

[66] GStA Merseburg, Staatsministerium, 25 November 1901.
[67] PA Bonn, Auswärtiges Amt, IA Preussen, no. 9, vol. 3, Wilhelm II to Foreign Office, 8 April 1904.
[68] Ibid., Rheinbaben to Wilhelm II, 9 April 1904 and Stengel to Foreign Office, 19 April 1904.
[69] See e.g. GStA Merseburg, Staatsministerium, 12 June 1908 for Wilhelm's views about monopolies.
[70] GStA Merseburg, Kronrat, 14 August 1903 and 28 January 1905.
[71] GStA Merseburg, Adjutantenjournale, 17 January 1904.

continued to see his personal preoccupations as synonymous with the interests of state and to regard his ministers as executive tools of the royal will whose main function was to do his bidding.

In 1906, when he called a rare Crown Council meeting at the palace on routine matters, the agenda reflected the Kaiser's initiatives in a wide variety of areas – how to improve the conditions of home workers, Prussian settlement policy in the eastern provinces, Germany's financial preparedness for war, measures to combat socialist penetration of the Army, and archaeological excavations in Prussia. In addition the Kaiser raised his concern about a Bill before the Reichstag which amended the *Reichsstempelgesetz* and envisaged a tax on automobiles. The ministers listened apparently without comment to his revelation that the Royal Automobile Club had expressed 'grave misgivings' about this move which had been worked out by men who were insufficiently oriented about the matter and had not consulted with those best able to assess its impact.[72]

How critical were the ministers and state secretaries of the Kaiser and how did they see their relationship with him? All were pronounced monarchists and many certainly began their ministerial careers in considerable awe of Wilhelm II. Men as different as Bismarck, Caprivi, Hohenlohe, and Bülow all at first found different reasons to admire the Kaiser, but eventually became disillusioned through having to work with him.

Hohenlohe persistently misread Wilhelm's attitude towards him, suspecting that Wilhelm treated him disrespectfully but easily being persuaded that this was not the case when he talked to Wilhelm personally. Even when he saw clearly that his role was to be 'a straw man' until the Kaiser had found the right Chancellor, Hohenlohe was convinced that he should stay and be 'more obedient to His Majesty'.[73] Bülow was effusive when, as State Secretary of the Foreign Office in 1898, he watched the Kaiser in action in a Crown Council meeting. 'I grow fonder and fonder of the Kaiser. He is so important!!' he wrote to Eulenburg afterwards.

In the Crown Council this morning I was completely overwhelmed! He gave an *exposé* of the terribly complicated waterways question – with all that entailed in the way of material and departmental problems – which no departmental Minister could have equalled for precision and accuracy. Yet it was done with a freshness, an attractiveness, a breadth of vision, in short with a brilliance far beyond the reach of any Minister.[74]

---

[72] GStA Merseburg, Kronrat, 13 January 1906.
[73] Röhl, *Eulenburg*, vol. III, Bülow to Eulenburg, 16 July 1897, p. 1846. See also Chlodwig zu Hohenlohe-Schillingsfürst, *Denkwürdigkeiten der Reichskanzlerzeit*, ed. Karl Alexander von Müller, Stuttgart and Berlin 1931, especially pp. 268f.; Röhl, *Germany without Bismarck*, pp. 209, 233.
[74] Röhl, *Germany without Bismarck*, pp. 259–60.

Bethmann, too, as a young Landrat, declared, 'More and more the kaiser captures my heart and undoubtedly matures in many ways.'[75] Hollmann was a state secretary who never ceased to be in awe of Wilhelm II. He was completely 'carried away by his magic' and continued to marvel 'that someone as unimportant as I, has won to such a large degree the trust of this man'.[76] Even the sober Loebell remained convinced as late as 1908 that Wilhelm always made the right decision in important questions.[77] By contrast, Dernburg maintained that he made up his mind to leave office in December 1908 after the Kaiser told him about a damaging conversation he had had with Sir Charles Hardinge in Homburg and hinted that he was considering making him Bülow's successor as Chancellor. 'I saw in that a lack of judgement as I possessed neither the intellectual stature, the necessary qualities and the previous experience for such a post, nor the necessary support from the political elite and the Court. The consequence was that I strongly withdrew.'[78]

Most of the ministers and state secretaries sought to avoid a confrontation with the Kaiser at all costs, many being timid and fearful about the consequences of standing up to him. Maximilian von Beseler, the Minister of Justice (1905–17) was, according to his Reich counterpart, 'a very kind and pleasant man but without firm and definite views and consumed (*beseelt*) by a terrible fear of the Kaiser'.[79] Schön, too, was not even prepared to warn Wilhelm when he was in danger of making inappropriate or indiscreet remarks in company which might compromise German foreign policy.[80] Bronsart clashed with Wilhelm over the issue of courts-martial reform and Bülow fell out with him after the *Daily Telegraph* affair, but both men were known to weep tears in the Kaiser's presence afterwards as they assured him of their loyalty and begged for forgiveness.[81] Dernburg, again, was less deferential, doubtless because he was recruited to the Berlin administration via an unusual route. He scandalized the all-male company at a Saturday evening dinner in 1910 by having the audacity to say to the Kaiser across the table, 'As Your Majesty rightly keeps on saying, "I really must put the wind up my ministers".'[82]

[75] Jarausch, *Enigmatic Chancellor*, p. 40.   [76] Hull, *Entourage*, p. 162.

[77] BA Koblenz, Schwertfeger Papers, 206, Loebell to Valentini, 21 July 1908.

[78] BA Koblenz, Wolff Papers, 8, Dernburg to Zedlitz, 4 January 1927.

[79] SA Cologne, Bachem Papers, 287, 'Besuch bei Nieberding anläßlich seines Abschiedes am 26 Oktober 1909'.

[80] Zedlitz-Trützschler, *Zwölf Jahre*, 4 April 1910, p. 248.

[81] Röhl, *Germany without Bismarck*, p. 141; HSA Munich, 699, Lerchenfeld's Report, 12 March 1909; Vierhaus, *Spitzemberg*, 25 March 1909, p. 501.

[82] Zedlitz-Trützschler, *Zwölf Jahre*, 21 February 1910, p. 234.

The unprecedented action of the State Ministry in forcing Wilhelm to accept Köller's resignation in 1895 was not undertaken lightly by men like Boetticher who believed it was 'not the Prussian way' to threaten mass resignations and argued that 'we could not cause the Kaiser trouble in difficult moments'.[83] The State Ministry repeated its threat to resign *en bloc* in the Podbielski crisis of 1906 and it also stood by Bülow in the *Daily Telegraph* affair since, in Bülow's words, 'it sensed the great gravity of the situation'.[84] But, even after his dismissal, when he was working on his later book *Deutsche Politik* in 1913 (and doubtless still had political ambitions), Bülow told Loebell, 'Above all, of course, I wish that there is nothing in the work which could appear in any way directed against our All-Gracious Master! Someone as thoroughly royalist as I am, and at the same time (despite everything) so completely and utterly devoted to our Master as I am, will never ever wish to attack the Crown.'[85]

Of course, after the collapse of the monarchy in 1918, many of Wilhelm's former ministers and state secretaries were openly critical of the Kaiser's personality and some, above all Bülow, produced damning memoirs.[86] Most remained loyal to the Hohenzollern monarchy as an institution and despised the newly established Weimar Republic; and Loebell, for example, attacked the Colonial Secretary, Wilhelm Solf (1911–18), a man he claimed to have suggested for the post, for his role in forcing the Kaiser's abdication in 1918.[87]

However, their ambivalence about Wilhelm personally was also very apparent. In his notes written after the war, Bülow wrote that his main task had been 'to protect and lead His Majesty'[88] but the unmistakable implication of his memoirs was that, first and foremost, he had had to protect Wilhelm from himself. Bülow also told the diplomat Monts that he had wanted to help Germany cope with the rule of Kaiser Wilhelm II, thus protecting the nation from the consequences of his exceptional individuality.[89]

Tirpitz, too, recalled that Wilhelm II had made life 'a perfect hell' for him, although his view was coloured by his negative experiences during

[83] Röhl, *Germany without Bismarck*, p. 122.
[84] See Lerman, *Chancellor as Courtier*, pp. 150–60; BA Berlin, Hammann Papers, 14, Bülow to Hammann, 11 November 1908.
[85] BA Koblenz, Bülow to Loebell, 3 March 1913; see also Bernhard von Bülow, 'Deutsche Politik', in *Deutschland unter Kaiser Wilhelm II*, vol. 1, Berlin 1914, and *Deutsche Politik*, Berlin 1916.
[86] See especially Bernhard von Bülow, *Denkwürdigkeiten*, 4 vols., Berlin 1930–1.
[87] BA Koblenz, Loebell Papers, 27, Loebell memoirs, Bl. 98.
[88] BA Koblenz, Bülow Papers, 33, Bl. 184.
[89] Anton Monts, *Erinnerungen und Gedanken des Botschafters Anton Graf Monts*, ed. Karl Nowak and Friedrich Thimme, Berlin 1932, p. 155.

the war.[90] Dernburg, the ministerial outsider, again had no reservations in 1927 about criticizing the Wilhelmine government system which, he was convinced, had contributed to Wilhelm's 'unfortunate development'. He maintained that all ministers before 1914 had been equally powerless and dependent on handling the King; if they had not done so, Germany could not have been ruled at all.[91]

Yet retrospective judgements may not be a true indicator of ministerial perspectives before 1914, especially given the bitter experience of defeat, revolution, and the Kaiser's abdication. Similarly, personal criticisms of Wilhelm may serve the biographer well but they are clearly less significant politically than evidence of a concerted effort by ministers to constrain the Kaiser or a readiness to consider reform.

In looking at the Berlin administration's attitude to political reform, it must be said that the ministers and state secretaries were not all die-hard conservatives, reluctant to embrace change and intent on preserving an untenable *status quo*. On the contrary, they clearly achieved reforms in a wide range of spheres before 1914 and, to a degree at least, the agenda of State Ministry meetings reflected an awareness of some of the major issues of the day – the concern to balance the needs of industry and agriculture, integrate former outsiders such as Catholics, counter the rise of socialism, investigate problems of unemployment, find a solution to the Polish problem and so on – even if ministers were also often pre-occupied with lesser matters, not least the material conditions of public officials.[92]

The Berlin administration also made repeated efforts to reform itself in the hope of thereby streamlining government processes and encouraging greater efficiency and co-ordination. Friedrich Althoff's plans to divide the Ministry of Education in 1907, Bethmann's hopes of stripping away some of the functions of the Reich Office of the Interior, Dernburg's initiative to create a Reich Trade Office in 1908, the attempt to reorganize the Foreign Office in 1909, all these were schemes which surfaced in a relatively short time-span though they were all too often shelved or curtailed because the obstacles and difficulties appeared too great.

The Kaiser, too, took an interest in reform, chairing a Crown Council meeting in February 1909 on the reorganization of the Prussian administration, much to the consternation of the Minister of the Interior, Friedrich von Moltke (1907–10) who had already developed his own plan for reform. 'H.M. happily has the desire to be involved in government affairs',

[90] Scheck, *Tirpitz*, p. 37.   [91] BA Koblenz, Wolff Papers, 8, Dernburg to Zedlitz, 4 January 1927.
[92] GStA Merseburg, Staatsministerium, 1 February 1908 and 30 November 1908.

Bülow informed the ministers ruefully since he no longer had Wilhelm's confidence and this was prior to their brief reconciliation in March,[93] 'and has always been an opponent of unbridled bureaucracy and tiresome and unnecessary formulae. H.M. wishes to simplify the administration and has wanted to call a Crown Council to discuss this for a long time'.[94]

In the event, Wilhelm II told the ministers that he had called the Crown Council (the first in over three years) to give the Minister of the Interior the opportunity to give a *Vortrag* on the reorganization of the Prussian administration, a reorganization which Moltke claimed was urgently necessary because of the increasing demands of legislation and the excessive centralization which had resulted from piecemeal reforms. The ensuing discussion, however, largely revolved around simplifying bureaucratic procedures, decentralization (provided this did not burden the local Landrat) and the extent to which they could use typewriters and female workers 'who are cheaper and are especially suited for precisely this kind of work'. Wilhelm was happy to confirm that in America all government papers, irrespective of their level of confidentiality, were typed by women and that thereby much time and money were saved.[95]

Despite these bureaucratic initiatives, however, the ministers and state secretaries in the Berlin administration took every opportunity to register their profound distaste for significant political reforms or moves towards greater democracy in Germany. Extreme Conservatives, like Rheinbaben and Podbielski, were understandably opposed to any concessions such as allowances for Reichstag deputies or the merest hint of a possible reform of the Prussian suffrage. Loebell, as Bülow's Chancellery Chief, categorically rejected the idea of Reich ministries responsible to the Reichstag in 1906 and resigned as Prussian Minister of the Interior over the issue of suffrage reform in 1917. But even the more enlightened conservative modernizers, Posadowsky and Bethmann, refused to contemplate an equal and direct male suffrage for Prussia before 1914 and were inclined to link a Prussian reform to a simultaneous reform of the Reichstag suffrage.[96] In late November 1908 the State Ministry was less exercised by the repercussions of the *Daily Telegraph* affair than by 'a regrettable democratic trait' (Rheinbaben) which had manifested itself in the Landtag committee looking into civil service salaries. The committee had increased the salaries of lower officials but not

[93] See Lerman, *Chancellor as Courtier*, pp. 228–35.
[94] GStA Merseburg, Staatsministerium, 13 February 1909.
[95] GStA Merseburg, Kronrat, 18 February 1909.
[96] GStA Merseburg, Staatsministerium, 1 December 1905; BA Koblenz, Loebell Papers, 27, unpublished memoirs, pp. 85–7; Jarausch, *Enigmatic Chancellor*, pp. 51–2, 75–9.

those of higher civil servants, a decision which the ministers wholeheart-edly condemned. 'This kind of lack of discipline and hubris which would not be tolerated in fully (*rein*) parliamentary countries must be vigorously opposed', Bülow agreed.[97]

Yet by 1910 it was becoming increasingly clear even to perceptive ob-servers at court that it was 'not just the socialist rabble and the Jews' who wanted to see a reform of the Prussian suffrage and that the government needed to display energy, courage, and determination in tackling necessary reforms.[98] Bethmann as Chancellor was convinced that Reich policy re-quired a liberal regime in Prussia, but he had no solution to the problem of how to break the Conservatives' stranglehold on Prussia without opening the floodgates to democratic or socialist radicalism. 'Has not the democ-ratization of parliament in all countries contributed to the brutalizing and diluting of political morals and to the hamstringing of progress which we need so dearly and to whose advancement the suffrage reform is being intro-duced?' he put to the Prussian Landtag in February 1910. He also deplored how the circumstances of Bülow's departure after the parliamentary defeat of the Reich financial reform had created 'a dangerous trend' in imperial German politics.[99]

Thus the Berlin administration felt under no pressure to re-think its relationship to the Kaiser before 1914. It remained the Kaiser's elite in that ministers and state secretaries saw themselves primarily as servants of the crown and were not prepared to seek support from the Reichstag for significant political reforms. Given the dearth of political talent within the higher civil service and the spectacular growth in support for the reformist parties on the eve of the First World War, it is scarcely surprising that, even under a relatively chastened and quiescent Kaiser, the government of Bethmann Hollweg could inspire little confidence in its domestic policy.

In April 1912 Ernst Bassermann, the National Liberal party leader, wrote to the former Chancellor Bülow that everything was going wrong in the Wilhelmstrasse.[100] The 'best man', the State Secretary of the Treasury since 1909, Adolf Wermuth, had left and his successor, Hermann Kühn, was 'completely spent'. 'Herr von Bethmann certainly has good intentions but no capacity to resist at all (*keinerlei Widerstandsfähigkeit*)', Bassermann asserted, 'and so the state ship sways in the wind and has lost its course.'

[97] GStA Merseburg, Staatsministerium, 30 November 1908.
[98] Zedlitz-Trützschler, *Zwölf Jahre*, 4 March 1910, pp. 238–9.
[99] Jarausch, *Enigmatic Chancellor*, pp. 73, 76.
[100] BA Koblenz, Bülow Papers, 107, Bassermann to Bülow, 3 April 1912. See also Bülow, *Denkwürdig-keiten*, vol. III, p. 89.

The shrewd parliamentarian had no doubts about the source of the problem and, unlike some with close knowledge of relationships in Berlin, he was not inclined to put all the blame on the personality of Kaiser Wilhelm II himself. Rather, Bassermann identified a more elemental weakness in the political structure of Wilhelmine Germany and one which struck at the heart of the Berlin administration: 'A system which appoints men completely lacking in influence to the responsible positions is not tenable', he concluded.

The evidence thus confirms that the Wilhelmine elite's approach to reform was essentially bureaucratic rather than political.[101] By contrast, chancellors and ministers could not tackle the key political questions left unanswered by the Bismarckian constitution, namely how to accommodate growing pressures for democratization and how to co-ordinate civil–military relations, which remained the exclusive preserve of the monarch. Neither of these issues was addressed even during the honeymoon period of Bülow's Chancellorship when the Kaiser was at his most malleable. Bülow himself had no interest in reforming a system that suited him so well, minimized the danger of social democracy, and did not dare to encroach upon the Kaiser's military prerogatives.[102]

---

[101] See especially Berlepsch, *Neuer Kurs im Kaiserreich*, p. 434.

[102] The Kaiser's 'personal rule' and the position of the Chancellors (but not the ministerial bureaucracy) is briefly discussed in Volker Ullrich, *Die nervöse Grossmacht 1871–1918*, Frankfurt 1997, chapter 2 (which devotes more space to the political parties). Thomas Nipperdey, *Deutsche Geschichte 1866–1918*, vol. II, *Machtstaat vor der Demokratie*, Munich 1992, discusses the administration (ch. 2), the role of the Kaiser after 1890 (ch. 4) and domestic policy under Bismarck's successors (ch. 5).

CHAPTER 4

Wilhelm, Waldersee, and the Boxer Rebellion

Annika Mombauer

His Majesty [Kaiser Wilhelm II] remarked further that in the near future decisions would be made not by diplomacy, but by the sword.[1]

In the spring and summer of 1900, the colonial powers in China experienced a violent backlash against their 'civilizing' and missionary undertakings in the country. In an effort to defend their interests against Chinese resistance during the so-called Boxer Rebellion, the war against the 'Boxers' marked one of the first occasions of international co-operation in the face of a perceived common enemy.[2] However, the unity between the Great Powers produced by the shared goal of defending the principles of the Occident against the Orient did not last much longer than the initial outrage with which the horrific violence of the revolt was received. The hope of future co-operation closer to home proved unfounded. None of the governments

---

[1] Derenthall to Count von Metternich, 21 August 1900, in Johannes Lepsius, Albrecht Mendelssohn-Bartholdy, and Friedrich Thimme (eds.), *Die Große Politik der Europäischen Kabinette 1871–1914. Sammlung der Diplomatischen Akten des Auswärtigen Amtes* (hereafter *GP*), 40 vols., Berlin 1922–7, vol. XVI, 4613, p. 93.

[2] A vast amount of literature exists on the Boxer Rebellion. This chapter focuses on the political and diplomatic developments that formed the background to Wilhelm's and Waldersee's reactions to the crisis. Many interesting facets of this story cannot be explored here in detail, such as the military dimensions of this event, the horrific acts of looting undertaken by the Allied troops, and the behaviour of the German troops towards the Chinese. For details, see e.g. Susanne Kuß, 'Deutsche Soldaten während des Boxeraufstandes in China: Elemente und Ursprünge des Vernichtungskrieges', in Susanne Kuß and Bernd Martin (eds.), *Das Deutsche Reich und der Boxeraufstand*, Munich 2002 and Sabine Dabringhaus, 'An Army on Vacation? The German War in China, 1900–1901', in Manfred F. Boemke, Roger Chickering, and Stig Förster (eds.), *Anticipating Total War. The German and American Experiences, 1871–1914*, Cambridge 1999, pp. 459–76. For recent accounts of the Boxer Rebellion, including the background to the Boxers' grievances, see e.g. Kuß and Martin (eds.), *Das Deutsche Reich und der Boxeraufstand*; Diana Preston, *The Boxer Rebellion. China's War on Foreigners*, London 2002; Frederic A. Sharf and Peter Harrington, *China 1900: The Eyewitnesses Speak*, London 2000. See also Victor Purcell, *The Boxer Uprising. A Background Study*, Cambridge 1963; T. Grimm, 'Die Boxerbewegung in China, 1898–1901', *Historische Zeitschrift*, 224 (1977), pp. 615–34; Joseph W. Esherick, *The Origins of the Boxer Uprising*, Berkeley, CA 1987. Wilhelm II's role in the events will be further illuminated in John C. G. Röhl's third volume of his biography *Wilhelm II.*, Munich, forthcoming, ch. 4.

involved really trusted the others, or played a straightforward game, and Germany under Wilhelm II's leadership was no exception.

In the war against the Chinese, as so often on other occasions during Wilhelm's reign, for Germany, and for Wilhelm, there was more at stake than avenging the horrors inflicted upon scores of foreign victims, or the assassination of the German envoy in Peking, or even of staking a claim in China. Rather, Wilhelm wanted to demonstrate to the world that Germany was a power to be reckoned with, and he wanted to be seen to be playing an important role in international affairs.[3] Moreover, although Wilhelm and the Auswärtiges Amt differed in their methods, each was anxious that other Great Powers, particularly Britain, but also Japan and Russia, should not get a chance to use the current crisis to their advantage by extending their influence in the region. For these reasons it was essential that Germany was involved prominently in whatever action would be decided upon by the major powers.

The Boxer Rebellion offers interesting insights into the foreign policy of Wilhelmine Germany. For Wilhelm, the event amounted to much more than a revolt in China. He considered it a fight between Asia and Europe (notwithstanding the fact that Japan fought on the side of the European powers, and that the United States were also involved). In this struggle, Wilhelm contended, the European powers had to be united if they were not to lose out to the 'yellow peril'. In this way, too, Germany's role went far beyond avenging the assassination of the German envoy Clemens von Ketteler, although that attack gave Wilhelm the pretext for demanding a prominent involvement of German troops. The episode is a brilliant example of how the Kaiser exercised his 'personal rule', and provides further evidence of the damage that could result from the Kaiser's influence over foreign policy and his often ill-considered interventions, particularly due to his personal command (*Kommandogewalt*) in military matters.

Wilhelm was not alone in having these ambitious plans for Germany, and for her troops' involvement in the Chinese war, as can be demonstrated by highlighting the attitudes of 'Weltmarschall' Alfred von Waldersee. The former Chief of the General Staff and long-time confidant of the Kaiser (his 'Ersatzvater' for many years), who was dispatched as the commander of the joint forces, shared the Kaiser's views about the Chinese, but he also had his own agenda. At the age of sixty-nine, and having just been promoted to Feldmarschall in May 1900, this finally was an opportunity

---

[3] A similar motivation could later be found behind Germany's policy in the First Moroccan Crisis, only then far more was at stake because Britain and France had just concluded the *Entente Cordiale*.

for proving his military skills and, as far as he was concerned, the more the conflict resembled a 'proper war', the better. By analysing how Waldersee came to command the joint allied forces, and by highlighting his reaction to the atrocities in China, this chapter offers valuable insights into the decision-making in Berlin in times of international crisis, and it also allows us a glimpse into the political and military culture of Imperial Germany at the turn of the century.[4]

For Germany, as well as for Wilhelm and Waldersee, the war in China seemed to present a great opportunity, and Waldersee was determined to stamp his mark on the military campaigns. However, the reality of joint command differed greatly from the much-eulogized ideal that was conjured up before Waldersee's departure. The campaign was almost over before he arrived in China, and the unity of the allied forces soon gave way to bickering and jealousies. In this context, Waldersee's understanding of his role, and of the role of the European powers, further illuminates German attitudes at this crucial time, not only *vis-à-vis* the perceived 'yellow peril', but also in the relations between Germany and the other Great Powers at a time when the rigid alliance system that would soon provide the framework for European diplomacy was still in the future. The experience that the Great Powers gained of each other did much to inform views about potential future allies. In many ways, relations between the different contingent armies in China replicated the hostilities which existed on the larger international stage. To her neighbours and potential future allies and enemies alike, Wilhelm II's Germany did not make the best impression.

GERMAN AND INTERNATIONAL REACTIONS TO THE BOXER REBELLION

> Do not rest until the opponent has been thrown to the ground and begs for mercy on his knees.
> Wilhelm II's farewell speech to officers, August 1900.[5]

When disaffected so-called Boxer rebels revolted against the increasing foreign influence in China in the spring of 1900 and committed acts of horrific cruelty both towards foreign nationals and fellow countrymen who had converted to Christianity, these atrocities, and the international military retaliation that followed, resulted in the deaths of tens of thousands

---

[4] This investigation of Waldersee's role in the Boxer Rebellion is part of a larger research project of which this essay presents only the first findings and tentative conclusions.

[5] Farewell speech to officers, no date, *Berliner Lokalanzeiger*, 14 August 1900, in Johannes Penzler (ed.), *Die Reden Kaiser Wilhelms II. in den Jahren 1896 bis 1900*, part 2, Leipzig 1904, p. 222.

of people. The violence of the Boxers towards their victims was terrifying. 'Chanting mobs surrounded the mission stations and dragged out their terrorized occupants. Some they killed on the spot; others they took to Boxer temples to be slowly tortured to death. Tens of thousands of Chinese converts, Protestant and Catholic, were murdered – hacked to pieces, skinned alive, set alight or buried still living.'[6] Foreign nationals in China did not fare better, and when news of these terrible deeds (much of it of a sensationalist nature) started arriving in Europe, and it became known that several hundred foreign nationals were besieged by the Boxers in Peking in increasingly desperate conditions, the Great Powers responded with international co-operation the like of which had not been seen before.

Britain, France, Germany, Austria-Hungary, Russia, Italy, Japan, and the United States as powers with trade or other colonial interests in the region all considered these worth defending against the Boxer backlash. Due to trade expansion in the region, German interests were also affected, and German nationals were among those trapped inside the Chinese capital. An involvement of German troops in any international reaction to the atrocities was therefore always on the cards. Since Germany's occupation of Kiaochow in 1897 had added this small territory in China to Germany's relatively modest colonial possessions, German interests were deemed sufficiently great to necessitate an involvement in whatever international response would be decided upon.

A significant German involvement became a certainty when the news arrived in early July that the German envoy Clemens von Ketteler had been brutally murdered, leading the outraged Kaiser to demand revenge. In Wilhelm II's judgement, Germany now needed to play a significant role in whatever action would be decided upon: 'The ocean is indispensable for Germany's power. But the ocean also demonstrates that no important decisions must be taken on it, far from Germany, without Germany and without the German Kaiser', he famously declared.[7] Public opinion also favoured a German involvement in China, as Waldersee reported in a letter of 26 August 1900: 'You cannot imagine the heightened mood at home. Something like this has not occurred since the outbreak of war [18]70; unfortunately it cannot stay this way and has to die down one day.'[8]

It is not surprising in the light of what is known of Wilhelm II's character that his reaction to these events was one of outrage and indignation, and that

---

[6] Preston, *Boxer Rebellion*, p. xvii.

[7] Speech on the occasion of the naming of the new ship of the line, *Wittelsbach*, 3 July 1900, Penzler, *Reden*, p. 208. Germany was, of course, at this time at the height of her fleet-building programme.

[8] Waldersee to von Liebert, 26 August 1900, Geheimes Staatsarchiv, Berlin (GStA), VI. HA, NL Waldersee (Waldersee papers), BI, no. 32, fo. 114R.

he was spoiling for a fight. His initial response was characteristically out of proportion. Bernhard von Bülow, then Foreign Secretary, later recorded in his memoirs that he had 'never seen Kaiser Wilhelm . . . in such excitement as during the first phase of the Chinese confusion'. According to Bülow, Wilhelm declared repeatedly: 'Now it is a joy to be alive!'[9] The Auswärtiges Amt, as usual powerless *vis-à-vis* the Kaiser's violent outbursts, was concerned about Wilhelm's rash actions, as Waldersee recorded, who thought he could particularly 'detect fear of England' among the diplomats.[10]

Although Wilhelm's response was certainly exaggerated, it is nonetheless worth considering it in the context of the general outrage with which the other Great Powers reacted to the Chinese developments, and of the often exaggerated news which was received from the Far East. In their concern for the safety of the trapped Europeans in Peking, they all hurriedly despatched troops to the region. It was even reported very confidentially that the Pope might encourage a crusade.[11] Wilhelm's reaction was thus to some extent on a par with that of other European leaders. The crucial difference to most of them was that he was in a position to make decisions without consulting the responsible politicians, and sometimes even against their counsel. Thus, he disregarded Bülow's advice to play a low-key role and allow the other nations to fall out over China, rather than risk inadvertently uniting the other powers by playing too prominent a role.[12] However, while the diplomats were horrified by Wilhelm's frequent *faux pas*, Waldersee was among those who approved of the Kaiser's belligerence: 'Our Kaiser was also the only one who wanted to tackle the Chinese properly; if one had followed him we would long have had peace.'[13]

---

[9] Bernhard von Bülow, *Denkwürdigkeiten*, 4 vols. Berlin 1930–1 vol. 1, p. 358.

[10] Waldersee memorandum on the Boxer Rebellion, Peking November 1900, GStA, VI. HA, NL Waldersee, AI, no. 27, fo. 5. (this section omitted in Meisner). (Waldersee's diaries and papers were published in the 1920s by Heinrich Otto Meisner, but his edition is far from reliable. Citations here are from the edition, unless omissions or alterations occurred which will be pointed out as above. See H. O. Meisner (ed.), *Denkwürdigkeiten des Generalfeldmarschalls A. Grafen Waldersee*, 3 vols., Stuttgart 1923–5). There certainly was concern over British intentions in the Yangtse question, and Germany demanded that no single power should be allowed to determine its outcome. See Norman Rich and M. H. Fisher (eds.), *The Holstein Papers*, Cambridge 1955, vol. 1, pp. 114–15. In October 1900, these differences were put aside temporarily when Britain and Germany concluded the Yangtse agreement in favour of an open-door policy in the region. See e.g. Thomas Nipperdey, *Deutsche Geschichte 1866–1918*, 2 vols., vol. II. *Machtstaat vor der Demokratie*, Munich 1992, p. 660.

[11] L. K. Young, *British Policy in China, 1895–1902*, Oxford 1970, p. 149.

[12] See also Konrad Canis, *Von Bismarck zur Weltpolitik. Deutsche Aussenpolitik 1890–1902*, Berlin 1997, p. 340.

[13] Waldersee to von Engelbrecht, 28 February 1901, GStA, VI. HA, NL Waldersee, BI, no. 16, fo.172. Waldersee must have referred to the Kaiser's earlier belligerent outbursts. On 5 June, for example, Wilhelm had already demanded of the Auswärtiges Amt that the city of Wech-huan near Kiaochow be bombarded and occupied 'if anything happens to a German'. Cited in Bernd Martin, 'Die Ermordung des deutschen Gesandten Clemens von Ketteler am 20. Juni 1900 in Peking und die Eskalation des "Boxerkrieges"', in Kuß and Martin, *Das Deutsche Reich*, pp. 85f.

Wilhelm evoked images of a crusade, and considered the current crisis to amount to a war between Occident and Orient.[14] Some of his most notorious public speeches were given in response to the Boxer Rebellion,[15] and his private and official correspondence of those months makes for equally shocking reading. As Thomas Nipperdey comments, 'the elaborate accompanying music and the new ideology of the "yellow peril" stood in no relation to the actual possibilities and results'.[16] On 18 June Wilhelm sent a telegram to Bülow, demanding 'exemplary punishment and preventive rules against repetition [of acts against European nationals]; i.e. armed intervention'.[17]

Although the Wilhelmstrasse was not keen on his violent reaction, the Kaiser moved swiftly by mobilizing two battalions of navy infantry as early as 19 June. His *Kommandogewalt* (authority to command the troops) meant that he was able to give such orders at a whim. Initially he even wanted to send an entire army corps, but Bülow managed to talk him out of this, much to the relief of many who had failed to see the sense in such a rash response.[18] In addition to the infantry battalions, the *Ostasiatisches Expeditionskorps*, a volunteer brigade, was formed by *Kabinettsorder*, under the leadership of Generalleutnant von Lessel.[19] The Kaiser saw off the first of its contingents on 2 July. In contravention with the constitution, Wilhelm failed to consult the Reichstag before ordering these measures, so bent was he on his 'campaign of vengeance (*Rachefeldzug*)'.[20]

Only in November, when German troops were already involved in fighting in China, did Wilhelm face the Reichstag with a justificatory speech, appealing to its members' patriotism and their outrage at the events in

---

[14] See e.g. Wilhelm II to Bülow, 19 June 1900, *GP*, vol. XVI, no. 4527.

[15] In particular the infamous 'Hun Speech' in Bremerhaven on 27 July 1900, which Bülow considered 'perhaps the most damaging speech that Wilhelm II ever held'. Bülow, *Denkwürdigkeiten*, vol. I, p. 359. On the authenticity of the published versions of the speech, and for a general discussion of its contents, see Bernd Sösemann, 'Die sog. Hunnenrede Wilhelms II. Textkritische und Interpretatorische Bemerkungen zur Ansprache des Kaisers vom 27. Juli 1900 in Bremerhaven', *Historische Zeitschrift*, 222 (1976), pp. 342–58. For a discussion of Maximilian Harden's contemporary critique of the speech and his view that Germany was in a 'monarchical crisis', see John C. G. Röhl, *Wilhelm II. Der Aufbau der Persönlichen Monarchie*, Munich 2001, pp. 1156–7.

[16] Nipperdey, *Deutsche Geschichte*, vol. II, p. 655.   [17] *GP*, vol. XVI, no. 4525, 18 June 1900.

[18] Gerd Fesser, *Der Traum vom Platz an der Sonne. Deutsche Weltpolitik 1897–1914*, Bremen 1996, p. 60.

[19] See e.g. Holger Afflerbach, *Falkenhayn. Politisches Denken und Handeln im Kaiserreich*, Munich 1994, pp. 35–9; Bülow, *Denkwürdigkeiten*, vol. I, p. 357.

[20] As early as 3 July, Hohenlohe told Bülow that due to the costs involved in the planned expedition, the Bundesrat and Reichstag would need to be consulted to approve credits for the expedition, and asked to be kept informed so that he could return to Berlin if this were to occur. Clearly neither the Kaiser nor Bülow took any notice of Hohenlohe's request, and Bülow even advised against summoning the Reichstag. Chodwig zu Hohenlohe – Schillingsfürst, *Denkwürdigkeiten der Reichskanzlerzeit*, edited by Carl Alexander von Müller, Osnabrück 1967, p. 577; Katharine A. Lerman, *The Chancellor as Courtier*, Cambridge 1990, pp. 56–7.

China.[21] However, not everyone was convinced of the need for German involvement in the war in China (the brutality of which was by now public knowledge due to the so-called 'Hunnen-Briefe'). August Bebel's criticism summed up what he thought was actually at the heart of the expedition:

No, this is no crusade, no holy war; it is a very ordinary war of conquest . . . A campaign of revenge as barbaric as has never been seen in the last centuries, and not often at all in history; . . . not even with the Huns, not even with the Vandals . . . That is no match for what the German and other troops of the foreign powers, together with the Japanese troops, have done in China.[22]

In the heated weeks of the summer of 1900, consulting the Reichstag could not have been further from Wilhelm's mind. He did not even consider it necessary to run his policies past Chancellor Hohenlohe (who was in any case away from Berlin during the summer months of 1900). When the first expeditionary corps left for China on 2 July, Wilhelm's speech was of bombastic proportions:

The torch of war has been thrown into the middle of the deepest peace, unfortunately not unexpected by me. A crime of unheard-of cheek, horrifying in its cruelty, has hit my trusted envoy and has killed him . . . The German flag has been insulted and the German Reich has been humiliated. This demands exemplary punishment and vengeance . . . Thus I send you out to avenge this injustice, and I shall not rest until German flags, united with those of the other powers, fly victoriously above those of the Chinese and, placed upon the walls of Peking, dictate the peace to them.[23]

---

[21] Penzler, *Reden*, Wilhelm's throne speech of 14 November 1900, pp. 241f. He brazenly declared: 'I would have liked to have gathered the Reichstag around me straight away when I heard of the outbreak of the quarrel in China.'

[22] August Bebel in the Reichstag, 19 November 1900, cited in Roland Felber and Horst Rostek, *Der 'Hunnenkrieg' Kaiser Wilhelms II. Imperialistische Intervention in China, 1900/01 (illustrierte historische hefte)*, East Berlin 1987, p. 43. See also Ute Wielandt und Michael Kaschner, 'Die Reichstagsdebatten über den deutschen Kriegseinsatz in China: August Bebel und die "Hunnenbriefe"', in Kuß and Martin, *Das Deutsche Reich*, p. 194; Canis, *Von Bismarck zur Weltpolitik*, pp. 343, 349. In private, at least, Helmuth von Moltke seems to have agreed with this interpretation, for he wrote to his wife on 11 July 1900: 'One should not comment on the actual motivating factor of the whole expedition, for if we were completely honest it is greed (*Geldgier*) which has encouraged us to cut into the big Chinese cake. We wanted to earn money, build railways, run mines, bring European culture, that means in one word, earn money. In this we are not an ounce better than the English in the Transvaal.' Eliza von Moltke (ed.), *Helmuth von Moltke, Erinnerungen, Briefe, Dokumente 1877–1916. Ein Bild vom Kriegsausbruch, erster Kriegsführung und Persönlichkeit des ersten militärischen Führer des Krieges,* Stuttgart 1922, p. 243.

[23] Penzler, *Reden*, pp. 205–7. Not everyone considered these speeches to have been deplorable. Baroness Spitzemberg commented in her diary: 'The Kaiser . . . held . . . a very good speech for the departing troops.' Rudolf Vierhaus (ed.), *Das Tagebuch der Baronin Spitzemberg. Aufzeichnungen aus der Hofgesellschaft des Hohenzollernreiches*, Göttingen, 3rd edn 1963, 3 July 1900, p. 397. According to Bülow's memoirs, the Kaiser gave speeches 'which were intended to impress not just the Chinese, but the entire world'. *Denkwürdigkeiten*, vol. I, p. 358.

But as far as German interests were concerned, there was one major problem: how to restrict the amount of influence that Germany's rivals on the
colonial stage might wield in such armed intervention, and the amount
of gain they might achieve following such a war with China. Wilhelm expressed concern that no single state, particularly Russia or Japan, should
under any circumstances be allowed to dominate proceedings in the Far
East, and advocated sending German naval and military troops to China.[24]
When more news started to arrive which indicated the severity of the attack
on the European delegations, Wilhelm considered this a 'grave embarrass-
ment of the Europeans in front of Asians' and demanded a 'grand military
action of a uniform nature'.[25]

Peking must actually be attacked and razed to the ground. For this the army must
be equipped with quick firing artillery and with siege artillery . . . I would gladly
perhaps supply the commanding general. Then the entire undertaking must be
placed in one firm hand, and a European one. We must never expose ourselves to
a situation in which Russia and Japan sort out the matter on their own and push
Europe out. The German envoy will be revenged by my troops. Peking must be
razed (*muß rasiert werden*).[26]

But Wilhelm's initial outrage soon died down and, following Bülow's objections, he changed his mind about the kind of military intervention
necessary in China, as a relieved Helmuth von Moltke (who had previously
expressed doubts about what a small European army could hope to achieve
against a numerically superior enemy in such a vast country) reported in a
letter of 9 July 1900:

There has been a complete change of heart here during the last twelve hours which I
am very glad about because the decisions which the Kaiser has now made conform
completely to what I have considered to be right. The campaign of vengeance
(*Rachefeldzug*) against Peking has been dropped. All troops which are en route or
still due to depart are ordered to Kiaochow. There a secure base will be created,
and peace and quiet will be restored and maintained. We will make do with that
for now . . . Thus we are outside of all political tangles, don't need to come to
blows with either Russia or England, and can present our bill later.[27]

There were many occasions in July and August 1900 where Wilhelm was
able to air his views about the Chinese, and about the task 'his' troops would
have to face in the Far East. Famously, he demanded of the volunteers of
the First East Asia infantry regiment who left for China on 27 July that

[24] *GP*, vol. xvi, no. 4525, 18 June 1900, see also no. 4526: 'All of Europe had to show its flags.'
[25] *GP*, vol. xvi, no. 4527, 19 June 1900.   [26] Ibid.
[27] Moltke, 9 July 1900, in Moltke, *Erinnerungen*, pp. 241–2.

they should 'take no prisoners', and that they should defeat the Chinese in such a way that no Chinese would ever dare as much as look askance at a German.[28] It is certainly true that the so-called 'Hun-speech' singled Germany out among the many powers who were involved in the Far East.[29] But other, less infamous speeches also deserve quoting, particularly as they reveal much about Wilhelm's attitude to the nature of the enemy that Germany and the allied troops were facing. On 2 August he declared: 'We are dealing with a cunning enemy who, if spared at one end, will emerge with deceit at the other. The Chinese [is] by nature cowardly like a dog, but also deceitful.'[30] Similarly in another farewell speech, the Kaiser was reported to have said to departing officers: 'Beware of underestimating the opponents . . . Always imagine you [are] fighting an equal opponent. But don't forget his deceitfulness.'[31]

In the face of such a 'cunning' enemy, it was particularly important for the allied forces to work closely together, and it soon became a priority to establish a unified command. Here, as usual, the Kaiser wanted to have his way, much to the despair of the responsible diplomats in the Auswärtiges Amt.

THE QUESTION OF A UNIFIED COMMAND

> Whether English or Russian, French or Japanese, we are all fighting against the same enemy, to safeguard civilization, [and] we particularly for our religion.
>
> Wilhelm II, 2 August 1900[32]

Despite the Kaiser's obvious desire to wage war against the Boxers, the Auswärtiges Amt wanted to avoid taking the lead in Chinese matters in the early days and weeks of the crisis. This, Bülow explained, was necessary so as to prevent the other European powers from uniting against Germany. Bülow feared that too prominent a role for Germany in East Asia might lead to closer relations between Russia, France, and Britain, not only in colonial matters, but ultimately also in European diplomacy. At the same

---

[28] See Sösemann, 'Die sog. Hunnenrede'; also Penzler, *Reden*, pp. 209–12. On Wilhelm's speeches see also Bülow, *Denkwürdigkeiten*, vol. I, pp. 358–61.

[29] Klaus Hildebrand, *Deutsche Aussenpolitik, 1871–1918*, Munich 1989, p. 33. Moreover, as Imanuel Geiss points out, it 'provided Allied propaganda with one of the most effective slogans to use against the German Empire during the First World War'. *German Foreign Policy*, London 1976, p. 85.

[30] Farewell speech on the steamer *Rhein*, 2 August 1900. Penzler, *Reden*, p. 220.

[31] Cited in ibid., pp. 221–3, from *Berliner Lokalanzeiger*, 14 August 1900. See also Oskar Klaussmann (ed.), *Kaiserreden. Reden und Erlasse, Briefe und Telegramme Kaiser Wilhelms des Zweiten. Ein Charakterbild des Kaisers*, Leipzig, 1902, p. 360.

[32] Penzler, *Reden*, p. 223 – Kaiser's farewell speech on the *Rhein*, 2 August 1900.

time, he was keen to encourage a deepening of the rifts between Russia, France, Britain, and Japan. He explained his hesitant policy to the Kaiser thus:

In my humble opinion German interests are best served the more distrustingly the other powers control each other. On the other hand it is to be expected that in the case of Germany emerging as the party with the main interest in Chinese matters, one or other of the powers would use this in order to direct the joint distrust of all towards Germany and to retain their unity at Germany's expense.[33]

Given the hatred and mistrust that existed between the Great Powers, Bülow doubted if the unity of aim currently displayed would last for the duration of the undertaking. His foresight was certainly confirmed by events in China during 1900 and 1901. But in the early summer of 1900, the Kaiser was convinced of the importance of swift action and co-operation with the other powers, as he also wrote in the margin of Bülow's telegram: 'There must not be a conflict of interests, otherwise the Europeans are simply doomed!'[34]

However, once it was clear that all involved countries would dispatch troops to the region, and when the question of supreme command created difficulties between Britain and Russia,[35] both Foreign Secretary Bülow and the Kaiser were keen to see Germany in contention when it came to naming a commander for the allied forces in China, although Bülow warned against playing too prominent a role in pushing for a German commander:

It would be useful for our prestige if [the supreme command] fell only to us. Perhaps the handing over of the supreme command to the more neutral Germany could result from the natural opposition between English–Japanese and Russian–French ambitions. But there is no talk of us pushing ahead of others in this regard.[36]

The negotiations regarding a supreme command over the unified troops were fraught. Britain and Russia in particular distrusted each other, and would not tolerate an extension of the other's influence in China by means of supreme command. Thus, the Russian Foreign Office declared that Russia was only prepared to participate in a joint offensive against Peking if 'Russian troops were not placed under an English, Japanese or American commander'.[37] However, this meant that a German officer in charge of joint military operations remained a possibility. Similarly, Japan objected to a Russian in charge of the joint forces, and hoped instead that Germany might

---

[33] *GP*, vol. XVI, no. 4528, 19 June 1900. See also Bülow, *Denkwürdigkeiten*, vol. I, p. 366.
[34] *GP*, vol. XVI, no. 4528, 19 June 1900.   [35] See Young, *British Policy*, p. 150.
[36] *GP*, vol. XVI, no. 4529, 22 June 1900.   [37] Ibid., no. 4548, 4 July 1900.

dispatch a general who would be given the command on grounds of age. Japanese officers would be happy to be led by a German general, the German envoy Count Botho von Wedel reported.[38] On 12 July, the Auswärtiges Amt learnt via Germany's Ambassador in St Petersburg, Count Radolin, that Britain wanted to keep her independence in the matter of command. Radolin had learnt from his French colleague 'that England . . . had expressed that she did not want to see her troops placed under a foreign command and would only work in co-operation with Japan', to which the Kaiser added indignantly in the margin: 'So the Japanese are no strangers for England! Only Germans, Russians etc.!!!'[39]

At the same time as these delicate negotiations were taking place, German political leaders began to express grave doubts about the Kaiser's mental state. On board the *Hohenzollern* during the Kaiser's annual North Sea cruise in July, an exasperated Eulenburg wrote to Bülow about the Kaiser's mad ravings and his liability to fly off the handle at the slightest provocation, and concluded: 'I have the impression that I am sitting on a powder keg and am *extremely* careful. Please limit your political reports *as much as possible* and request decisions only where they are unavoidable.'[40] In other words, despite the fact that the international situation required sensitive and shrewd decision-making, the 'supreme warlord' could not be consulted freely for fear of his irrational reactions and needed to be sheltered as much as possible from news about developments in China and closer to home.

In the meantime, negotiations regarding a united command continued. By 18 July, Russia still considered a united advance on Peking 'only with the greatest reluctance'.[41] In Bülow's opinion, this was due to the fact that Russia's interests in China differed from those of the other powers. Bülow suspected that while the other Great Powers had considerable economic interests in China, Russia was more concerned to try and keep foreigners out of the country. Although the Russian Ambassador passed on a request to the European capitals to come to an arrangement about a joint command, at this point Britain was still opposed to any such plan.[42] Clearly, despite the common threat they faced in China, there still could be no talk of unity among the international community at this time. Bülow continued to urge

---

[38] Ibid., no. 4561, telegram, Wedel to Auswärtiges Amt, no date, arrived 9 July 1900.

[39] Ibid., no. 4568, 12 July 1900.

[40] Eulenburg to Bülow, 14 July 1900, in John C. G. Röhl (ed.), *Philipp Eulenburgs Politische Korrespondenz*, 3 vols., Boppard am Rhein 1976ff., vol. III, p. 1984. The next day he added: 'I don't see any other solution but to wait quietly and ask God not to let some complicated matter approach H.M.' Ibid., p. 1985.

[41] *GP*, vol. XVI, no. 4573, 18 July 1900.

[42] Ibid. See also Young, *British Policy*, pp. 149–59, for the appointment of the Chief Command.

for a measured approach and was opposed to pushing for a German general to command the joint troops. However, his Kaiser had different ideas and was keen to see 'his' man in a prominent position in China.

WALDERSEE AS *WELTMARSCHALL*

All of Europe, and Asia, America, even Africa will be looking at you.

Holleben to Waldersee, 10 August 1900[43]

Given such mutual mistrust and suspicion of the motives of the other parties, it is surprising that the question of joint command was nonetheless resolved. Against Bülow's advice,[44] Wilhelm pushed for a German Oberbefehlshaber (an idea he had harboured at least since early June when he had asked Waldersee if he were willing to serve in this role), and the fact that Britain and Japan did not trust Russia to lead the joint forces, and Russia in turn did not trust them, worked in Germany's favour. However, it seems as though Wilhelm pursued the idea of a German commander rather too vigorously. Hermann Freiherr von Eckardstein commented later:

the unworthy way in which Wilhelm II went begging with the powers in order to achieve that Field Marshal Count Waldersee, whom he had already chosen for this post, would be suggested, was in no way helpful in increasing the German Reich's standing. On the contrary, he only made himself and thus the Reich appear ridiculous in the highest degree in the eyes of the foreign countries.[45]

Initially Britain was approached with a view to getting London's support for the suggestion of a German general for the supreme command. This suggestion was discussed in London at a ministerial council on 19 July.[46] While negotiations were still taking place with a reluctant Salisbury, and while the German Ambassador Hatzfeldt implored that it was 'urgently necessary that England makes the suggestion in question',[47] Wilhelm announced to the world that his friend, the Emperor of Russia, had asked him to make Waldersee available for the supreme command. However, Wilhelm's version of events did not match up with reality, for it was in

[43] GStA, vi. HA, NL Waldersee, BI, no. 25.

[44] Bülow had not been informed by the Kaiser of his decision to appoint Waldersee. See Lerman, *The Chancellor as Courtier*, p. 40. Likewise Hohenlohe had not been informed before the announcement and did not welcome the appointment; neither did Tirpitz, who feared that the other powers would only be waiting for Germany to embarrass herself. See Peter Winzen, *Die Englandpolitik Friedrich von Holsteins 1895–1901*, Cologne 1975, pp. 291–2.

[45] Hermann Freiherr von Eckardstein, *Lebenserinnerungen und politische Denkwürdigkeiten*, 3 vols., Leipzig 1921, vol. ii, p. 187.

[46] Young, *British Policy*, p. 152.   [47] *GP*, vol. xvi, no. 4578, 20 July 1900.

fact he who had approached the Tsar, rather than the other way around. Following Bülow's advice, Wilhelm had sent a telegram to the Tsar, enquiring if he wanted a Russian general for the supreme command and, if not, suggesting Waldersee. Nicholas II replied that he would not object to Russian troops being led by a German general.[48] The Kaiser immediately made this public knowledge, albeit with a different spin, as he informed, for example, his uncle Edward in London: 'On the Emperor of Russia's proposal Field Marshall Count Waldersee is designated as Commander in Chief of the allied armies in China. His great experience guarantees with the help of Providence the success of the campaign which is to begin in September.'[49]

Once the announcement had been made (before the other major powers had agreed to Waldersee!) it was up to the diplomats to try to win the other capitals over. As a result, the Auswärtiges Amt 'bombarded' the embassy in London with the most urgent official and private telegrams, because 'H.M. attaches great importance to the matter', and because a scandal was feared if Britain decided not to back Waldersee whose appointment had already been announced in Berlin in the meantime.[50] The diplomats faced a difficult dilemma, as Hatzfeldt outlined to Eckardstein:

> Now that the matter has been raised here and it is known that we *wish* to have the supreme command, a failure would undoubtedly be interpreted in Berlin as if we would have to keep reckoning with the incorrigible evil intentions of the English government.[51]

In other words, Wilhelm would interpret a refusal of his wish as a declaration of British hostility, and it was likely that future German policy would be shaped by this potential break-down of diplomatic relations between the two powers. With the stakes as high as this, it is unsurprising that the responsible politicians feared Wilhelm's erratic interferences.

According to Bülow, the fact that the Tsar accepted Waldersee was 'the result of weeks of diplomatic work and a great amount of patience, and finally also skill' on his part.[52] As far as Wilhelm was concerned, however, his personal policy had delivered the desired result. Now it was the job

[48] Wilhelm II to Bülow, 6 August 1900, ibid., no. 4602.
[49] Wilhelm II to Albert Edward Prince of Wales, 7 August 1900, RA Q16/632a, cited in Röhl, *Wilhelm II.*, vol. III (forthcoming), ch. 4, who points out that it is curious that Wilhelm repeats this lie to his friend Eulenburg. See also *Eulenburgs Korrespondenz*, vol. III, no. 1424.
[50] Hatzfeld to Eckardstein, 18 July 1900, Eckardstein, *Lebenserinnerungen*, p. 189, relaying a message from Holstein.
[51] Hatzfeld to Eckardstein, 20 July 1900, ibid., p. 191.
[52] Bülow to Eulenburg, 23 August 1900, *Eulenburgs Korrespondenz*, p. 1990.

of the Auswärtiges Amt to secure the consent of the other major powers, which Wilhelm and the diplomats of the Wilhelmstrasse did by intimating that Russia had suggested Waldersee's nomination, rather than it having been the Kaiser's wish.[53] Even the Reichstag was told that Germany had been invited by the Tsar to put Waldersee forward.

This whole protracted and confusing episode demonstrates one thing perfectly: how diplomacy was conducted in Imperial Germany under Wilhelm II, who felt authorized and qualified to meddle in diplomacy and decision-making at every level. In important matters, the Kaiser would not listen to his responsible ministers, whose job it was to pick up the pieces of his 'personal diplomacy' and try to avert the worst embarrassments by working busily behind the scenes.

Moreover, even in the light of the threat from the East that he clearly perceived, Wilhelm was still not willing to give up his prejudice and downright hostility towards his European neighbours. His Russophobe tendencies, for example, were not dampened by the experience of having a new, shared enemy. Likewise the Tsar became increasingly disenchanted with his German counterpart, as he had been during the previous months.[54] Many of Germany's diplomats were well aware that Germany had embarrassed herself in these early months of the crisis, due to the Kaiser's insensitive and rushed interferences and public outbursts. When the matter of the supreme command was decided in Germany's favour, however, Wilhelm received praise from his sycophantic courtiers, among them Philipp zu Eulenburg, who wrote to congratulate him, adding: 'it will be a calming influence on the musicians [of the famous European concert] that there is *finally* a conductor: Kaiser Wilhelm and Germany under the incognito of a Count Waldersee',[55] Wilhelm himself considered Waldersee's appointment 'the most shining justification' of Germany. 'I am extremely pleased for Waldersee about the unqualified acceptance from all sides', he added, seemingly unaware that in fact Salisbury's agreement had, in Eulenburg's words, been only 'bitter-sweet'.[56]

In mid-June, even before all these diplomatic wrangles had taken place, Wilhelm had approached Waldersee about the possibility of his taking over the command in China. After confirming that he would be delighted to

---

[53] Schwertfeger, *Die diplomatischen Akten des Auswärtigen Amtes 1871–1914*, Berlin 1927, pp. 122–3; Young, *British Policy*, pp. 153–4.
[54] On the increasingly strained relations between the two monarchs see Roderick R. McLean, *Royalty and Diplomacy in Europe, 1890–1914*, Cambridge 2001, pp. 38–9.
[55] Eulenburg to Wilhelm II, 11 August 1900, *Eulenburgs Korrespondenz*, vol. III, p. 1987.
[56] Wilhelm to Eulenburg, 17 August 1900, and Eulenburg to Wilhelm II, 11 August 1900. Ibid., pp. 1988 and 1987.

take on this task, Waldersee heard nothing further (and assumed the whole thing had come to nothing), until he received a telegram on 7 August advising him of his appointment.[57] When his selection was made public, many in German military and political circles were of the opinion that he was exceptionally well qualified for this unprecedented position. Commentators also stressed the unique nature of this command. Never before had a German general headed international troops in such a way,[58] and this was seen as confirmation of Waldersee's unique abilities. However, his suitability for the command was much exaggerated by his supporters, leading to ridicule in the German press in the days before his departure for China. It was in this context that the term 'Weltmarschall' was first coined, intended as a sarcastic description of the inflated expectations of the general's role in East Asia. The *Berliner Tageblatt* commented later in its obituary for Waldersee: 'It was his misfortune that over-eager friends, who speculated on the laurels to be earned, embarrassingly celebrated him in advance.' The result was a certain amount of unpopularity, the paper concluded.[59] But this was just one side of the story, for there was also much patriotic fervour on display. Crowds of people gathered outside Waldersee's home and greeted him at every railway station on his way to Berlin and onwards to Naples, where he was to embark for his journey to China.[60]

Among his military friends, expectations of Waldersee were high, and he received many letters and telegrams congratulating him on this prestigious appointment. Albrecht, Prince of Prussia, for example, congratulated Waldersee on his new position, 'which is unique in its kind, as far as I know history, and for which only few [people] in the world might be suitable'.[61] Some had visions of the effect the co-operation of the Great Powers might have on future European diplomacy. Thus Colmar von der Goltz expressed the hope that Britain's ambitions might well be curbed by such a venture in the long run, and that Germany's relations with France might become more cordial in future:

The co-operation of all great European peoples and Tsars in an event can be of great consequence. Perhaps this way we will also manage the initiation of a gradual reconciliation with France, something which would not be without importance for us in view of growing English over-enthusiasm.[62]

[57] GStA, VI. HA, NL Waldersee, AI, no. 27, Waldersee, diary, fos.1–2. (Cf. also Meisner, *Waldersee*, vol. III, pp. 1–3).

[58] Hans Mohs, *Generalfeldmarschall Alfred Graf von Waldersee in seinem militärischen Wirken*, Berlin 1929, p. 404.

[59] *Berliner Tageblatt*, 6 March 1904.   [60] GStA, VI. HA, NL Waldersee, diary, AI, no. 27, fos. 3R, 4.

[61] Telegram, 12 August 1900, cited in Mohs, *Waldersee*, p. 405.

[62] GStA, VI. HA, NL Waldersee, B.I., no. 21, Korrespondenz von der Goltz, letter of 10 August 1900.

Many generals expressed their desire to fight for Germany in China, among them von der Goltz and Helmuth von Moltke. Friedrich von Bernhardi regretted the fact that he had to forego this chance to fight a war, which he considered 'perhaps the only opportunity for military action . . . that life will offer me'.[63]

Waldersee was immensely proud to have been chosen. He thought that anything like the European forces going to China 'had not been seen since the building of the tower of Babel', but he also recognized that the only real shared goal of the Great Powers was to punish the Chinese. Beyond this, 'nobody trusts the other one'.[64] Clearly, unlike Bülow, neither Waldersee nor the Kaiser concerned themselves with the political dimensions of the crisis or considered the possibility of international co-operation leading to a *rapprochement* with other Great Powers. Rather, they focused only on the military prestige that the crisis might entail.

But to the disappointment of many, it looked as if Waldersee might arrive too late, as Bernhard Meiningen, for example, explained to his father in a letter of 16 August 1900:

I fear that Waldersee will arrive too late, for these days one hears of the conquering of Peking unless – what can neither be hoped nor wished – the Allies are defeated in front of the city gates. They are reputed to be only 25 kilometres away. If they do not manage to enter now, then the lives of the unfortunate embassies and the Europeans are lost. What Waldersee was then to achieve there is beyond me, for, if Peking is taken, the Chinese opposition is certain to collapse. These Orientals are brutal, blood-thirsty, but also cowardly.[65]

Indeed, before Waldersee finally went on board the *Sachsen-Coburg* in Naples, the news was received that the British, Japanese, and Russian troops that were already fighting in the region, without the involvement of any German troops, had surprisingly taken Peking on 15 August.[66] Thus the main task of the expeditionary corps had already been fulfilled, and Germany was in danger of not playing a part in the victory. The Kaiser's disappointment was such that, according to Bülow, he had been 'completely

---

[63] GStA, vi. HA, NL Waldersee, BI, no. 7 (Bernhardi), letter, 12 August 1900. See also Baronin Spitzemberg's diary entry, 12 July 1900: 'The military are in a state of the greatest excitement, all want to go along to China, but while the sons are begging imploringly out the front to be taken along, the fathers are begging out the back for the signing-up to be turned down.' Vierhaus, *Tagebuch*, p. 399.

[64] GStA, vi. HA, NL Waldersee, BI, no. 34, letter to Loë, 13 August 1900, fo. 119R.

[65] Bernhard Meiningen, 16 August 1900, Thüringisches Staatsarchiv Meiningen, HA 341. (I would like to thank John Röhl for making this document available to me.)

[66] For a contemporary account of the siege and liberation of the legations, see Robert Hart, *The Peking Legation: A National Uprising and International Episode*, Shanghai 1900.

thrown off-balance' by the news and ordered the Foreign Office to come to an agreement with Japan, an order which Bülow managed to prevent.[67] Waldersee later also recorded the Kaiser's reaction to the news, which was received in Wilhelmshöhe on 17 August:

Of course this was initially a great disappointment for the Kaiser. He had firmly convinced himself of the fact that the envoys, together with the entire staff, had long been murdered, and the joint advance on Peking was to begin following my arrival . . . under my supreme command, and thus the glory of having conquered Peking was to be mine. That dream was now gone.[68]

It is likely that the disappointment he described was his own as much as the Kaiser's ('he [Waldersee] has been waiting since [18]70', Baroness Spitzemberg recorded in her diary![69]), for both seemed to have hoped to be able to defeat the Chinese in a large-scale battle,[70] but he managed to convince Wilhelm that rather than cancel the expedition, much remained to be done and the German force should actually be increased in size. Waldersee was relieved that the Imperial Chinese Court had fled: 'If it had been captured in Peking, it would probably not have been difficult to conclude the peace, I would certainly have come too late, and we would probably not have played a decisive role in the peace', he commented.[71] Moreover, he felt that because the Imperial Court had fled into the 'interior of the vast country, it was very likely that there could be no talk of peace for some time and that I could still go to East Asia as Oberbefehlshaber'.[72]

Despite this 'disappointing' news, the Kaiser received Waldersee in Kassel with much pomp and saw him off at his Residenzschloss on 18 August. In his farewell speech, the Kaiser stressed the potential benefits for European peace that might be reaped from this undertaking: 'In the interest of our people I wish that our joint expedition will become a firm bond of mutual respect and mutual peace for the European powers, like H.M. the Emperor of Russia had tried to achieve last year in another area. Perhaps what could not be in peace time can now be achieved with weapons in hand.'[73] But Wilhelm's mood soon turned against the Russians, as they declared that they regarded the campaign in China as finished, following

---

[67] Bülow, *Denkwürdigkeiten*, vol. I, p. 456. See also *Eulenburgs Korrespondenz*, vol. III, p. 1983, n. 3.

[68] GStA, VI. HA, NL Waldersee, AI, no. 27, fo. 5 (Cf. also Meisner, *Waldersee*, vol. III, pp. 5–6).

[69] Vierhaus, *Tagebuch*, p. 400.   [70] See also Bülow, *Denkwürdigkeiten*, vol. I, p. 369.

[71] GStA, VI. HA, NL Waldersee, AI, no. 27, fo. 6 (a shortened version in Meisner, *Waldersee*, vol. III, p. 6).

[72] GStA, VI. HA, NL Waldersee, AI, no. 27, fo. 6 (omitted in Meisner).

[73] Penzler, *Reden*, p. 229.

the liberation of Peking by the allied troops, something which Wilhelm considered 'deplorable and surprising in the highest degree'.[74]

As far as Germany was concerned, and given that the Chinese Empress and her court had fled Peking and had avoided capture, the main task remained that of forcing the Chinese government to submit itself to the demands of the other powers. Moreover, there was still the significant matter of revenge for the assassinated envoy. Wilhelm was in no mood to accede to Russia's plans to let diplomacy take over from military action, as the Russian War Minister General Kuropatkin had suggested. He wrote to the Auswärtiges Amt in response to the latest intelligence from Russia:

To utter this at the moment at which Count Waldersee is just about to go off to China on his [Kuropatkin's] behest, when Peking is reputed to have been taken, but is supposed to be a sea of flames and filled with battles which might not even be going well for the allies, demonstrates such utter ignorance of the circumstances and lack of orientation over the situation as is well-near devastating.[75]

His disappointment at what he considered Russia's betrayal ('lies and lack of consideration') of the joint cause was evident, and he was not prepared to agree to Russian suggestions to abandon further military action, now that Russia had 'Manchuria in her pocket'. As far as Wilhelm (and Waldersee) were concerned, there was still an important mission to be achieved. 'We must attempt, under all circumstances, to capture Li-Hung-chang [viceroy of Kwangtung and Kwangsi] as soon as he leaves Shanghai, and to be sure of him as a valuable hostage', he advised the diplomats in the Wilhelmstrasse. At talks with the Prince of Wales on 22 August, Wilhelm spoke decidedly against Russia's desire 'to conclude a premature rotten peace against all our interests'.[76]

As far as Waldersee was concerned, this was to be his chance to demonstrate his abilities as a military leader in times of war, and he would not let a 'set back' such as the early liberation of the legations get in the way of his plans or agree to early peace negotiations. Not only was this a welcome opportunity for war when he had seemingly come to the end of his career, but he was also pleased once again to be in the Kaiser's good books after a period of declining relations with the monarch (and the dashing of his hope of perhaps one day becoming Chancellor).[77]

Waldersee departed from Naples as planned on 22 August, and arrived in Hong Kong on 17 September, where he took over the command over

[74] Wilhelm II to the Auswärtiges Amt, 21 August 1900, *GP*, vol. XVI, no. 4615.   [75] Ibid.
[76] Wilhelm II to the Auswärtiges Amt, 22 August 1900, ibid., no. 4617, pp. 97–8.
[77] See e.g. Bülow, *Denkwürdigkeiten*, vol. I, pp. 363ff.

all German land and sea forces. His reports to the Kaiser recorded the pleasant reception he received from the Governor of Hong Kong, but noted anti-Russian feelings among the British officers and the Governor.[78] He continued his journey via Taku and arrived in Tientsin on 27 September. On 17 October, Waldersee entered Peking ('a world-historic moment'[79]) and installed himself in the Dowager Empress's palace in the Forbidden City. In his diary he recorded his impressions of the place, noting in particular the devastation of towns along the way, as well as of Peking itself, for which he blamed both the Boxers and the fighting and looting of the Allied troops.[80]

Although the main objective of the allies, that of liberating the embassies inside Peking, had been achieved many weeks before, Waldersee nonetheless embarked upon his tasks with 'feverish activity', for example by ordering no fewer than seventy-five punitive expeditions in which countless Chinese, including many women and children, met their deaths.[81] At that time (October), the total number of Allied troops from eight countries in China was approximately 55,600 (rising to 58,300 by December), of which Germany and France made up the largest contingents (10,200 and 12,500 in October; 17,000 and 15,000 in December, respectively). Austria-Hungary's force was the smallest, with around 400 troops.[82] The total rose to 68,659 in April 1901.[83] Although this was a relatively large military force, it could be of little effect in a country as vast as China, and it would only ever be possible to take possession of a small part of that country. Therefore, as far as the allied powers were concerned, and in line with their military capabilities, they only considered themselves at war with the province of Chihili, while the provinces of Shantung and the Yangtse were regarded as neutral territories.[84]

Following Waldersee's arrival in China and his taking over of the joint command, his task of achieving an Allied victory had to begin in earnest. It was in no small measure due to Wilhelm II and his desire to rule personally with the help of just a few trusted confidants that Waldersee had been sent to China without specific instructions. The General was pleased about this

---

[78] Waldersee, diary, 25 September 1900, Meisner, *Waldersee*, vol. III, pp. 15–17.
[79] 'Generalleutnant Freiherr von Gayl, Gedächtnisworte zur Enthüllung des Denksteins an die China-Expedition', GStA, VI. HA, NL Waldersee, D, no. 3.
[80] Waldersee, diary, 17 October 1900. GStA, VI. HA, NL Waldersee, fos. 55–7, 64.
[81] Fesser, *Traum*, p. 61.   [82] Mohs, *Waldersee*, p. 409.
[83] Sharf and Harrington, *China 1900: The Eyewitnesses speak*, p. 211. (These were broken down as follows: Austria-Hungary: 300, Italy: 2,155, Japan: 6,408, Russia: 2,900, United States: 1,750, Britain: 18,181, France: 15,670, and Germany: 21,295.) According to Fesser, the total number of Allied troops was 87,700. *Traum*, p. 61.
[84] Mohs, *Waldersee*, p. 411.

independence, and he prided himself on making his own decisions without asking for advice or approval from the responsible diplomats in Germany, as he recorded in his diary after a few months in the Far East on 1 January 1901: 'It fills me with a certain amount of satisfaction that I have not bothered anybody back home with a request in the four months that I have been absent from Berlin. Hopefully it will be possible to keep this up until the end.'[85] Throughout Waldersee's time in China, the Auswärtiges Amt complained about not being kept informed about events, and not having any influence on German military policy in China. As on so many occasions, the diplomats were kept in the dark about important international developments because the Kaiser and his close military advisors wanted to stage-manage events themselves without any 'interference' from civilians. Waldersee observed 'that the Kaiser, even in important questions, does not always ask Bülow . . . ; the Chancellor is of course consulted even less'. He also remarked that he had occasion to notice that both put up with this treatment without opposition.[86] The importance of the Kaiser's *Kommandogewalt* is underlined by such statements – it was his right to make decisions and give orders as he saw fit, without any obligation to consult his ministers, and on this as on other occasions, the 'supreme warlord' made use of this prerogative.[87]

Unsurprisingly, Chancellor Hohenlohe complained later that he had not been consulted by the Kaiser:

The entire Chinese matter has been put into effect without my participation; I was neither informed in advance of the armaments, nor the troop-sending or the appointment of Waldersee to Oberfeldherr. Everything which bears relation to foreign policy is discussed and decided by H.M. and Bülow [Foreign Secretary] . . . All questions of personnel are being decided without my advice and even without my knowledge.[88]

In October 1900, Hohenlohe asked for his retirement, as his position *vis-à-vis* the Kaiser had become untenable. As expected, the Kaiser replaced him with his Foreign Secretary, Bülow.[89]

---

[85] Waldersee, diary, 1 January 1901, Meisner, *Waldersee*, vol. III, p. 79.

[86] Waldersee, Memorandum, November 1900, GStA, VI. HA, NL Waldersee, AI, no. 27, fo. 5 (a shortened version in Meisner, *Waldersee*, vol. III, p. 6).

[87] On the Kaiser's *Kommandogewalt*, see e.g. Annika Mombauer, *Helmuth von Moltke and the Origins of the First World War*, Cambridge 2001, pp. 17–18.

[88] Hohenlohe, *Denkwürdigkeiten der Reichskanzlerzeit*, p. 582.

[89] This replacement had long been on the cards. See e.g. Hohenlohe's letter of 7 January 1900, 'that I increasingly am of the conviction that I have to prepare myself for my departure. A Chancellor who avoids the Kaiser has a ridiculous position.' Ibid., p. 554. See also Bülow's account of his appointment, *Denkwürdigkeiten*, vol. I, pp. 372ff.

During his time in China, Waldersee did not keep the Chancellor or even the Auswärtiges Amt informed, and sent despatches only to the Kaiser. Moreover, the military authorities in Berlin, and in particular the General Staff and its Chief, Alfred von Schlieffen, did not become involved in Waldersee's affairs in China, and were merely keen for news from the theatre of war, which was reported daily to Schlieffen.[90] Waldersee was thus able to conduct himself, and German military policy in China, as he saw fit, and was answerable to nobody but the Kaiser. The *Frankfurter Zeitung* commented later: 'the way in which this influence [Waldersee's on Wilhelm] demonstrated itself during the China expedition may have caused Count Bülow some uneasiness'.[91] After all, Waldersee had once before been aiming to become Chancellor, and there was every chance he would use his restored good relations with the Kaiser to this effect.[92]

If the Auswärtiges Amt wanted to find out what Waldersee was reporting to Wilhelm, they needed to do so unofficially, and one way was via the Kaiser's friend Eulenburg. On 27 September 1900, Oswald von Richthofen approached the Prince to ask for his help in establishing what Waldersee was sending by telegram to the Kaiser. 'It would be of great importance to us, as far as possible, always to have knowledge of that which Count Waldersee telegraphs. Given that, as I have been told by Count Schlieffen, the Count only sends telegrams directly to the Kaiser, it will not always be very easy to find out about their content.'[93] As far as Wilhelm was concerned, Waldersee's mission was a strictly *military* one which was of no concern to the Auswärtiges Amt and which in addition was to be directed by the Kaiser alone from the saddle (*aus dem Sattel*). 'This point of view', Eulenburg commented, 'is neither politically or militarily possible and must lead to catastrophe.'[94] However, although the Auswärtiges Amt was able to get access to Waldersee's despatches via Eulenburg, the fact remained that both Waldersee and Wilhelm attempted and were able to run the Chinese affair entirely without briefing the responsible diplomats.

[90] Mohs, *Waldersee*, p. 410.   [91] *Frankfurter Zeitung*, 6 March 1904.

[92] See e.g. also Eulenburg to Bülow, 19 August 1900: Waldersee 'has departed [for China] with the "Reichskanzler-thought". But His Majesty does not even think about doing him this favour.' *Eulenburgs Korrespondenz*, vol. III, p. 1989.

[93] Richthofen to Eulenburg, 27 September 1900, ibid., p. 1998. See also Eulenburg to Bülow, 30 September 1900: asked by Eulenburg whether he had passed a telegram from Waldersee 'to Berlin', the Kaiser replied: 'It goes to the General Staff – it is military.' Eulenburg avoided further discussion, but ordered that such messages 'be passed to the General Staff *via* the Auswärtiges Amt'. Ibid., p. 2003.

[94] Eulenburg to Bülow, 3 October 1900, ibid., p. 2006.

THE REALITY OF WALDERSEE'S MISSION

A unified command of eight powers is an impossibility . . .
                                    Waldersee diary, 5 May 1901

Germany's generals and military commentators were disappointed with
the nature of the war that Germany and her allies had fought in China.
As we have seen, the first set-back was the fact that the war was almost
decided before Waldersee had even arrived. Once *in situ*, there were further
disappointments. Due to the size of the country, and the relatively limited
numbers of allied troops, it had been impossible to wage the anticipated
large-scale battles or engage in co-ordinated campaigns involving the different troops. German officers were also disappointed by the nature of the
enemy who, informed of the allies' actions by good communications, usually managed to avoid a confrontation with the opponent – in the eyes of
the German military this made them an enemy who 'lacked an energetic
will to fight' and who did not fight according to the rules. For this reason,
and also because of the difficulties imposed on the allied troops due to
the terrain, it was impossible to achieve 'overwhelming military successes
(*militärische Glanztaten*), measured against European examples', as Hans
Mohs commented in 1929.[95] Rather than the 'proper' war that Waldersee
and others had craved, the military effort in China assumed 'the character
of an occupation' – a shame for Waldersee, as Mohs concludes: 'From a
purely military point of view, fate did not extend its hand to Waldersee, for
him to display fully his great military ability in front of the entire world.'[96]
In addition, the Kaiser steadily lost interest in the campaign in the Far East,
following the liberation of the foreign nationals on 15 August, and only a
few months later he did not want to hear anything more about the matter.[97]
Little wonder that Waldersee was keen for the peace negotiations to yield
results, so that he could come home as soon as possible.[98]

   However, the real difficulty for Waldersee's mission did not emanate from
military matters. Rather, it was the fact that the powers present in China
had such diverging interests, that they had their own regulations regarding
military tactics, military law, disciplinary matters, and so on, that they were
unable to communicate with one another due to the number of different

---

[95] Mohs, *Waldersee*, p. 411.   [96] Ibid., p. 412.
[97] Bülow, *Denkwürdigkeiten*, vol. I, p. 370.
[98] An account of the German army's conduct in China is beyond the scope of this essay, but details of
Germany's military involvement can be found in Dabringhaus, 'An Army on Vacation?', pp. 459–76
and Susanne Kuß, 'Deutsche Soldaten während des Boxeraufstandes in China'.

languages spoken among them, and that they regarded each other with constant suspicion and jealousy, even hatred.[99]

While they were united by the common goal to free the envoys inside Peking and restore order to the province, the various contingents cooperated militarily, but once this aim had been achieved, separate interests soon took over. It had not taken the allied troops long to defeat the Chinese, but settling their scores with them proved more difficult. Much to Waldersee's annoyance, the negotiations prior to the peace treaty dragged on, 'due to the miserable quarrelling of the diplomats'.[100] He recorded his frustrations at the actions of the other powers, particularly those of Russia (whom he blamed for initiating separate negotiations with China), in his diary on several occasions. Not unlike Russia, Britain also tended to go its own way, at least in secret, Waldersee thought,[101] while relations with the French contingent were particularly delicate, due to their 'national sensitivity'.[102]

On the whole, Waldersee's authority as supreme commander was accepted by the other contingent armies. The British, Italian, and Austrian troops were willing and obedient, he reported to the Kaiser on 26 October, the Japanese troops bowed to his authority, and Russian troops claimed to accept his command, although he felt unsure if they could be trusted. Relations with the French troops were 'curious', for, having initially been very polite and accommodating to Waldersee, General Boyron later withdrew his offer to second an officer to the Supreme Command, and initiated several smaller sorties of his troops without informing Waldersee. American and French troops were not under Waldersee's command in Peking,[103] while British interests were concentrated primarily in the Yangtse area (although General Gaselee accepted Germany's supreme command over the allied troops).

Waldersee soon realized the limitations of the attempt at international cooperation in China (and his own inability to co-operate with his allies[104]), complaining frequently about the distrust and even hatred that existed between the different contingent armies, and on their differing, and often opposing, aims. On 20 November he commented in his diary on the difficult peace negotiations: 'The interests of the European powers are totally different and an honest collaboration is completely out of the question.

[99] Mohs, *Waldersee*, p. 412.   [100] Meisner, *Waldersee*, vol. III, p. 130.
[101] Waldersee, diary, 23 January 1900, ibid., p. 89.   [102] Mohs, *Waldersee*, p. 413.
[103] Waldersee, diary, 23 January 1900, Meisner, *Waldersee*, vol. III, pp. 40–1.
[104] This was a failing he shared with his two successors as Chiefs of the General Staff, Schlieffen and the younger Moltke, who had been unable to conduct proper relations with Germany's ally Austria-Hungary. See Mombauer, *Moltke*, pp. 80–2, 213–16.

If an understanding is reached in an area, then in reality nobody actually trusts the other one.'[105] A few days later he wrote: 'Russian and English officers have sometimes been close to shooting at each other. The English, Russians, French tell me, each of the others, that they are thieves, robbers, arsonists, [all] qualities which all three attribute to the Italians.'[106]

Particularly the difference between Britain and Russia is frequently referred to in his diaries and reports. 'The hatred between the two contingents is so strong that it could come to hostilities', he recorded on 9 November.[107] British and French troops were also not on friendly terms.[108] In the light of this experience, and nearing the end of his time in China, Waldersee summed up: 'A united military action by eight powers is an impossibility; that this is not entirely recognized by the great public, and that no open arguments ensued between the allies, I believe is in a small part thanks to me.'[109] However, it seems even his presence was not able to prevent all hostilities. The day before Waldersee's departure, British, German, French, and Japanese soldiers clashed in Tientsin, leading to the death and injury of some of them.[110]

Waldersee finally left China via Japan on 3 June 1901, before the peace treaty was signed on 27 September, and returned to Germany a celebrated hero in some quarters, but 'politically a dead man'. Wilhelm's interest in the expedition was at this point almost non-existent, and he did not even consider it necessary to meet Waldersee when he returned to Hamburg.[111] The sarcasm with which Waldersee's appointment to 'Weltmarschall' had initially been greeted was only briefly transformed into public celebration of Waldersee the heroic military leader (although at all times, some critics voiced concerns about Germany's involvement in the Chinese war[112]).

---

[105] Waldersee, diary, 20 November 1900, Meisner, *Waldersee*, vol. III, pp. 50–1.

[106] Waldersee, diary, 11 October 1900, ibid., p. 45, n. 2.

[107] Waldersee, diary, 9 November, ibid., p. 45; report of 24 November, p. 55; report of 21 March, pp. 108f. – on alleged British insult of Russian flag; report of 23 March, p. 111 – including description of quarrels between Russian and British troops and violent outburst of French troops towards British soldiers.

[108] Waldersee, report of 24 November, ibid., p. 55.

[109] Waldersee, diary, 5 May 1901, ibid., vol. III, p. 131.

[110] *Schulthess Geschichtskalender*, 2 June 1901, 16. Jahrgang 1900, Munich 1901, p. 312.

[111] Winzen, *Englandpolitik*, p. 306.

[112] In addition to criticism from the Social Democrats, see e.g. the obituary in the *Frankfurter Zeitung*, 6 March 1904: 'Of course, these deeds [Waldersee's deeds in China] are in no relation to the "*Vorschußlorbeeren*" [premature praise] with which the '*Weltmarschall*' had amply provided himself, and also not quite with the subsequent eulogies in which other troops were denigrated without effort. The costs of that Chinese expedition still burden the Reich's finances today, and there cannot be any doubt today that the same result could have been achieved with a lesser show of force (*Machtentfaltung*).'

Waldersee himself had raised such heightened expectations of the campaign that disappointment was inevitable.[113] Nonetheless, although the campaign never lived up to its promise, Waldersee maintained a certain myth that the expedition to China marked the successful climax of a long military career, although his long-standing dream of becoming Chancellor was never fulfilled, as the *Frankfurter Zeitung* commented on his death in 1904:

> Count Waldersee's speeches following his return led to the conclusion that his political ambitions had been revived, that he wanted to become Chancellor. It did not come to that, and even if Waldersee had lived longer he would always have remained the 'up and coming' man.[114]

For Wilhelm, the results were less positive still; his heated speeches and ill-judged reactions just confirmed what his critics had known for some time: that the German Kaiser, while desirous of ruling Germany almost single-handedly, was ultimately ill-equipped to do so, and was in many ways a dangerous liability for Germany's relations with her European neighbours. The hopes that better relations between the European powers might result from this joint effort were dashed and it was not long before Britain would relinquish her 'splendid isolation' for alliances and ententes that did not include Germany.

CONCLUSION

A number of conclusions can be drawn from this brief account. Firstly, Wilhelm's and Waldersee's reaction to the events in China highlights their attitudes towards Asia, and the racial stereotypes which prevailed throughout Europe, as well as a sense in which Germans considered it their duty to colonize and cultivate the 'uncivilized' Asian countries. Both Wilhelm and Waldersee displayed an air of superiority and prejudice *vis-à-vis* the Chinese. Their alleged 'cunning' was frequently mentioned by the monarch in his speeches to departing troops, and Waldersee echoed similar sentiments in his diary: 'Only if one behaves harshly and ruthlessly against them can one make progress with them', he wrote on 7 December.[115] On 30 December, he recorded why negotiations with the Chinese Court were still

---

[113] See also Bülow's critique, *Denkwürdigkeiten*, vol. 1, p. 370.

[114] *Frankfurter Zeitung*, 6 March 1904. On Waldersee's earlier hopes of becoming Chancellor following Bismarck's dismissal, see John C. G. Röhl, *Wilhelm II. Der Aufbau der Persönlichen Monarchie*, Munich 2001, pp. 365ff.

[115] Cited in Mohs, *Waldersee*, p. 420.

potentially fraught: 'Because one cannot ever trust the Chinese completely, one still has to be careful here until the last moment.'[116]

Secondly, the events highlighted the question of Germany's relations with her European neighbours. Closer to home, the Kaiser's reaction revealed some of the hostilities German decision-makers fostered towards the other Great Powers, and the sense of insecurity of Germany's position *vis-à-vis* them. The events in China unfolded against a volatile European background at a time when the two rivalling alliances that were to dominate pre-war European politics were not yet formed and there was, for Germany, still everything to play for in terms of perhaps coming to an arrangement with Britain. France and Russia had, of course, allied in 1894, but the co-operation between German and French troops nonetheless suggested to some that there might now be scope for a future friendship. In this context of uncertainty regarding Germany's future the Kaiser was keen to prove to the world that Germany was a power to be reckoned with, and one whose friendship was worth coveting.

Wilhelm and his future Chancellor Bülow certainly hoped to turn the international European situation to Germany's advantage while playing an underhand game of waiting to see if the other European powers, particularly Russia, Britain, and France, would perhaps fall out over the Chinese matter. This was the reason for Bülow's caution when the Kaiser demanded 'an immediate big military joint action' in June 1900. Allowing the other powers to fall out over China was to Bülow even more important than defending or extending Germany's influence in the region.[117] The Kaiser, however, feared that Europe 'would be lost' (in an unspecified way) in case of a conflict between the other European powers over China.[118]

Thirdly, the events demonstrate the detrimental effect that the Kaiser's *Kommandogewalt* could have in times of crisis. Without the need for consultation with the responsible politicians or the Reichstag, the Kaiser, with the help of one or two confidants, could dispatch ships and men, could solicit support or cause affront to possible allies, and could wage war. The Chancellor, the Chief of Staff, the Chief of the Reich Navy Office, all leading men acquiesced, and the Kaiser was allowed to co-ordinate this military campaign with the help of 'his' man Waldersee. This was an extraordinary amount of power for a hereditary ruler at the beginning of the twentieth century to hold, and it was supported by spineless (Hohenlohe) or self-serving (Bülow) Chancellors, and a military elite which sought only

---

[116] GStA vi. HA, NL Waldersee, AI, no. 27, Waldersee, diary (omitted in Meisner, *Waldersee*).
[117] See Wilhelm's telegram of 19 June, demanding that Peking be razed to the ground, and Bülow to Wilhelm, 19 June, *GP*, vol. xvi, nos. 4527 and 4528.
[118] Ibid., marginal notes.

to preserve its own privileges or seize an opportunity to practise war in earnest.

Finally, and perhaps most importantly, Germany's actions during the Boxer Rebellion need to be seen in the context of German history at the end of the nineteenth century. The country's involvement in the Boxer Rebellion forms only part of a string of foreign-policy engagements, most of which did not make Germany appear in a positive light. German policy appeared, in the words of Klaus Hildebrand, to be 'directionless and aimlessly drifting', and it led to the alienation of the other powers. Germany's acquisition of Kiaochow, her attitude in the war between the United States and Spain and regarding the Samoa question, as well as the purchase of some territories in the Pacific, deepened the rift between Germany and the other Great Powers, and made it difficult to gauge the country's real intentions.[119] It amounted, in Hildebrand's words, to a policy of 'wanting to be rewarded simply for being strong and present'.[120]

The conflict occurred at a crucial time when the Tirpitz Plan and Bülow's desire to keep a 'free hand' until Germany was strong enough to be able to take on Britain necessitated a measured foreign policy, while at the same time half-hearted alliance negotiations took place between Britain and Germany between 1898 and 1901. A less heavy-handed approach to the question of a German commander for the allied forces, for example, might have helped to make friends of, rather than further alienate, Britain.

Following the international co-operation in China, Wilhelm certainly hoped that closer relations might be possible with Germany's European neighbours, for example in pursuing a possible alliance with Britain and Russia, or a *rapprochement* with France. As we have seen, this was also considered a possibility by leading military commentators, like, for example, Colmar von der Goltz. On 23 August 1901, Goltz recorded the results of a conversation between Wilhelm and King Edward VII and the British ambassador Lascelles, in which the Kaiser referred back to their recent collaboration, remarking:

Who would, for example, have thought just ten years ago that French and German troops would fight together against a third party under a German general? The blood that was spilled jointly had worked miracles, and we now got along quite well with the neighbours the other side of the Vosges.[121]

---

[119] Klaus Hildebrand, *Deutsche Aussenpolitik 1871–1918*, Munich 1989, p. 33. See also Klaus Hildebrand, *Das vergangene Reich*, Stuttgart 1995, p. 193.

[120] Hildebrand, *Das vergangene Reich*.

[121] Erwin Hölzle, *Quellen zur Entstehung des ersten Weltkrieges. Internationale Dokumente 1901–1914*, Darmstadt 1978, p. 259.

However, Wilhelm failed to understand the effects of his erratic and sometimes even duplicitous policies (as in the case of Waldersee's appointment) which meant that on this as on future occasions (for example, following the First Moroccan Crisis), he did not comprehend that, rather than making new allies, he was alienating potential friends even further. For Wilhelm and his advisors, the 'encirclement' of Germany over the next fourteen years seemed damning evidence of Germany's precarious position, and yet, her own 'exclusion' (*Auskreisung*) had begun almost as soon as Wilhelm had come to power. The Boxer Rebellion and Germany's reaction to it was just one important stepping-stone in this fateful direction.

CHAPTER 5

Dreams of a German Europe:
Wilhelm II and the Treaty of Björkö of 1905

Roderick R. McLean

I

'The 24th of July 1905 is a cornerstone in European politics', Kaiser Wilhelm II declared in a letter to Tsar Nicholas II of Russia on the 27th of the same month, 'and turns over a new leaf in the history of the world'.[1] The occasion to which Wilhelm referred was the signing of a treaty of alliance between Germany and Russia by himself and Nicholas at Björkö, off the southern coast of Finland. The treaty, although restricted to Europe, would have had the effect of neutralising the Dual Alliance between France and Russia which had been concluded in 1894, thus freeing Germany from the danger of a war on two fronts. In addition, it was designed to pave the way for a continental league, involving the participation of all the Great Powers of the European mainland, including France, against the British Empire. The aim of the treaty was therefore to effect a diplomatic revolution that would have left Germany with *de facto* mastery of the European continent. The Kaiser would have achieved the objective that he had set himself early in his reign, when he had declared to his closest friend and political confidant Philipp Count zu Eulenburg-Hertefeld that the 'fundamental principle' of his European policy was '*leadership* in the peaceful sense – a sort of Napoleonic supremacy'.[2] Wilhelm was therefore correct in relation to the potential importance of the agreement which he had concluded with the Tsar. The whole history of Europe and of the world could have been different as a result of the Treaty of Björkö.

The agreement between the two Emperors, however, never came into effect. Within a year, Russia was more firmly anchored than ever to its alliance with France and was in the process of taking initial steps towards

---

[1] Wilhelm II to Nicholas II, 27 July 1905 in W. Goetz (ed.), *Briefe Kaiser Wilhelms II. an den Zaren, 1894–1914*, Berlin 1920, p. 373.
[2] John C. G. Röhl, 'A Document of 1892 on Germany, Prussia and Poland', *Historical Journal*, 7 (1964), p. 144.

an understanding with Britain. St Petersburg's support for Paris against Berlin at the Algeciras Conference which concluded the First Moroccan Crisis and the refusal of the Kaiser to allow German banks to participate in an international loan to Russia in the spring of 1906 created a significant breach between the Tsarist Empire and the Kaiserreich.[3] Relations between Russia and Germany continued to deteriorate, with various ebbs and flows, from 1905–6 onwards, and when war came in 1914 it was unsurprising that the two Empires found themselves on opposing sides. The Treaty of Björkö therefore marked not the start of a peaceful German supremacy in Europe, but the initiation of a process that was to lead to permanent estrangement, and eventually to armed conflict, between Berlin and St Petersburg.

Because the agreement between the two Emperors was never implemented, historians have tended to be dismissive about the episode and it rarely receives attention from them. Johannes Paulmann, a prominent historian of dynastic relations in the era before the First World War, maintains that the Treaty of Björkö was 'a non-event'.[4] David McDonald, an expert on Tsarist Russia's foreign policy, takes a similar line, describing it as 'little more than a curious episode in Russian diplomacy'.[5] An examination of this subject is not, however, the futile exercise that Paulmann and McDonald imply, for it can provide insights into the strengths and weaknesses of the Kaiserreich's policy towards Russia, as well as allowing an assessment of the ability of the Kaiser and the Tsar to influence the course of German–Russian relations and an analysis of the constraints upon such influence.

II

The outbreak of the Russo-Japanese War in February 1904 presented Germany with an opportunity to reverse a decade of diplomatic setbacks, which had begun with the conclusion of the Franco-Russian alliance in 1894. The reason for this was that France was in the process of negotiating a colonial agreement with Britain, which had since 1902 been the ally of Russia's enemy, Japan. The outbreak of war in the Far East therefore raised the possibility that Germany might be able to drive a wedge between

---

[3] Bernard F. Oppel, 'The Waning of a Traditional Alliance: Russia and Germany after the Portsmouth Peace Conference', *Central European History*, 5 (1972), pp. 326–9.

[4] Johannes Paulmann, '"Dearest Nicky . . .": Monarchical Relations between Prussia, the German Empire and Russia during the Nineteenth Century', in Roger Bartlett and Karen Schönwälder (eds.), *The German Lands and Eastern Europe: Essays on the History of their Social, Cultural and Political Relations*, Basingstoke 1999, p. 176.

[5] David M. McDonald, *United Government and Foreign Policy in Russia, 1900–1914*, Cambridge, MA 1992, p. 77.

Russia and France, resurrect the traditional alliance between Berlin and St Petersburg and then compel Paris to join it. In addition, the possibility that Russia might emerge victorious from its war with Japan implied that its expansionist energies would continue to be directed towards north-east Asia and away from the Balkans where they were likely to clash with those of Germany's ally Austria-Hungary. Even before the outbreak of the war, the 'grey eminence' of the German Foreign Office, Friedrich von Holstein, had drawn attention to the benefits to Germany of Russia's interest in the Far East. He wrote to his cousin, 'Our situation has eased since Russia has been pursuing an active East Asian policy . . . As a consequence, the danger of France and Russia together falling on Germany can be set aside for the forseeable future.'[6]

The re-establishment of an alliance between the German Empire and Russia had been an aim pursued fairly consistently by the Kaiser since the mid-1890s.[7] However, it had never come to pass, primarily due to the reluctance of the Tsar and the Russian government to enter into such an arrangement. As Wilhelm wrote on one occasion, following a statement by the then Russian Finance Minister, Sergei Witte, in favour of a continental league: 'I have indeed . . . been prepared for it, but at the last moment a firm will and purposeful action has always been absent in Russia.'[8] Wilhelm saw Russia's war with Japan as a perfect opportunity to mount a new diplomatic offensive at St Petersburg. Indeed, the Kaiser had proved most unsubtle in his attempts to urge Nicholas to take measures against the Japanese. As early as November 1902, he had warned the Tsar that 'certain symptoms in the East seem to show that Japan is becoming a rather restless customer'.[9] In a further letter to Nicholas, a few weeks before the outbreak of the Russo-Japanese war, Wilhelm proclaimed, 'it is evident to every unbiased mind that Korea must and will be Russian'.[10] In private, the Kaiser was even more eager to see Russia embroiled in a conflict in the Far East.

---

[6] Friedrich von Holstein to Ida von Stülpnagel, 21 January 1904 in Helmuth Rogge (ed.), *Friedrich von Holstein: Lebensbekenntnis in Briefen an eine Frau*, Berlin 1932, p. 228.

[7] Roderick R. McLean, *Royalty and Diplomacy in Europe, 1890–1914*, Cambridge 2001, pp. 20–48; Lamar Cecil, 'William II and his Russian Colleagues', in Carole Fink, Isabel V. Hull, and MacGregor Knox (eds.), *German Nationalism and the European Response, 1890–1945*, Norman, OK and London 1985, pp. 95–134; Barbara Vogel, *Deutsche Rußlandpolitik: Das Scheitern der deutschen Weltpolitik unter Bülow, 1900–1906*, Düsseldorf 1973, esp. pp. 9–22; Peter Winzen, *Bülows Weltmachtkonzept: Untersuchungen zur Frühphase seiner Außenpolitik, 1897–1901*, Boppard am Rhein 1977.

[8] Wilhelm II's comment on Radolin to Hohenlohe, 2 April 1899 in *Die Große Politik der Europäischen Kabinette, 1871–1914*, in Johannes Lepsius, A. Mendelssohn Bartholdy, and F. Thimme ed., 40 vols., Berlin 1922–7 (hereafter *GP*) vol. XIII, no. 3537, p. 211, note 12.

[9] Wilhelm II to Nicholas II, 1 November 1902. PAAA Berlin R10691.

[10] Wilhelm II to Nicholas II, 3 January 1904. Goetz, *Briefe*, p. 335.

Nicholas, he told the Chancellor Bernhard Count von Bülow, was 'damaging the monarchical principle through his shilly-shallying'. The 'yellow race' would be at the gates of Moscow if the Tsar did not stand up to the Japanese.[11]

Given the extent of Wilhelm II's enthusiasm for Russian expansion in the Far East, it is not surprising that of all the strategies used by Germany to win over Russia during the Russo-Japanese War, the most prominent one was the Kaiser's attempt to win over the Tsar directly through correspondence. It was during the war in the Far East that a high proportion of the letters in the twenty-year exchange between Wilhelm II and Nicholas II – the infamous 'Willy–Nicky' correspondence – was written, and it was also during the conflict that the letters took on their most overtly political character. The emphasis on winning over Russia by wooing the Tsar directly reflected the Kaiser's view that Nicholas II decided Russia's foreign policy and that if the Tsar came out in favour of a *rapprochement* with Berlin, his ministers would have no alternative but to follow him. 'The two of us make history and determine fates!', Wilhelm asserted.[12] Bülow, who had the task of vetting the letters and advising the Kaiser on the best methods of winning Nicholas's trust, shared Wilhelm's view of the Tsar's importance. He declared on one occasion that: 'The experience of many years tells us that much less can be achieved with Russian diplomats than through direct contact between His Majesty and the Tsar.'[13]

In his letters to the Tsar, Wilhelm presented himself as Nicholas's mentor and loyal colleague and drew attention to the extent of German sympathy for Russia in its struggle with the Japanese. In addition, three further themes recurred in the correspondence. The Kaiser emphasized that Germany and Russia were united by political conservatism and their commitment to the monarchical principle and were therefore natural allies. He stressed his support, and that of his government, for Russian expansion in the Far East, as part of a civilizing Christian mission, and drew attention to the actions of the British, and to a lesser extent the French, which he presented as undermining the chances of a Russian victory. In a letter in the spring of 1904, for example, the Kaiser suggested to Nicholas that the aim of the

[11] Bernhard Prince von Bülow, *Memoirs*, 4 vols., English translation, London 1931, vol. II, pp. 60–1; cf. Wilhelm II's comments on Count von Arco to the German Foreign Office, 13 January 1904. *GP*, vol. XIX (i), no. 5937, pp. 27–8; Wilhelm II's comments on Bülow's note, 14 February 1904, ibid., no. 5961, pp. 62–3.
[12] Wilhelm II's comment on Alvensleben to Bülow, 18 February 1902. *GP*, vol. XVIII (ii), no. 5900, p. 824.
[13] Bülow to the German Foreign Office, 12 August 1905, PAAA, R2097.

Anglo-French *Entente*, which had just been concluded, was 'to stop the French helping you!'[14]

The letters, at least in the short term, undoubtedly did have an effect on the Tsar's attitude towards the Kaiser and Germany. Nicholas's personal distaste for Wilhelm, whom he had described on one occasion prior to the war as 'raving mad',[15] gave way to a sense of gratitude at the Kaiser's support for Russia in its struggle with Japan. Sergei Witte informed Bülow during a visit to Germany in the summer of 1904: 'Since the outbreak of the war Emperor Nicholas knows where he is with your Kaiser. He is now full of trust in your Kaiser and, more than that, he genuinely likes your Kaiser. Everything in the Tsar's nature derives from how he feels personally.'[16] Other observers also remarked on the change that had taken place in the Tsar's attitude towards Wilhelm II.[17] Some of them went further and speculated that this might lead, as the Kaiser and Bülow indeed wished, to the resurrection of intimate ties between Berlin and St Petersburg.[18]

The German strategy for winning over Russia during its war with Japan involved more than epistles from the Kaiser to the Tsar. There were also more practical steps, such as royal visits and exchanges of emissaries. Prince Heinrich, the Kaiser's brother and the Tsar's brother-in-law, visited St Petersburg on two occasions during the Russo-Japanese War: in the summer of 1904 and the spring of 1905.[19] Heinrich's visits were useful from the point of view of German diplomacy on two grounds. First, he was able to emphasize German support for Russia against Japan directly to the Tsar, and in so doing to increase Nicholas's resolve to continue the conflict and his favourable inclinations towards the Hohenzollern dynasty and Germany. Secondly, the impressions Heinrich obtained during his visits to

---

[14] Wilhelm II to Nicholas II, 6 June 1904, Goetz, *Briefe*, p. 341; on the wider point, cf. Wilhelm II to Nicholas II, 11 February 1904, 19 August 1904 and 10 October 1904, ibid., pp. 337–8, 342–6.

[15] A. A. Mossolov, *At the Court of the Last Tsar*, English translation, London 1935, pp. 202–3; cf. Margaret M. Jefferson, 'Lord Salisbury's Conversations with the Tsar at Balmoral, 27 and 29 September 1896', *Slavonic and East European Review*, 39 (1960), p. 220; note by Hanotaux, 12 October 1896, *Documents Diplomatiques Français*, ed. Ministère des Affaires Etrangères, 32 vols., Paris 1929–62 (hereafter *DDF*), 1st series, vol. XII, no. 472, p. 781; Maurice Paléologue, *Guillaume II et Nicolas II*, Paris 1935, pp. 20–4, 90–3.

[16] Bülow to Wilhelm II, 15 July 1904, *GP*, vol. XIX (i), no. 6043, p. 200.

[17] Cf. Hugo Prince von Radolin to Bülow, 28 February 1904, PAAA, R1986; Bompard to Delcassé, 15 July 1904, *DDF*, 2nd series, vol. V, no. 269, pp. 317–19.

[18] Bompard to Delcassé, 25 February 1904, *DDF* 2nd series, vol. IV, no. 317, pp. 419–23; Bihourd to Delcassé, 26 March 1904, ibid., no. 366, pp. 506–7; Spring-Rice to Lascelles, 27 September 1904, Lascelles Papers, Public Records Office, London, Foreign Office (hereafter PRO FO) 800/12.

[19] Roderick R. McLean, 'Monarchy and Diplomacy in Europe, 1900–1910', DPhil dissertation, University of Sussex 1996, pp. 213–14, 221–3; Vogel, *Rußlandpolitik*, p. 173.

Russia provided Bülow and the Kaiser with valuable intelligence on the Tsar's opinions and attitudes, together with those of his principal advisors, which could be exploited later for political ends.

Heinrich's visit to Russia in 1904, for the christening of Nicholas II's heir, the Tsarevitch Alexei, demonstrated the advantages of the German strategy. The Prince was impressed by the extent of gratitude in all circles at St Petersburg for the support given by Germany and the Kaiser to Russia during her war with Japan, but noted that there was an atmosphere of despondency as a result of the lack of success in the Far East.[20] Russian defeatism was a sentiment which the German government did not wish to encourage, given the strategic advantage that the Kaiserreich had gained as a result of the absence of a military threat on her eastern frontier and the potential danger that a premature end to war with Japan would precipitate a revolution and cost the Tsar his throne. Bülow, referring to these two factors, took the view that Nicholas should not make peace until there had been some Russian victories:

If the Tsar holds his nerve and does not conclude a precipitous and weak peace without a prior military success, my instinct still tells me that the Russian Empire and the Romanov House which is still fairly firmly anchored in the emotional life of 100 million Muzhiks [Russian peasants] will withstand its present certainly very serious test.[21]

The argument that the survival of the Russian autocracy depended on the avoidance of a premature peace was consequently the line that Prince Heinrich was advised by the Chancellor to take in his discussions with the Tsar[22] and put forward in the letter from the Kaiser to Nicholas which Heinrich took to Russia. 'I have no doubt', Wilhelm wrote, 'you will and must win in the long run, but it will cost both money and many men; as the enemy is brave and well led and can only be beaten by overwhelming numbers and time and patience.'[23] These sentiments accorded with Nicholas II's own instincts and Heinrich received a cordial welcome from the Tsar and his courtiers. Even the Prince was astounded by the extent of Nicholas's optimism and his conviction 'that everything will come perfectly right', despite the military reverses which his army had suffered.[24] The visit reinforced the German leadership's view that the Russian court was favourably disposed

---

[20] Alvensleben to Bülow, 25 August 1904, PAAA, R10670.

[21] Bülow to Wilhelm II, 2 August 1904. Geheimes Staatsarchiv Preußischer Kulturbesitz Berlin Hausarchiv (hereafter GStA HA) Rep. 53 J Lit. B no. 16a vol. III.

[22] Bülow to the German Foreign Office, 20 August 1904. PAAA R10670.

[23] Wilhelm II to Nicholas II, 19 August 1904, Goetz, *Briefe*, p. 344.

[24] Wilhelm II to Bülow, 28 August 1904. *GP*, vol. XIX (i), no. 6049, p. 216.

towards Berlin and appeared to confirm that even Count V. N. Lamsdorff, the Tsar's Foreign Minister and an ardent supporter of the Franco-Russian alliance, was now in favour of closer ties with Germany.[25]

In addition to royal visits, a relationship of confidence between the two imperial courts was fostered by the resurrection, in the autumn of 1904, of the practice whereby both Wilhelm and Nicholas received military plenipotentiaries from each other, who were attached to their respective suites.[26] That the Tsar accepted the Kaiser's suggestion that the practice should be revived was itself significant, as in 1894 he had refused to countenance such a step on the grounds that 'it would provoke all kinds of gossip'.[27] By agreeing to the appointment of a Prussian military plenipotentiary, Nicholas was demonstrating symbolically that relations between the Russian and Prussian courts had become more intimate than at any previous point during his reign. This fact did not go unnoticed by the diplomats of other powers. Boutiron, a senior French diplomat at St Petersburg, observed that the exchange of plenipotentiaries was a clear sign that Wilhelm II 'wishes to establish close relations between the two courts, if not between the two nations'. The Kaiser's ultimate objective, Boutiron correctly surmised, was the destruction of the Franco-Russian alliance.[28] In reality, however, the revival of the practice proved less significant than Wilhelm for one had hoped. The Tsar rarely met the Prussian plenipotentiary, nor spoke openly to him.[29] The Kaiser complained that he was unable to gain benefit from the presence of the Russian plenipotentiary in Berlin, Colonel Schebeko. 'Schebeko never comes into my presence', Wilhelm remarked, 'and most of the time I speak to him only about the weather!'[30] When Wilhelm did raise less banal matters with the Russian plenipotentiary, his tendency to speak bluntly and indiscreetly could backfire to the detriment of German diplomacy. This was demonstrated soon after Schebeko's arrival. The Kaiser denounced his uncle, the British monarch King Edward VII, in conversation with the Russian plenipotentiary, instructing him to tell the Tsar 'that the King of England speaks and writes very well, but always lies'. Schebeko immediately communicated the Kaiser's remark to the French.[31]

[25] Alvensleben to Bülow, with comment by Wilhelm II, 31 August 1904, PAAA, R10671.
[26] Wilhelm II to Nicholas II, 6 June 1904, *Briefe*, pp. 340–2.
[27] Nicholas II to Wilhelm II, November 1894, Chlodwig Fürst zu Hohenlohe-Schillingsfürst, *Denkwürdigkeiten der Reichskanzlerzeit*, ed. Karl Alexander von Müller, Berlin 1931, p. 9; cf. Count Gustav Graf von Lambsdorff, *Die Militärbevollmächtigten Kaiser Wilhelms II. am Zarenhofe, 1904–1914*, Berlin 1937, pp. 94–5.
[28] Boutiron to Delcassé, 26 October 1904. *DDF*, 2nd series, vol. v, no. 394, pp. 471, 472.
[29] Lambsdorff, *Militärbevollmächtigten*, pp. 104–8.
[30] Wilhelm II's comment on report by Major Count von Lambsdorff, 19 September 1904, ibid., p. 232.
[31] Boutiron to Delcassé, 24 October 1904, *DDF*, 2nd series, vol. v, no. 385, p. 464.

Of greater value were the measures that the Germans took to supply Russia with military and naval intelligence. Captain Paul von Hintze, in particular, the German naval attaché at St Petersburg, was highly valued by the Tsar and his military entourage. Prince Orloff, the Tsar's personal naval cabinet chief, asked Hintze to write confidential memoranda for Nicholas, on the basis that this would ensure that the Russian Emperor was 'as well informed as the Kaiser'.[32] In addition, Russia's debt towards Germany was further enhanced by the decision by the HAPAG shipping line, headed by the Kaiser's friend Albert Ballin, to supply coal to the Russian Baltic fleet, to allow it to sail round the world to confront the Japanese navy.[33] German banks also participated in a financial loan to Russia in the autumn of 1904, helping to give Berlin financial leverage as well as political influence at St Petersburg.[34]

These steps were, however, counterbalanced, to some extent, by actions which the Germans took to gain from Russia's weakness during its war with Japan. The German–Russian Commercial Treaty of 1904 was the most prominent example of this tendency. It was concluded on terms that were extremely unfavourable to Russian goods, and which facilitated German penetration of Russian markets. Both Sergei Witte, the Chairman of the Russian Council of Ministers, and Nicholas II agreed to the terms of the treaty only with considerable reluctance. In a letter to the Kaiser, Nicholas indicated that he was prepared to accept the treaty on Berlin's terms primarily because the Germans had revealed themselves to be 'real friends' of Russia in her war with Japan. 'I have given directions to Witte to meet the German proposals as far as possible', he wrote.[35] The agreement provided a foretaste of what economic subservience to Germany would mean for the Tsarist Empire.

The Kaiser and Bülow made one attempt to extract a treaty of alliance from the Tsar prior to the meeting between the two Emperors at Björkö in the summer of 1905. This was in the autumn of 1904. The offer of an alliance was made at that point, because the circumstances appeared to be particularly favourable. The Dogger Bank incident, in which the Russian Baltic fleet had fired on British fishing vessels which it had mistaken for

---

[32] Jonathan Steinberg, 'Germany and the Russo-Japanese War', *American Historical Review* 75, 7 (1970), pp. 1969–70.

[33] Lamar Cecil, 'Coal for the Fleet that had to Die', *American Historical Review* 69, 4 (1964), pp. 990–1005; cf. Nicholas II to Wilhelm II, 15/28 September 1904. *GP*, vol. XIX (i), no. 6088, pp. 263–5.

[34] Count Sergei Witte, *The Memoirs of Count Witte*, ed. Sidney Harcave, London 1990, p. 391; Ernst von Mendelssohn-Bartholdy to Bülow, 1 November 1904, PAAA, R10671; James Long, 'Franco-Russian Relations during the Russo-Japanese War', *Slavonic and East European Review*, 52 (1974), pp. 220–4.

[35] Nicholas II to Wilhelm II, 19 May/1 June 1904, *GP*, vol. XIX (ii), no. 6034, pp. 181–2; cf. Witte, *Memoirs*, pp. 389–90; Lascelles to Lansdowne, 4 August 1904; Spring-Rice to Lascelles, 27 September 1904. Lascelles Papers, PRO FO 800/12; Vogel, *Rußlandpolitik*, pp. 25, 45.

Japanese vessels, had just occurred. It had caused a crisis in Anglo-Russian relations and had incited the Tsar against the English. Nicholas referred in his diary to the 'impertinent behaviour' of Russia's 'mangy enemies'.[36] As a result of the incident and fearing British retribution for German coaling of the Russian navy, Wilhelm and the Chancellor considered that Nicholas might be ready to sign an agreement with Berlin. After consulting Holstein and Bülow, the Kaiser sent a telegram to the Tsar proposing a German–Russian defensive alliance as a first step towards a continental league including France, directed against Britain.[37] On the spur of the moment, Nicholas indicated that he would support the Kaiser's proposal 'that Germany, Russia and France should at once unite upon an agreement to abolish Anglo-Japanese arrogance and insolence'. He asked Wilhelm to draw up a draft treaty and declared, somewhat naively, that once Russia had signed the agreement, 'France is bound to join her ally.'[38] No treaty of alliance was signed at that time, however, because it quickly became apparent that the Russian Foreign Minister, Count Lamsdorff, the vast majority of Russian diplomats, and the French government, and particularly its Foreign Minister Théophile Delcassé, would not countenance such an agreement.[39] As the Tsar would not sign an alliance with Germany without a guarantee of French participation, and as the Kaiser and Bülow knew that the only way to get the French to participate would be to present them with a *fait accompli*, this effectively ended the negotiations.[40]

III

The second German attempt to form an alliance with Russia, at Björkö, was made possible because the situation both within Russia and internationally had changed in a way that appeared potentially beneficial to Berlin's geo-political interests. During the winter of 1905 the war against Japan went badly for Russia. It was defeated on land by the Japanese in a decisive battle at Mukden in Manchuria in February 1905. Domestic developments within

[36] Nicholas II, diary entry, 15–16 October 1904, in Andrew M. Verner, *The Crisis of the Russian Autocracy: Nicholas II and the 1905 Revolution*, Princeton, NJ 1990, p. 111.

[37] Wilhelm II to Nicholas II, 27 October 1904, in Herman Bernstein (ed.), *The Willy–Nicky Correspondence: Being the Secret and Intimate Telegrams Exchanged between the Kaiser and the Tsar*, New York 1918, pp. 72–3.

[38] Nicholas II to Wilhelm II, 15/28 October 1904, ibid., pp. 73–5.

[39] Maurice Paléologue, *The Turning Point: Three Critical Years, 1903–1906*, English translation, London 1935, diary entries, 3 and 9 November 1904, pp. 134, 140.

[40] Nicholas II to Wilhelm II, 10/23 November 1904, *Willy–Nicky Correspondence*, p. 83; Wilhelm II to Nicholas II, 26 November 1904, ibid., pp. 83–4; Wilhelm II to Bülow, 23 November 1904, *GP*, vol. XIX (i), no. 6126, pp. 316–17; cf. Wilhelm II's comments on Nicholas II to Wilhelm II, 24 November/7 December 1904, PAAA, R2094.

Russia also made the Kaiser and his Chancellor optimistic of being able to secure an agreement with the Tsar. Revolution had broken out in Russia in January 1905. This had had the consequence of severely undermining the Tsar's confidence and rendering him more isolated and therefore potentially vulnerable to the influence of persuasive outsiders. The German leadership took full advantage of this situation. When the Kaiser's brother Prince Heinrich visited Russia in April 1905, he found Nicholas to be on the verge of a nervous collapse. Heinrich reported subsequently to Wilhelm about the Tsar's behaviour during their meeting: 'I told him things which ought to have had the consequence of my being immediately transported to the frontier under escort. Instead of which, as was actually the case, [he] came near to me and thanked me with tears of emotion for my "open-heartedness".'[41] Heinrich had been instructed by Bülow before the visit to urge the Tsar to introduce limited reforms and not to make peace with the Japanese until Russia had regained the military initiative and the revolution had been crushed.[42] As this emphasis on the need to avoid a premature peace coincided with Nicholas's own inclinations, Heinrich's visit proved a resounding success. Bülow told the Kaiser after the Prince's return from Russia that it was evident that Nicholas, 'now feels deep gratitude and heartfelt devotion for Your Majesty'.[43] Less self-interested observers than the Chancellor also noted that the Tsar appeared more determined than ever to continue the war with Japan after Prince Heinrich's visit. The British diplomat Cecil Spring-Rice speculated after the visit that the signs now pointed again to the possibility of a renewed effort by Germany to detach Russia from France. He observed, in a letter to King Edward VII's Private Secretary, Viscount Knollys:

Germany can offer the Czar security on the Western frontier, supplies for the war, money, and so on, and security against Revolution. In return all she asks is to be allowed a free hand in Western Europe, where after all Russia has no interests – and against that nation which is the source and origin of all Revolutions [France]. It would be impossible to deny the force of this argument.[44]

French concerns that such a prospect might become a reality in the aftermath of Prince Heinrich's visit led Count Lamsdorff to assure Maurice

[41] Prince Heinrich to Wilhelm II, 11 April 1905, GStA HA Rep. 52 VI no. 13.
[42] Bülow to Prince Heinrich (draft), 30 March 1905. PAAA R10136.
[43] Bülow to Wilhelm II, 10 April 1905, GStA HA Rep. 53 J Lit. B no. 16a. vol. III.
[44] Spring-Rice to Knollys, 2 May 1905, Royal Archives, Windsor Castle (hereafter RA), W46/3. On the Tsar's renewed determination to continue the war, cf. Hardinge to Knollys, 12 April 1905, RA W45/156; Hardinge to Lansdowne, 12 April 1905, Hardinge Papers, University Library, Cambridge, vol. 6. The author would like to thank HM the Queen for permission to cite from the Royal Archives, and the Syndics of Cambridge University Library for permission to cite the Hardinge Papers.

Bompard, Paris's Ambassador at St Petersburg, that Russia would remain faithful to the Dual Alliance, despite the efforts being made by Germany to resurrect intimate relations with St Petersburg.[45] Even Russia's defeat at sea by the Japanese at Tsushima in May 1905, which seemed to undermine the wisdom of the German leadership's earlier advice to the Tsar to continue the war in the Far East, did not diminish the Kaiser's attempts to convince the Tsar of Germany's good faith. Soon after the débâcle, which, together with the continuing revolution within Russia, indicated that a Russian victory against Japan was no longer possible, Wilhelm wrote to Nicholas in sympathetic tones, commiserating with him, recalling their 'firm feeling of mutual friendship', and offering to secure the services of President Roosevelt of the United States as a mediator between St Petersburg and Tokyo.[46]

By the spring of 1905, other developments also appeared to augur well for the success of German *Rußlandpolitik*. Two prominent opponents of close relations with Germany within the Romanov family, the Tsar's uncle, the Grand Duke Sergei, and his mother, the Dowager Empress Marie Feodorovna, were no longer in a position to influence Nicholas. In the case of Sergei – whom Wilhelm regarded as the Kaiserreich's 'most determined enemy' at the Russian court[47] – this was the result of political assassination at the hands of the revolutionaries.[48] The Dowager Empress, an enthusiastic supporter of better relations with Britain[49] and a fanatical Germanophobe,[50] by contrast, had quarrelled with Nicholas over domestic reform and appointments within the executive, temporarily alienating her son as a result.[51]

France, too, seemed to be in a much weaker position to block a German–Russian alliance and to resist the formation of a continental league than it had been in the autumn of 1904. This was because the First Moroccan Crisis had broken out in the spring of 1905, in which Berlin contested Paris's attempts to turn the North African kingdom into a French protectorate and

[45] Bompard to Delcassé, 10 May 1905, *DDF*, 2nd series, vol. VI, no. 424, pp. 500–2.
[46] Wilhelm II to Nicholas II, 3 June 1905, Goetz, *Briefe*, pp. 370–3.
[47] Wilhelm II to Hohenlohe, 20 October 1896, *GP*, vol. XI, no. 2868, p. 370.
[48] Radolin to Bülow, 18 February 1905; Wilhelm II's comments on Alvensleben to Bülow, 22 February 1905; Schoen to Bülow, 24 February 1905, PAAA, R10672.
[49] Hardinge to Queen Alexandra, 4 June 1904, Hardinge Papers, vol. 6.
[50] Dominic Lieven, 'Pro-Germans and Russian Foreign Policy, 1890–1914', *International History Review* 2, 1 (1980), p. 42; Alexander Isvolsky, *The Memoirs of Alexander Iswolsky: Formerly Russian Minister of Foreign Affairs and Ambassador to France*, ed. Charles L. Seeger, London 1920, p. 22; McDonald, *United Government*, p. 158; Bülow, *Memoirs*, vol. II, p. 63; Lambsdorff, *Militärbevollmächtigten*, pp. 58–9; see also the many hostile remarks about the Kaiser and Germany in her letters to Nicholas: Edward J. Bing (ed.), *The Letters of Tsar Nicholas and Empress Marie*, English translation, London 1937.
[51] Witte, *Memoirs*, p. 374; Verner, *Crisis*, pp. 104–52; Dominic Lieven, *Nicholas II: Emperor of All the Russias*, London, 1993, pp. 134–5, 147–8; Alvensleben to Bülow, 17 March 1905, PAAA, R10672.

sought to test the strength of the recently concluded Anglo-French *Entente*. The German strategy in the crisis was designed to convince the French that their new agreement with Britain was without value, by demonstrating that London could not save France from the threat of a German invasion.[52] Shortly before the Kaiser travelled to Björkö, Germany had scored a major diplomatic success in the crisis. The French Foreign Minister and architect of the Anglo-French *Entente*, Théophile Delcassé, had resigned as a result of German threats of war.[53] Bülow in particular believed that the removal of this fierce opponent of the Reich would lead to a more accommodating attitude towards Germany on the part of the French government.[54]

It is clear, despite Bülow's prominence in promoting a *rapprochement* between Berlin and St Petersburg, that Wilhelm II played the central part in securing the Tsar's signature to the Treaty of Björkö. During the Baltic cruise, which preceded his meeting with the Tsar, the Kaiser hid the specific purpose of the journey from his entourage.[55] Prince Otto Wittgenstein, who was on board the *Hohenzollern* as it steamed towards the Finnish skerries, subsequently recalled, nonetheless, that the Kaiser had discussed his diplomatic objectives in general terms, 'The Emperor William's talk is ever of alliances and political combinations and he gave utterance on the cruise to his cherished idea of now being able to effect a coalition between Germany, France and Russia, to the exclusion of Great Britain.'[56]

The tactics which Wilhelm employed to secure Nicholas's signature to the treaty indicated that it was his understanding of the Russian Emperor's character and naivety that helped him to ensure the Tsar's support for the idea of a continental league directed against Britain. Wilhelm played on Nicholas's resentment towards the British, whose support for the Japanese the Tsar blamed for Russia's humiliation in the Far East. He also tried to incite Nicholas against King Edward VII, by implying that the British monarch was a duplicitous presence on the international scene. In this he proved most successful, as Heinrich von Tschirschky und Bögendorff, who attended the talks on behalf of the German Foreign Office, observed:

His Majesty found the Tsar to be most enraged against England and particularly King Edward. He spoke with indignation about the policy of intrigues pursued by

---

[52] Mark Hewitson, 'Germany and France before the First World War: A Reassessment of Wilhelmine Foreign Policy', *English Historical Review* 115, 462 (2000), pp. 585–8.

[53] Christopher Andrew, *Théophile Delcassé and the Making of the Entente Cordiale: A Reappraisal of French Foreign Policy, 1898–1905*, London 1968, ch. 14.

[54] Bülow to the German Foreign Office, 22 July 1905, PAAA, R2095.

[55] Helmuth von Moltke, *Erinnerungen, Briefe, Dokumente, 1877–1916*, ed. Eliza von Moltke, Stuttgart 1922, 26 July 1905, pp. 325–6.

[56] Reginald Tower to Lord Lansdowne, 13 August 1905, Lansdowne Papers, PRO FO, 800/130.

the King and, punching the table, gave His Majesty an assurance that he, the Tsar, would never allow himself to make a pact with England and least of all [undertake] anything against the German Kaiser.[57]

During the discussions between the two Emperors, Wilhelm made light of the Tsar's reservation that the French might object to an alliance between Germany and Russia, by exaggerating the extent of the improvement that had occurred in Franco-German relations since Delcassé's dismissal.[58] After succumbing to Wilhelm's blandishments, Nicholas agreed to sign a treaty. However, in a striking assertion of his own right to make foreign policy, Wilhelm placed a treaty in front of the Russian monarch that differed in one important respect from that which he and Bülow had sought to conclude with Nicholas in the autumn of 1904. Russia and Germany would now only be required to go to each other's assistance in the event of an attack on one or other of them 'en Europe' rather than 'par une puissance européenne' anywhere in the world as in the draft treaty provided by the German foreign office. The restriction to the scope of the treaty had been made by the Kaiser without Bülow's knowledge or approval,[59] reducing as a consequence the chance that it would secure the Chancellor's support.

Nicholas had no prior knowledge that Wilhelm would seek his agreement to an alliance during their meeting. He was therefore surprised to find himself pressurized into signing such an agreement.[60] He was without high-level advice and had the treaty countersigned by his aged Minister of the Marine, Admiral Birilev, who was ignorant of high politics and from whom he hid the text of the agreement.[61] The evidence indicates that Nicholas was not in a fit psychological state at Björkö to sign a document of such potential significance. The Tsar appeared to be on the point of nervous collapse. After signing the treaty, the Kaiser recalled that Nicholas had become highly emotional and dependent on him: 'Then he fell into my arms and wept, so that the tears came pouring down, [saying:] "You are really my only true friend."'[62] The Russian Foreign Ministry, which was traditionally pro-French, was ignorant of the discussions between the two Emperors. Nicholas promised the Kaiser that he would not reveal the content of the treaty to his Foreign Minister, Count Lamsdorff, until after

[57] Tschirschky to Bülow, 24 July 1905, PAAA, R2096.
[58] Note by Bülow, 18 August 1905, *GP*, vol. XIX (ii), no. 6240, pp. 502–3.
[59] Wilhelm II to Bülow, 30 July 1905, PAAA, R2096.
[60] Alexander Savinskii, 'Guillaume II et la Russie: ses dépêches à Nicolas II, 1903–1905', *Revues des deux mondes* 92, 12 (1922), p. 799.
[61] Isvolsky, *Memoirs*, p. 60; McDonald, *United Government*, p. 79.
[62] Notes by Eulenburg, 25 September 1905, in John C. G. Röhl (ed.), *Philipp Eulenburgs Politische Korrespondenz*, 3 vols., Boppard 1976–83 (hereafter *EK*), vol. III, no. 1509, p. 2118.

the conclusion of peace between Russia and Japan. Lamsdorff therefore remained in ignorance of the Björkö agreement until the end of August, after the conclusion of the Treaty of Portsmouth between St Petersburg and Tokyo.[63] At Björkö, the Kaiser had placed absolute faith in Nicholas's ability to dictate Russia's foreign policy. That faith soon proved to have been misplaced.

The first obstacle to ratification of the treaty, however, came from the German, not the Russian, side. Both Holstein and Bülow initially welcomed the Björkö agreement as a diplomatic triumph for the Kaiser and the Reich. The Chancellor seemed particularly moved by the news: 'Your Majesty's gracious telegram from Björkö received with deep emotion and heartfelt thanks. Your Majesty alone is to be congratulated on this success, because Your Majesty alone made this turn of events possible and brought it about.'[64] Holstein's support for the treaty was more measured. Pointing to potential opposition among Russian ministers and to the precarious internal situation in the Tsarist Empire, he told Bülow, 'This deal is a great success, provided that the Tsar succeeds in remaining at the helm and alive.'[65] But once the changes that Wilhelm had made to the text of the draft treaty were revealed, the Chancellor's attitude changed. Bülow asserted that the Kaiser's decision to restrict the operation of the treaty to Europe had rendered it worthless in the event of a conflict between Germany and Britain. He urged Wilhelm to seek the Tsar's agreement to amend the treaty to allow it to operate on a global basis and, when the Kaiser initially refused to do so, Bülow tendered his resignation as Chancellor.[66]

There has been a lively debate among historians about Bülow's motives in taking such a dramatic step. Gerd Fessler and Terry Cole both believe that the Chancellor was genuinely incensed by the changes that the Kaiser had made to the carefully worded draft treaty.[67] The Chancellor had indeed informed the Kaiser shortly before he met the Tsar at Björkö that a treaty between Germany and Russia would have considerable value if it operated on a global basis, because the British would be deterred from mounting an attack on Germany by the knowledge that this would lead to a Russian assault on India. 'The concern of the English about an attack on India is greater than they outwardly reveal', the Chancellor had observed.[68]

[63] Savinskii, 'Guillaume II', pp. 798–9; McDonald, *United Government*, p. 79.

[64] Bülow to Wilhelm II, 24 July 1905, PAAA, R2095.

[65] Holstein to Bülow, 25 July 1905, ibid.   [66] Bülow, *Memoirs*, vol. II, pp. 133–41.

[67] Gerd Fessler, *Reichskanzler Bernhard von Bülow*, Berlin 1991, p. 88; Terry Cole, 'Kaiser Versus Chancellor: The Crisis of Bülow's Chancellorship, 1905–6', in Richard J. Evans (ed.), *Society and Politics in Wilhelmine Germany*, London 1978, p. 52.

[68] Bülow to the German Foreign Office, 22 July 1905, PAAA, R2095.

Bülow repeated this view as a justification for offering his resignation as Chancellor after Björkö, in refuting Wilhelm's contention that it was 'illusory' to think that the Russians would be capable of mounting a successful attack on India.[69] The Chancellor responded in strong terms: 'The view that a Russian assault against India would be hopeless is not shared by the most powerful elements in England, as was demonstrated recently in the dispute [between] Mr Curzon [and] Kitchener and the whole English literature produced on India.'[70] In making this statement, Bülow exhibited an astute understanding of the anxieties of British military planners and policy-makers, who were becoming alarmed that Russian railway building in Central Asia might make an attack by the Tsarist Empire on India through Afghanistan a realistic strategic goal for the first time.[71]

As Katharine Lerman has pointed out, however, the Björkö agreement as it stood, with its scope restricted to Europe, was still better than no German–Russian alliance at all.[72] In addition, given Bülow's commitment to good relations with Russia both as State Secretary of the German Foreign Office in the late 1890s and as Chancellor,[73] it seems baffling that he was prepared to reject the agreement that had been concluded between the two Emperors simply because its scope was not as wide as he would have wished. Therefore, as virtually all historians who have studied the episode have agreed, it is apparent that the changes that the Kaiser had made to the draft treaty were the pretext for Bülow's offer of resignation, not the cause. The real cause was the Chancellor's growing frustration with Wilhelm II's irresponsible exercise of power in the sphere of foreign policy.[74] The Chancellor believed that the Emperor's behaviour had damaged German interests and that his threat of resignation would help to end it. Wilhelm had certainly been indiscreet on frequent occasions during 1905. The most serious incident prior to Björkö had been Wilhelm's assurance to a group of French officers that Germany would in no case go to war over Morocco and wished to solve its dispute with France peacefully.[75] This was in direct contradiction to the official German policy, devised by Holstein and Bülow,

---

[69] Wilhelm II to Bülow, 30 July 1905, PAAA, R2096. [70] Bülow to Wilhelm II, 30 July 1905, ibid.

[71] Beryl Williams, 'The Strategic Background to the Anglo-Russian Entente of August 1907', *Historical Journal* 12, 3 (1966), pp. 360–73.

[72] Katharine A. Lerman, *The Chancellor as Courtier: Bernhard von Bülow and the Governance of Germany, 1900–1909*, Cambridge 1990, pp. 128–9.

[73] Winzen, *Weltmachtkonzept*, esp. pp. 140–75; Fessler, *Bülow*, pp. 50–1.

[74] Cole, 'Kaiser versus Chancellor', pp. 51–3; Lerman, *Chancellor*, p. 130; Lamar J. R. Cecil, *Wilhelm II: Emperor and Exile, 1900–1941*, Chapel Hill, NC and London 1996, pp. 101–2; Christopher M. Clark, *Kaiser Wilhelm II*, Harlow 2000, pp. 99–100, 141.

[75] Holstein to Radolin, 14 June 1905, in Norman Rich and M. H. Fisher (eds.), *The Holstein Papers*, 4 vols., Cambridge, 1955–63 (hereafter *HP*), vol. IV, no. 891, pp. 342–3.

which depended on securing French concessions through threats of German aggression.[76] At various stages in the course of 1905, the Kaiser had appeared to undermine the policy of *rapprochement* with Russia. In conversation with his Anglo-German relative Prince Louis of Battenberg in the spring of 1905, for example, Wilhelm had contradicted his own government's pro-Russian policy by declaring that he now favoured co-operation between 'the three great Anglo-Saxon races, as represented by Germany, Great Britain and the United States'.[77] The Kaiser had also made indiscreet comments to French diplomats about the Tsar's conduct during the Russian revolution.[78] The changes made by the Kaiser to the text of the Björkö agreement were therefore the 'last straw' as far as the Chancellor was concerned.

Bülow's position in the summer of 1905 appeared to be sufficiently strong for him to resort to the risky course of offering his resignation, because the Chancellor knew that the Kaiser could not dispense with his services at a time of continuing tension with France and Britain over Morocco. Bülow had made the correct calculation. Wilhelm panicked when faced with the prospect of losing his Chancellor at such a critical time and agreed to seek Nicholas II's support for amendments to the Björkö agreement that would extend its scope to the whole globe.[79] Although Bülow's threat of resignation may have strengthened his position in the short term, in the medium to long term it proved counter-productive. This is unsurprising, given that by acting out of what the Kaiser considered to be 'injured vanity, because he had not secured the treaty himself',[80] Bülow had forgotten that his political power depended in the last instance on his ability to retain Wilhelm II's favour and trust – on the operation of what John Röhl has defined as the 'kingship mechanism'.[81] The Chancellor may, in fact, have realized his mistake soon after the event. The letter he wrote to the Kaiser on 12 August, rescinding his offer of resignation, was notably obsequious in tone, even for a master of flattery such as Bülow, suggesting that he was trying to recover his standing with Wilhelm. He compared the Kaiser to Friedrich the Great, praised him as 'the embodiment of the national idea

---

[76] Norman Rich, *Friedrich von Holstein: Politics and Diplomacy in the Era of Bismarck and Wilhelm II*, 2 vols., Cambridge 1965, vol. II, pp. 699–710.

[77] Prince Louis of Battenberg, Notes of a conversation with the German Emperor on board HMS *Drake*, 1 April 1905, Lansdowne Papers, PRO FO, 800/130.

[78] Bihourd to Delcassé, 18 March 1905, *DDF*, 2nd series, vol. VI, no. 158, pp. 203–4.

[79] Bülow, *Memoirs*, vol. II, pp. 139–41; cf. Bülow to the German Foreign Office, 5 August 1905, PAAA, R2096.

[80] Eulenburg's notes, 25 September 1905, *EK*, vol. III, no. 1509, p. 2119.

[81] John C. G. Röhl, *The Kaiser and his Court: Wilhelm II and the Government of Germany*, Cambridge 1994, pp. 107–30.

and the future of the German Empire', and sought to deny the charge that 'arrogance' had been the cause of his resignation.[82]

The Chancellor's actions over the Björkö agreement failed to alter the Kaiser's behaviour. Instead, Wilhelm decided to bypass Bülow in the negotiations to secure revisions to the agreement. He did this by encouraging Philipp Eulenburg, who had emerged from a three-year-long retirement from public life, to open up a private channel of communication with Sergei Witte.[83] Wilhelm's injudicious interventions in diplomacy did not come to an end until the twin public-relations disasters of the 'Hale Interview' and the *Daily Telegraph* affair in the autumn of 1908 caused a political crisis which came close to forcing his abdication.[84] Bülow's resignation offer over Björkö and the Kaiser's capitulation in the face of the threat of losing his Chancellor, therefore, although at first looking like a victory for the head of government over the monarch was actually nothing of the sort. It was a move which backfired because the power structure of the Reich made the retention of the Kaiser's confidence the crucial factor for any Chancellor who wished to remain in office. Bülow's action over the treaty resulted in a loss of an element of that confidence, while failing to curb the irresponsible exercise of power by Wilhelm II.

The failure of the Björkö agreement to come into effect was not, however, the result of Bülow's reservations about the document. The Kaiser's and Bülow's greatest mistake was to believe that the conclusion of a treaty between Wilhelm and the Tsar would of itself secure an alliance between Germany and Russia. They overestimated Nicholas II's power and his ability to persuade his ministers and Russia's French ally of the desirability of entering a combination with Germany. It soon became evident that the Tsar could persuade neither and was not inclined to force the issue. When Nicholas informed Lamsdorff of the treaty's existence, on 30 August 1905, the Russian Foreign Minister immediately raised objections to it. He informed the Tsar that the text of the Björkö agreement was incompatible

---

[82] Bülow to Wilhelm II, 12 August 1905, GStA HA Rep. 53 J Lit. B no. 16a vol. III.

[83] Witte, *Memoirs*, pp. 454–7; Bülow to Eulenburg, 22 September 1905; Eulenburg to Bülow, 23 September 1905, *EK*, vol. III, nos. 1506–7, pp. 2112–14; Wilhelm II to Bülow, 27 September 1905, *GP*, vol. XIX (ii), no. 6246, pp. 508–11; Eulenburg to Bülow, 26 September 1905, Bülow, *Memoirs*, vol. II, pp. 165–6.

[84] Ralph R. Menning and Carol Bresnahan Menning, '"Baseless Allegations": Wilhelm II and the Hale Interview of 1908', *Central European History* 16, 4 (1983), pp. 368–97; Terence F. Cole, 'The Daily Telegraph Affair and its Aftermath: The Kaiser, Bülow and the Reichstag, 1908–1909', in John C. G. Röhl and Nicolaus Sombart (eds.), *Kaiser Wilhelm II: New Interpretations*, Cambridge 1982, pp. 249–68. For the *Daily Telegraph* affair and the Hale Interview see now the document collections edited by Peter Winzen, *Das Kaiserreich am Abgrund. Die Daily-Telegraph-Affäre und das Hale-Interview von 1908*, Stuttgart 2002.

with that of the Franco-Russian alliance. If Russia were to ratify the Treaty, she would be in the invidious position of being committed to aiding France and Germany simultaneously in an armed conflict. The fact that Nicholas had signed the treaty with Germany under false pretences was revealed in his response to Lamsdorff. Nicholas told his Foreign Minister, 'I did not understand the Treaty of Björkö as you did. In signing it, I did not believe for a single moment that my agreement with Emperor William could be directed against France; it was exactly the reverse; I always had in mind to incorporate France into it.'[85] This remark indicates the extent to which the Tsar had succumbed to the Kaiser's powers of persuasion at Björkö.

At the Tsar's insistence, Lamsdorff agreed to sound out the French government to see if it would agree to an understanding with Germany.[86] However, when Nelidov, the Russian Ambassador to Paris, raised the issue with the French Prime Minister, Rouvier, the latter ruled out French participation in forceful terms. 'I can't see either the value or the possibility of such a grouping', Rouvier told the Ambassador. 'You know the lines of our foreign policy; it is based on alliance with Russia and friendship with England. These are all we require . . . can you see public opinion in France accepting the idea of a German alliance? Can you see William II received in Paris?'[87] The French government, despite Wilhelm's and Bülow's wishful thinking, had always been likely to object to a continental league directed against Britain.

French objections to such a combination had a crucial bearing on the outcome of the discussions at St Petersburg on the course of Russian foreign policy in the autumn of 1905. That this was the case can be attributed to two factors. First, the Tsar, in particular, had a sense of honour and obligation towards the French. He saw the Franco-Russian alliance as the cornerstone of Russian foreign and security policy and also as a sacred inheritance from his father Alexander III. Throughout his reign, he never wavered in his 'steadfast' commitment to it[88] and he went cold on the idea of an alliance with Germany as it gradually dawned him that France could not be brought into such a combination. On 7 October 1905, in a letter to the Kaiser, Nicholas stated that he was opposed to the Treaty of Björkö coming

---

[85] Savinskii, 'Guillaume II', pp. 801–2.

[86] McDonald, *United Government*, pp. 80–1; Witte, *Memoirs*, pp. 462–4.

[87] Paléologue, diary entry, 16 October 1905, *Turning Point*, p. 303.

[88] Louis to Cruppi, 4 March 1911, *DDF*, 2nd series, vol. XIII, no. 173, pp. 313–14; cf. General de Boisdeffre to Hanotaux, 17 November 1894, *DDF*, 1st series, vol. IX, no. 284, p. 427; Nicholas II to M. Casimir-Périer, President of the French Republic, 11 November 1894, ibid., no. 277, p. 417; Touchard to Pichon, 7 May 1909 and 9 June 1909, *DDF*, 2nd series, vol. XII, nos. 182, 214, pp. 228, 292.

into effect 'until we know how France will look upon it'.[89] On 23 November 1905, by which time there was no longer any doubt that France would under no circumstances involve itself in Wilhelm II's proposal for a continental league against Britain, the Tsar again sent a letter to the Kaiser. This time, Nicholas suggested that a declaration be added to the Treaty of Björkö, rendering it inapplicable in the case of a war between Germany and France. He emphasized that he could not act disloyally towards the Franco-Russian alliance and, invoking the memory of Alexander III, declared that 'what was signed by my Father . . . cannot be struck off by a stroke of the pen'.[90] As the Kaiser appreciated, Nicholas's proposed declaration represented 'a direct annulment of the treaty in the event of a war with France'.[91]

Second, Russia was heavily dependent on loans from the Paris money markets. This financial dependence gave the French political leverage at St Petersburg, particularly in the context existing in the autumn of 1905 where Russia had been defeated in war, was beset by revolution and facing economic collapse. The German money markets would not have been able to make up the shortfall that would have resulted from the withdrawal of French financial support for Russia. That the need for a loan was a key factor in the decisive orientation of Russia away from Germany in the winter of 1905–6 can be illustrated with reference to the behaviour of two of the leading political actors: Witte and the Tsar. Witte's initial enthusiasm for an alliance with Germany was genuine. He told Philipp Eulenburg, after being informed of the treaty, 'Björkö is the greatest relief of my life! The only means of achieving a stable policy.'[92] Although concerns over the difficulty of securing French involvement in a continental league soon tempered his enthusiasm,[93] Witte's eventual rejection of a German alliance can be linked explicitly to the issue of finance. The 'loan that saved Russia', as he subsequently called it in his memoirs, could more easily be raised in Paris and London than in Berlin.[94]

The need for a loan was also a factor in the Tsar's *volte face* over the Björkö agreement. As has been shown, Nicholas, unlike his Foreign Minister,

[89] Nicholas II to Wilhelm II, 24 September/7 October 1905, PAAA, R2097; *GP*, vol. xix (ii), no. 6347, pp. 512–13.

[90] Nicholas II to Wilhelm II, 10/23 November 1905, PAAA, R2097.

[91] Wilhelm II to Bülow, 26 November 1905, ibid.

[92] Eulenburg to Bülow, 26 September 1905, Bülow, *Memoirs*, vol. ii, pp. 165–6; cf. Hardinge to Lansdowne, 1 October 1905, *British Documents on the Origins of the War, 1898–1914*, ed. G. P. Gooch and Harold Temperley, 11 vols., London 1926–38 (hereafter *BD*), vol. iv, no. 193, pp. 202–3.

[93] Witte to Eulenburg, 8 October 1905, PAAA, R2097.

[94] Witte, *Memoirs*, pp. 561–72; Howard D. Mehlinger and John M. Thompson, *Count Witte and the Tsarist Government in the 1905 Revolution*, Bloomington, IN 1971, pp. 209–41.

had actively wanted to explore the possibility of bringing France into a German–Russian alliance. Nicholas had also been, as indicated in relation to the Dogger Bank incident and his statements at Björkö, most hostile to the British. Indeed, as late as 23 November 1905, Nicholas had told the Kaiser that he had 'not the slightest intention' of opening negotiations with England 'for an understanding about Asiatic frontier questions'.[95] The Tsar was being disingenuous. Pressure from his own advisors, the French and British governments, coupled with the lure of access to the financial markets of the City of London, had already compelled Nicholas to alter Russia's stance towards Britain, if not his own private feelings.[96] On 24 October 1905, Nicholas had conceded that Russia would give priority to improving its relations with Britain, when he responded favourably to an overture to that effect from the British Ambassador at St Petersburg, Sir Charles Hardinge.[97] Maurice Paléologue, a senior official in the French foreign ministry, noted approvingly on the same day that the Tsar had 'recovered his balance' and accepted that co-operation with France and Britain was now the only realistic course open to Russia.[98] Finance also played a key role in the decision which, more than any other, finally sealed the fate of the Treaty of Björkö. In return for a further loan from the Paris money markets, Nicholas appeared in December 1905 to promise the French government Russia's unconditional support at the forthcoming Algeciras Conference to resolve the Moroccan Crisis between Paris and Berlin.[99]

It would be misleading, however, to conclude that the need for loans, and Paris's and London's greater ability to furnish them than Berlin's, was the crucial factor in Russia's reluctance to ratify the Treaty of Björkö. In reality, Russian policy was determined by an assessment of the Empire's vital interests. In the face of French reluctance to join a continental league, Russia had to choose between Paris and Berlin. The choice was not a difficult one to make, because, for all its faults, the Franco-Russian alliance had the semblance of being a partnership of equals and helped to maintain a military balance in Europe. By contrast, if Russia had decided to ally herself with the Kaiserreich against France, she would have helped to ensure German dominance of the continent and would have seen her own status diminish from that of a Great Power to that of a client state of Berlin. The point

---

[95] Nicholas II to Wilhelm II, 10/23 November 1905, PAAA, R2097.
[96] Paul Cambon to Rouvier, 20 and 27 October 1905, *DDF*, 2nd series, vol. VIII, nos. 65, 87, pp. 91–8, 123–6; Hardinge to Lansdowne, 21 October 1905; Lansdowne to Bertie, 25 October 1905, *BD*, vol. IV, nos. 201, 203, pp. 214–15, 217–18.
[97] Hardinge to Edward VII, 24 October 1905, Hardinge Papers, vol. 6.
[98] Paléologue, diary entry, 24 October 1905, *Turning Point*, pp. 304–5.
[99] Mehlinger and Thompson, *Witte*, pp. 218–19.

was made most ably by Lamsdorff in the autumn of 1905. 'From many years' experience', the Russian Foreign Minister declared, 'I have brought the conviction that in order to be on the best relations with Germany we need the alliance with France. Otherwise we lose our independence and a heavier yoke than the German I do not know.'[100]

Holstein and Bülow both believed that the Russian revolution of 1905 and Russia's rejection of the Björkö agreement had put an end to the dynastic solidarity that had allowed Germany and Russia to co-operate in the past. Holstein drew the conclusion that 'The old Russia, where one only asked about the opinion of the Tsar and his Foreign Minister, has sunk out of sight and the Russian people, who will in future have more or less influence on policy, have already given free rein to their hatred of the Germans.'[101] Bülow concurred. 'What we are currently experiencing', he informed the Kaiser in June 1906, 'is . . . the collapse of the Russian autocratic system . . . that for hundreds of years has been the hope and now and then the bastion of monarchical and conservative Europe'. The Chancellor observed that the Tsarist system had many features of Germanic origin. By contrast, the 'real' Russia was Asiatic and most unlikely to be a friend of the Kaiserreich.[102]

These predictions proved to be misplaced, most obviously because the Tsarist regime withstood the revolution of 1905–6, but also because the decision-making process did not change fundamentally. While it is true that in the years immediately following the 1905–6 revolution Nicholas retreated into the role of 'legal sovereign',[103] he still controlled government appointments and was ultimately responsible for Russian foreign policy.[104] The relationship between the Kaiser and the Tsar remained an important factor in German–Russian relations during these years, a point that was conceded by the British Ambassador to Russia, Sir Arthur Nicolson. In his annual report on Russia, submitted to the Foreign Office in January 1907, Nicolson presented an extremely favourable picture of the relations between the Prussian and Russian courts. He wrote that these were 'at the present time intimate and cordial. I should go further and state that German influence is to-day predominant at the Court and in Government circles.'[105]

---

[100] Lamsdorff to Nelidov, 9 October 1905, D. W. Spring, 'Russia and the Franco-Russian Alliance, 1905–14: Dependence or Interdependence', *Slavonic and East European Review*, 66 (1988), pp. 583–4.
[101] Holstein to Bülow (draft), January 1906, *GP*, vol. IV, no. 919, p. 381.
[102] Bülow to Wilhelm II, 17 June 1906, GStA HA Rep. 53 J Lit. B no. 16a vol. III.
[103] McDonald, *United Government*, p. 106.
[104] Dominic C. B. Lieven, *Russia and the Origins of the First World War*, London 1983, p. 54.
[105] Nicolson, Annual Report for Russia 1906 (extract), *BD*, vol. IV, no. 243, p. 256.

What had changed was that the Kaiser and others in the leadership of
Imperial Germany had a much more realistic conception of the limits of
what could be achieved through dynastic diplomacy than had been the case
prior to the débâcle over the Treaty of Björkö. They were aware that warm
words for Germany from the Tsar did not compensate for the fact that
Russia was firmly committed to her alliance with France. As Holstein observed prior to the meeting between Wilhelm and Nicholas at Swinemünde
in August 1907, 'Because the Russian Government cannot conclude an alliance with us both because of the antipathy of its people towards Germany
and because of its constant dependence on the French market, it must be
fully reassured on this point.'[106] The Kaiser himself had come to regard the
Tsar as a pathetic figure, unable to withstand the pressure from his advisors
for an accord with Britain. 'The Emperor is not false but weak!', he noted
on a despatch from St Petersburg in the spring of 1907, 'Weakness is not
falseness, but it takes its place, and fills its functions!'[107]

IV

Philipp Eulenburg observed in 1917 that Wilhelm II's decision, on the
advice of his then Chancellor General Leo von Caprivi and the German
Foreign Office, to fail to renew the Reinsurance Treaty with Russia in 1890
had been the most damaging error in Berlin's policy towards St Petersburg
before 1914.[108] Eulenburg was correct. That decision opened the way for
the Franco-Russian alliance that was concluded in 1894. By 1905–6, the alliance had become an enduring feature of the diplomatic scene, supported
by military co-operation and lavish French loans for the economic development of Russia. It was the existence and seeming permanence of the alliance
that fatally weakened the Kaiser's and Bülow's attempt during the Russo-
Japanese War to find a route out of Germany's encirclement by negotiating
an alliance with Nicholas II. German policy towards Russia therefore failed
so spectacularly to achieve its objectives because it did not take proper account of the political realities. It placed too much emphasis on winning
over Nicholas II and on contact between the Kaiser and the Tsar. While
both were the leading political figures in their respective capitals, neither
had full autonomy. This was illustrated when the Björkö agreement began

[106] Holstein, diary entry, 13 August 1907, *HP*, vol. IV, no. 1046, pp. 486–7; cf. Note by Tschirschky, 7
August 1907, *GP*, vol. XXII, no. 7387, pp. 67–8; Wilhelm II's comments on Miquel to Bülow, 27
September 1907, *GP*, vol. XXV (i), no. 8537, pp. 45–7.
[107] Wilhelm II's comment on Schoen to Bülow, 16 March 1907, *GP*, vol. XXII (i), no. 7877, p. 161.
[108] Note by Eulenburg, February 1917, *EK*, vol. III, no. 1563, p. 2230.

to unravel: Wilhelm was willing to appease his Chancellor by seeking revisions to the treaty and Nicholas stepped back from entering an alliance with Germany when he realised that his ministers and the French government would never tolerate such a combination, even if extended to encompass France.

The fact that the Treaty of Björkö did not come into effect should not, however, be taken as evidence that Wilhelm II was a marginal figure in the conduct of German diplomacy. Instead, the evidence shows that the Kaiser played a prominent role in the attempt to win over the Tsar in 1904–5. The letters that he sent to Nicholas were a central instrument in the German campaign to bring about a treaty of alliance with Russia. It was Wilhelm who secured the Tsar's signature to the treaty at Björkö, through his own powers of persuasion and skilful manipulation of Nicholas during their meeting. Nonetheless, the episode undoubtedly indicates that there were significant constraints on the Kaiser's ability to influence the course of Germany's relations with Russia. Wilhelm had severe weaknesses as a diplomatist, most notably the fact that he was indiscreet and inconsistent in his approach. Bülow, and to a lesser extent Holstein, provided the political direction in German policy towards Russia which the Kaiser could not. Wilhelm's panic when Bülow tendered his resignation over the treaty indicated that he was not willing to take over the day-to-day business of policy-making himself. Wilhelm, like Bülow, also underestimated the significance of the structural forces that prevented Russia from entering an alliance with Germany. The Tsar was not omnipotent. He could sign a treaty, but he could not compel his ministers and his French allies to support it, against their own inclinations and their perceptions of their countries' financial, strategic and national interests. The failure of the Treaty of Björkö to come into effect indicates therefore that an agreement between Emperors could not lead to an alliance between Empires in the early twentieth century, if such an alliance was perceived to be against the vital interests of one of the states involved. National interest had replaced the will of the sovereign as the primary determinant of foreign policy. This point was made, albeit with some exaggeration, by Helmuth von Moltke, the then Chief of the German General Staff, following the summit between the Kaiser and the Tsar at Swinemünde in August 1907. 'The interests of states are not determined by meetings between monarchs', Moltke observed, 'they follow their own course and lead consequently and inexorably either to clashes or understandings.'[109]

[109] Moltke, *Erinnerungen*, 4 August 1907, p. 348.

From a German perspective, however, what is striking is that having correctly identified the implications of the events of 1905–6 for Russia, the Kaiser and his advisors failed to draw the appropriate lessons for the Reich itself. The failure of the Björkö agreement to come into effect indicated that a German–Russian alliance was not a realistic diplomatic objective, but there was no fundamental reassessment of *Weltpolitik* in Berlin in the years after 1906. This was despite the fact that the anti-British orientation of the policy was predicated on Germany's ability to come to terms with Russia. The result, therefore, was a disastrous deterioration in Anglo-German relations without a commensurate improvement in the atmosphere between Berlin and St Petersburg. Similarly, despite recognizing the limits of Nicholas II's power, there was no real change in Wilhelm II's conception of diplomacy as the conduct of relations by and between monarchs as a result of the Björkö fiasco. The Kaiser's interventions in German foreign policy continued, to the detriment of the Reich's international standing, until the *Daily Telegraph* affair in the autumn of 1908 brought about a political crisis in Berlin that forced Wilhelm, albeit temporarily and with ill grace, to retreat from the diplomatic limelight.

CHAPTER 6

The uses of 'friendship'. The 'personal regime' of Wilhelm II and Theodore Roosevelt, 1901–1909

Ragnhild Fiebig-von Hase

'Dynastic diplomacy' had played an important role in German foreign policy ever since Wilhelm II had established his 'personal regime' during the 1890s. Since the Kaiser believed in the outstanding qualities of his personal diplomatic skills, he frantically tried to improve not only the Russo-German, but also the Anglo-German relationship through cultivating his contacts to his royal relatives in Russia and England. But these endeavours did not fall on fertile ground, since the 'Royals' in London and the Russian Tsar perceived them not only as troublesome and obstructive, but also as dishonest and manipulative. Too often foreign-policy performance and military preparations of the German Empire contradicted the Kaiser's verbal affirmations of friendship and goodwill.[1]

It is much less well known that, in 1902, Wilhelm II also built up a personal relationship with Theodore Roosevelt, President of the United States since September 1901. This is remarkable because, while the Emperor's family ties easily explain his personal contacts with the ruling houses of Europe, Wilhelm II did not know Roosevelt personally until they met in May 1910, when the latter had already left office.[2] Thus, the so-called Willy–Teddy relationship consisted of written communications[3] and the verbal messages of the two men to each other, which were delivered through

---

[1] John C. G. Röhl, *Wilhelm II. Der Aufbau der Persönlichen Monarchie 1888–1900*, Munich 2001, pp. 534–65.

[2] Roosevelt came privately to Berlin on a tour through Europe that he undertook to accept the Nobel Peace Prize awarded to him in 1906. For Roosevelt's own description of his tour see his letter to the British historian Sir George Trevelyan, 1 October 1911, in Elton E. Morison and John M. Blum (eds.), *The Letters of Theodore Roosevelt* (hereafter Roosevelt, *Letters*), vol. VII, Boston 1951–4, pp. 390–9.

[3] The correspondence between the two men can be consulted in the Theodore Roosevelt Papers in the Library of Congress in Washington, DC (hereafter Roosevelt Papers), but some are also in the State Department Records in the National Archives (NA, DS, RG 59), and the Records of the Politische Abteilung, Auswärtiges Amt (AA-PA), Berlin. A few documents have been printed in the *Die Große Politik der Europäischen Kabinette, 1871–1914*, ed. Johannes Lepsius, Albrecht Mendelssohn-Bartholdy, and Friedrich Thimme, 40 vols, Berlin 1922–27 (*GP*); and in *Papers Relating to the Foreign Relations of the United States*, Washington 1902–19 (*FRUS*).

the German and American Ambassadors in Berlin and Washington as well as other emissaries chosen for such purposes.

Until now, only biographers of Theodore Roosevelt,[4] but not of Wilhelm II[5] have shown an interest in the relationship of the two men. Almost unanimously, Roosevelt is praised for his efficient and wise handling of Wilhelm's difficult personality as well as his successful efforts to integrate the Kaiser into his peace mediation during the Russo-Japanese war, and to ban the threatening Franco-German war during the Morocco Crisis in 1905–6. Publications on German–American relations before the First World War also describe the relationship in highlighting the following episodes: the Kaiser's initiative to send his brother Prince Heinrich to the United States in January 1902; the monarch's co-operation with Roosevelt to save the integrity of China and the open-door policy during the Russo-Japanese War, and the endeavours to end the war in 1904–5; Roosevelt's mediation efforts during the first Moroccan Crisis; and, finally, Wilhelm II's belief in co-operation with Roosevelt in East Asia against the 'yellow peril'. With few exceptions, the personal intercourse between the Kaiser and the President is described as a relatively positive asset within the otherwise problematical German–American relationship.[6]

The following contribution deconstructs the so-called 'friendship' by questioning, although not denying, the 'personal' factor, and by stressing political motives as the essential reason for the development of the relationship. Thus, it analyses the process of 'personalization' in the official diplomatic intercourse between Germany and the United States through

[4] Cf. Henry F. Pringle, *Theodore Roosevelt. A Biography*, New York 1931; Joseph B. Bishop, *Theodore Roosevelt and His Times*, New York 1920; Howard K. Beale, *Theodore Roosevelt and the Rise of America to World Power*, Baltimore, MD 1956; William H. Harbaugh, *The Life and Times of Theodore Roosevelt*, London 1975; Lewis L. Gould, *The Presidency of Theodore Roosevelt*, Lawrence, KA 1991; H. W. Brands, *T. R. The Last Romantic*, New York 1997; Nathan Miller, *Theodore Roosevelt. A Life*, New York 1992; Edmund Morris, *Theodore Rex*, New York 2001.
[5] See Michael Balfour, *The Kaiser and His Times*, New York 1972; Lamar Cecil, *Wilhelm II*, vol. II: *Emperor and Exile, 1900–1941*, Chapel Hill, NC and London 1996; Willibald Gutsche, *Wilhelm II. Der letzte Kaiser des Deutschen Reiches. Eine Biographie*, Berlin 1991.
[6] Alfred Vagts, *Deutschland und die Vereinigten Staaten in der Weltpolitik*, New York 1935, especially pp. 1932–48; Howard K. Beale, 'Theodore Roosevelt, Wilhelm II. und die deutsch-amerikanischen Beziehungen', *Die Welt als Geschichte*, 15 (1955), pp. 155–87; Manfred Jonas, *The United States and Germany. A Diplomatic History*, Ithaca, NY and London, 1984, pp. 65–94; Ragnhild Fiebig-von Hase, *Lateinamerika als Konfliktherd der deutsch-amerikanischen Beziehungen, 1898–1903. Vom Beginn der Panamerikapolitik bis zur Venezuelakrise von 1902/03*, Göttingen 1986, especially pp. 943–66; Ragnhild Fiebig-von Hase, 'Die Rolle Kaiser Wilhelms II. in den deutsch-amerikanischen Beziehungen, 1890–1914', in John C. G. Röhl (ed.), *Der Ort Kaiser Wilhelms II. in der deutschen Geschichte*, Munich 1991, pp. 223–57; Reiner Pommerin, *Der Kaiser und Amerika. Die USA in der Politik der Reichsleitung 1890–1917*, Cologne and Vienna 1986; Raimund Lammersdorf, *Anfänge einer Weltmacht. Theodore Roosevelt und die transatlantischen Beziehungen der USA 1901–1909*, Berlin 1994.

Wilhelm's interferences and Roosevelt's responses. It describes the image the two men had of each other, discusses the authorship of their letters, and finally concentrates on the political motives behind the relationship and the impact it had on foreign affairs in both countries. The underlying hypothesis is that the initiative for this kind of 'personal diplomacy' originated with the Kaiser, and that the Teddy–Willy relationship from 1902 to 1911 can be studied as a revealing model for the functioning of Wilhelm II's 'personal regime' in foreign policy. President Roosevelt's perception of Wilhelm II as Emperor of Germany and his reactions to the Kaiser's proposals serve as a mirror image magnifying certain traits of the 'personal regime'.

Focusing on personal factors does not mean neglecting the importance of structural preconditions shaping foreign policy. But it is interesting to note that the historical controversy about the general methodological problem of whether structures or persons are more important in shaping history is closely connected with the evaluation of Wilhelm II's role within the German political system.[7] There is no equivalent contemporary historical discussion of Roosevelt's presidency, although the power of the executive was immensely expanded during his years in the White House, and although the awareness of historians of this process is reflected in phrases like 'Theodore Rex', 'imperial presidency', 'personalized presidency', or 'autocratic tendencies'. While, in the past, historians have condemned Roosevelt's expansionism in foreign affairs as an aberration from the righteous path of American republicanism, today, the modernity of his presidency is stressed. In many ways, Theodore Roosevelt was the first modern President in the White House. He was a man gifted with a keen awareness of the new forces shaping industrial America, of the country's new role in world affairs, and the new challenges to the Federal Government emanating from interior as well as global developments.[8]

The newer historical discussion of Wilhelm II's role within the German power structure is far more complex and controversial. Three different approaches can be distinguished: first, the traditional approach which interprets Wilhelm II's contributions as deplorable and damaging, but also irrelevant for the otherwise rational conduct of German foreign affairs. In this view, the Chancellors of the Reich, and among them especially Bernhard von Bülow and the experienced diplomatic personnel of the Auswärtiges Amt in the Wilhelmstrasse, were at the centre of foreign-policy

---

[7] See e.g. Volker Berghahn's contribution to this volume, pp. 281–93.
[8] Morris, *Theodore Rex*; Gould, *Presidency*.

decision-making. Peter Winzen gives this general interpretational pattern
a different turn: the Kaiser was an extremely dangerous political asset in
international relations before 1914, but, even more so, Bülow's incompetence, inefficiency, and lack of orientation, as well as his constant efforts
to manipulate Wilhelm with flatteries and lies, instead of pursuing a clear
and realistic political concept, were responsible for the blunders of German
foreign policy under the 'personal regime' in the crucial years from 1897 to
1909.[9]

The second, 'structural' approach is a reaction to the fact that diplomatic
history with its concentration on Great Powers and great men neglected the
impact of social, economic, and institutional structures on the shaping of
decisions in foreign affairs. Structuralists interpret Wilhelmine naval policy
and *Weltpolitik* as an outflow of domestic policy, as a 'social-imperialistic'
strategy used to distract the masses and preserve the socio-economic *status
quo* without changing the immense structural deficits of the political system.
The leaders of the parties, economic pressure groups, and nationalistic
associations come into sight as major agents, while the Kaiser appears as
only one of the actors in the 'polycratic chaos' at the centre of governmental
power.[10]

Finally, the third, 'personalizing' approach of John C. G. Röhl and others argues that Bismarck's political system proved flexible enough to permit
Wilhelm II to establish his autocratic 'personal regime' without a *coup
d'état*. The main pillar of his quasi-absolutistic regime was his grip on
the bureaucracy and the military. He could select men for top positions
without regard to their qualifications, men who had gained his confidence
and were willing to subject themselves to his will. Thereby, the deficiencies of the bureaucratic apparatus and its political mistakes were closely
related to the ineptitude and inefficiency of Wilhelm II as a statesman.
The result was the 'Byzantinism' which characterized Wilhelm II's reign
in general and particularly the decision-making process in domestic and
foreign affairs. The chancellorship of Bülow and his blunders in foreign
policy are interpreted as an integral part of Wilhelm's II 'personal regime'.[11]
With regard to foreign affairs, the 'structural' and the 'personalized' approach do not exclude, but rather supplement each other: while internal

[9] Peter Winzen, *Bülows Weltmachtkonzept. Untersuchungen zur Frühphase seiner Außenpolitik 1897–
1901*, Boppard 1977; Peter Winzen, 'Zur Genesis von Weltmachtkonzept und Weltpolitik', in Röhl,
Der Ort Kaiser Wilhelms II., pp. 189–222.
[10] Hans-Ulrich Wehler, *Deutsche Gesellschaftsgeschichte*, vol. III: *1849–1914*, Munich 1995, pp. 1000–81
and 1129–52.
[11] John C. G. Röhl, *Kaiser, Hof und Staat. Wilhelm II. und die deutsche Politik*, Munich 1987, 4th edn
1995; Isabel V. Hull, *The Entourage of Kaiser Wilhelm II, 1888–1918*, Cambridge 1982; Isabel V. Hull,
'Persönliches Regiment', in Röhl, *Der Ort Kaiser Wilhelms II.*, pp. 3–23.

developments and pressures confronted German foreign policy with challenges to which there was no easy solution, the decisions themselves were made by the men at the top – by Wilhelm II and his chosen advisors – his Chancellors, the officials of the Auswärtiges Amt, and the diplomatic corps.[12]

Although the following investigation, concentrating on the relationship between the two heads of state of Germany and the United States, can profit from these interpretative patterns, it has to transcend them and use the international history approach, which goes beyond the restricted perspective of national history. It perceives foreign affairs not only as emanating from intra-national factors, but also from inter- and trans-national interactions in an interdependent global environment.[13] In Germany as well as in the United States, political decision-making processes were shaped by socio-economical developments and socio-political and cultural processes closely connected with the emergence of both countries as the two leading industrial nations besides England. But, at the same time, the perception of the 'Other' and, in addition, international economic, political, and cultural developments, were important. Wilhelm II's world view was deeply influenced by anxieties caused by his perception of growing American world power and his hopes of utilizing the young American nation's abounding power potential for the advancement of his own political aims through cultivating personal relations with Roosevelt. At the same time, the growing distrust in America towards the political aims of the German Empire, which Roosevelt shared, was decidedly magnified by the foreign-policy ambitions and tactics of Wilhelm II and his closest advisors.[14]

I

To insist on the political importance of the Willy–Teddy relationship does not mean to deny that there was mutual personal respect between the two men, although this was certainly more visible in Wilhelm's II utterances

---

[12] Even Hans-Ulrich Wehler has to admit this despite his harsh criticism of the 'monarcho-centric interpretation'. Wehler, *Deutsche Gesellschaftsgeschichte*, vol. III, pp. 1017, 1147. Paul M. Kennedy, 'The Kaiser and German Weltpolitik: Reflections on Wilhelm II's Place in the Making of German Foreign Policy', in John C. G. Röhl and Nicolaus Sombart (eds.), *Kaiser Wilhelm II. New Interpretations. The Corfu Papers*, Cambridge 1982, pp. 143–68, is an excellent plea for the combination of both approaches.

[13] See among others Akira Iriye, 'The Internationalization of History', *American Historical Review*, 94 (1989), pp. 1–10.

[14] Vagts, *Deutschland*; Fiebig-von Hase, *Lateinamerika*; Ragnhild Fiebig-von Hase, 'The United States and Germany in the World Arena, 1900–17', in Hans-Jürgen Schröder (ed.), *Confrontation and Co-operation. Germany and the United States in the Era of World War I, 1900–1924*, Providence, RI and Oxford 1993, pp. 33–68.

about Roosevelt than vice versa. Already in his first personal telegram to Roosevelt of 10 January 1902, Wilhelm II stated that he was sending his brother Prince Heinrich over to the United States so he 'could express to you my sincere feelings of friendship for the United States and their illustrious head'. Roosevelt shortly afterwards answered that the Prince's visit 'is eminently calculated to strengthen the bonds of friendship that knit together this country and yours', and he also insisted that 'such friendship is to a very high degree a guaranty of the peace of the world'. The Kaiser replied: 'May heaven bless our relations with peace and good-will between the two great nations.'[15] The phraseology never really changed until the end of the correspondence.

The Kaiser was magically attracted by the manly character and virtues of the Rough Rider in the White House and enjoyed identifying himself with Roosevelt, whom he believed to be one of the strong personalities the world needed as leaders.[16] In January 1904 he wrote to Roosevelt in one of his handwritten letters that 'to elicit praise from a man like you is enough to make any ruler proud for the rest of his life', and he continued:

Your unlimited power for work, dauntless energy of purpose, pureness of motives, moving towards the highest ideals, this all crowned by an iron will, form qualities which elicit the highest admiration from everybody over here. They are the characteristics of a 'man', and as such most sympathetic to me. The 20th century is sadly in want of men of your stamp at the head of great nations and there are few of them I own [sic!]. But let us rejoice that, thank Heaven, the Anglo-Saxon-Germanic Race is still able to produce such specimen. You must accept it as a fact that your figure has moved to the foreground of the world + that mens [sic!] minds are intensely occupied by you.[17]

In July 1908, he explained to the American journalist William B. Hale in the famous interview he gave to him on board the *Meteor* in Norway:

It isn't genius the world needs, nor brilliancy, nor profound learning, half so much as personality. The man with convictions of righteousness, who is ready to fight for them and never give them up, indifferent to abuse and careless of lying and howling adversaries – he is the man to whom all will come and before whom all things will yield.[18]

---

[15] Wilhelm II to Roosevelt, telegram, 10 January 1902; Roosevelt to Wilhelm II, telegram, 17 February 1902 and Wilhelm II to Roosevelt, telegram, 12 March 1902, Roosevelt Papers.

[16] Bernhard Fürst von Bülow, *Denkwürdigkeiten*, vol. 1, Berlin 1930–1, 573; Beale, 'Theodore Roosevelt, Wilhelm II', p. 182.

[17] Wilhelm II to Roosevelt, 14 January 1904, Roosevelt Papers.

[18] William B. Hale, 'An Evening with the German Emperor'. A copy of this suppressed article is in the Frank Polk Papers, Yale University Library, Walter H. Page (London) to Robert Lansing, 21 December 1917.

Roosevelt represented in Wilhelm II's eyes all the virtues which made him such a man.

The Kaiser's attraction to Roosevelt was strengthened by the belief that he could manipulate the President by personal favours and by honouring him with medals and gifts. In view of the Kaiser's high self-esteem, the assumption that a bourgeois president would feel particularly susceptible to such imperial acts of grace is not astonishing.[19] But it was also characteristic for the 'personal regime' that German diplomats knew the Kaiser's preference for such acts and tried to please and encourage him by describing Roosevelt as exceedingly vain and highly receptive to royal flatteries. Diplomatic reports also stressed Roosevelt's 'monarchic' behaviour and thus made it easier for Wilhelm II to overcome the social difference and communicate with the American President as an equal.[20] However, the image thus created did not correspond to reality. 'Roosevelt's vanity was oddly leavened with modesty,' as Roosevelt's latest biographer, Edmund Morris, remarks.[21] As a proud Republican who believed in the superiority of the American political system, Roosevelt felt partially amused, sometimes annoyed, and finally stunned and molested by the Kaiser's advances and almost all of his insensitive and even preposterous gifts.[22] But Roosevelt was shrewd enough

---

[19] Theodor Schiemann, editor of the influential conservative *Kreuz-Zeitung*, even insisted that 'His Majesty the Emperor has President Roosevelt in his pocket.' Quoted in Paul Graf von Wolff-Metternich to Bülow, 8 December 1906, AA-PA, Vereinigte Staaten von Nord-Amerika (VStNA) 16, R 17341.

[20] See e.g. Quadt to Bülow, 18 October 1901, and Holleben to Bülow, 11 December 1901, AA-PA, VStNA 11, R 17286; Holleben to Bülow, 12 April 1902, VStNA 16, R 17332.

[21] Morris, *Theodore Rex*, p. 237.

[22] This was the case with the statue of Friedrich the Great which Wilhelm II had forced Roosevelt to accept in the name of the American people in April 1902. Wilhelm never considered that, in American eyes, the Prussian King was a symbol of the highly unpopular Prussian autocracy and militarism. Roosevelt got into trouble with Congress when he accepted the gift, and the statue was never erected in a public place in Washington as the Kaiser had wished. Vagts, *Deutschland*, pp. 1940–3; Pommerin, *Kaiser*, pp. 282–8. The Kaiser presented to Roosevelt another statue in the spring of 1905. This time it was an enormous heavy bronze bust of Wilhelm II himself, which, as Roosevelt complained, 'caused me real anguish'. Roosevelt stowed it away in the White House before it could be stored in the basement of an art gallery. Roosevelt to Thomas H. Warren, 7 June 1916, Roosevelt, *Letters*, vol. VIII, pp. 1057–8. For a description of how Roosevelt personally thanked the Kaiser for 'all those execrable presents' in 1910, see Archie Butt, *Taft and Roosevelt: The Intimate Letters of Archie Butt, Military Aide*, Garden City, NY 1930, pp. 425–6. Butt describes a conversation between Taft and Roosevelt after his return from Europe, in which Roosevelt sarcastically ridiculed the Kaiser's personal gifts: 'the bust of himself, which is now over at the Corcoran Art Gallery, the books on religion, of which he knows little, the work on art, of which I found he knows nothing, and the hideous vase with nymphs for handles . . . The nymphs are built after the German *hausfrau* order and are clumsily thrown against the sides of the vase and look as if they are too fat to hang there another minute.' Wilhelm's II last gift to Roosevelt was a book on the German war of annihilation in 1906 in South-West Africa. Roosevelt remained polite and replied that the accounts about 'the feats of the German "Rough Riders" – as you so kindly call them' was 'fascinating reading' and exclaimed:

to take advantage of the Kaiser's high opinion of him. To Secretary of State John Hay he wrote in April 1905 with regard to the Kaiser's fears of an English attack and British aggressive designs in China:

The Kaiser has become a monomaniac about getting into communication with me every time he drinks three pen'orth of conspiracy against his life and power; but as has been so often the case for the last year, he at the moment is playing our game – or, as I should more politely put it, his interests and ours [in ending the Russo-Japanese War through bilateral negotiations between the combatants and without interference by neutral powers], together with those of humanity in general, are identical.[23]

Roosevelt professed to have difficulties understanding Americans who were fascinated by Wilhelm II. He regretted 'that there are certain Americans who seem to be wholly unable to withstand contact with royalty', who 'have been profoundly affected by meeting the German Emperor and having him courteous to them'.[24]

Only after their personal encounter in Berlin, in May 1910, did the Kaiser's interest in Roosevelt diminish, since the latter seemed too much involved in the peace movement sponsored by prominent Anglo-Americans like Andrew Carnegie, and too much insisting on republican virtues. In Wilhelm's presence, the ex-President lectured in the Friedrich-Wilhelms-Universität on the development of a tolerant, civil, and westernized world culture,[25] and in their personal encounters he stressed the necessity to reduce international tensions through naval disarmament.[26] These subjects were anathema to the Kaiser and his entourage. Wilhelm was in his element when the two men attended the manoeuvre in Döberitz for several hours. Pictures of them on horseback were taken and presented to Roosevelt with the Kaiser's inscriptions on the back. These short sentences illustrate Wilhelm's wishful thinking with regard to Roosevelt, as he wrote: 'The argument

'What an extraordinary campaign it was, and how difficult it is for men in highly civilized countries to realize what grim work is needed in order to advance the outposts of civilization in the world's dark places!' Roosevelt to Wilhelm II, 2 January 1909, original in Roosevelt's handwriting, Roosevelt, *Letters*, vol. VI, p. 1441. It is hard to imagine that Roosevelt felt pleased by the comparison of his own performance in Cuba during the Spanish-American War with the butchery of the German troops against the Hereros, or that Wilhelm II realized the irony of Roosevelt's letter.

[23] Roosevelt to Hay, private, 2 April 1905, ibid., vol. IV, pp. 1156–8.

[24] One of them was Nicolas M. Butler, the prominent President of Columbia University, whom Roosevelt believed to be 'much more royalist than the King himself'. Roosevelt was especially disappointed that Butler seemed to accept the Kaiser's views about the Anglo-German estrangement and blamed England for the naval armament race. Roosevelt to Arthur Hamilton Lee, 16 September 1910, ibid., vol. VII, p. 129.

[25] Theodore Roosevelt, 'The World Movement', in his *Presidential Addresses and State Papers, European Addresses, 8.12.1908 – 7.6.1910*, New York 1910, pp. 2223–56.

[26] Roosevelt's most extensive report on his visit to Berlin and his encounters with Wilhelm II can be found in a letter to Sir George O. Trevelyan, 1 October 1911, Roosevelt, *Letters*, vol. VII, pp. 377–99.

driven home! The Germanic + Anglo Saxon Races combined will keep the world in order!' Another phrase proclaimed: 'Total agreement about the general maxims of life + policy between Amerika + Germany!', and the two remaining ones show a strong aversion against the peace movement that Andrew Carnegie – the 'old Peacebore' – promoted.[27] But despite this, the Emperor was disappointed, as Bülow remembered later,[28] the spell of Roosevelt's personality was gone, and the correspondence ended.

Roosevelt's judgements about the Kaiser's personality were far more complex and reveal signs of opportunistic insincerity. Already before he acceded to the Presidency, Roosevelt had lauded Wilhelm II as 'far and away the greatest crowned head of the present day' and as a 'fit successor of the Ottos, the Henrys, and the Fredericks of the past' in a letter to his German friend, the diplomat Hermann Speck von Sternburg.[29] At the same time, he conveyed to his close American friend, Senator Henry Cabot Lodge, his impression that 'a little common sense' should be instilled 'into the Kaiser'.[30] This calculated ambivalence – flatteries of the Kaiser especially towards German interlocutors and critical comments only to very close American and English friends – remained typical of Roosevelt's references to Wilhelm II. In his letter of 2 December 1903, Roosevelt's flatteries were extreme, doubting that 'Your Majesty' had anywhere 'more sincere admirers than in America', describing his own deep interest in German history and especially in that of the house of Hohenzollern. He continued:

You yourself have already left your mark deep on the times in which you have lived; and even nations not your own have felt the thrill of admiration which must ever be caused by the sight of a ruler who has worked at his many and heavy tasks with such brilliant mastery and in the spirit of such lofty adherence to noble ideals. You have played well a great part; you have added to the heritage of honor you have received from your fore-fathers; and, as one who believes in and admires the German people, I wish you Godspeed.[31]

But when this outwardly friendly reception of the Kaiser's advances created irritation among his English friends and the British government alike, he ridiculed the idea that he stood under Wilhelm's influence. He insisted to Lodge 'that nothing would persuade me to follow the lead of or enter into a close alliance with a man who is so jumpy, so little capable of continuity of action, and therefore, so little capable of being loyal to his friends or

[27] Pictures in Stefan Loran, *The Life and Times of Theodore Roosevelt*, Garden City, NY 1959.
[28] Bülow, *Denkwürdigkeiten*, vol. I, pp. 574f.
[29] Roosevelt to Sternburg, 27 November 1899, Roosevelt, *Letters*, vol. II, pp. 1062–3; Beale, 'Theodore Roosevelt, Wilhelm II.', pp. 182–3.
[30] Roosevelt to Lodge, 28 August 1899, Roosevelt, *Letters*, vol. II, pp. 1097–8.
[31] AA-PA, VStNA II, quoted in Vagts, *Deutschland*, p. 1944.

steadfastly hostile to an enemy'.[32] In May 1905 he professed to one of
his British friends, the diplomat Sir Cecil Arthur Spring Rice, that he
admired much about the Kaiser, but thought him 'altogether too jumpy,
too volatile in his policies, too lacking in the power of continuous and
sustained thought and action' to recognize him even as a man of the calibre
of American politicians like William H. Taft or Elihu Root. He confessed
that he got 'exasperated with the Kaiser because of his sudden vagaries' like
his Moroccan policy or his 'yellow peril' speeches, with the result that 'I
cannot of course follow or take too seriously a man whose policy is one of
such violent and often wholly irrational zigzags.' Roosevelt did not intend
to rely on Wilhelm II: 'If the Kaiser ever causes trouble it will be from
jumpiness and not because of long thought out and deliberate purpose.
In other words he is much more apt to be exasperating and unpleasant
than a dangerous neighbor.'[33] His friends advised to the contrary, as Lodge
warned from London on 3 June 1905: 'He seems to me easily understood.
He is unstable, crazy for notoriety – not to be trusted. Not a man to rely
on at all – with a saving sense of the danger of war and a strong inclination
to bully up to the verge of war.'[34] Roosevelt always took great care that
his disparaging remarks about Wilhelm II remained top secret. This was
especially true with regard to his British friends like Spring Rice, whom he
trusted and used as channels for informal and confidential communication
with the British government. At the same time he was most concerned that
King Edward VII could get hold of his letters, as he feared indiscretions
'on the part of the royal entourage'.[35]

[32] Roosevelt to Lodge, 15 May 1905, Roosevelt, *Letters*, vol. IV, pp. 1179–81.

[33] Roosevelt to Sir Arthur Spring Rice, 13 May 1905, ibid., pp. 1177–9.

[34] Lodge to Roosevelt, 3 June 1906, Henry C. Lodge (ed.), *Selections from the Correspondence of Theodore Roosevelt and Henry Cabot Lodge, 1884–1918*, vol. II, New York 1925, p. 128.

[35] Remarks on a copy of Spring Rice's letter to Roosevelt, 7 December 1904, sent to the British Secretary for Foreign Affairs, Lord Lansdowne, Cambridge University, Churchill College, Cecil Arthur Spring Rice Papers (hereafter Spring Rice Papers). To the British Ambassador in Washington, Henry Durand, Roosevelt explained: 'Whatever you do, don't let anything get round to Germany.' Durand to Lansdowne, telegram, 10 March 1905, Public Record Office, Foreign Office (PRO, FO) 800/144, Lord Lansdowne Papers; see also Roosevelt to Reid, 14 January 1907, Roosevelt, *Letters*, vol. V, p. 552. Spring Rice, who served as Counsellor at the British Embassy in St Petersburg from 1903 to 1906, was also a close friend of Secretary of State John Hay and of Senator Henry Cabot Lodge, who were involved in Roosevelt's informal communication network with the British government. Spring Rice constantly informed Roosevelt through these friends, Roosevelt's wife, and the American Ambassador to St Petersburg, George von Lengerke Meyer, about events in Russia, Wilhelm II's influence on the Tsar, and his efforts to build a Continental European alliance. See the correspondence in the Roosevelt Papers, and in the Library of Congress (LC), John Hay Papers (Hay Papers), and the Massachusetts Historical Society, Henry Cabot Lodge Papers and George von Lengerke Meyer Papers. Among Roosevelt's other close and trusted English friends was Arthur Lee, who served as Lord of the Admiralty from 1903 to 1905. William N. Tulchin, *Theodore Roosevelt and the British Empire: A Study in Presidential Statecraft*, New York 1997.

Roosevelt wanted to keep German–American relations 'on a good footing' and therefore used Wilhelm's preference for a personal relationship and the monarch's illusion about his influence over him for his own ends. But to Spring Rice he insisted: 'It is a simple wild nightmare to suppose that he can use me to the detriment of any other nation.'[36] The more the President began to understand Germany's far-reaching global plans, the more negative his image of Wilhelm II became.[37] The lowest point was reached when he learned of the so-called Hale Interview of July 1908, which bluntly uncovered Wilhelm II's far-reaching animosities towards England and Japan and his aggressive global aims. Perplexed, he wrote to Elihu Root, John Hay's successor as Secretary of State: 'The Kaiser had spent two hours talking to this unknown newspaperman in language which would invite an international explosion if made public.' Roosevelt was shocked that Wilhelm II was not only troublesome, but a real threat to the peace of the world, and he helped to prevent the publication of the interview.[38] He was no longer amused by the idea that people liked to compare him to the Kaiser, as he explained to Oscar K. Davis, the White House Correspondent of the *New York Times*:

He [the Kaiser] is, of course, very jumpy and nervous . . . and often does things which seem jumpy. But most people say that about me, whereas I never act except upon the most careful deliberation . . . They say the Emperor and I are alike, and have a great admiration for each other on that account. I do admire him, very much as I would a grizzly bear.[39]

Yet Roosevelt continued to flatter Wilhelm II, when he wrote to him shortly before he left his office as President of the United States in December 1908: 'The combination of your personality and your position render you the most influential and powerful of living men; and your hearty good will to America has been of real moment to my fellow countrymen.'[40] Whether Wilhelm II understood the ambivalence of such words remains questionable.

Unlike modern historians, Roosevelt was never plagued by the problem of the 'personal regime', and he never questioned the Emperor's

[36] Roosevelt to Spring Rice, confidential, 16 June 1905, Roosevelt, *Letters*, vol. IV, pp. 1233–4.
[37] Already during the Moroccan Crisis Roosevelt confessed to his friend, the French Ambassador Jules Jusserand, that 'his impressions of the Emperor had been very much changed to his disadvantage'. Jusserand to the French premier, Maurice Rouvier, 8 June 1905, *Documents Diplomatiques Français (1871–1914)* (*DDF*), 2nd series, Ministère des Affaires Etrangères (ed.), 41 vols., Paris 1929–36, vol. VII, pp. 7–8.
[38] Roosevelt to Root, 8 August 1908, Roosevelt, *Letters*, vol. VI, pp. 1163–5.
[39] Oscar K. Davis, *Released for Publication*, Boston 1925, pp. 86–8.
[40] Roosevelt to Wilhelm II, 26 December 1908, Roosevelt, *Letters*, vol. V, pp. 1441–2.

responsibility for German foreign policy. This corresponded to his perception of his own role as head of state, but also to his impression that the
Kaiser was one of the mightiest men in Europe. Therefore, he was naturally disappointed, when he met him in Berlin in May 1910 and realized
the loss of power Wilhelm II had suffered since the *Daily Telegraph* affair.
To the British historian Sir George O. Trevelyan he confided in 1911 that
he was

not a little surprised to find that the Emperor was by no means as great a character
in Berlin as outsiders supposed him to be, and that both the men highest in politics
and the Administration, and the people at large, took evident pleasure in having
him understand that he was not supreme, and that he must yield to the will of the
Nation on any point as to which the Nation had decided views.

In this letter Roosevelt heavily criticized Wilhelm's international behaviour,
insisting that 'he at times acts as a bully, and moreover a bully who bluffs
and then backs down'. Therefore, the ex-President did not regard 'him nor
Germany – as a pleasant national neighbor', although he clearly perceived
Wilhelm's desire for co-operation with England and the United States 'in
all matters of world policy'.[41] The two men met again at the funeral of
King Edward VII in London, which Roosevelt attended as Taft's representative, but, on this occasion too, the Kaiser's rude behaviour to some of
his fellow monarchs was not likely to change Roosevelt's opinion about
him.[42]

II

A thorough investigation of the Willy–Teddy correspondence clearly
demonstrates that, on both sides, the relationship was not considered a
private affair, but a carefully designed scheme to advance specific political
aims. Handwritten letters were the exception. The bulk of the correspondence consists of telegrams, and for the historian it is impossible to identify
those messages as being personally written either by Wilhelm II or Roosevelt
or by officials in the Wilhelmstrasse or the State Department. Roosevelt
usually drafted his letters himself, consulted his Secretary of State, and had
them rewritten or even translated into German in the State Department.
One should not underestimate the part played by the State Department in
the Willy–Teddy correspondence, as it seems to have been responsible for
much of the stereotype flatteries in Roosevelt's letters and telegrams.[43]

[41] Roosevelt to Trevelyan, 1 October 1911, ibid., vol. VII, p. 393.
[42] Roosevelt to David Gray, 5 October 1911, ibid., pp. 409–11.
[43] Roosevelt to Department of State, 2 December 1908, ibid., vol. VI, p. 1405.

Most of Wilhelm's II letters were drafted by officials in the Auswärtiges Amt. They were submitted to Chancellor Bernhard von Bülow for his consent, and finally reached the Kaiser, before they were sent or cabled to the German Embassy in Washington and then delivered directly to Roosevelt or indirectly through the State Department.[44] Thus, the Kaiser's letters were an integral part of foreign policy decision-making in Berlin, not an alien element disturbing an otherwise rational process. As a rule, Bülow was in consonance with Wilhelm II or agreed to his proposals to communicate with Roosevelt, although there were three remarkable exceptions: first, Wilhelm II announced the visit of his brother Prince Heinrich to the United States on 10 January 1902 without the consent of Bülow, who thought the christening of the Kaiser's new sports yacht *Meteor* not sufficiently important for such a demonstration of royal benevolence.[45] Second, the Emperor personally and decisively intervened in German Far Eastern policy during the Russo-Japanese War with his message of 4 June 1905 to Roosevelt, which the American Ambassador in Berlin, Charlemagne Tower, was asked to cable to the White House. A courier delivered the message to the Ambassador during the festivities of the Crown Prince's wedding, and the Auswärtiges Amt was informed only afterwards.[46] Third, Wilhelm II again tried to evade the Wilhelmstrasse when he instructed the Naval Attaché at the German Embassy in Washington, Commander Georg Hebbinghaus, to deliver his letter of 4 September 1905 and three pictures to Roosevelt.[47] Although the letter revealed the Kaiser's deepest anxieties about the 'yellow peril', British perfidy against the 'White race', and the future 'fight for life and death between the 'White' + the 'Yellow', and although one of the pictures was a copy of the famous painting 'Peoples of Europe save your holiest possessions!', Bülow did not feel particularly alarmed when he finally got to read it on 22 September. He advised State Secretary Oswald von Richthofen that the letter could be delivered if its secrecy were

[44] See e.g. Wilhelm II to Roosevelt, 6 February 1907, Roosevelt Papers. There were long discussions about whether to send a letter or a telegram between Kaiser, Chancellor, and the Auswärtiges Amt (AA) before this letter was finally sent. Wilhelm II got angry when the AA and Bülow suggested a telegram, after Bülow had at first consented to a letter, and insisted on a letter exclaiming: 'I do not let myself be pushed around like a bureaucrat!' Bülow's notes, 22 January 1907, Tschirschky to Wilhelm II, 23 January 1907 with the Kaiser's remarks, and draft of the letter to Roosevelt, 6 February 1907, AA-PA, VStNA 16 secr., R 17380.

[45] Wilhelm II to Roosevelt, telegram, 10 January 1902, *FRUS* 1902, 422. Report of the Austrian Ambassador in Berlin, Ladislaus von Szögyényi-Marich, 26 February 1902, as quoted in Katharine Lerman, 'The Decisive Relationship: Kaiser Wilhelm II and Chancellor Bernhard von Bülow, 1900–1905', in Röhl and Sombart, *Kaiser Wilhelm II*, p. 227.

[46] Wilhelm II to Reginald Tower, strictly confidential, 4 June 1907, in Tower to Roosevelt, 9 June 1905, Tower to Roosevelt, telegram, 4 June 1905, Roosevelt Papers. For more details on this letter see below.

[47] Wilhelm II to Roosevelt, 4 September 1905, AA-PA, VStNA 16 secr., R 17380.

assured, and if Roosevelt was told that the letter was strictly confidential. The slick Chancellor wanted to deflect Wilhelm's wrath, which was to be expected if he opposed the letter. Instead, the American President was supposed to act as an accomplice in hushing up the irresponsible remarks of the monarch. Only the German Ambassador in Washington, Hermann Speck von Sternburg, had the courage to raise serious doubts about this procedure and to warn against the delivery. Bülow did not back him up, but rather hid behind him and telegraphed to Wilhelm: 'I liked the letter very much, but Sternburg urgently advises against the sending', and then he begged Wilhelm II to follow Sternburg's counsel. Finally, Hebbinghaus was directed by the Auswärtiges Amt not to deliver letter and the picture, but this order did not reach him before he arrived in New York. Even two years later, Wilhelm II still grumbled that 'Specky, Auswärtiges Amt, and the Chancellor' had 'forced me to recall the letter and take the picture back!!'[48]

The events leading to the *Daily Telegraph* affair and the Hale Interview in 1908 suggest that the opportunistic handling of Wilhelm's letter by Bülow was not an exception but had become the rule under the 'personal regime' during Bülow's chancellorship. Only Sternburg's courage in opposing the Kaiser prevented a catastrophe of similar dimensions to that of 1908.[49] The character traits of the men Wilhelm II had chosen as his closest advisors, and their intense dependence on the Kaiser's will were heavy liabilities for a rational conduct of foreign policy. Bülow was known as 'Bernhard the Obliging', as a man who seldom contested the monarch's will directly, who regarded himself as the tool of the Kaiser, and who believed in the 'personal rule' of Wilhelm II. His mostly charming, often also ridiculous flatteries were essentially the result of falseness and a shallow, but also extremely ambitious, character. His 'Byzantine sycophancy'[50] reinforced not only the Kaiser's inflated self-perception, but also his misperception of the political environment.[51] Bülow constantly supported Wilhelm's illusions

[48] Bülow to Richthofen, 13 September 1905, Richthofen to Sternburg, 16 September 1905, Sternburg to Richthofen, 17 September 1905, Bülow to Wilhelm II, 19 September 1905, report by Hebbinghaus, 2 October 1905, and Wilhelm's remarks on Sternburg's letter to the AA, February 1907, all in AA-PA, VStNA 16 secr., R17380.

[49] For a thorough investigation and documentation see Peter Winzen, *Das Kaiserreich am Abgrund. Die Daily-Telegraph-Affäre und das Hale-Interview von 1908. Darstellung und Dokumentation*, Stuttgart 2002; Ralph R. Menning and Carol B. Menning, '"Baseless Allegations": Wilhelm II and the Hale Interview of 1908', *Central European History*, 16 (1983), pp. 368–97.

[50] Lerman, 'Decisive Relationship', p. 226.

[51] Katharine A. Lerman, *The Chancellor as Courtier: Bernhard von Bülow and the Government of Germany 1900–1909*, Cambridge 1990; Röhl, *Wilhelm II.*, vol. II, pp. 642–9; Lamar Cecil, *The German Diplomatic Service, 1871–1914*, Princeton 1976, pp. 281–8; Isabel V. Hull, 'Bernhard von Bülow', in

that Roosevelt was a friend towards whom confidence and intimacy were appropriate, if this helped him to gain the Kaiser's support for his policies. Thus in August 1905 he advised Wilhelm that he should not forget 'that the President is a great admirer of Your Majesty and would like to rule the world hand in hand with Your Majesty, as he certainly conceives himself to be the American pendant to Your Majesty', while Wilhelm II accepted such praise as 'very flattering to me'![52]

The German Ambassador in Washington, Hermann Speck von Sternburg, also played an important role as mediator in the Willy–Teddy relationship. Wilhelm II had personally picked Roosevelt's friend Sternburg for the post as a favour to the President when tensions between the United States and Germany had dangerously escalated during the Venezuela crisis in January 1903. Sternburg became the Kaiser's mouthpiece and the medium for his efforts to influence Roosevelt. Using his personal relationship with Roosevelt, he could circumvent the State Department, and deliver the messages from Berlin directly to the President. In 1904–6 he also became the tool of Bülow and Friedrich von Holstein, the 'grey eminence' in the Auswärtiges Amt, in their efforts to engage Roosevelt for their political aims in China and Morocco.[53] Encouraged by Bülow, Sternburg adopted the habit of speaking in the Kaiser's name when he presented his political messages to Roosevelt. This gave his notes and verbal communications substantially more weight, but also exposed the monarch as being personally responsible for German day-to-day political decisions. Thus in 1905, when Roosevelt saw himself confronted with Germany's political brinkmanship in Morocco, he immediately assumed that the Kaiser's 'pipe dreams' were responsible for the diplomatic bluff which actually originated with Bülow and Holstein.[54] At the same time, Sternburg constantly endeavoured to flatter the Kaiser through magnifying Roosevelt's sympathy for the monarch, and thereby contributed to his misperception of Roosevelt's attitude.

III

Wilhelm II decided to start his 'personal diplomacy' with Roosevelt by sending Prince Heinrich to the United States in a time when economic

---

Wilhelm von Sternburg (ed.), *Die deutschen Kanzler von Bismarck bis Schmidt*, Königstein/Ts. 1985, pp. 69–85.
[52] Bülow to Wilhelm II, 31 August 1904, *GP*, vol. XIX, 1, pp. 535–7; Beale, *Roosevelt*, p. 433.
[53] Stefan H. Rinke, *Zwischen Weltpolitik und Monroedoktrin: Botschafter Speck von Sternburg und die deutsch-amerikanischen Beziehungen, 1898–1908*, Stuttgart 1992.
[54] Roosevelt to Taft, 8 April 1905, Roosevelt, *Letters*, vol. IV, p. 1159.

competition, a growing perception of cultural and political differences, and the clashing interests of the two expanding nations in South America, East Asia, and the Pacific had created a climate of distrust and enmity in Germany and the United States. Germans were talking about the 'American peril (*amerikanische Gefahr*)', a catchword expressing German anxieties about a future world dominated by America through its economic superiority, and Americans discussed the 'German danger', which reflected American worries about German expansionistic aims and possible military interventions in Latin America. Under these circumstances, German–American friendship was not very popular in either country. But, in cultivating the Willy–Teddy relationship, Wilhelm II and Roosevelt refused openly to exploit the potential of the German–American antagonism in the sense of a manipulative social-imperialistic strategy.[55]

Not domestic politics, but considerations concerning international relations were decisive for both men. It is possible to recognize a clear modification in Wilhelm's attitude towards the United States at the beginning of 1902, although this was a change only in tactical behaviour, not in deeper convictions. Until then, Wilhelm II had fully supported those groups of the ruling elite which had constantly used the slogan of the 'amerikanische Gefahr' for agitation. He had utilized the image of an American enemy in his endeavours to create a united continental Europe under German hegemony. Already in 1896–7 he had warned the Tsar against the 'amerikanische Gefahr' and had pressed him to agree to a continental German–Russian–French alliance economically directed against America.[56] In September 1897 he had tried to use the escalating Spanish–American conflict over Cuba as a lever to unite the European monarchs in solidarity for the Spanish crown against the 'Americano-British company for international robbery and war instigation'.[57] During 1901 he had approached the British Foreign

---

[55] Fiebig-von Hase, *Lateinamerika*, pp. 742–88, 961–6.

[56] Wilhelm II to Auswärtiges Amt, telegram, 9 September 1896, secret memorandum of Chancellor Chlodwig Fürst zu Hohenlohe-Schillingsfürst about a conversation with the Russian Tsar Nicholas in Breslau, 10 September 1896, Wilhelm II to Hohenlohe-Schillingsfürst, telegram, 20 October 1896, *GP*, vol. XI, pp. 360–2, 369–70; Memorandum of State Secretary Adolf Freiherr Marschall von Bieberstein about his conversation with the Russian Foreign Minister Count Michael Muraview, 31 January 1897, Bülow from St Petersburg to Auswärtiges Amt, telegram, 10 August 1897, ibid., vol. XIII, pp. 56–61, 75–6.

[57] In German: 'Amerikano-Britische Aktiengesellschaft für Internationale Raub- und Kriegsanstiftung', Wilhelm II to Bülow, 28 September 1897, AA-PA, Spaniens Besitzungen in Amerika 2, vol. I.

Minister Lord Lansdowne,[58] King Edward VII,[59] the French Ambassador in Berlin,[60] and the French journalist Count Pierre de Ségur,[61] with the idea of a European alliance against the 'American peril' and American pretensions in East Asia. Wilhelm II's anti-American statements were widely published in the international press. Bülow's efforts to deny the authenticity of such reports[62] were not very effective, especially since the Kaiser's remarks reflected a wider movement of German public opinion. As the American Ambassador Andrew D. White wrote from Berlin as early as January 1898: 'On the Continent there has never been a time, probably, when ill will towards the United States has been so strong as at present.' American public opinion responded similarly. Holleben reported from Washington that 'Germany is here the absolutely most hated country'.[63]

International developments, and particularly the deterioration of Anglo-German relations and British efforts to cultivate the relationship with the United States brought about the change in the Kaiser's attitude towards America. Both developments indicated that the international environment was changing in a direction which endangered the imperial strategy of the 'policy of the free hand', which Wilhelm II, Bülow, and Admiral Alfred von

---

[58] In January 1901, Wilhelm II feared Russo-American co-operation in the Far East against Germany and England. He reported to Bülow from Osborne, where he had met Edward VII, that he had explained to the astonished Lansdowne that, 'on one side, there stood Russia and America as states with non-European interests, and on the other side Europe that had to be reunited to constitute a counterweight. In my considerations I did not take only the present into account but had also the future before my eyes.' Eckardstein to AA, telegram, 29 January 1901, and Wilhelm II to Bülow, 29 January 1901, *GP*, vol. XVII, pp. 23–9; Lansdowne's notes on the conversation with Wilhelm II are in PRO, FO, 800/130, Lansdowne Papers.

[59] Wilhelm II urged Edward VII during the latter's visit to Wilhelmshöhe on 23 August 1901 that England should give up her policy of 'splendid isolation' and cooperate with the Continent. Wilhelm II to Bülow, 23 August 1901, *GP*, vol. XVII, p. 97.

[60] Wilhelm II spoke to Ambassador Emmanuel Marquis de Noailles about the fight of the Occident against the Asian world, as part of which he counted Russia, Japan, and America, against whom England, France, and Germany should ally themselves to build a united front. Next to the 'danger asiatique' he warned about 'le grand danger' for Europe, the 'Américains'. Marquis de Noailles to the French Foreign Minister Théophile Delcassé, Berlin, 1 March 1901, *DDF*, 2nd series (1901–11), vol. I, Paris 1930, pp. 147–50.

[61] Wilhelm II had given de Ségur an interview on board the *Hohenzollern* in Odde, Norway. The interview was published in several French and American papers. An official denial was impossible because the Kaiser himself had confirmed the interview's authenticity. Memorandum of Friedrich von Holstein for Bülow, 3 November 1901, notes of Otto Hammann, chief of the Press Bureau in the AA, 5 November 1901, and report of the German Embassy in Washington to Bülow, 9 November 1901, AA-PA, VStNA 16 secr., R 17380.

[62] Report of the American Ambassador to Berlin, Andrew D. White, about a conversation with Bülow, 26 March 1898, NA, DS, RG 59, DD Germany.

[63] White to Secretary of State, John Sherman, 7 January 1898, NA, DS, RG 59, DD Germany; Holleben to Hohenlohe-Schillingsfürst, 1 January 1898, AA-PA, VStNA 1.

Tirpitz had initiated in the context of *Weltpolitik* and the two fleet laws of 1898 and 1900. The underlying idea was that German foreign policy should keep out of all international conflicts, until the strong battleship fleet, which was being built according to the Tirpitzplan, was available and could be used as a lever to extort overseas concessions from the main sea powers. Until that moment, German foreign policy would pass through a 'risk period', during which its main function was to dispel possible suspicions among foreign powers, which could effectively block Germany's long-range plans. As Volker Berghahn and others have demonstrated, the ultimate aim of this strategy was to depose England as the leading sea power. The Imperial government hoped to preserve the international *status quo* during the period of German naval weakness only to revolutionize it as soon as the German power base was strong enough to make the Empire a bold bidder for a leading place among the world powers.[64] But international developments did not wait until Germany believed herself ready to ask for her 'place in the sun', while at the same time the extensive naval propaganda campaign created inflated expectations about future gains overseas among economic interest groups and nationalistic circles alike. Already around the turn of the century the first signs of these developments indicated that the Kaiser's 'free hand' strategy would end in an impasse. But Wilhelm II, Bülow, and Tirpitz possessed neither the insight into the fatal political shortcomings of the Tirpitzplan nor the will to readjust their foreign policy expectations and long-term strategy to actual global developments. They would much rather muddle through with *ad hoc* tactical manoeuvres, which aimed at increasing tensions among the leading powers and preventing a consolidation among them. As Spring Rice remarked to John Hay in 1905, German foreign policy excelled in 'a policy of exciting one nation against the other by means of personal suggestions or offers of friendly offices in case of trouble'.[65] Thus, the 'zig-zag' course was not the result of imperial irrationality and jumpiness, as Roosevelt at first believed, but a consequence of unrealistic political aims and a failed general strategy. The Kaiser's 'jumpiness' only made things worse.

---

[64] For the anti-British foundation of the Tirpitzplan: Volker R. Berghahn, *Der Tirpitz-plan. Genesis und Verfall einer innenpolitischen Krisenstrategie unter Wilhelm II.*, Düsseldorf 1971, pp. 380–415; Volker R. Berghahn, *Germany and the Approach of War in 1914*, 8th repr., Houndsmills and London 1988, pp. 25–64; Michael Epkenhans, *Die wilhelminische Flottenrüstung 1908–1914. Weltmachtstreben, industrieller Fortschritt, soziale Integration*, Munich, 1991, pp. 15–51; Paul M. Kennedy, *The Rise of Anglo-German Antagonism, 1860–1914*, London 1980, pp. 415–31; Klaus Hildebrand, *Das vergangene Reich. Deutsche Außenpolitik von Bismarck bis Hitler*, Stuttgart 1995, pp. 190–221.

[65] Memorandum by Spring Rice for Hay, January 1905, Hay Papers.

Wilhelm's decision to send his brother Prince Heinrich to the United States was one of these 'means of personal suggestions'. The improvement of German–American relations by such means became necessary when the failure of the Anglo-German alliance talks in the autumn of 1901 indicated a rapid deterioration in Anglo-German relations and when, at the same time, the successful conclusion of the Hay–Pauncefote Treaty in October 1901[66] signalled a remarkable Anglo-American *rapprochement*.[67] Despite this, Wilhelm II believed that he could contain the British with the help of the United States. An article in the *National Review* in October 1901 caused the German Ambassador in London to warn that a 'radical change of British foreign policy', going as far as including British collaboration with Russia and Japan in China, could be imminent. Wilhelm II reacted angrily by proposing to seek commercial co-operation with the United States with the ultimate goal to 'smash British world trade and, together with the Americans, inflict such heavy losses on the English that they will be willy-nilly forced to seek a better political understanding with us'. He also dreamed that in this case all other nations would join Germany and a completely different result would be reached than that which Metternich had forecast.[68]

Wilhelm II presumed that his brother's visit to the United States could cement such a German–American understanding directed against England on the basis of a political compromise about South America. Such an assumption seems justified because the Prince believed in a political mandate and intended to negotiate with the American government about such hot issues as the planned German intervention in Venezuela and the creation of a German sphere of influence in South America. The Wilhelmstrasse became highly alarmed when the Prince refused 'to take political considerations into account even when performing a political mission' and to discuss the opportunity of his plans with the Auswärtiges Amt. Since he belonged to the Imperial household and was an Admiral of the Navy, he insisted that he would take orders only from the Kaiser. Bülow had to apply to Wilhelm II to prevent the Prince's trip becoming 'more advantageous to our enemies and enviers than to German interests'. Finally Wilhelm II advised his brother: 'Keep your eyes open and your mouth shut' and the trip was thus

---

[66] In this treaty Great Britain renounced her rights to participate with the Americans in building a trans-Isthmian canal.

[67] For the Anglo-German alliance talks see Kennedy, *Anglo-German Antagonism*, pp. 223–50; Hildebrand, *Das vergangene Reich*, pp. 213–21; for the Anglo-American *rapprochement* see Bradford Perkins, *The Great Rapprochement: England and the United States 1895–1914*, London 1969, pp. 173–85.

[68] Metternich to AA, telegram, 22 October 1901, with Wilhelm II's remarks, AA-PA, VStNA 16 secr., R 17380.

reduced to what Holstein later called a 'fairly useful pleasure trip'.[69] Prince
Heinrich was much welcomed by American society circles and by German–
Americans, but the political impact of his visit was marginal. Yet Wilhelm
II firmly believed in a major improvement, until the Anglo-German inter-
vention in Venezuela abruptly ended that dream in December 1902. The
Kaiser's misperception was due to his vanity and exposed the anachronistic
nature of his personal approach to foreign policy.[70]

That the Kaiser's and Bülow's anti-British tactics were utterly out of step
with American reality in 1902 was verified when Bülow ordered Holleben
to start a campaign against the highly respected British Ambassador, Sir
Julian Pauncefote, accusing him of anti-American machinations during
the Spanish–American War. While Holleben believed in the success of this
'diplomatic war against England', the truth was that his own reputation and
that of his government were damaged. Secretary of State John Hay asked
Roosevelt: 'Is this the speech of great nations or the shrieks of angry house-
maids pulling caps over the policeman?' The American press interpreted
Holleben's efforts as obnoxious slander.[71]

To Roosevelt, deeds were more important than imperial flatteries, and
what preoccupied him in 1902 was Germany's obvious intention to intervene in Venezuela and force the Venezuelan President to pay long-
outstanding debts. Roosevelt had been warned by his naval advisors that
Germany would either use the intervention as a pretext for the acquisition
of a naval base, or to establish a customs receivership in Venezuela, and
thereby gain control over the country. Since such actions would *de facto*
mean an infringement of the Monroe Doctrine, Roosevelt prepared for a
possible naval show-down with Germany over Venezuela, and ordered the
American fleet to Puerto Rican waters for winter manoeuvres. When the
Anglo-German blockade of the Venezuelan coastline began in December

---

[69] Holstein's memorandum concerning Prince Heinrich's trip to the United States, 29 January 1902,
Bundesarchiv Koblenz, Bernhard von Bülow Papers; Bülow to Prince Heinrich, 30 January 1902,
GP, vol. xvii, p. 243; A. O. Klausmann (ed.), *Kaiserreden. Reden und Erlasse, Briefe und Telegramme
Kaiser Wilhelms des Zweiten. Ein Charakterbild des Deutschen Kaisers*, Leipzig 1902, p. 328; Holstein
to Johanna von Radolin, 31 January 1902, Norman Rich and M. H. Fisher (eds.), *The Holstein Papers*,
vol. iv, Cambridge 1963, p. 251; Fiebig-von Hase, *Lateinamerika*, pp. 943–53; Pommerin, *Kaiser*, pp.
107–13.

[70] Sternburg to Roosevelt, 15 December 1902, Roosevelt Papers; remarks of Wilhelm II regarding
Sternburg's letter to Bülow, 26 November 1902, AA-PA, VStNA 16 secr., R 17380. For differences
in the historiographical evaluation of Prince Heinrich's visit to the United States compare Vagts,
Deutschland, pp. 1939–40; Fiebig-von Hase, *Lateinamerika*, pp. 943–66; Lammersdorf, *Anfänge*, pp.
45–54; Pommerin, *Kaiser*, pp. 104–13.

[71] Hay to Roosevelt, 15 February 1902, Roosevelt Papers; Vagts, *Deutschland*, pp. 1400–10; Nelson M.
Blake, 'Ambassadors at the Court of Theodore Roosevelt', *Mississippi Valley Historical Review*, 42
(1955–6), pp. 183–6.

1902, the American navy was on the spot, and Roosevelt was able to force Germany into accepting arbitration of the outstanding issues. Roosevelt later claimed that he had taught the Kaiser a lesson.[72] When Roosevelt explained to Sternburg that the American and German navies had already viewed each other as future adversaries during the crisis, this certainly did not encourage Wilhelm's enthusiasm for personal diplomacy with the President during the coming months.[73]

In December 1903, Russo-Japanese tensions over Manchuria threatened to explode into war, and American interests in the region were also affected. Now it was Roosevelt who courted the Kaiser with excessive flatteries which climaxed in his remark to Sternburg that people in America realized more and more 'that the steering wheel of the global ship was in two hands, those of the German Emperor and those of President Roosevelt, and that the loss of one of these men would have far-reaching consequences for civilization'.[74] The President hoped to get German co-operation against Russia's expansion in Manchuria and tried to encourage Wilhelm to expand into Eastern Europe, because that would keep Russia busy in Europe and make it more co-operative in China. Wilhelm II reacted with elaborate personal flatteries but without any encouragement for such political proposals. He did not want to be talked into a conflict with Russia, but rather insisted on expansion in South America.[75] His answer reflected the fact that German and American interests and strategies with regard to the Russo-Japanese conflict could not be harmonized, although both the American and the German governments at first welcomed the war and hoped that Russia and Japan would be weakened.

But American and German motives were not the same: the Roosevelt government fought for the open-door policy and the integrity of all of China, therefore condemned Russian occupation of Manchuria, and welcomed the energetic Japanese moves to throw Russia out of the region. The President was convinced that the Kaiser was partly responsible for the war,

---

[72] Roosevelt to William B. Thayer, 21 August 1916, Roosevelt, *Letters*, vol. VIII, pp. 1102–4; for a detailed analysis: Fiebig-von Hase, *Lateinamerika*, pp. 846–1083; Ragnhild Fiebig-von Hase, 'The German Challenge to American Hegemony in the Caribbean: The Venezuela Crisis of 1902–3', in Walther L. Bernecker (ed.), *1898: su significado par y Centroamérica y el Caribe*, Frankfurt am Main 1998, pp. 77–112; Morris, *Theodore Rex*, pp. 177–92.

[73] There are only some ceremonial letters by Wilhelm II for the year 1903. Wilhelm II to Roosevelt, 29 March 1903 and 25 June 1903, Roosevelt Papers.

[74] Roosevelt to Wilhelm II, 2 December 1903, Sternburg to Bülow, 12 December 1903, and 20 December 1903 (quotation), AA-PA, VStNA 16, R 17336.

[75] Wilhelm II to Roosevelt, 14 January 1904, Roosevelt Papers; Wilhelm's remarks on Sternburg's telegram of 12 December 1903 were: 'Cheers, the Russians are there! No, South America is our goal, old boy.' AA-PA, VStNA 16, R 17336.

as 'he has done all he could to bring it about'.[76] Since the beginning of the conflict, Roosevelt was determined to enter the war on Japan's side if the continental European powers tried to withhold from Japan the fruits of her victories against Russia, as they had done after the Chinese–Japanese War of 1894–5.[77] During 1904, Roosevelt repeatedly approached the Kaiser through Sternburg to reach an understanding on terms which would permit an early peace on the basis of Manchuria's return to China, Japan's predominance in Korea, and the integrity and open door of China as an entity. He showed himself interested in saving the balance of power between Russia and Japan in the Far East.[78]

In contrast, Wilhelm II and his advisors were indifferent to Manchuria's fate, encouraged and quietly supported Russia's engagement there, and were only concerned to uphold the open door in the Yangtse basin, where German ambitions and British interests collided. They encouraged Roosevelt to support the open-door principle, mainly in the Yangtse region, but intended to keep themselves in the background and did not commit themselves to anything, especially not in Manchuria.[79] This pattern was visible in Bülow's proposal to Roosevelt of February 1904, according to which the Powers should bind themselves to respect China's neutrality, with the exception of the war zone, that is, Manchuria. But Roosevelt and Hay changed this proposal to fit their own intentions, and sent out their 'neutralization' circular on 8 February which contained the request to observe the neutrality of the 'entity' of China.[80] The whole manoeuvre did not lead to concrete results, although the powers consented, except for the Russian government learning about the German authorship and feeling duped.[81]

Roosevelt's interest in the war centred on events in the Pacific, and he realized the European dimension of the conflict only later. In contrast,

---

[76] Roosevelt to Spring Rice, 24 July 1905, Roosevelt, *Letters*, vol. IV, pp. 1283–7.

[77] John Hay diary, 28 May 1904, LC, John Hay Papers. After the outbreak of the war America's naval strategists worked on plans for a campaign assuming war between a coalition of Germany, France, and Russia opposed to an alliance of England, Japan, and the United States. NA, RG 225, Joint Board Records, draft of Rear Admiral Henry Taylor, 10 June 1904.

[78] John Hay diary, 10 August 1904, Hay Papers; Bülow to Wilhelm II, 31 August 1904, *GP*, vol. XIX, 1, pp. 535–7; Sternburg to AA, 5 December 1904, AA-PA, VStNA 16.

[79] Bülow to Wilhelm II, 31 August 1905, Bülow to Sternburg, telegram, 5 September 1904, Bülow to Embassy Washington, telegram, 22 October 1904, *GP*, vol. XIX, 1, pp. 535–7, 541, 543–4.

[80] Bülow to Embassy Washington, telegram, 5 February 1904, *GP*, vol. XIX, 1, pp. 98f.; Sternburg's memorandum, 5 February 1904, NA, DS, RG 59, Notes from Foreign Missions, Germany (NFMG); Hay diary, 7 and 8 February 1904, Hay Papers.

[81] Report of the German Ambassador to St Petersburg, Friedrich Count von Alvensleben to AA, telegram, 12 February 1904, *GP*, vol. XIX, 1, pp. 106–7.

Wilhelm's and Bülow's enthusiasm for the war had mostly to do with European affairs: they saw Germany in the role of the *tertius gaudens*, and hoped to change the power balance in continental Europe to Germany's advantage during the war. Because Russia's military power was distracted in the Far East, France's position in Europe was indirectly weakened, and since England was allied to Russia's foe, Japan, an Anglo-Russian *rapprochement* seemed improbable. Germany remained uncommitted and thus was, as they believed, in a position to tip the scales. In Holstein's eyes, America's anti-Russian policy in the Far East also reinforced the improbability of an Anglo-Russian compromise: 'America had sided against Russia, and England would and had to stay on the same side as America.'[82] The changed balance of power would ultimately enable Germany to broaden its global power base through unifying the European continent under German hegemony. Friendly, although non-committal, support for Russia in East Asia would be helpful in inducing Russia to sign an alliance treaty with Germany. Wilhelm II flattered the Tsar as the saviour of Europe against the 'yellow peril' to encourage the Russian adventure in East Asia.[83] At the same time, warnings from the Auswärtiges Amt and Tirpitz that an alliance with Russia would endanger relations with America, might even lead to a British preventive stroke against the German navy, would push America into the arms of England, and, therefore, would mean an early end to *Weltpolitik*, demonstrated once more the dangerous contradictions which the subordination of imperial foreign policy under the dictates of the rigid Tirpitzplan with its long-term anti-British perspective implied. Support for the Russian fleet on its move to East Asia brought Germany to the brink of war with England during the Hull incident in October 1904, and German diplomatic activities aroused increasing mistrust in all of Europe.[84] Despite all the efforts undertaken, the Kaiser's hopes for an alliance with Russia were disappointed in December 1904 when the Tsar rejected his advances. He had become suspicious of Germany's motives, and insisted on France's

---

[82] Holstein to Bülow, 17 January 1904, *Holstein Papers*, vol. IV, pp. 277–8.

[83] Wilhelm II's deliberate use of the 'yellow peril' slogan was more than a personal idiosyncrasy and fitted into the general pattern of German foreign policy under his regime, i.e. to encourage Russia's Far Eastern adventures and later to sow discord between the United States and Japan. Not the substance, but only the form of Wilhelm II's 'yellow peril' propaganda disturbed the official policy of the Wilhelmstrasse. Ute Mehnert, *Deutschland, Amerika und die 'Gelbe Gefahr'. Zur Karriere eines Schlagworts in der Großen Politik, 1905–1917*, Stuttgart 1995, pp. 110–19.

[84] Memorandum of Secretary of State Oswald von Richthofen, no date, but early in July 1904, *GP*, vol. XIX, 1, pp. 194–6; Volker R. Berghahn, *Der Tirpitz-plan*, pp. 386–90, 407–11.

agreement as a precondition. But France definitely refused to consider such an alliance.[85]

As Wilhelm's and Bülow's fears grew that Germany might become isolated or even be attacked by England, co-operation with the American President became attractive again, and Bülow started a new series of Imperial flatteries towards Roosevelt.[86] To Wilhelm he outlined his policy towards America on 26 December 1904: Germany could not support America's Far Eastern aims just to please her and had to follow a course that would not manoeuvre her into conflict with Russia. But at the same time the 'so important relations of Your Majesty with the American President and the slowly improving friendly relations of Germany with America should not be imperilled'. Because Roosevelt admired the Japanese, Bülow advised Wilhelm to drop the 'yellow peril' argument the Kaiser cherished so much, and to stress instead the danger that France and England might mediate peace. The result would be, as Bülow insisted German diplomacy should argue, that a new concentration of powers – the combination of the Anglo-Japanese and the Franco-Russian alliance – would appear, and that those powers would then carve up China among themselves. Roosevelt was to be warned that only close German–American co-operation could possibly prevent the formation of such a 'quadruple alliance'. Thus, Bülow hoped to get Germany out of its self-inflicted isolation with the help of America and also improve relations with Japan. Wilhelm II reluctantly consented.[87] After the fall of Port Arthur in January 1905, Bülow repeated the diplomatic procedure of the preceding year: the German chargé d'affaires at Washington was to warn Roosevelt in the name of Wilhelm II about the quadruple alliance and suggest that the President should ask the powers to pledge themselves not to seek compensations after the war and to respect the integrity of China with the exception of the North of China, that is, Manchuria.[88]

---

[85] For Germany's policy toward Russia 1904–5, see Barbara Vogel, *Deutsche Rußlandpolitik. Das Scheitern der deutschen Weltpolitik unter Bülow 1900–1906*, Düsseldorf 1973, pp. 45–6, 169–73, 189–231; Jonathan Steinberg, 'Germany and the Russo-Japanese War', *American Historical Review*, 75 (1970), pp. 1965–86.

[86] Bülow used the unveiling of the statue of Friedrich the Great by Roosevelt to initiate a press campaign of eulogies about Roosevelt as 'man, thinker, and statesman'. He also saw to it that these articles reached Roosevelt. Bülow to Hammann, 20 November 1904, Richthofen to Sternburg, 25 November 1904, AA-PA, VStNA 16, R 17338.

[87] Bülow to Wilhelm II, 24 December 1904 and 26 December 1904, Holstein's memorandum, 28 December 1904, *GP*, vol. XIX, 2, pp. 547–9, 400–3, 551–6.

[88] Bülow to Bussche, telegram, 4 January 1905, ibid., pp. 556–7.

Roosevelt, who was by now suspicious about Wilhelm's aspirations in China and Europe,[89] decided 'to nail the matter with him'. He asked Sternburg to express to the Kaiser his full accord and thanks, and then ordered Hay to send out his 'self-denying' circular asking respect for the 'entity' of China. To the satisfaction of the President, Wilhelm and Bülow understood that they had to consent to their 'own' proposal.[90] Thus, the veiled diplomatic help for Russia which the Kaiser had intended was nullified, and the whole move only angered the Russians.[91] When the powers reacted positively and pledged their disinterestedness, Roosevelt became more and more suspicious that the Kaiser wanted to exploit the situation and was playing a double game. His mistrust grew during the following months when Wilhelm's and Bülow's agitation against England increased, and he realized that they obstructed his cautious attempts at peace mediation.[92] Roosevelt's confidence in Wilhelm II was further undermined when the latter publicly warned against the 'yellow peril' in May, and this damage could not be repaired by Wilhelm's assurances that these were only 'lies' which were spread by the 'hostile and especially the British press'.[93]

Finally, the imperial government started its campaign against France in Morocco to weaken the Anglo-French Entente and force France to give up her resistance against the planned Russo-German-French alliance. Bülow and Holstein firmly believed that they could neutralize British assistance for France by gaining Roosevelt's co-operation. They also assumed that the American President would be willing to insist on the preservation of the

---

[89] In October 1904 Roosevelt had already been informed by the American embassy at St Petersburg about the possibility of a German–Russian alliance. Spencer Eddy to Hay, 29 October 1904, Hay Papers; Sternburg to AA, telegram, 5 December 1904, AA-PA, VStNA 16, R 17338. In January 1905, Spring Rice was in Washington for informal talks with Roosevelt about the European and East Asian situation. He informed Roosevelt and Hay about the Kaiser's efforts to create a European continental alliance with Russia and France, and to 'shut out England + America'. Hay diary, 2 and 3 February 1905, Hay Papers.

[90] Bülow to Bussche, telegram, 5 January 1905, *GP*, vol. xix, 2, pp. 556–7; Bussche to Roosevelt, 5 January 1905, Roosevelt Papers; Hay's Circular, 13 January 1905, *FRUS* 1905, pp. 1–4; Roosevelt to Sternburg, 10 January 1905, in Bussche to AA, telegram, 11 January 1905, Tower to Richthofen, 14 January 1905, Bülow to Bussche, 17 January 1905, Roosevelt to Sternburg, 18 January 1905, in Bussche to Bülow, 18 January 1905, *GP*, vol. xix, 2, pp. 557–9, 562–3.

[91] Hay diary, 31 January 1905, Hay Papers.

[92] Sternburg to AA, telegram, 21 March 1905, Bülow to Sternburg, telegrams, 22 and 23 March 1905, Sternburg to AA, telegram, 1 April 1905, *GP*, vol. xix, 2, pp. 582–7, 590–1; Roosevelt to William Taft, private, 30 March 1905, Roosevelt, *Letters*, vol. iv, p. 1150; Roosevelt to Sternburg, 31 March 1905, Roosevelt Papers.

[93] Roosevelt referred to Wilhelm's speeches in Strassburg and Wilhelmshaven. Sternburg to Bülow, telegram, 13 May 1905, AA-PA, Preussen pers. 1, no. 13. These passages were omitted when the document was published in *GP*, vol. xx, 2, pp. 622–3. Wilhelm II to Roosevelt, telegram, 15 May 1905, AA-PA Deutschland 135, secr., 4a, 1c.

open door policy not only in China, but also in Morocco.[94] But already on 7 March 1905, when Sternburg proposed such a co-operation in the name of the Kaiser for the first time, Roosevelt declared that his country's interests in Morocco were too small to justify an American involvement. Hay was perplexed about Wilhelm's indiscretion, because already 'by giving England and France the least hint of what he has said to us in the last few weeks we could make very serious trouble'.[95] Despite Roosevelt's negative answer, Bülow and Holstein were certain that they could count on the President's co-operation. Due to Sternburg's exuberantly optimistic reporting, they completely over-estimated Roosevelt's sympathies for the Kaiser and the German cause. Again and again they instructed Sternburg to warn Roosevelt about the quadruple alliance and the inner connection between the Far Eastern war and the Morocco question. They impressed on him the necessity to assemble the signatory powers of the Morocco Treaty of 1880 for a conference to discuss Morocco's future. The reason for their tenacity was that in their tactical calculations Roosevelt's consent was essential to overcome British opposition to the conference plan. If Great Britain accepted the Sultan's invitation to the conference, France would be left isolated, humiliated, and exposed to Germany's pressures and war threats until she agreed to the Morocco conference and in the long run acceded to the planned continental alliance.[96] The Anglo-French *Entente* would be ruined and Germany's position definitely strengthened *vis-à-vis* her true foe, England. Thus Roosevelt's support for the conference idea became a keystone in Germany's plans to change the European balance of power.[97]

Roosevelt was stunned by the Kaiser's language,[98] but remained friendly and uncommitted, because he could not count on the approval of Congress

---

[94] For the Moroccan Crisis see Heiner Raulff, *Zwischen Machtpolitik und Imperialismus. Die deutsche Frankreichpolitik 1904–5*, Düsseldorf 1976, especially pp. 84–125; Stefan Rinke, 'A Diplomat's Dilemma: Ambassador von Sternburg and the Moroccan Crisis, 1905–6', *Mid-America*, vol. 75 (1993), pp. 165–95.

[95] Sternburg to Roosevelt, 7 March 1905 with memorandum, Roosevelt Papers; Sternburg to AA, telegram, 9 March 1905, AA-PA, Marokko 4; Hay diaries, 7 March 1905, Hay Papers.

[96] Wilhelm II later told Eulenburg at Rominten that they had to play *gros jeu* and that the German Morocco action was meant as a 'cleansing thunder storm to clear the path for the entente between us and France'. Eulenburg's notes, 25 September 1905, Röhl (ed.), *Eulenburg*, vol. III, pp. 2115–16.

[97] Rinke, 'Diplomat's Dilemma', p. 172; Fiebig-von Hase, 'Amerikanische Friedensbemühungen', pp. 288–91; Raulff, *Machtpolitik*, pp. 98–108.

[98] To Spring Rice he wrote on 26 May 1905: 'The Kaiser, both through personal dispatches, through communications from the AA and the communications of his Ambassador, in repeating these statements has shown an astonishing willingness to put down in black and white what his feelings are. Evidently he regards me as a gentleman and feels confident that the letters would never be published against him – a confidence which is entirely justifiable.' Roosevelt, *Letters*, vol. IV, p. 1194.

for intervention in Europe and did not intend to become the tool of Germany's far-reaching European plans. As he let Wilhelm know, he would accept the invitation to a conference only if France also agreed to it.[99] In the meantime, the defeat of the Russian fleet in the battle of Tsushima on 27 May further weakened Russia, and again encouraged Bülow's hopes that the Tsar would become more accessible to the alliance idea. German pressure on France intensified, but France still refused to accept the conference, and Bülow became desperate. As a consequence, Sternburg was instructed on 30 May to impress on Roosevelt that, in case the conference idea failed, Germany had to choose between war with France, or alternatively a Franco-German understanding about Morocco that would lead to a continental alliance and a Franco-German-Russian understanding in the Far East. Events in Morocco, Sternburg told Roosevelt, were not an isolated problem, but part of an 'historical phase of universal dimensions', and not only Germany's, but also America's position in Eastern Asia was endangered in an Anglo-French war against Germany. But despite these threatening disclosures of German intentions, the President 'did not see how America could join in any conference regarding Morocco unless France acquiesced'.[100]

Finally, the prospects of a war in Europe threatening the chances of peace in the Far East induced Roosevelt to change his attitude. As he wrote a year later:

It really did look as if there might be a war, and I felt honor bound to try to prevent the war if I could, in the first place, because I should have felt such a war to be a real calamity to civilization; and in the next place, as I was already trying to bring about peace between Russia and Japan, I felt that a new conflict might result in war that would literally be a world conflagration; and finally for the sake of France.[101]

The possibility of peace in the Far East increased when Japan approached the President on 3 June to act as a mediator, and France pressed Russia for help and insisted on how much the Far Eastern war contributed to the dangerous situation in Europe.[102] But suddenly, on the same day, Wilhelm

---

[99] Sternburg to AA, telegrams, 2 and 9 June 1905, AA-PA, Marokko 4; Jusserand to Delcassé, 6 June 1905, *DDF*, 2nd series, vol. VI, p. 596; Roosevelt to Reid, 6 June 1905, Roosevelt, *Letters*, vol. IV, p. 1207.

[100] Bülow to Sternburg, telegram, 30 May 1905, *GP*, vol. XX, 2, pp. 386–8; Sternburg's memorandum for Roosevelt, 31 May 1905, NA, DS, RG 59, NFMG; Sternburg to AA, telegram, 2 June 1905, AA-PA, Marokko 4. This part of Sternburg's report was omitted in *GP*, XIX, 2 no. 6311, pp. 606–7; Roosevelt to Whitelaw Reid, telegram, 6 June 1905, Roosevelt, *Letters*, vol. IV, p. 1207; Sternburg to Roosevelt, 9 June 1905, AA-PA, Marokko 4.

[101] Roosevelt to Reid, 28 April 1906, Roosevelt, *Letters*, vol. V, p. 236.

[102] Also for the following Dennett, *Theodore Roosevelt*, pp. 184–214.

II also intervened and proposed to the Tsar that he should ask Roosevelt to mediate peace. This was nothing less than a *volte-face* in Germany's Far Eastern policy.[103] The Kaiser's fear that the growing revolutionary unrest in Russia might endanger not only the Tsar's throne and life, but also spread to Germany, gained the upper hand over all other tactical considerations. He told the Auswärtiges Amt only later that he had also privately informed Roosevelt through Ambassador Tower about this step, as he intended to keep the correspondence with Roosevelt on this issue in his own hands. This was 'personal diplomacy' in its pure form.[104] Scared by revolution at home and advised by the French, Wilhelm II, and Roosevelt, the Tsar agreed to negotiations with Japan on 12 June 1905.[105]

The President realized that prospects of a European war grew when Germany did not stop threatening France even after the dismissal of the French Minister of Foreign Affairs, Théophile Delcassé, on 6 June. To Delcassé Wilhelm II and Bülow atttributed much of the French resistance. Sternburg brought Roosevelt another message from the Kaiser, in which the warnings about a world conflagration were repeated.[106] Further information made Roosevelt understand how much the alternative of either a European war or a Franco-German agreement on Morocco would damage American national interests, if the outcome of both could possibly be a European continental alliance under German hegemony. The President showed himself 'embarrassed' and he spoke of 'the gravity of possible consequences' when he learned during an interview with the French Ambassador that a separate French–German agreement on Morocco, which the Emperor had

---

[103] On 2 June, Bülow and Wilhelm II had still criticized the advice to seek peace which Sternburg had given to the Russian Ambassador in Washington, Count Cassini, as 'really wrong and very inopportune'. Sternburg to AA, telegram, 2 June 1905 with Bülow's remarks, and Bülow to Sternburg, telegram, 3 June 1905, *GP*, vol. XIX, 2, pp. 606–7.

[104] The delivery of the Kaiser's message to Roosevelt was unusual. One of Wilhelm's couriers handed Wilhelm's letter to Tower on 4 June at the door of the Berlin cathedral immediately after the Crown Prince's wedding. Wilhelm II to Reginald Tower, strictly confidential, 4 June 1905, in Tower to Roosevelt, 9 June 1905, and Tower to Wilhelm II, telegram, 4 June 1905, Roosevelt Papers; Tower to Wilhelm II, 4 June 1905, with remarks of the Kaiser, *GP*, vol. XIX, 2, pp. 607–8. Wilhelm II also instructed Tower, as Tower reminded him in his letter of 16 August 1905, 'that any replies received from the President of the United States to letters addressed by me [Tower] to him [Roosevelt] in communicating Your Majesty's views regarding the question of peace between Russia and Japan, should be transmitted directly to Your Majesty in person'. *GP*, vol. XIX, 2, pp. 615–16.

[105] Roosevelt to Meyer, 5 June 1905, Roosevelt Papers; Sternburg to AA, telegram, 5 June 1905, *GP*, vol. XIX, 2, pp. 608–7; Roosevelt to Lodge, 5 June 1905, Roosevelt, *Letters*, vol. IV, pp. 1202–6; Meyer to Roosevelt, telegram, 12 June 1905, as printed in Dennett, *Roosevelt*, p. 226.

[106] Bülow to Sternburg, telegram, 10 June 1905, *GP*, vol. XX, 2, pp. 626–8; Sternburg's memorandum for Roosevelt, 11 June 1905, NA, DS, RG 59, NFMG. Although Bülow had originally signed this letter, Roosevelt understood the memorandum as coming from the Kaiser. Roosevelt to Reid, 28 April 1906, Roosevelt, *Letters*, vol. IV, pp. 235-6.

mentioned in one of his letters, was indeed a possibility.[107] The President was well enough acquainted with the strategic considerations of his naval advisors to know that a German sphere of influence and a port in Morocco would negatively affect America's capability to win a German–American war over the Monroe Doctrine.[108] And he also realized that the creation of a continental European alliance under German hegemony including Denmark or the Netherlands would bring the West Indian possessions of these countries in the reach of German control. To the British Ambassador, Henry Durand, he confided that 'if Germany developed designs upon Holland he sh[oul]d at once take over and hold in pledge all Dutch possessions in this part of the world'. He expressed a similar attitude to the French Ambassador Jules Jusserand, while Lodge and the American press warned him about German designs on Denmark.[109]

America's global interests would not remain unaffected in case of war in Europe, and therefore Roosevelt decided to do whatever was possible to prevent it. The problem was that the German government saw itself confronted with the stubborn opposition of France and England and felt cornered. Bülow's and Holstein's political brinkmanship in Morocco threatened to bring about war, not because they wanted it, but because they saw no other way out without losing face. At this moment Wilhelm's fraternizing remarks to French officers attending the manoeuvres in Döberitz increased the tension. While Holstein and Bülow went to the extreme and threatened France with war, Wilhelm II exclaimed that he would never go to war for Morocco, expressed his love for France and exposed his Chancellor's policy

[107] Jusserand to French premier Rouvier, telegram, received 15 June 1905, *DDF*, 2nd series, vol. VII, pp. 68–9. In his memoirs, Eckardstein reported that Rouvier had hinted to him on 3 May 1905 that he was willing to cede a naval base in Morocco to Germany in case of a bilateral Franco-German agreement on Morocco. Hermann Freiherr von Eckardstein, *Lebenserinnerungen und politische Denkwürdigkeiten*, vol. III, Leipzig 1921, p. 3.

[108] The General Board of the Navy stated as early as May 1900 that in case of operations against the United States in the West Indies, it was of the 'first importance' for Germany 'to secure another base in the Eastern Atlantic', and recommended that the United States should 'prevent the acquisition by Germany of such an intermediate base or station in the Eastern Atlantic'. 'Germany versus the United States–West Indies', paper by Captain C. D. Sigsbee, 21 May 1900, NA, Department of the Navy, RG 80, General Board Records no. 425–1, War Portfolio 1.

[109] Durand's report to Lansdowne on his interview with Roosevelt, 27 June 1905, copy in Durand Papers, School of Oriental and African Studies, London, Accession no. 257247; Jusserand to Delcassé, 11 June 1905, *Ministère des Affaires Etrangères*, Paris, new series, Etats-Unis 7, Politique étrangère, Dossier Générale, 1897–1914, pp. 119–20; Lodge to Roosevelt, 10 June 1905, Henry C. Lodge (ed.), *Selections from the Correspondence of Theodore Roosevelt and Henry Cabot Lodge, 1884–1918*, vol. II, New York 1925, pp. 135–8; *Washington Post*, 'Emperor William's Ambition', 18 June 1905. The Kaiser had already talked about drawing Belgium and Denmark into the closer circle of Germany to the kings of those two countries in 1904. *Holstein Papers*, vol. IV, no. 904.

as a 'bluff'. Naturally, Bülow and Holstein felt doubly cornered.[110] Now the
government's prestige at home and in the world would no longer permit a
retreat. War could only be prevented if it were possible to find a solution
which would permit the Kaiser and his government to save face. Roosevelt's
solution was to advise France to give way and accept the conference plan.
But at the same time he promised the French that he would support them at
the conference table and 'would not sanction any unjust attack by Germany
upon French interests'.[111] The French government hesitated, as it also feared
a loss of face, and demanded a conference programme before accepting.
Tensions grew in Berlin. Again, Roosevelt tried his flatteries on Wilhelm II
and congratulated him on his overwhelming diplomatic success.[112] But
Bülow and Wilhelm were not yet satisfied and refused to negotiate a programme, because they needed the complete humiliation of France to make
her obedient enough to accept their alliance plans later. Roosevelt grew
impatient and in a further letter to Sternburg he admonished Wilhelm in
a strange mixture of flatteries and threats, claiming that his prestige as a
peace-loving monarch was at stake:

I feel he stands as the leader among the sovereigns of today who have their faces
set toward the future, and that it is not only of the utmost importance for his own
people but of the utmost importance to all mankind that his power and leadership
for good should be unimpaired. I feel now, having obtained what he asks, it would
be most unfortunate even to seem to raise questions about minor details, for if
under such circumstances the dreadful calamity of war should happen, I fear that
his high and honorable fame may be clouded.[113]

---

[110] Bülow to the German Ambassador to Paris, Prince Radolin, 10 June 1905, *GP*, vol. xx, 2, pp. 429–30;
Holstein to Radolin, 14 June 1905, *Holstein Papers*, vol. iv, no. 891; R. Zedlitz-Trützschler, *Zwölf
Jahre am deutschen Kaiserhof*, Berlin and Leipzig 1924, pp. 173–5.

[111] For Roosevelt's detailed description of his strategy during this stage of the crisis see Roosevelt to
Reid, 28 April 1906, Roosevelt, *Letters*, vol. v, p. 236.

[112] Roosevelt explained to Jusserand that probably 'his only chance to make himself useful was to
flatter the excessive vanity of Emperor Wilhelm, to whom he attributed a great deal of the present
difficulties. Profiting consequently by the communications system that had been established between
them on the initiative of the Emperor himself through the German ambassador as intermediary,
Mr. Roosevelt dictated in my presence a letter to the latter.' Roosevelt considered the French
wishes for a programme as entirely justified and then asked Sternburg 'vivaciously to congratulate
Emperor Wilhelm on the success of his diplomacy'. But he also warned that if he did not concede
'he would necessarily cause a war of which the whole world would disapprove'. Roosevelt also told
Jusserand that he did not think this was a certain method to convince the Kaiser, but 'this was all he
could think of now'. Jusserand to Rouvier, without date (24 June 1905), *DDF*, 2nd series, vol. vii,
pp. 126f.

[113] Bülow to Sternburg, telegram, 24 June 1905, Bülow to Wilhelm II, who was attending the regatta
at Kiel, 25 June 1905, with Wilhelm II's remarks, *GP*, vol. xx, 2, pp. 466–7; Roosevelt to Sternburg,
25 June 1905, Roosevelt, *Letters*, vol. iv, pp. 239–40.

Bülow realized that Roosevelt would not support any further manoeuvring and he knew that war with France could only be avoided if Roosevelt continued his mediation. Therefore he understood that it was time to yield, but Wilhelm refused to send a personal telegram to the President, as Bülow had suggested in an effort to put responsibility solely on the Kaiser. Therefore Bülow cabled Sternburg to explain to Roosevelt that the fact

that, in view of the international situation, which the President recapitulated so appropriately, war would have been for us just as unattractive as for France, does not have to be discussed. Germany's Emperor and Germany's people, both equally peacefully disposed, will always be grateful, that President Roosevelt contributed to spare us such a war.[114]

When the French finally accepted the conference invitation on 8 July 1905, Wilhelm II saw himself as the victor. The road seemed to be free for his continental European alliance, and he jubilantly persuaded Tsar Nicholas II to sign a Russian–German alliance treaty when he met his cousin at Björkö at the end of July. France and Germany had buried their antagonism, he explained to the Tsar.[115]

Bülow also interpreted his diplomacy as a success, as he firmly believed that Germany could count on Roosevelt's support at the conference table. To strengthen the President's belief in the peaceful intentions of the Kaiser in Morocco, he even promised to follow Roosevelt's advice in case there was another impasse during the coming negotiations with France. Sternburg transformed this message in the usual way into one coming from Wilhelm personally and explained to the President that Wilhelm would follow his advice at the coming Morocco conference in case there would be an impasse.[116] Roosevelt was stunned about this blunder, and finally the letter enabled him to force the German government to retreat during the conference at Algeciras in March 1906. When the conference reached an impasse, he reminded Sternburg of the letter, and threatened to publish all his correspondence with Sternburg on the Morocco issue. Bülow was aghast when he calculated the dimension of the possible damage.[117] Simply to punish Sternburg, Roosevelt's friend, would not suffice, as this would

[114] Bülow's notes, 26 June 1905, and Tschirschky to Bülow, 26 June 1905, AA-PA, Marokko 4, vol. 71a; Bülow to Sternburg, telegram, 26 June 1905, *GP*, vol. XX, 2, pp. 475–6.
[115] For the Björkö treaty see Vogel, *Deutsche Rußlandpolitik*, pp. 222–31; see also Roddy McLean's contribution to this volume, pp. 119–42.
[116] Bülow to Sternburg, telegram, 27 June 1905, *GP*, vol. XX, 2, pp. 481–2; Sternburg to Roosevelt, 28 June 1905, NA, DS, RG 59, NFMG.
[117] Rinke, 'Diplomat's Dilemma', pp. 184–95; Beale, *Roosevelt*, pp. 370–89; Lammersdorf, *Anfänge*, pp. 311–54.

only expose the whole system of the strange Willy–Teddy 'friendship', and Bülow had reasons to fear Wilhelm's reactions. In this situation, Bülow decided to end Germany's resistance to the proposals of the majority of the powers in Algeciras and thereby give way to Roosevelt's demands.

The result of Wilhelm II's 'personal diplomacy' towards President Roosevelt during the years 1904 to 1906 was a disaster. When the risky German threats towards France during the Morocco crisis escalated in June 1905 and threatened to provoke war, Roosevelt worked out the compromise formula which satisfied the French and helped the Kaiser to save face. But for Wilhelm II and his political advisors this was a questionable victory, as all their far-reaching hopes came to nothing. As Russia's government refused to accept the Björkö treaty, the Kaiser's dreams of continental hegemony evaporated, and the results of the conference at Algeciras no longer left any doubts that Wilhelm II and his Chancellor had manoeuvred Germany into international isolation. Wilhelm II continued to correspond with the American President during the following years until Roosevelt's presidency ended. However, with Germany weakened and isolated, their relationship no longer had the relevance in international relations it had had during the years 1904 to 1906.

Comparing Wilhelm II's 'personal diplomacy' with Roosevelt's states-manship reveals the extreme weaknesses of the first. Roosevelt and his ad-visors excelled in their rational evaluation of international developments, their country's strength, the international environment, and even the psyche of their counter-players. They adapted their political strategy and actions accordingly. The same cannot be said of Wilhelm II and his top political advisors. Not only were their far-reaching political aims based on unrealistic assumptions, but so was their perception of the global environment and of foreign statesmen. The reasons for this must be sought in a political system which enabled a man like Wilhelm II to be at the centre of power. He was responsible for the fact that men like Bülow and Sternburg, who oppor-tunistically adhered to his wishes and advanced their own personal careers to the detriment of the nation, became so influential in German–American re-lations and German foreign policy in general. In the Byzantinistic 'personal regime' it became more important to please and satisfy the vanities of the Kaiser than to pursue a rational foreign policy and present Germany as a reliable partner in the community of nations. In 1910, Roosevelt realized that for the Kaiser the outward appearance of power had become more important than ruling his country, and that this was a central weakness of his role within the German political system. Returning from Europe, he reported to President Taft about his experiences with Wilhelm II:

'I must say on the whole I was disappointed with him. I found him vain as a peacock. He would rather ride at the head of a procession than govern an empire. That is what has contributed mostly to his downfall, for he certainly has had a downfall.'[118] Seen against the background of the functioning American political system in its relations to the outside world, the behaviour of the leading political men in the powerful German Empire appears not like that of statesmen, but more like that of actors performing an operetta.

---

[118] Butt, *Taft and Roosevelt*, p. 421.

CHAPTER 7

Military diplomacy in a military monarchy? Wilhelm II's relations with the British service attachés in Berlin, 1903–1914

Matthew S. Seligmann

That Kaiser Wilhelm II revelled in the paraphernalia of military life is a matter of historical record. His fondness for uniforms, medals, and decorations; his delight in parades, marches, and army ceremonies; and his enthusiasm for the grand spectacle of the annual manoeuvres, and especially for the grand cavalry charges that occurred there, are all well documented.[1] Equally well known is that he liked the company of Prussian officers and included many such persons within his immediate entourage, much to the irritation of the Reich's civilian politicians who found themselves constantly displaced from the centre of governance by the presence of these martial interlopers. Indeed, so great was the magnitude of the Kaiser's preference for military men over ministers that some officials feared that Wilhelm intended to dispense entirely with his civilian advisors, replacing them with those of his soldierly companions whom he found most congenial, namely his aides-de-camp. One such fearful individual was the senior Foreign Office counsellor, Friedrich von Holstein. As he vehemently complained: 'Internal conditions, especially at court, are less pleasant. The . . . aides-de-camp are becoming more and more an organized secondary Government.'[2]

While it was undoubtedly members of the German central administration who suffered most from this situation, the danger of being marginalized by the presence of military men at the German court was, nevertheless, not a problem that was faced exclusively by Reich officials. Foreign diplomats stationed in Berlin encountered similar difficulties, in that the Kaiser's delight in the company of serving officers extended beyond members of his

---

[1] For a recent summary of these matters, see Annika Mombauer, *Helmuth von Moltke and the Origins of the First World War*, Cambridge 2001, pp. 18–19; on the Kaiser and cavalry, see Eric Dorn Brose, *The Kaiser's Army: The Politics of Military Technology in Germany during the Machine Age, 1870–1918*, Oxford 2001, pp. 116–17; Isabel V. Hull, *The Entourage of Kaiser Wilhelm II, 1888–1918*, Cambridge 1982, p. 11.

[2] Friedrich von Holstein to Hugo von Radolin, 22 March 1896. Quoted in Norman Rich and M. H. Fisher (eds.), *The Holstein Papers*, Cambridge 1961, vol. III, p. 601.

own nation's armed forces to encompass those foreign military and naval personnel who were accredited as attachés to the various embassies of the imperial capital. Such officers, normally intended by their own governments to be mere adjuncts to the diplomatic effort in Germany, often found that they were treated with a warmth and respect that was not accorded to their civilian counterparts. Writing in his memoirs, the Vicomte de Faramond, who had been French naval attaché in Germany during the years 1910 to 1914, recalled the extraordinary position accorded to him and his fellow service attachés by Kaiser Wilhelm II:

In those countries where the sovereign personally commands the land and sea forces, the position of military and naval attachés is quite special. Wilhelm II considered the foreign officers attached to the embassies as accredited more to his person than to the German government . . . He invited them to all the court balls and concerts, even though the secretaries to the embassies were not themselves present at a single ball in the winter season. It was always the military or naval attaché who accompanied the ambassador to the annual diplomatic dinner offered by the Emperor to those chiefs of mission holding the rank of ambassador.[3]

Faramond's opinion was hardly unique. Lieutenant-Colonel the Hon. Alexander Russell, a contemporary of Faramond's, who served as British military attaché in Berlin from 1910 to 1914, echoed many of these sentiments in his post-war 'Reminiscences'. 'The position of a Military Attaché in Berlin', he explained,

[was] a more brilliant one on account of the special attention which the Emperor . . . invariably paid to the military representatives of foreign powers. The number of parades, military functions, gala operas, etc., to which we were invited was larger, I am convinced than at any other Court, and on nearly all these occasions the foreign Military Attachés were . . . 'made a fuss of' by the Emperor.[4]

Though Faramond's and Russell's observations were written some years after the event, this should not be taken to imply that this assessment of Wilhelm's behaviour was only made in retrospect. On the contrary, numerous contemporary accounts recorded the same phenomenon and attested in comparable terms to the advantages that could accrue from possessing a military bearing when on service in Germany. Thus, for instance, when, in 1906, Richard Burdon Haldane, Britain's recently appointed and decidedly unsoldierly-looking Secretary of State for War was invited to Berlin to attend the autumn army manoeuvres, it was noted that Edward VII had

[3] Amiral de Faramond, *Souvenirs d'un Attaché Naval en Allemagne et en Autriche 1910–1914*, Paris 1932, p. 24. (My translation.)
[4] A. V. F. V. Russell, 'Reminiscences of the German Court', *The Fighting Forces*, 1 (1924), p. 58.

reservations about the value of his trip. 'The King has always thought', explained his private secretary, Lord Knollys, 'that a *civilian* . . . Secretary of State for War is rather out of place at foreign . . . military manoeuvres, especially when [he] can only appear in civil uniform.'[5] Such a statement would have been nonsensical if applied to either Republican France or the United States. Given that it was raised in the specific context of a visit to the German capital, it is inevitable that the Kaiser's insatiable love of martial attire did much to inform this judgement. As King Edward correctly recognized, those people clad in warrior's garb were held in the highest esteem and given preferential treatment at Wilhelm's court.[6]

Other members of the British establishment were equally aware of the Kaiser's preferences, and likewise recognized that this had implications for the management of Anglo-German relations. Hence, when surveying the manifold difficulties of conducting diplomacy in Berlin, the influential British Foreign Office senior clerk, Eyre Crowe, referred to 'the well-known idiosyncrasies of the German Emperor and his preference for naval and military persons'.[7] This fact, he felt, meant that the British service attachés in Berlin required close monitoring. Only thus could it be ensured that 'communications of importance, which may hereafter have to be referred to and made use of in diplomatic negotiations, should pass through the authoritative channel'.[8] Crowe's anxiety that, if given the opportunity, the Kaiser would eschew the professional diplomats and undertake diplomacy through the soldiers and sailors assigned to the Berlin embassy – it is in this sense that the term 'military diplomacy' will be understood in this essay – suggests that, like King Edward, he, too, recognized that important consequences flowed from the Kaiser's military preferences.

As the above citations illustrate, contemporary observers clearly recognized that Wilhelm II preferred the company of officers to officials and was inclined, where possible, to conduct state business – including diplomatic contacts – with the former rather than the latter. In spite of this, however, when it has come to assessing the significance of the foreign military and naval attachés stationed in Berlin, historians have diverged markedly in their views. Some, such as Paul Kennedy, have stressed the importance of

[5] Lord Knollys to Richard Burdon Haldane, 5 August 1906, Haldane Papers, National Library of Scotland, Edinburgh, MS 5907, fo. 71.
[6] Haldane was aware of the reasoning behind the King's misgivings. As he wrote in his autobiography: 'King Edward was afraid lest I should show to disadvantage in the company of the German officers.' See Richard Burdon Haldane, *An Autobiography*, Garden City, NY 1929, p. 215.
[7] Minute by Eyre Crowe, 12 September 1910, Public Record Office (hereafter PRO), FO 371/901 fos. 41ff.
[8] Ibid.

the attachés' proximity to the Kaiser. As he put it in his seminal text, *The Rise of the Anglo-German Antagonism*:

In a military monarchy, where the opinions and influence of the chief of the Prussian General Staff before the emperor might be as important as those of the Chancellor himself . . . military attachés . . . had an importance quite distinct from their roles as *rapporteurs* of the affairs of the German army.[9]

Others, however, have taken quite a contrary perspective. Lamar Cecil, for example, in a recent biography of Wilhelm, maintains that 'after the turn of the century, the Kaiser had little to do with the British military and naval attachés'.[10] Given the existence of such clearly contrasting views, this is a matter that evidently needs exploring. Was Crowe correct to suggest that the Kaiser liked to indulge in diplomacy conducted through service personnel, a view with which Paul Kennedy would seem to concur? Or is Cecil nearer the mark in implying that this phenomenon has been largely overstated?

It must be acknowledged at the outset that there are two separate components to Lamar Cecil's statement. First, there is the implicit suggestion that prior to 1900 there was a process of active engagement between the Kaiser and the British service attachés, a proposition entirely in line with Paul Kennedy's conclusion. Second, there is the contention that, after 1900, this process, if not actually ended, was greatly reduced.

The initial point, concerning the Kaiser's manifold dealings with the attachés in the earlier part of his reign, is undoubtedly correct. We know, for example, on the basis of several well-recorded incidents from this period, that the Kaiser was quite willing to undertake important business through the British attachés. Frequently cited are two meetings between Wilhelm and Colonel Leopold Swaine from late 1895. Swaine, who was both a personal friend and someone with whom Wilhelm had had useful dealings even before his accession to the throne,[11] was a regular interlocutor of the Emperor's. This did not mean, however, that he was prepared when, on 24 October, he found himself on the receiving end of a long tirade in which the Kaiser 'gave free rein to his irritation with Britain'.[12] Over the course of an extended conversation, during which the colonel allegedly 'winced', the Kaiser unburdened himself of all his manifold vexations with

[9] Paul Kennedy, *The Rise of the Anglo-German Antagonism, 1860–1914*, London 1982, p. 136.
[10] Lamar Cecil, *Wilhelm II: Emperor and Exile 1900–1941*, Chapel Hill 1996, p. 126.
[11] John C. G. Röhl, *Young Wilhelm: The Kaiser's Early Life, 1859–1888*, Cambridge 1998, pp. 440, 445, 689.
[12] Norman Rich, *Friedrich von Holstein: Politics and Diplomacy in the Era of Bismarck and Wilhelm II*, Cambridge 1965, vol. II, p. 457.

London. He accused the British government of, among other things, 'selfishness and bullying', of harbouring designs over the Dardanelles, and of threatening Germany with war over its relationship with the Transvaal. It was an astonishing performance that left the colonel, in the Kaiser's own words, 'deeply moved and shaken'.[13] Yet, it was not an isolated case. Two months later, the Kaiser cornered Swaine once again, this time levelling the unlikely charge that Britain was planning an Anglo-Russian condominium over Constantinople.[14] The accusation produced an official denial from Lord Salisbury, who was by now becoming quite accustomed to major policy initiatives from the Emperor coming to him via the military attaché.[15] Clearly, therefore, there are good grounds for concluding that before 1900 important contacts existed between the Kaiser and the British service attachés.[16]

However, Cecil's main proposition that, in the succeeding years, such interactions were reduced to the point where 'the Kaiser had little to do with the British military and naval attachés', is more open to debate. To begin with, the basis for this judgement – which, given the Kaiser's military proclivities, can only be described as counter-intuitive – is the infrequency with which reports concerning audiences between the Kaiser and the British service attachés appear in the published diplomatic record, *British Documents on the Origins of the War*. As Cecil explains:

Colonel Frederick Trench was the British military attaché from 1906 to 1910, but his five audiences with the Kaiser were inconsequential. See B[ritish] D[ocuments], . . . a source that also indicates how rarely Wilhelm saw Captains Dumas, Heath, and Watson, the British naval attachés from 1906 to 1913.[17]

While the logic of this argument is clear-cut, it is problematic in one respect. George Gooch and Harold Temperley's collection of diplomatic documents, while an excellent compendium that admirably fulfils its purpose of providing an overview of British foreign policy before the First World War, was never intended as a guide to the activities of Britain's military and naval attachés. It includes, for example, only seven of the more than

---

[13] Kaiser Wilhelm II to Freiherr von Marschall, 25 October 1895. Quoted in Johannes Lepsius, Albrecht Mendelssohn-Bartholdy, and Friedrich Thimme (eds.), *Die Grosse Politik der Europäischen Kabinette 1871–1914*. Sammlung der Diplomatischen Akten des Auswärtigen Amtes, 40 vols, Berlin 1922–7, vol. XI, pp. 8–11.

[14] Memorandum by Freiherr von Marschall, 21 December 1895. Quoted in ibid., vol. X, p. 255.

[15] Lord Salisbury to Sir Frank Lascelles, 21 December 1895, ibid., p. 258.

[16] A doctoral dissertation based upon archival materials for the years up to 1902 came to the same conclusion. See Lothar Hilbert, 'The Role of Military and Naval Attachés in the British and German Service with Particular Reference to those in Berlin and London and their Effect on Anglo-German Relations, 1871–1914', doctoral dissertation, University of Cambridge 1954, esp. p. 81.

[17] Cecil, *Wilhelm II*, p. 395n.

170 memoranda and dispatches written by Colonel Trench – less than 5 per cent – and omits many of the documents which detail discussions between him and the Emperor.[18] Indeed, an inspection of the original papers in the Foreign Office political files reveals six major conversations between the Kaiser and Trench in 1906 alone.[19] This represents more discussions in nine months (Trench arrived in April) than Cecil, relying on Gooch and Temperley, acknowledges for the full four-year period of Trench's posting. And this pattern of editing permeates the entire series. Accordingly, we find that *British Documents* is similarly incomplete as a guide to the work of Trench's immediate successor, Lieutenant-Colonel Russell,[20] and of the naval attachés, Dumas, Heath, Watson, and Henderson. In short, it cannot be used to sustain the claim that the attachés rarely saw the Kaiser, an opinion, which in Trench's case at least, is also flatly contradicted by the British ambassador, Sir Frank Lascelles. He recorded in an official letter to the Foreign Secretary: 'I am personally grateful to Colonel Trench for keeping me fully informed of his conversations with the German Emperor on the frequent occasions on which his military duties give him the opportunity of meeting His Imperial Majesty.'[21] So clear a statement from the attaché's head of mission cannot be ignored.

In addition to offering evidence of regular encounters between the British service attachés and the Kaiser, the archival record also shows that throughout this period Wilhelm took a special interest in them, even to the point of interfering in the selection and appointment of the officers chosen to serve in Berlin.[22] When in 1903 Colonel W. H. H. Waters was replaced by Lord Edward Gleichen, the Kaiser wrote a long letter to his uncle, King Edward, to complain about the procedures adopted in making the new appointment. His particular gripe was that, as Gleichen had been prevented by existing duties in Egypt from taking up his position in Berlin until many months after the departure of his predecessor, his selection had left an unwelcome gap in Wilhelm's military retinue. The process, he requested, should be changed to ensure that this should not happen again:

---

[18] For more information on Trench as military attaché, see Matthew S. Seligmann, 'A View from Berlin: Colonel Frederick Trench and the Development of British Perceptions of German Aggressive Intent, 1906–1910', *Journal of Strategic Studies*, 23, 2 (2000), pp. 114–47.

[19] The conversations can be found in PRO, FO 371/77–9.

[20] Of Russell's 169 major dispatches only ten appear in *British Documents*. For further details on Russell, see Matthew S. Seligmann, '"A Barometer of National Confidence". A British Assessment of the Role of Insecurity in the Formulation of German Military Policy before the First World War', *English Historical Review*, 127 (2002), pp. 333–55.

[21] Sir Frank Lascelles to Sir Edward Grey, 22 October 1908. PRO, FO 371/462.

[22] Alfred Vagts has recorded a similar phenomenon in respect to the appointment and recall of the American and French military attachés in Berlin. See Alfred Vagts, *The Military Attaché*, Princeton 1967, pp. 303–4.

I may venture to suggest that the next time the War Office intends to change the milit. attaché here, they would be more sensible if they recalled the old one *after* the new one has been presented to me & to the authorities with whom he is to treat & correspond. But not as was the case this time, recall the acting one, *before* they knew who was to replace him, & leave the post vacant for many months![23]

While this comment from one sovereign to another on the workings of the latter's government might be considered impertinent, such interference in the appointment of military attachés was far from unique, as the nomination of Gleichen's successor illustrates. In this instance, the Kaiser's involvement owed less to a concern over the process than to an interest in the character of the future appointee and stemmed from the fact that Gleichen's posting had been marred by deep personal frictions between the Kaiser and the attaché. The two men simply did not get on, even to the extent that they clashed dramatically on several occasions. Their most bitter contretemps concerned a violently Anglophobic German book, written by a serving guards officer called Jecklin, which Gleichen had sent back to the War Office in 1904 as part of a routine dispatch. Entitled *The Military Interpreter*, the volume purported simply to be a compendium of translation exercises tailored to suit regular users of military terminology. However, as the passages for translation contained highly inflammatory material, such as stories about British soldiers murdering innocent Boer civilians, it was clear that politics rather than linguistic excellence was at the heart of the publication. Nevertheless, nothing would have come of this had the book not been passed to King Edward, who, unfortunately for Gleichen, chose to raise the matter in jest with Wilhelm during a royal visit to the German port of Kiel. The Kaiser was mortified and blamed Gleichen for ruining the entire visit, an offence for which he never forgave him.[24] Thereafter he continuously found fault with Gleichen's conduct, an attitude that, quite naturally, produced additional fraught moments.[25] One such occasion concerned a relatively minor violation by Gleichen of the correct dress code for a formal reception, an error at which the Kaiser took disproportionate offence. Commenting on this incident, Lord Knollys observed that the 'Emperor appears to have made a mountain out of a molehill in regard to Gleichen's uniform . . . I don't believe the former has either forgotten or forgiven the latter for the Kiel incident, and if Gleichen is wise he will be

---

[23] Kaiser Wilhelm II to King Edward VII, 16 August 1903, Royal Archives (hereafter RA) X37/57. I am indebted to Roderick McLean for drawing my attention to this incident.

[24] Lord Edward Gleichen, *A Guardsman's Memories: A Book of Recollections*, Edinburgh and London 1932, pp. 263–5.

[25] For a discussion of Gleichen's problems in Berlin see Roderick R. McLean, 'Monarchy and Diplomacy in Europe, 1900–1910', DPhil dissertation, University of Sussex 1996, pp. 62–4.

extra careful in all his dealings with the Emperor.'[26] Unfortunately, as time was to show, no amount of care could salvage Gleichen's position at court. The upshot of such unpleasantness was that the Kaiser took a particular interest in the matter of Gleichen's successor, who he was determined should be more to his taste. This he achieved when he secured the appointment of Colonel Trench.

The Kaiser had first met Trench in Gibraltar in 1903 and had developed such a partiality for the colonel that the latter soon became the recipient of a stream of All Highest favours. Following an invitation in 1904 to attend the German Army manoeuvres, he was given the opportunity the next year to accompany the Reich's forces in their campaign against the Herero tribesmen in South-West Africa. Finally, in 1906, he became 'the Emperor's own selection' to replace Gleichen in Berlin.[27] At a personal level, Trench's appointment to Berlin was an unqualified success. For one thing, the new attaché, unlike his predecessor, was extremely sensitive to the Kaiser's fondness for outward shows of respect and did everything that he could to pander to this predilection. Thus, for example, having heard Wilhelm mention his status as a British Field Marshal on more than one occasion, Trench requested that a specially bound copy of the *Army List* be sent to Berlin so that it could be presented to Wilhelm to mark the anniversary of his appointment. Needless to say, this gesture was very well received and, accordingly, the ever-solicitous Trench requested that, not only should this practice be continued, but that in future, a copy of the *Army List* should be printed in advance so that it could be presented to the Kaiser on his birthday.[28] Clearly, in pushing for Trench's appointment, the Kaiser ended up with an attaché after his own heart.

These personal interventions in the appointment of the service attachés suggest that the Kaiser took a keen interest in the officers stationed in Berlin. This begs the question: was this interference an end in itself – often the case with the mercurial and superficial Kaiser – or did he have a more substantive motive for his involvement? The evidence suggests that Wilhelm's interest was no idle matter, but stemmed from the fact that he regarded these officers as having a very particular role to play in two key areas of his discourse with Britain. First, there was the conduct of the Anglo-German diplomatic dialogue; then there was the management of relations

[26] Lord Knollys to Sir Frank Lascelles, 7 March 1905, PRO, FO 800/12. Once again, I am grateful to Dr McLean for providing me with this reference.
[27] Sir Charles Hardinge to Sir Edward Goschen, 7 December 1908, Cambridge University Library, Hardinge of Penhurst Papers, vol. 13, fos. 162–5.
[28] See Trench Report, nos. 32 and 44, 31 January 1907 and 27 March 1907, PRO, FO 244/682.

between the British and Prussian royal houses, especially with regard to the military and ceremonial features of their intercourse.

Beginning with the first of these areas, it is clear that with respect to Anglo-German diplomatic relations the Kaiser regarded the service attachés as useful intermediaries. Accordingly, he frequently employed them in his attempts to arrange ministerial and other visits designed to impress public opinion with signs of the harmony present between the two countries. Possibly the best-known illustration of this phenomenon was the trip to Berlin undertaken by Secretary of War Richard Burdon Haldane in 1906. The visit occurred as a result of a chance conversation between the Emperor and Colonel Trench, the newly appointed military attaché. Trench, who had gone to Potsdam to observe the resident garrison's Spring Parade, was discussing general military matters with the Kaiser when the latter suddenly shifted the subject: 'Haldane', he told Trench,

knows German well and has studied the German Army; but what good is that? One must see for one's self; he only knows what he reads and is told. . . . he should write to his colleague here that he is coming over, and come and see the army for himself. We would be very glad to see him.[29]

The Kaiser's message was not ignored. As Haldane's biographer records: 'The report of this conversation was soon followed by a formal invitation', one that Haldane was more than happy to accept.[30]

Of course, the many direct requests and broad hints extended through the service attachés did not always produce such positive results, as the Kaiser's attempts to lure Winston Churchill to Kiel in the summer of 1914 demonstrate. After extending invitations in various forms from as early as Easter without producing a definitive outcome, Wilhelm resorted to sending an informal but pressing message via the new British naval attaché, Captain Wilfred Henderson, who was then attending an aeronautical display organized by the Kaiser's brother, Prince Heinrich. A letter from Henderson to Churchill explains what occurred:

[Prince Heinrich] took us aside and said that he had had a long talk with the Emperor yesterday about the visit of our fleet to Kiel, & the Emperor had said that he had invited you (& any of your colleagues on the board who wished to come) *officially* . . . the point he wanted us to convey to you clearly was that the Emperor will undoubtedly be hurt if you and at least one other member of the board do not appear . . . To make a long story short, what is evidently hoped for is that you and the First Sea Lord will both be at KIEL in the 'Enchantress'.[31]

[29] Frederick Trench to Sir Frank Lascelles, 1 June 1906, PRO, FO 371/78, fo. 111.
[30] Dudley Sommer, *Haldane of Cloan: His Life and Times, 1856–1928*, London 1960, p. 177.
[31] Wilfred Henderson to Winston Churchill, 16 May 1914, CHAR 13/45/9–10, Churchill Papers, Churchill Archives Centre, Churchill College, Cambridge.

This letter was not without some impact. Churchill himself was very keen to go to Germany and made representations to this effect to the Prime Minister. However, the Foreign Office declined to sanction the visit and so, notwithstanding the Kaiser's desires and the naval attaché's assistance, the First Lord of the Admiralty did not end up as a guest at Kiel week.[32]

Equally fruitless was an attempt to encourage a meeting between the British Channel Fleet and the German Baltic Squadron during the former's summer cruise in 1906, a proposal that the Kaiser and the serving naval attaché, Commander Philip Dumas, bandied about over several conversations in June of that year. Raised informally at a ceremonial inspection of the Lehr Battalion at Potsdam on 4 June, the matter was discussed again on 25 June at Kiel, where the Kaiser and Dumas agreed that it would be an excellent idea if the visit should allow the officers of the British and German fleets to meet. Unfortunately, the turbulent state of Russian domestic politics made it doubtful whether foreign sailors would be well received in Russian ports and so, despite the fact that extensive preparations had already been made, the entire cruise was cancelled.[33] As Dumas bemoaned in his diary: 'so all my pleasant conversation with the Emperor is wasted'.[34] Nevertheless, that such discussions took place at all shows the role that the naval attaché had in the Kaiser's conception of managing Anglo-German relations.

In addition to the aforementioned diplomatic duties, service attachés also played a part in the equally complex and taxing sphere of the familial relations between the British and Prussian royal houses. Despite being closely tied as blood relatives, many members of the Hohenzollern and the Saxe-Coburg dynasties heartily disliked each other, with the inevitable result that their mutual dealings and exchanges needed careful management. Although many different agencies were involved in this prickly process, the service attachés filled a particular niche, especially with regard to the military and ceremonial dimension to relations between the royal houses.

The awarding of honorary positions in the Royal Navy and British Army to the Kaiser and his immediate family highlights the attaché's role. As Roderick McLean's important recent study has noted, the bestowal of such outward signs of approval by his British relatives was something that the ever-insecure Kaiser particularly 'craved'.[35] To obtain them along with the

---

[32] Randolph S. Churchill (ed.), *Winston S. Churchill, 1874–1965: Volume II Companion, Part 3, 1911–1914*, London 1969, pp. 1978–81.

[33] Admiralty File D322, 'Proposed visit of the Channel Fleet to the Baltic. Owing to troubles in Russia the entire cruise abandoned.' PRO, ADM 1/7865.

[34] Dumas Diary, 4 June, 25 June, and 14 July 1906, Imperial War Museum (hereafter IWM).

[35] Roderick R. McLean, *Monarchy and Diplomacy in Europe, 1890–1914*, Cambridge 2001, p. 78.

full privileges and dignities that pertained to them, the imperial family were not above making their desires known, and the British military attaché in Berlin was the obvious person through whom hints could be channelled. This aspect of life as an attaché was something that would become very evident to Lieutenant-Colonel Russell during the first year of his tour of duty in Berlin. A conversation with the Kaiser in March 1911, for instance, led to the revelation that Wilhelm was 'very hurt that though admiral of the British fleet he has never been allowed on board a Dreadnought!'[36] Naturally, as the Kaiser well knew, this message that Wilhelm felt denied some of the privileges of his honorary rank was passed back to the Royal Court at Windsor. In a similar vein, Russell reported in April 1910 that, during a dinner given by the Commander of the Guard Corps, the Crown Prince had intimated to him that he wished to belong to a Scottish regiment. The Colonel immediately reported this singular penchant to the King's Assistant Private Secretary, along with the supplementary information that it appeared to be founded on sartorial grounds. 'H.R.H.', he wrote, 'would particularly like to wear a kilt.' Would it not be feasible, he asked, to make him 'an honorary colonel in some Highland regiment, as the King of Norway is in the Norfolk Yeomanry'?[37]

In so far as such requests could be met, the British authorities endeavoured to satisfy them. The granting of such favours could, however, generate complications and, when this happened, it naturally fell to the military attaché to sort things out. For example, in 1911 the Kaiser's position as honorary Colonel-in-Chief of the 1st Royal Dragoons (the 'Royals') created a singular mix up. In March of that year, this regiment was due to return from India to Britain, a move that would result in their missing George V's coronation at the Delhi Durbar. Somehow – it later transpired that it was all a misunderstanding – their desire to remain for the ceremony was conveyed to the Kaiser along with the impression that they hoped that he would be able to arrange the matter for them. Ironically, the Kaiser had actually made a point of opposing the stationing of this regiment in India when the possibility had first been mooted in 1903. As Gleichen, the then military attaché, had reported:

H.M. referred with considerable displeasure to the fact that 'his' regiment, the 'Royals', were going to be sent to India, in defiance of the pledge given by His late Majesty George III that, as a reward for their services in the Union Brigade at Waterloo, they would never be sent out of England in time of peace.[38]

[36] Alick Russell to Sir Frederick Ponsonby, 4 March 1911, RA PS/GV/F 138/1.
[37] Alick Russell to Sir Frederick Ponsonby, 23 April 1910, RA VIC/X 23/31.
[38] Lord Edward Gleichen to Sir Frank Lascelles, 24 October 1903, PRO, FO 64/1574.

Now, however – or so it appeared – Wilhelm was being asked to reverse his stance and help them stay in the subcontinent! Herein lay an awkward situation, for, as the Kaiser well knew, his interference on such a point was out of the question; as he put it: 'Of course I cannot help them in this matter.' Equally, having, as he thought, been requested to intercede, he felt honour bound to do something. As he implored Lieutenant-Colonel Russell: 'My dear fellow, I am in a dreadful fix and I want you to help me out of it!'[39] Smoothing over such matters, thereby ensuring the Kaiser's good will, was part of the ordinary routine of the military attaché.

However, there was a less pleasant side to being stationed in Berlin. While the Kaiser, as described above, often employed the service attachés as conduits for initiatives designed to improve relations between the United Kingdom and Germany, they proved just as suitable as a channel for calculated diplomatic snubs designed to express All-Highest displeasure with Britain, a fact of which Wilhelm took frequent advantage. The farewell audience (*Abschiedsaudienz*), traditionally accorded to departing diplomats, provided one venue at which the Kaiser could deliver a pointed diplomatic put down to an unsuspecting attaché. One officer to discover this, albeit in a minor way, was Colonel W. H. H. Waters, whose formal departure from Berlin in 1903 exhibited some novel characteristics evidently designed to detract from the solemnity and splendour of the occasion. Rather than taking leave of the Emperor, as custom dictated, in the grand surroundings of the imperial palace, the outgoing attaché found himself taking part in a ceremony held in the altogether less salubrious environs of a platform at Potsdam railway station. Those in the know had no doubts as to the reason for this undignified breach of protocol. As the former attaché Leopold Swaine, now a major-general, informed Arthur Davidson, King Edward VII's assistant private secretary: 'This has been purposely done to play to the Teutonic gallery as an affront to our army.'[40] Fortunately, on this occasion, few people noticed, least of all Colonel Waters, who continued to be an admirer of the Kaiser's, to the extent that he regularly visited him in his exile after 1918.

Yet 'disagreeable' circumstances surrounding the departure of a service attaché could not always be overlooked so easily, as the 'cut direct' delivered to the naval attaché, Captain Herbert Heath, upon his departure from Berlin in August 1910 amply illustrates. Trouble arose on this occasion because of the German perception that Heath had played a major role in the so-called

[39] Alick Russell to Sir Frederick Ponsonby, 4 March 1911, RA PS/GV/F 138/1.
[40] Major-General L.V. Swaine to Colonel Arthur Davidson, 21 May 1903, RA VIC/X1/2.

'acceleration scare', a diplomatic spat that erupted in 1909 over British fears that Germany intended to increase the tempo of its naval construction and surreptitiously out-build the Royal Navy.[41] Although some circumstantial evidence of an 'acceleration' did exist, historians have generally concluded that the German navy had no plans to speed up its shipbuilding programme and Tirpitz, the State Secretary at the Reich Naval Office, consistently and vigorously denied the accusation both in public and in private.[42] Yet, his protestations were to no avail. However remote, the mere possibility that Germany's fleet might conceivably overtake the Royal Navy produced up-roar in Britain, where the government was forced by popular pressure to authorize a massive new construction programme. An unprecedented eight dreadnoughts were ordered in 1909–10 and justified to parliament on the grounds of the German 'acceleration'. The Kaiser was outraged. As the British Foreign Secretary acknowledged: 'the German Emperor had been very much hurt by our failure to accept the assurances given by his govern-ment with regard to the number of ships which Germany would have by the end of 1912. In spite of these assurances, public feeling in this country had been worked up.'[43] Yet angry though he was with the British government for doubting the word of his ministers, Wilhelm was especially indignant towards Heath, who he believed 'had spread lies, told nonsense and agitated [against Germany]'.[44] The unfortunate Heath would discover that he bore the brunt of the Kaiser's displeasure when he attempted to take his leave in the summer of 1910.

On 23 July, Sir Edward Goschen, the British Ambassador in Berlin, wrote to the German government 'requesting that the pleasure of the Emperor might be taken as to the granting of a farewell audience to Captain Heath on the termination of his appointment as Naval Attaché to this Embassy'.[45] The reply, received on 5 August, was negative. The Kaiser, so Goschen was informed, having already left Berlin and being, furthermore, 'wholly occupied with other duties', would not be able to receive the outgoing attaché.[46] This response, which would have been deemed extraordinarily

---

[41] A good summary of the 'acceleration scare' can be found in Peter Padfield, *The Great Naval Race: The Anglo-German Rivalry, 1900–1914*, London 1974, pp. 194ff.

[42] Jonathan Steinberg, 'The German Background, 1905–1914', in F. H. Hinsley (ed.), *British Foreign Policy Under Sir Edward Grey*, Cambridge 1977, pp. 210–12.

[43] Sir Edward Grey to Sir Edward Goschen, 9 June 1909, Grey Papers, PRO, FO 800/61.

[44] Marginal comment by Wilhelm on Captain Widemann to Admiral von Tirpitz, 29 April 1910. Quoted in *GP*, vol. XXVIII, p. 317.

[45] Sir Edward Goschen to Sir Edward Grey, 6 August 1910, PRO, FO 371/906, fos. 40–2.

[46] Alfred von Kiderlen-Wächter to Sir Edward Goschen, 5 August 1910. Enclosed in ibid.

uncivil at the best of times, was received especially badly because it did not ring true. As the Ambassador indignantly noted, 'between the time when my application was made and the answer to it was received, the Emperor had spent several days in Berlin and had received many people (including the Chinese)'.[47] Clearly, had he so desired, he could also have received Captain Heath and, consequently, as Goschen concluded in his diary, his refusal to do so was 'evidently a "parti pris"'.[48] To Grey's private secretary, Sir William Tyrell, Goschen was even more forthright. The Kaiser, he wrote, having been 'poisoned' against Heath, 'who was held responsible here for what they consider misstatements on the part of Mr. Asquith and the First Lord with regard to German naval construction', deliberately concocted an 'ostentatious breach of ordinary custom' as an 'apparent slight'.[49] This was certainly the prevalent view among the officials of the Foreign Office in London, many of whom expressed outrage at the Kaiser's behaviour. Walter Langley, the Assistant Under Secretary of State, recorded in the departmental minutes that 'there was no reason why he [Heath] should not have been received as H.M. came to Potsdam for two days and the Embassy had given three weeks notice of Captain Heath's departure. It was certainly a slight.'[50] The Admiralty agreed wholeheartedly; as the First Lord put it, the treatment accorded to Heath was 'a piece of rudeness without precedent'.[51] Clearly, as these minutes show, if the Kaiser's object in cutting Captain Heath had been to reciprocate the offence he felt over the accusations of a German 'acceleration', then he had eminently succeeded.

Yet, the matter did not end there. Having refused to see Captain Heath when he had asked for an audience, thus forcing the departing attaché to leave Berlin 'under a cloud' and without the customary order of chivalry awarded on such occasions, the Kaiser then inexplicably attempted to call him back. On 9 August, after Heath had left Berlin, the British Ambassador was informed that Wilhelm would be willing to receive him on 1 September. The Emperor's bad timing was unlikely to have been accidental. For one thing, as the Kaiser well knew, Heath was scheduled to hoist his pennant on board a new command in mid-August. Returning to Berlin would, there-fore, have been almost impossible. Moreover, given the manner in which he

---

[47] Sir Edward Goschen to Sir William Tyrell, 10 August 1910, PRO, FO 800/62.
[48] Goschen Diary, 6 August 1910, quoted in Christopher H. D. Howard (ed.), *The Diary of Edward Goschen, 1900–1914*, London 1980, p. 216.
[49] Sir Edward Goschen to Sir William Tyrell, 10 August 1910, PRO, FO 800/62.
[50] Minute on Sir Edward Goschen to Sir Edward Grey, 6 August 1910, PRO, FO 371/906.
[51] Minute by the First Lord of the Admiralty, 18 August 1910, ibid.

had been dispatched from the German capital, the British government was never likely to have regarded it as even remotely incumbent upon Captain Heath to accept such an invitation. Indeed, to do so might justifiably have been regarded, under the circumstances, as a further humiliation. Why, then, did he bother to issue this belated invitation at all? The most plausible explanation is that this action constituted a subtle form of diplomatic damage control. The original refusal to meet Heath was, as one Foreign Office clerk bluntly stated, a 'distinct snub'. While the undoubted intention, the problem was, as the same clerk further noted, that it was 'hardly likely to have a good effect on the relations between the two countries'.[52] It was probably in this context that an invitation to Heath was eventually issued. Such an offer, while in no way undoing the preceding snub, nevertheless allowed the German official Wilhelm von Stumm to inform an incredulous Goschen 'that it was at all events all right now as the Emperor had shown by his last message that he had meant to receive Capt Heath'. As Goschen wrote to Tyrell, 'I was obliged to accept this, but I confess that to me the second message seems under the circumstances slightly thin.'[53] And so it was. The Kaiser had effectively concluded his castigation of Heath by offering a rather limp olive branch to the British government. It failed to convince, but it did underscore his desire to end the matter there and then.

Of course, even when a naval attaché was received for a farewell audience, the event itself could still become a venue for Wilhelm to exhibit his displeasure with the British government. Such, in any event, was the experience of Heath's successor, Captain Hugh Watson, whose final meeting with the Kaiser on 4 October 1913 included more than just the usual valedictory sentiments expressed to a distinguished and well-liked officer. In addition to such pleasantries, the Emperor treated his guest to some unexpectedly forthright criticisms of British ministers and officials, most especially of Lord Haldane and Sir Charles Hardinge. Indeed, so plain speaking was the Kaiser on this occasion that Sir Edward Goschen advised Watson that the contents of the conversation were not suitable for a regular dispatch, and, in the end, Watson's record of the meeting was communicated as a private letter. Yet, even in this format, the text had to be carefully composed, for, as Goschen noted, the Emperor made numerous 'lurid' comments about many members of the British government. 'It passes belief', Goschen concluded, that Wilhelm 'should have selected Watson as a proper recipient of

---

[52] Minute of 15 August 1910, ibid.
[53] Sir Edward Goschen to Sir William Tyrell, 10 August 1910, PRO, FO 800/62.

his grievances'.[54] With respect to protocol this was certainly an accurate observation. However, as the examples already cited have shown, with respect to the Kaiser's past behaviour, utilizing the naval attaché in this manner was far from unusual.

In addition to using service attachés as a medium for demonstrating All-Highest displeasure at the British government, the Kaiser also employed them as a vehicle for expressing his disapproval of the British media. Once again, farewell audiences could act as the venue for this process, as Captain Reginald Allenby, the departing naval attaché, discovered in early 1906. Received by Wilhelm on 16 January, Allenby was subjected to a most unexpected tirade against 'the iniquities of the press' on the occasion of the Moroccan Crisis, in particular in *The Times*, the *National Review*, and the *Daily Mail*. However, as Allenby reported, the Kaiser's irritation was much more general. 'His Majesty,' so the attaché wrote, '. . . appeared to keenly feel and resent the imputations in the press . . . under which he has suffered.' 'For ten years', Wilhelm told the startled Allenby, 'I had to face German music because I was too friendly to England, and now for the last ten years I have to face English music because I am German . . . It is getting too tiring always to be misjudged.'[55]

Unfortunately for Wilhelm, his tendency to manipulate farewell audiences for specific political purposes was not unknown in informed diplomatic circles. Thus, the Kaiser's exaggerated display of pique towards the departing naval attaché was treated with some suspicion at the British Embassy, where it was noted that Allenby's farewell audience had been arranged unusually far in advance of the attaché's actual departure from Berlin. This led the ambassador, Sir Frank Lascelles, to conclude that it had been specifically staged to afford the Kaiser 'a good opportunity for reiterating his complaints of being the victim of misrepresentation', and to do so at the very moment when the Algeciras conference was getting started.[56] While this showed a certain awareness of the Kaiser's diplomatic methods, it remained the case that, whatever Wilhelm's motives for expressing these views, they were not sentiments that the British government could just ignore. In consequence, Allenby's account of his farewell audience was extensively circulated in Whitehall and even led to King Edward taking up the matter with the German ambassador in London.[57]

---

[54] Sir Edward Goschen to Sir Arthur Nicolson, 11 October 1913 enclosing Watson's Memorandum of 9 October 1913. Quoted in Gooch and Temperley, *British Documents*, vol. x, pt. 2, pp. 707–10.

[55] Allenby, Report no. 2/06, 29 January 1906, PRO, ADM 1/7902.

[56] Sir Frank Lascelles to Sir Edward Grey, 17 January 1906, PRO, FO 244/655.

[57] Graf von Metternich to Bernhard von Bülow, 4 February 1906, Politisches Archiv des Auswärtigen Amtes, England, no. 78 secr., vol. 8.

Of course, the *Abschiedsaudienz* was not the only occasion when the Kaiser railed against British newspapers. Dinner parties also provided an opportune venue for Wilhelm to vent his spleen at the press, as several attachés had the misfortune to discover. A dinner at the Imperial Yacht Club at Kiel, for example, attended by the naval attaché, Commander Dumas, was one such occasion. Mingling after the meal, Wilhelm found the perfect opportunity to accost the attaché about a 'nasty article in the *Standard'*. Fortunately, Dumas had not read it and could consequently make no comments, with the result that the conversation remained good-humoured.[58] Yet, these little discussions about the British press were not always so amicable. At another dinner, this time at the British Embassy, Wilhelm complained about 'a particularly venomous article about him that had appeared in the *National Review'*. His victim on this occasion was the military attaché, Lord Edward Gleichen, whose attempt to correct some of the Emperor's facts about the piece did not, as the attaché later admitted, make this a happy moment.[59]

Even more fraught was a discussion that took place in May 1912 between Wilhelm and the then military attaché, Lieutenant-Colonel Russell, this time on the subject of the writings of the military correspondent of *The Times*, Colonel Charles à Court Repington.[60] In his 'Reminiscences', published in 1924, Russell described the conversation as a 'serious row' and went on to record that he and the Emperor 'both more or less called each other liars!' So dramatic, indeed, was this tête-à-tête in Russell's memory that he further observed:

I lost my temper completely, and so did he. The French Military Attaché, who was standing close by, but could not hear what was going on during this conversation, rushed back to his Ambassador and told him that war must be imminent between Great Britain and Germany.[61]

Russell's official report from 1912 confirms all but the most theatrical aspects of this story. As he recorded:

the Emperor took me by the arm and led me out of earshot of any bystanders. His Majesty then commenced a violent diatribe against press correspondents in general and Colonel Repington in particular. His Majesty said that the military

---

[58] Dumas Diary, 25 June 1906, IWM.
[59] Gleichen, *A Guardsman's Memories*, p. 263.
[60] Useful information on Repington can be found in A. J. A. Morris (ed.), *The Letters of Lieutenant-Colonel Charles à Court Repington CMG, Military Correspondent of the Times, 1903–1918*, Sutton 1999; see also Bernd F. Schulte, *Die Deutsche Armee 1900–1914: Zwischen Beharren und Verändern*, Düsseldorf 1977.
[61] Russell, 'Reminiscences', pp. 67–8.

correspondent of *The Times* had written the most horrible things about the German army and had been making untold mischief in America, France and other places by his writings on this subject.[62]

Following this, the Kaiser threatened to retaliate against these perceived calumnies by refusing in future to allow any other British officers to attend German army manoeuvres. However, while it was certainly true that Repington was one of the sharpest critics of the German army and had published numerous articles to this effect, he was not, at the time his words were printed, a serving officer in the British army. His writings, thus, had no official sanction, a fact Russell attempted unsuccessfully to point out to Wilhelm:

Although I did my best even to the extent of interrupting His Majesty to a greater extent than is perhaps compatible with customary deference, I was, I fear, unable to explain to, or adequately convince His Majesty that Colonel Repington's articles were merely the result of journalistic enterprise and had nothing whatever to do with the British officers attending manoeuvres. I fear that the Emperor is unable to disassociate the two ideas in his mind.[63]

Whether or not Russell's stretching of the 'customary deference' constituted the 'serious row' that he later remembered is impossible now to say, but Wilhelm's anger at Repington is not in doubt. It is also a fact that the Emperor chose to voice this anger to the British military attaché rather than to another member of the diplomatic corps. Indeed, as Russell noted, he seemed to have been deliberately keeping the matter back for their meeting. 'I have not', he wrote, 'had an opportunity of speaking with His Majesty since the offending articles appeared and am inclined to think that he has been nursing the grievance till this moment occurred when it was possible to air it unreservedly.'[64] If Russell was right in this assessment, then the Kaiser's inclination for using service attachés as a channel for expressing his anger at the writings of the British press comes into particularly sharp relief.

Returning then to the proposition that 'after the turn of the century the Kaiser had little to do with the British military and naval attachés', it is clear that this judgement needs modification. In reality, far from being marginalized after 1900, the service attachés in Berlin acted as important intermediaries between the Kaiser and the authorities in London. Through them, Wilhelm was able to request British ministerial visits, involve himself in the ceremonial aspects of British military affairs, indicate his annoyance

---

[62] Russell, Report no. 23/12, 27 May 1912, PRO, FO 371/1376, fos. 88–91.
[63] Ibid.   [64] Ibid.

with British government policy, and rail against the iniquities of the British press. Of course, there were other – more correct – avenues through which he could have maintained these very same dialogues, but, largely owing to his military predilections, he preferred to engage with the attachés. Indeed, Wilhelm treated with them in a manner, if not always with a cordiality, that significantly exceeded their station. As a result of this idiosyncrasy, the service attachés played a very particular and significant part in the Anglo-German diplomatic discourse, thereby truly illustrating Paul Kennedy's notion of military diplomacy in a military monarchy.

CHAPTER 8

Wilhelm II as supreme warlord in the First World War

Holger Afflerbach

WILHELM II: A SHADOW KAISER?

'The Beast of Berlin' was the name of an American film, made in 1918, which depicted Wilhelm II as a militaristic monster. This title reflected public opinion among the Allied Powers at the end of the First World War. 'Hang the Kaiser!' was the motto which won Lloyd George the election of 1918. And in Article 227 of the Versailles Treaty the victorious powers in the First World War called for Wilhelm II to be publicly indicted for the 'most serious infringement of international moral law'.[1] He was never brought to trial, only because the Netherlands, where the ex-Kaiser had fled, refused to extradite him.

The desire to punish the Kaiser for the war was based on the assumption that, as the highest-ranking person in charge of German policy, he was partly to blame for the war, and responsible for its bloody course. This assumption did not seem to be unjustified. After all, Wilhelm II had been astonishing and irritating his contemporaries with his autocratic and militaristic pronouncements for decades. His unpredictable volatility, in particular, raised doubts. Bismarck once disapprovingly remarked that Wilhelm II had an opinion about everything, but that it was a different one every day. And indeed, the Kaiser was known to the people around him as *Wetterhahn* (weathercock) or *Ballon* (balloon), who always blew with the prevailing wind. One day he wanted to join Britain in attacking Russia, the next to join Russia in attacking Britain,[2] and the day after that, to join

---

This essay is a shortened and revised version of an article published in *War in History*, 5 (4) (1998), pp. 427–49. The author would like to thank Arnold publishers for permission to reprint this revised version.

[1] Walter Schwengler, *Völkerrecht, Versailler Vertrag und Auslieferungsfrage, Die Strafverfolgung gegen Kriegsverbrechen als Problem des Friedensschlusses 1919/20*, Stuttgart 1982, pp. 365f.; James Joll, *Die Ursprünge des Ersten Weltkrieges*, Munich 1988, pp. 9–11; Holger Afflerbach, *Falkenhayn. Politisches Denken und Handeln im Kaiserreich*, Munich 1996, p. 496.

[2] A striking example is the Kaiser's speech of 26 January 1893, when he praised Russia and her monarchic traditions. J. Lepsius, A. Mendelssohn-Bartholdy, and F. Thimme (eds.), *Die Große Politik der*

Britain in attacking Japan; one day he wanted to bring peace to the world, and the next to behave like a soldier-king and warlord in the tradition of his Prussian ancestors. Added to these mood swings and changing opinions was Wilhelm's tendency to make spur-of-the-moment decisions. Baron Marschall von Bieberstein, the Foreign Secretary, complained: 'A monarch must have the last word. His Majesty, however, always wants to have the first one. That is a cardinal fault.'[3]

All this and a whole series of other 'peculiar character failings'[4] meant that contemporaries and future generations frequently asked whether Wilhelm II could really ever have ruled his Reich by himself. Here, however, we are interested less in the whole of his reign than in his role during the First World War. Historians, in contrast to the Allied Powers during the First World War, generally seem to have assumed that Wilhelm II had no say during the First World War, and that he slipped into complete insignificance because of his lack of any specialist knowledge.[5] Yet even the leading specialist on Wilhelm II, John Röhl, who accused Hans-Ulrich Wehler, and with

Europäischen Kabinette, 40 vols., Berlin, 1922–7, vol. VII, p. 424); four days earlier, on 22 January 1893, he had praised the Duke of Edinburgh and reflected on the fighting of the British and the German navy shoulder to shoulder.

[3] Wolfgang J. Mommsen, *Großmachtstellung und Weltpolitik. Die Außenpolitik des Deutschen Reiches 1870–1914*, Frankfurt am Main 1993, p. 130.

[4] Isabel Hull, 'Persönliches Regiment', in J. C. G. Röhl (ed.), *Der Ort Kaiser Wilhelms II. in der deutschen Geschichte*, Munich 1991, p. 22.

[5] Walter Görlitz, for example, published his edition of the diaries of Admiral von Müller, who as Chief of the Naval Cabinet formed part of the Kaiser's daily entourage, under the title 'Did the Kaiser rule?': *Regierte der Kaiser? Kriegtagebücher, Aufzeichnungen und Briefe des Chefs des Marine-Kabinetts Georg Alexander von Müller 1914–1918*, Göttingen 1959. Görlitz also published Müller's pre-war diaries: *Der Kaiser . . . Aufzeichnungen des Chefs des Marinekabinetts Admiral Georg Alexander von Müller über die Ära Wilhelms II.*, Göttingen 1965. The answer to this question emerges clearly on every page of the work: no! In 1948, Erich Eyck wrote of Wilhelm II: 'For the duration of the war, in any case, personal rule was over': *Das Persönliche Regiment Wilhelms II.*, Zürich 1948, p. 785. Michael Balfour, biographer of Wilhelm II, also claims that Wilhelm's lack of consistency meant that he was banished to the sidelines during the war: *Der Kaiser. Wilhelm II. und seine Zeit*, Berlin 1973 (*The Kaiser and his Times*, London 1964), p. 423. This opinion was shared by many of the Kaiser's contemporaries, in particular the generals and the conservatives, who had already complained about his weak leadership during the war, and also by important historians such as Gerhard Ritter (*Staatskunst und Kriegshandwerk*, 4 vols., Munich 1954–68; see vols. II–IV) or Karl-Heinz Janßen (*Der Kanzler und der General, Die Führungskrise um Bethmann Hollweg and Falkenhayn, 1914–1916*, Göttingen 1967). Thomas Nipperdey (*Deutsche Geschichte 1866–1918*, vol. II: *Machtstaat vor der Demokratie*, Munich 1992), writes: 'The war pushed the Kaiser more and more into the background: his position became increasingly weak, despite his retention of the important power of appointment and dismissal' (p. 787, my translation); Wilhelm Deist: 'Kaiser Wilhelm II. als Oberster Kriegsherr', in Röhl (ed.), *Der Ort Kaiser Wilhelms II.*, writes: 'The indispensable nature of imperial decisions can be observed also during the world war, when Wilhelm II, as a 'shadow Kaiser', clearly failed in the immense duties demanded of his position . . .' (p. 38, my translation). This is the current, and well-founded, historical view. Lamar Cecil, *Wilhelm II*, vol. II: *Emperor and Exile, 1900–1941*, Chapel Hill, NC 1996, writes: 'The man who in peace had believed himself omnipotent became in war a "shadow Kaiser", out of sight, neglected, and relegated to the sidelines in Imperial Germany's hour of trial' (p. 212). All these historians seem

him the whole Bielefeld School, of attempting to write the 'history of the Kaiserreich without the Kaiser, and of Wilhelminism without Wilhelm' (in Nicolaus Sombart's words), concludes, rather surprisingly, that there is no controversy about the fact that during the First World War, Wilhelm II was little more than a 'Schattenkaiser', a 'shadow emperor'.[6]

At the same time, however, in his brilliant thesis of a *Königsmechanismus* or 'kingship mechanism' John Röhl argues that Wilhelm II had a significant influence on the whole history of imperial Germany.[7] Yet if this was the case, it is difficult to understand why this influence suddenly stopped on 4 August 1914. For everything that suggested that Wilhelm was incapable of active involvement in government – his peculiar character failings, his volatility and laziness, his lack of specialist knowledge and his banality, must have been apparent since 1888, and not just since 1914.

Moreover, what does the term 'Schattenkaiser' (which was, incidentally, already used by contemporaries[8]) actually imply? Someone who does not act by himself? Or someone who has no influence on what happens? After all, there is a significant difference between these two positions. This chapter will examine more closely the widely accepted view that Wilhelm II had no significance for the history of German leadership during the First World War, and will address the question of the Kaiser's role within the German Leadership in the years 1914 to 1918.[9]

to share the view that the Kaiser had been an insignificant figure, to be ignored with impunity. This is also the opinion of Hans-Ulrich Wehler, who in any case concentrates on social structures and regards the individual as playing a comparatively unimportant part in historical developments. Thus the fact that he saw Wilhelm II as a 'feeble figure' in peacetime, and assumes the same to have been true during the war, is hardly surprising. H.-U. Wehler, *Das deutsche Kaiserreich 1871–1918*, Göttingen 1973, pp. 60ff., esp. pp. 63–9.

[6] John C. G. Röhl, *Kaiser, Hof und Staat*, Munich, 4th edn 1995, ch. 4: 'Der "Königsmechanismus" im Kaiserreich', p. 126.

[7] The same opinion is shared by Paul Kennedy, 'Reflections on Wilhelm II's Place in the Making of German Foreign Policy', in J. C. G. Röhl and Nicolaus Sombart (eds.), *Kaiser Wilhelm II: New Interpretations*, Cambridge 1982, pp. 157–64.

[8] Röhl, *Kaiser, Hof und Staat*, p. 140, citing Bülow using the expression 'Schattenkaiser'; H.-U. Wehler, *Deutsche Gesellschaftsgeschichte. Dritter Band: Von der 'Deutschen Doppelrevolution' bis zum Beginn des Ersten Weltkrieges 1849–1914*, Munich 1995, p. 1001, citing Hans Delbrück.

[9] In the meantime a number of relevant books and articles have been published, e.g. Annika Mombauer, *Helmuth von Moltke and the Origins of the First World War*, Cambridge 2001 (an important contribution which explains the relations between Moltke and Wilhelm II and also the reasons for his appointment very clearly). A very valuable essay on Wilhelm II was published by Matthew Stibbe: 'Kaiser Wilhelm II: The Hohenzollerns at War', in Matthew Hughes and Matthew Seligmann (eds.), *Leadership in Conflict 1914–1918*, Barnsley 2000, pp. 265–83. Forthcoming is the edition of primary sources by Holger Afflerbach, *Kaiser Wilhelm II. als Oberster Kriegsherr 1914–1918. Quellen aus der militärischen Umgebung des Kaisers*, Munich 2003, which will contain the diaries and war-letters of the Generals and General Adjutants Hans Georg von Plessen and Moriz von Lyncker. The detailed introduction in this volume will deal with many problems and questions concerning Wilhelm II, Plessen, and Lyncker, which cannot be mentioned here for reasons of limited space.

THE KAISER: AN UNWARLIKE COMMANDER-IN-CHIEF?

The first question to consider is whether the Kaiser wanted this war. Could it be said that he deliberately brought it about? The sources, as is almost always the case with Wilhelm II, reveal a kaleidoscopic picture: it would be possible to draw from them the picture of a peace-loving Kaiser – and also the contrary. A significant factor in any discussion of the Kaiser's role in the outbreak of the First World War is the 'Kriegsrat', the so-called 'War Council' of 8 December 1912. The Kaiser, impressed by the diplomatic tensions caused by the First Balkan War, discussed with his military entourage the necessity of preparations for a major war which was predicted in 1914. The importance of this council remains controversial. Some historians argue that the Kaiser and his entourage agreed that a war was to start in 1914.[10] But the majority believe that the major source which reports on this event, the diary of Admiral von Müller, is right: 'The result of this conversation was more or less zero.'[11] Either way, it has still not proved possible to draw a continuous line from 1912 to the actual outbreak of the war, and thus to establish a connection.[12] We will restrict ourselves to what the sources demonstrate with certainty. Did the Kaiser want a great war, a war among the Great Powers? The answer is most likely no. It is true that Wilhelm II was no pacifist and felt himself to be the complete soldier, missing no opportunity to make tactless and belligerent speeches. Nor did he want to stop rearmament, and especially not naval rearmament. But ultimately, according to everyone around him, including foreign observers, this man did not want a great European war.[13] Bülow's

[10] Fritz Fischer, *Krieg der Illusionen. Die deutsche Politik 1911–1914*, Düsseldorf 1969; J. C. G. Röhl, 'An der Schwelle zum Weltkrieg. Eine Dokumentation über den "Kriegsrat" vom 8. Dezember 1912', *Militärgeschichtliche Mitteilungen* 21 (1977), pp. 77–134, and J. C. G. Röhl, *The Kaiser and his Court, Wilhelm II and the Government of Germany*, Cambridge 1994, ch. 8.

[11] Görlitz, *Regierte der Kaiser*, Diary entry, 8 December 1912; Mommsen, *Großmachtstellung und Weltpolitik*, pp. 253–6, argues that there was no plan for an aggressive war, but that the War Council demonstrated the war fatalism in the German elite. A very similar argument is made in Klaus Hildebrand, *Das vergangene Reich, Deutsche Außenpolitik von Bismarck bis Hitler*, Stuttgart 1995, pp. 288–90. J. C. G. Röhl, 'Vorsätzlicher Krieg? Die Ziele der deutschen Politik im Juli 1914', in Wolfgang Michalka (ed.), *Der Erste Weltkrieg. Wirkung, Wahrnehmung, Analyse*, Munich 1994, pp. 193–215, has a very different view. Röhl argues (pp. 205–9) that the decision for war was the result of war plans of the German government which began with the second Morocco Crisis, at the latest in spring 1912. For Röhl's views on the War Council, see also *The Kaiser and his Court*, ch. 8.

[12] Röhl, as the strongest supporter of the importance of the 'War Council', admits some uncertainties in the evidence, see Röhl, 'Vorsätzlicher Krieg?', p. 206.

[13] Examples are the two Moroccan Crises, in which the Kaiser personally voted for peace. Otto Hamann, a member of staff of the Foreign Office and responsible for public information, commented after the war: 'Of all the roles played by Wilhelm II, that of "peace Kaiser" was the truest. The population, including a large proportion of the working class, remained convinced, before and after the crisis of

memoirs contain the following statement made by the Chancellor to the Kaiser:

Your Majesty has l'esprit batailleur. But unlike Napoleon I, Charles XII of Sweden, and Friedrich the Great, you do not have une âme guerrière. You don't even want war! You have never wanted it, and will never want it. You have often told me yourself that your ideal would be to prepare, like Friedrich Wilhelm I, to forge weapons for your son, or even better, your grandson, to use. Why, since your intentions are so peaceful, risk annoying your neighbours or making them suspicious?[14]

Bülow depicted Wilhelm II as a second soldier-king, who armed his country and created a navy for Germany, but who did not himself actually want to wage war. If this is how Wilhelm II saw himself, it would certainly tie in with the events of the July crisis. It is true that, at the beginning of July 1914, Wilhelm II had rather unwisely taken a tough line, calling for Austria to punish Serbia harshly. He did not refrain from rash, belligerent comments. It is certain that he wanted Vienna to punish Serbia by war and demonstrate that the old Habsburg monarchy was, in spite of its internal problems with the nationalities, still able to act as a great power. Yet obviously neither he nor his entourage believed that it would really come to a major war.[15] It seems that they actually doubted whether their Austrian allies, whom they regarded as rather weak, would be able to manage any sort of action against Serbia. This is why Wilhelm II did not change his annual routine, but was sent by Bethmann Hollweg on his usual North Sea cruise on the *Hohenzollern*. The Chancellor wanted to play his diplomatic game without being disturbed by the Kaiser, and to demonstrate to the other powers that nothing unusual was going to happen. En route Wilhelm II continued to brag both orally and in writing, while Bethmann Hollweg in Berlin pursued a highly dangerous foreign policy without the participation of the Kaiser or the generals.[16] The Austrian government, strongly encouraged by the Kaiser and by the German foreign ministry, issued a stern ultimatum to Serbia.

From that point it was clear that things were getting serious, and the danger of a European war became imminent. Immediately the Kaiser's mood changed. To the horror of his belligerent entourage, Wilhelm repeatedly

---

1908, that despite the image he had created by his pompous speeches, Wilhelm would never drag his people into war through desire for conquest or carelessness', *Deutsche Weltpolitik 1890–1912*, Berlin 1925.

[14] Bernhard von Bülow, *Denkwürdigkeiten,* vol. II, Berlin 1930, p. 65.

[15] Afflerbach, *Falkenhayn*, pp. 149–51. Annika Mombauer, 'A Reluctant Military Leader? Helmuth von Moltke and the July Crisis of 1914', *War in History,* 6, 4 (1999), pp. 417–46.

[16] Afflerbach, *Falkenhayn*, p. 151.

tried to prevent the outbreak of war. As early as the second Morocco crisis, the *Post* had already mocked him as 'Guillaume le timide' for his allegedly exaggerated love of peace.[17] Returning to Berlin from his trip on 27 July, the Kaiser was ready to compromise. He was satisfied by the Serbian reply to Austria's ultimatum, and noted that he would never have ordered mobilization in response.[18] Among the people around him the impression was strengthened that the Kaiser was determined to avoid a war. On 28 July 1914 the Prussian war minister, Erich von Falkenhayn, one of the strongest advocates of war in the government, noted in his diary after a discussion with the Kaiser in the Neues Palais in Potsdam: 'He makes confused speeches. The only thing that emerges clearly is that he no longer wants war, even if it means letting Austria down. I point out that he no longer has control over the situation.'[19] This was true. The people around him and, even more, actual events with the real and alleged military constraints governing them, could push the protesting, vacillating Kaiser in a particular direction.[20] Wilhelm II was trapped by his own belligerent posturing and forceful words from the quarter-century and more of his rule. On the other hand, he had the strongest desire to avoid a continental war. Throughout the second half of the July crisis, he vacillated between a desire for peace, a fatalistic attitude – the ball had been set rolling and could no longer be stopped[21] – and a desire to adopt the military bearing that his surroundings expected from 'a German Kaiser, a Prussian king'.[22] Where opportunities to prevent war still offered themselves, he attempted to intervene immediately. On 1 August 1914 it seemed as if British diplomacy promised British neutrality if Germany did not attack France. Thereupon the Kaiser simply instructed his chief of staff, Helmuth von Moltke, not to put the Schlieffen Plan into action. This prohibition stayed in force as long as the British offer held.[23]

---

[17] Ibid., p. 76.   [18] Ibid., p. 153.

[19] Falkenhayn diary, 28 July 1914, cited in ibid., p. 154.

[20] On the outbreak of the Second World War, Wilhelm II is reported to have said: 'The machine is gone with him [Hitler], as it has gone with me.' (A comment made to me by John Röhl.)

[21] Falkenhayn diary, 29 July 1914, cited in Afflerbach, *Falkenhayn*, pp. 155f.

[22] Falkenhayn diary, 31 July 1914, cited in ibid., p. 160. I would like to thank John Röhl for telling me that the Empress also joined in this game and asked her husband in front of his entourage to 'be a man' and to sign the mobilization order. The influence of Empress Auguste Victoria on her husband in the years 1914 to 1918 will be discussed in more detail in Holger Afflerbach, *Wilhelm II. als Oberster Kriegsherr*, Introduction (forthcoming).

[23] The way in which Wilhelm II intervened on 1 August 1914 was often described as highly amateurish. This was especially the opinion of Moltke himself. For Moltke's view see Mombauer, *Moltke*, pp. 219–26. But there are new sources available which offer quite a different view, suggesting that the Kaiser acted reasonably and according to military possibilities. See Afflerbach, *Wilhelm II. als Oberster Kriegsherr*, Lyncker diary, 1 August 1914, and footnotes, especially the Mutius papers, BA-MA, N 195.

Moltke sat in the general staff, raging with frustration and powerlessness. Jules Cambon, the French Ambassador to Berlin, was not speaking purely rhetorically when he said to his British colleague on the outbreak of war: 'This evening there are three people in Berlin who regret that the war has started: you, me, and Kaiser Wilhelm.'[24]

When war actually broke out, the Kaiser gave a highly successful performance with his speech: 'I no longer recognize any political parties, all I see is Germans!'[25] This is generally held to be the most successful speech that he ever delivered, and the one with which he introduced the domestic 'truce' (*Burgfrieden*) – without which Germany would not have been able to carry on the murderous struggle for so long. Throughout the war he continued to give speeches, especially to his soldiers, but also to factory workers and other civilians.

WILHELM II AND OPERATIONAL PLANNING

With the outbreak of hostilities, Wilhelm II became Commander-in-Chief of the German army. According to Article 63 of the Reich constitution, he was Commander-in-Chief of the 'Reich's entire land powers'.[26] In the time of Moltke the elder, however, the Kaiser's powers had been transferred from Wilhelm I to the Chief of the General Staff, who formally possessed no authority to command. This transfer meant that the latter became *de facto* Commander-in-Chief of the army in place of the Kaiser. Thus the Kaiser had given up personal operative leadership of the army. However, throughout the war he kept open the option of intervening in the decision-making process. In order to underline the fact that he was Commander-in-Chief, he did not stay in Berlin, but followed the General Staff first to Koblenz, then to Luxemburg, Mézières, Pless, Kreuznach, and finally to Spa. During the entire war he and his entourage stayed at general headquarters. He took as his model his grandfather, Wilhelm I, who had also taken the field with his armies during the wars of unification instead of staying in the capital. And the Chief of the General Staff had to appear before him daily, usually at 11 a.m., to deliver an hour-long report on the situation.

What happened at these meetings? Apart from the Kaiser, they were attended by the Chief of the General Staff, the Chief of the Imperial Military

---

[24] Balfour, *Der Kaiser*, p. 385.

[25] Afflerbach, *Falkenhayn*, p. 176. Wilhelm's speeches are now the subject of a PhD thesis by Michael Obst at the Heinrich-Heine-Universität, Düsseldorf.

[26] Eckart Busch, *Der Oberbefehl. Seine rechtliche Struktur in Preußen und Deutschland seit 1848,* Boppard am Rhein 1967, p. 23.

Cabinet (that is, the army's highest personnel office), General von Lyncker, the Imperial Adjutant General, von Plessen, and sometimes the Prussian Minister of War; occasionally the Chief of Staff invited military experts or assistants, and the Kaiser might ask the Chief of the Naval Cabinet, Admiral von Müller, to attend. Given this high-ranking attendance at the daily briefings, can we assume that the Kaiser was always in the picture about military events? Wilhelm's second and favourite Chief of Staff during the war, Erich von Falkenhayn, claimed in his memoirs that he had informed the Kaiser about all the important decisions taken during his period in office.[27] But even if this had been true – it was not! – the Kaiser and his advisors had no chance to compete against the superior military competence of the whole general staff. The closest military advisors of Wilhelm II also had different strategies: General Adjutant von Plessen wanted to protect Wilhelm II's influence over the decision-making process, but Lyncker tried to hinder the Kaiser from intervening.[28] The supreme warlord could only approve the arrangements made by his Chief of General Staff without raising major objections. This is also the impression we get from Hindenburg's memoirs.

In peacetime, Wilhelm II liked to bask in the illusion that in war he would be 'his own chief of staff', and announced this to mollify those who criticized the younger Moltke's abilities on the latter's appointment. Yet experts were well aware that the Kaiser's operative abilities were not sufficient 'to lead three soldiers over the gutter'.[29] It was thus only to be expected that the monarch was not really involved in planning operations during the war, and that in many cases, despite the reports made to him, he was not even adequately briefed about events. This was deliberate. The responsible political and military figures systematically excluded the Kaiser because they feared his interference. As early as August 1914 Falkenhayn, at that time still Prussian War Minister, told the military representative of Bavaria, General von Wenninger, that the Kaiser

is not told more than diplomats and courtiers. The main thing is the numbers of POWs, cannons, etc. Now he is no longer told about anything that is at the planning stage; all he hears about is what has already happened, and only the favourable events.[30]

---

[27] Erich von Falkenhayn, *Die Oberste Heeresleitung in ihren wichtigsten Entschließungen*, Berlin 1919, p. 3.

[28] Afflerbach, *Wilhelm II. als Oberster Kriegsherr*, Introduction (forthcoming).

[29] On Waldersee's critique of Wilhelm II's military abilities see John C. G. Röhl, *Wilhelm II. Der Aufbau der Persönlichen Monarchie 1888–1900*, Munich 2001, pp. 470–2. On Wilhelm's ambitions to be his 'own chief of staff' in war time, see Mombauer, *Moltke*, p. 67.

[30] Wenninger diary, 31 Aug. 1914, cited in Bernd Felix Schulte, 'Neue Dokumente zu Kriegsausbruch and Kriegsverlauf 1914', *Militärgeschichtliche Mitteilungen (MGM)*, 25 (1979), p. 161.

The Kaiser, of course, noticed that he was not being kept up to date, and complained about this as early as September 1914.[31] On 6 November 1914 he let off steam to the Chief of the Naval Cabinet, Admiral von Müller. He made a semi-ironic comment that has greatly influenced historians, and has cemented the image of a powerless Commander-in-Chief:

The general staff tells me nothing and does not even consult me. If people in Germany imagine that I command the army, they are much mistaken. I drink tea and chop wood and like to go for walks, and from time to time I find out what has been done, just as it pleases the gentlemen.[32]

Was the Kaiser, the Commander-in-Chief, really only Germany's chief tea-drinker during the war? Wilhelm's continual complaints to the people around him about his lack of say in the planning of operations could create this impression. A characteristic example is Plessen's diary entry of 23 November 1914:

His Majesty very *mauvais humeur!* He claims that he is being completely sidelined by the chief of staff and that he does not find out anything. He complains that he is expected just to say 'yes' to everything, and says he could do that just as well from Berlin![33]

The Kaiser also often complained to the War Minister, Wild von Hohenborn, an old school-fellow from their days at Kassel Gymnasium, that he was not adequately informed about military planning. In June 1916 the Kaiser told Wild that he had only found out about a major attack on Verdun from the newspapers. 'If he was so little needed, he said, he might as well live in Germany.'[34]

It is true that the Kaiser's opportunities to influence operational technicalities were limited. This is underlined by a direct comparison with the German leadership during the Second World War. In endless discussions in the Führerhauptquartier, Adolf Hitler dictated the movements of every individual division. He had his decisions minuted, and woe betide anyone who ignored them! Wilhelm II, by contrast, could consider himself lucky if he received a more or less serious overview of events.

---

[31] Afflerbach, *Falkenhayn*, p. 236, n. 410.
[32] Müller, *Regierte der Kaiser?*, diary entry for 6 November 1914.
[33] Plessen diary, 23 November 1914, in Afflerbach, *Wilhelm II. als Oberster Kriegsherr*.
[34] A. Wild von Hohenborn, *Briefe und Tagebuchaufzeichnungen des preußischen Generals als Kriegsminister und Truppenführer im Ersten Weltkrieg*, ed. Helmut Reichold and Gerhard Granier, Boppard am Rhein 1986, p. 168; diary entry for 25 June 1916.

THE KAISER AS CO-ORDINATOR OF GERMAN STRATEGY

It is debatable, however, whether it was the head of state's duty to devote himself entirely to technical military details. It could be argued that he should have been more concerned with the grand sweep of policy and strategy. It is a striking continuity in the supreme command of Germany during two world wars that both Wilhelm II and Hitler saw their place as being at the map table, planning operations, and only occasionally showed an interest in other issues. In Hitler's case, companions such as Joseph Goebbels and Albert Speer were surprised at the extent to which the dictator concerned himself with military details. They wondered whether he would not have been better off leaving these to the military experts and devoting himself instead to central issues, such as the overall direction of the war, grand strategy, and foreign policy. Wilhelm II, too, who saw himself as the complete soldier, largely lost sight of his other tasks. Much more serious than the fact that he did not participate in the work of the General Staff was that constitutionally the Kaiser's job was to co-ordinate the efforts of politicians, the army, and the navy,[35] and thus, ultimately, to define the aims of the war.[36] The Chancellor of the Reich had no authority over the armed forces, and the navy led a largely independent existence next to the army. The co-ordinator at the highest level, Wilhelm II, however, was quite incapable of fulfilling his duty of bringing together the efforts of individual departments and directing them at a single goal. This is why the Freiburg historian Wilhelm Deist has recently made much of the lack of strategic leadership in Germany before and during the First World War. On the one hand he blames Wilhelm II for floundering out of his depth, and on the other the leadership structures that allotted him such an immense task.

The Kaiser's failure as co-ordinator of German strategy was undoubtedly dramatic, and had an adverse effect on the country's war effort. But if we look at the whole period of the war, it becomes apparent that negative effects came not so much from lack of co-ordination between army, navy and policy, as from unity in pursuing the wrong goals. Examples include the question of annexation, and the lack of a constructive peace policy, as expressed, for example, in the Reichstag's peace resolution of 1917 which did

---

[35] This is the main argument of Deist, 'Kaiser Wilhelm II.'.

[36] Wilhelm Deist, 'Strategy and Unlimited Warfare in Germany: Moltke, Falkenhayn and Ludendorff', in Roger Chickering and Stig Förster (eds.), *Great War, Total War. Combat and Mobilization on the Western Front, 1914–1918*, Cambridge 2000, pp. 265–80. See pp. 265f. for a definition of strategy advanced by Andreas Hillgruber: 'the integration of domestic and foreign policy, of military and psychological planning, and the administration of the economy and armaments by the top-level leadership of a state, in order to carry out a comprehensive ideological and political plan'.

not accord with the leadership's aims. This attitude reflected the mentality of the Wilhelmine leadership elite, with all its faults.[37]

In other respects, too, Wilhelm exercised direct or indirect influence on strategic decisions, in particular the declaration of unlimited submarine warfare – an act of stupidity which influenced the outcome of the conflict, in that it led to the entry of the United States into the war. In this case the Kaiser's contribution was important because Germany's military and civilian leaders disagreed bitterly on this issue, and thus the role of umpire fell to the Kaiser. He had the last word; he had to decide between Bethmann Hollweg on the one hand and Falkenhayn (later on Hindenburg, Ludendorff, and the navy) on the other. In frequent meetings, about whose difficult nature the Kaiser complained, he was quite up to his job of making decisions. He had strong moral and political reservations about unlimited submarine warfare, and in retrospect these were fully vindicated. Wilhelm II was of the opinion that 'to torpedo big passenger liners full of women and children is an act of incomparable barbarian brutality with which we will bring upon ourselves the hatred and poisonous rage of the whole world'.[38] The decision was difficult: 'On the other hand, he has to ask himself whether he can justify prolonging the war for humanitarian reasons and contrary to the advice of his military advisors, thus sacrificing more worthy soldiers? He was facing the most difficult decision of his life.'[39] The Kaiser could easily have decided in favour of submarine warfare as early as spring 1916, but he did not.

The third and crucial U-boat crisis followed in January 1917. Against the background of the 'turnip winter', growing food shortages, and the exhaustion of the Central Powers in terms of material and men, the general view was that a decision had to be reached on the matter. In addition, the Entente's rejection of the Central Powers' peace offer in December 1916 seemed to present a politically favourable moment to declare unlimited submarine warfare. In this case the army and navy leaders, the people around the Kaiser, and above all the Kaiser himself were all agreed. Even Bethmann Hollweg, weary and uncertain, abandoned his opposition to unlimited submarine warfare. Wilhelm II, relieved of the function of umpiring between substantively divergent views, agreed.

This discussion about U-boat warfare, which had catastrophic consequences for Germany, demonstrates that there was indeed a sort of strategic

---

[37] As an example, see Lyncker's and Plessen's war aims throughout the war, in Afflerbach, *Wilhelm II. als Oberster Kriegsherr.*

[38] Plessen diary, 10 January 1916, in ibid.

[39] Müller diary, 15 January 1916, in Görlitz, *Regierte der Kaiser?*, p. 147.

decision-making forum over which the Kaiser presided, and in which military and political leaders participated. Admittedly, this must be qualified
by pointing out that Wilhelm II was capable only to an extremely limited
extent of giving these negotiations a unified, consistent direction. Lyncker
indeed was of the opinion that the Kaiser was unable to lead these confer-
ences effectively.[40] His views about the enemy – the French, the British, and
the Russians – about war aims, about the general prospects of the fighting,
and about annexations were too changeable and contradictory. For this
reason any source-based analysis of whether the Kaiser regarded the war as
being primarily against Russia, Britain, or France, or against all of them at
once, would be of only limited value.

Wilhelm's vacillations also gave the people around him the impression
that he was helpless. As in peacetime, he liked to flee from brutal reality
into other worlds, and would have newspaper reports read to him for hours
about, for example, Hittite translations. Or he would go hunting in moments of crisis, appearing at dinner in the uniform of a Hofjagdmeister.
Or he would boast and surprise his retinue by proclaiming war aims that
changed almost daily, from radical plans for annexation to a dejected desire for a peace of renunciation. The people around him interpreted this
behaviour as a mechanism which he used to escape from depressing reality.
A quotation from Lyncker's war letters illustrates this. On 20 July 1918 he
reported heavy reverses in France, and wrote: 'The Kaiser calls this a victory
and fantasizes about the enemy's enormous losses. I cannot deny that I am
worried. So is the Kaiser; he is in very low spirits, and fantasizes more than
ever; with him this is never a good sign.'[41]

Let us put all this together. The Kaiser's contribution to operational
planning was insignificant; but the same cannot be said of his direct and
indirect contributions to major strategic issues. It has already become clear
that his importance for the decision-making process was less in deciding
things himself, than in whom he appointed to the top military and civilian
posts, and how the personalities and groups around him had to compete
to bring their views to bear.

THE KAISER'S PERSONNEL POLICY

These are the essential components of the 'kingship mechanism' which, as
John Röhl has shown, was already a central element of the Kaiser's power in

[40] Afflerbach, *Wilhelm II. als Oberster Kriegsherr*, no. L 345 (letter dated 3 March 1916). On the question
of unlimited submarine warfare, see also Matthew Stibbe's contribution to this volume, pp. 217–34.
[41] Lyncker to his wife, 20 July 1918, in Afflerbach, *Wilhelm II. als Oberster Kriegsherr*.

peacetime. By appointing certain people and removing others from office, Wilhelm II had always been able to dictate the basic outlines of policy. This mechanism remained in force during the war. In close co-operation with his three cabinets – the Civil Cabinet under Rudolf von Valentini (1908–18), the Military Cabinet under General Moriz von Lyncker (1908–18), and the Naval Cabinet under Admiral von Müller (1906–18) – he was able to lay down guidelines for strategy by selecting appropriate civilian and military appointees.

Let us first turn to the especially significant appointment to the post of Chief of the General Staff. Colonel General Helmuth von Moltke, who had succeeded Schlieffen, had been personally selected for the job by the Kaiser. In the July crisis, however, he proved to be so nervous that by the beginning of August 1914 the Military Cabinet was starting to look around for a successor. Erich von Falkenhayn (1861–1922), hitherto Prussian War Minister, was envisaged for this post.

Like Moltke, Falkenhayn was Wilhelm's personal choice. He had been considering Falkenhayn for this sort of appointment since at least 1912, and Falkenhayn already owed his promotion to the position of Prussian War Minister in 1913 to the Kaiser's support. And in September 1914 he became the Kaiser's candidate for the position of Chief of the General Staff, despite the fact that his appointment in autumn 1914 aroused controversy in the army.[42] Some were offended by Falkenhayn's arrogance, others envied him the post for which they felt themselves to be predestined. A serious and not unjustified point of criticism was his responsibility for the catastrophic outcome of the battles in Flanders in November 1914. Because of this, the army in general questioned his leadership abilities, as did the politicians, especially Bethmann Hollweg. In short, by the autumn/winter of 1914 a situation had arisen in which the controversial military leader could have been ousted, especially as his dismissed predecessor, Moltke, had joined forces with Bethmann Hollweg, Hindenburg and Ludendorff – leaders of Germany's eastern army and highly popular after the victory of Tannenberg – to try to have Falkenhayn replaced at the turn of 1914–15. But supported by his military cabinet, the Kaiser held on to Falkenhayn, who, he informed one of Falkenhayn's most vociferous critics, was 'an outstanding general'. The Kaiser even went so far as to compare Falkenhayn with Moltke the elder.[43]

---

[42] Afflerbach, *Falkenhayn*, pp. 211–17.
[43] Eckehard P. Guth: 'Der Gegensatz zwischen dem Oberbefehlshaber Ost und dem Chef des Generalstabs des Feldheeres 1914/15. Die Rolle des Majors v. Haeften im Spannungsfeld zwischen Hindenburg, Ludendorff und Falkenhayn', *MGM*, 35 (1984), p. 104.

Falkenhayn, kept in office by the Kaiser and the military cabinet alone, advocated a basic strategy which Hans Delbrück, an expert on military history, after the war described as a 'strategy of attrition'. From autumn 1914, Falkenhayn could no longer believe in victory and large-scale annexations. 'If we do not lose this war, we have won it', he said repeatedly to the people around him.[44] An alternative to Falkenhayn's idea of a compromise peace was Ludendorff's competing recipe for victory. Ludendorff believed that it was possible to inflict a crushing defeat on the Russians. Then, he argued, the Western Powers could be beaten in a second step, and a victorious peace achieved.

The question arises as to whether Wilhelm supported Falkenhayn against all opposition until August 1916 because he believed in Falkenhayn's strategy, or whether it was simply an act of defiance and stubbornness on the Kaiser's part in which the urgent question of a peace with victory or a compromise peace was only secondary. Numerous statements by the Kaiser suggest that, even if we take his mood swings into account, he not only thought highly of Falkenhayn, but also considered his basic strategic line correct, that is, renunciation of the Utopian notion of a decisive victory against Russia, pursuit of smaller, not decisive victories more appropriate to Germany's strength, the attempt to find a political balance with Russia and fighting against Britain – or at least that Falkenhayn managed to exert an amazing influence over his supreme commander on how to conduct a land war. Nevertheless it is impossible to distinguish a clear strategical line in this decision of personnel policy. It is much easier to understand Lyncker's reasons for keeping Falkenhayn in office; and, perhaps, Lyncker is at least as much a key figure in the question concerning 'kingship mechanism' as is Wilhelm II himself.[45] His initiative was decisive; without his intervention neither Moltke nor Falkenhayn would have been dismissed.

In the summer of 1916, the Kaiser and the military cabinet had to choose between Falkenhayn and Hindenburg–Ludendorff. For Wilhelm II this alternative was associated with further highly personal considerations. For there was one area in which Wilhelm never wavered throughout his entire period in office, and in which he was firmly and consistently determined to assert his position of power: the matter of his image, and of maintaining his own myth.

This could be attributed to Wilhelm's naive and deeply held belief in the divine right of kings. But there was a further component. To clarify this we must see the Kaiser as an actor. After all, contemporaries as different as

---

[44] Afflerbach, *Falkenhayn*, p. 198.   [45] See Afflerbach, *Wilhelm II. als Oberster Kriegsherr*.

Sarah Bernhardt and Conrad von Hötzendorf described him as such. He was prepared to play almost any role, as long as it was the leading part. This did not change throughout his entire period of rule; sometimes he played the protector of the lower classes, sometimes the part of the reactionary, sometimes that of the belligerent, sometimes that of the concerned preserver of European peace. The main thing was that he, the Kaiser, should be always at the forefront. The Kaiser's programme was simply that he was the Kaiser; the rest, while not unimportant, was negotiable, but this was not. Nor was this simply a subconscious, naive process, but rather the result of a deliberate, almost cynical calculation of its effects on the outside world.[46] During the Falkenhayn era, Wilhelm said after the Battle of Gorlice, when he was complaining that the Chief of the General Staff took no notice of him: 'After all, I put my oar in as little as possible, but for the outside world Falkenhayn must maintain the fiction that I personally order everything.'[47] Here we have the true, unchanging core of the Kaiser's programme, not only during the First World War but probably for his whole period in office. It did not matter that others did the real work; as far as the outside world was concerned, he was the Kaiser and he decided, and woe betide anyone who revealed the true state of affairs to the rest of the world. On this point the Kaiser had absolutely no sense of humour, and he placed the very highest value on maintaining this fiction.

This also largely explains the Kaiser's aversion to Hindenburg and Ludendorff. After the victory at the Battle of Tannenberg against the Russians in 1914, both enjoyed immense popularity in Germany. They could count on wide popular support, which made the Kaiser distrust them. He was most receptive to Falkenhayn's warnings that Hindenburg was another Wallenstein, and he increasingly opposed Hindenburg's power as long as possible. Only the serious military and political crisis of the summer of 1916 was able to persuade him gradually to let go of Falkenhayn and appoint Hindenburg and Ludendorff. Yet he was most reluctant, and said he might as well abdicate at once and let Hindenburg take over as a tribune of the people. The idea of appointing Hindenburg was terrible to the Kaiser, and could put him in a bad mood for days. Moreover, the Kaiser disliked Ludendorff as a person, regarding him as a dubious character, tainted by personal ambition.

On 28 August 1916 Falkenhayn was replaced as a result of Romania's entry into the war, something that the general had not foreseen at this

---

[46] A striking example of this kind of manipulation was, for example, his talk with Minister Drews at the beginning of November 1918. For a detailed description and interpretation see ibid., Introduction.

[47] Letter from Wild to his wife of 7 June 1915, in Wild, *Briefe*, p. 64.

point in time. At this news Wilhelm was ready to give up the war, and
thought that the Central Powers would now have to sue for peace. The
people around him – Valentini, Müller, Plessen and, most importantly,
Lyncker – urged him to make the replacement and used his moment of
despondency to persuade him to give up Falkenhayn. The Kaiser found
this decision difficult to make – after all, just a few days before he had
assured Falkenhayn that he wanted to keep him to the end of the war –
and he only finally made it after having consulted other advisors such as
War Minister Wild. Only then could he bring himself to take this step.

Gerhard Ritter has rightly described Falkenhayn's replacement by Hindenburg and Ludendorff as marking a highly significant stage in the history
of Imperial Germany.[48] The Kaiser lost much of the indirect control which
he had possessed during the Falkenhayn period. The nadir of his power
was the Third Supreme Army Command's heyday, when his decisions were
heavily dependent on the Hindenburg–Ludendorff tandem. This also applied to personnel decisions. Given that Germany would not tolerate their
dismissal, the two generals, by threatening to resign, could put considerable pressure on the Kaiser on almost every question. Thus, for example,
on their urging he replaced the moderate Chief of the Civil Cabinet, von
Valentini, with the conservative and fanatical die-hard von Berg.[49]

But even as the Kaiser's power reached its lowest point, he was able
to secure an important part of his decision-making role. This, however,
meant that the decision-making structures at the top of the German Reich
became even more complicated. One example will serve to illustrate these
confused power relations: Bethmann Hollweg's dismissal in July 1917. This
was considered one of the most spectacular coups executed by the two
generals. They are said to have forced the Chancellor's replacement by
themselves threatening to resign. Bethmann Hollweg forestalled this at the
last minute by offering his own resignation.

However, one thing must first be clarified. Hindenburg's and Ludendorff's threat to resign was certainly an important component in the affair,
but Bethmann Hollweg was dismissed only after he had lost the confidence
of the majority of the party leaders in the Reichstag, leaving the Chancellor
with no basis among the people, in the army leadership or in parliament.
The search for a successor revealed the whole confusion of Wilhelmine
personnel policy. It will be illustrated here by quoting from a highly in-
formative source, the diary of the imperial Adjutant General, Colonel
General Hans von Plessen. On 13 July 1917 he described how the men at

---

[48] Ritter, *Staatskunst*, vol. III, p. 249.   [49] Ibid., vol. IV, pp. 124–31.

headquarters responsible for appointments racked their brains to find a successor:

Hindenburg–Ludendorff, who had both handed in their resignations, arrived at Schloß Bellevue. Reason: they could not work with Bethmann Hollweg. In the meantime, however, Bethmann Hollweg had handed in his resignation, and it had been accepted. Reason: because the Crown Prince had received the leaders of all the parties in the Reichstag individually, and had been told pointblank by four of the six gentlemen that they could no longer deal with Bethmann Hollweg. This information had persuaded His Majesty to accept Bethmann Hollweg's resignation. Now it is a matter of finding a successor. Valentini, Chief of the Civil Cabinet, had proposed Graf Hertling, the 72-year-old Minister President of Bavaria. But Graf Hertling refused. As I had predicted. Now there is a real crisis. I met Valentini in the military cabinet. At a complete loss. Ditto Lyncker. In my presence, they went through all the conceivable and inconceivable candidates again: Dallwitz, Bülow, Tirpitz, Gallwitz, Bernstorff, Rantzau. In Valentini's view, there were reasons why none of them was suitable. Silent reflection. Thereupon I suggested Dallwitz again. Rejected, because he was once said to have declared that he would never accept this office. Thereupon I suggested Hatzfeld. His Majesty did not want him, or Bülow, or Tirpitz. Then I thought of Deputy Under-Secretary of State Michaelis, who was considered by all to be clever, energetic and reliable. Valentini delighted! Michaelis would be a suitable force. Valentini, Lyncker and I go to Hindenburg with the proposal first. He and Ludendorff agree. Now all three of us go to His Majesty, who declares himself in favour, although he has only seen Michaelis once; he is small, he says, a dwarf. Now I take Valentini to Michaelis and leave him to his fate. To this day, I do not know whether he accepted this desperately difficult position or not.[50]

The absurdity of this procedure is in inverse proportion to the significance of the appointment. The search to fill the highest political office in the German Reich, to find the fifth successor to Bismarck, produced, more or less by chance, a compromise candidate who had offended neither the Kaiser nor the military high command. Wilhelm's banal comment about the candidate's smallness was a striking illustration of his lack of seriousness. But we have seen to what extent the Kaiser had reserved at least a power of refusal – he categorically rejected certain candidates such as Tirpitz or ex-Chancellor Bülow. And although Hindenburg and Ludendorff would have been happy with either of these men, there was nothing to be done. John Röhl has described this method of exercising power based on negation in the pre-war period as 'negative personal rule', and correctly ascribes great political significance to it.[51] Michaelis remained in office only for a few months. In sum, this scene – which was by no means unique – casts light

---

[50] BA-MA, W 10–50656.   [51] Röhl, *Kaiser, Hof und Staat*, p. 126.

on the chaotic and arbitrary decision-making mechanisms at the top in Germany. However, a further source which tells us about German decision-making structures casts quite a different light on the image of a military dictatorship by Ludendorff, and the Kaiser's role under the Third Supreme Army Command. I refer to the writings of Walter Rathenau, the director of AEG (Allgemeine Elektrizitäts-Gesellschaft) and, during the war, head of the department for procuring raw materials. Rathenau was of the opinion that the incredible chaos in the leadership could not continue, and placed his hopes on Ludendorff. In a number of conversations during 1917 he tried to make clear to Ludendorff that he was 'exercising an unconscious dictatorship and that, if he were to appeal to his real power-base, he would have the support not only of parliament, but the whole of public opinion against any government department'.[52] Rathenau appealed to Ludendorff, pointing out that he was underrating his power, that he already possessed power bordering on dictatorship and therefore also had some responsibility. And, Rathenau went on, history would look to him. Ludendorff disagreed.

He replied that I [Rathenau] was over-estimating his power, that he could not get through to the Kaiser, and that he was bound on all sides. I answered by emphasizing the incredibly confused channels through which power flows: the under-secretaries of state can do nothing because the Chancellor blocks them. The Chancellor can do nothing without the confirmation of headquarters. At headquarters Ludendorff is hemmed in by Hindenburg. Hindenburg, in turn, gives in as soon as the Kaiser taps his shoulder. The Kaiser himself feels bound by the constitution, and thus the circle is closed.[53]

What are the implications for the Kaiser's role? Rathenau insisted that the Kaiser as Commander-in-Chief still had full authority over Hindenburg, and other sources agree. Ludendorff's power was perhaps more circumscribed than has often been claimed.[54] The Kaiser was by no means completely powerless, not because of his personality, but because his office gave him such a decisive role that it was impossible to exclude him from important political decisions. This was to receive clear confirmation in October 1918. In view of the defeat, Germany's political leaders insisted on Ludendorff's immediate dismissal. Yet the Kaiser managed to get rid of Ludendorff while persuading Hindenburg, who was very loyal to the Kaiser, to stay.

---

[52] Special Archive, Moscow, Rathenau Papers, 634-1-286, minute of a conversation with Ludendorff of 16 February 1917.

[53] Ibid., 10 July 1917. On Rathenau and Ludendorff, see also Hartmut Pogge von Strandmann's contribution to this volume, pp. 259–80.

[54] This is also the thesis of the newest Ludendorff biography. Cf. Franz Uhle-Wettler, *Erich Ludendorff in seiner Zeit, Soldat-Stratege-Revolutionär, Eine Neubewertung*, 2nd edn, London 1996.

The result of this was a permanent rift between the previously inseparable 'Dioscuri'.

This act in particular demonstrates that even on the eve of parliamentarization, to which he himself subscribed, and just a few weeks before his flight to Holland, Wilhelm II still had enough freedom of movement within his system to enable him to play a significant part in the course of events via the lever of personnel policy.

EXILE OR SACRIFICIAL DEATH?

Under the imminent threat of defeat the Kaiser, like the whole of Germany's political order, was swept away by general despair. By the autumn of 1918 the person of the Kaiser had absolutely no significance for the soldiers in the field, according to an opinion poll among officers in the Western army. Army and people were more than ready to sacrifice the Kaiser in return for better peace conditions. But did this not also apply to all of Germany's political and military leaders? The mood was less that of a politically motivated anti-monarchical revolution than of a mass refusal to fight by hungry and disillusioned men who had been placed under enormous strain and who now cared about nothing. Or, as Colonel Heye, who investigated the mood of the troops, judged:

The troops will not march against the enemy now, not even with Your Majesty in the lead . . . The only thing they want is a quick armistice . . . Under its generals alone the army will march home in an orderly fashion; it is still firmly under the control of its leaders. If Your Majesty were to march with the army, it would be pleased. But the army no longer wants to fight, neither abroad nor at home.[55]

In this situation of certain defeat, the Kaiser's entourage played a guessing game. What was to become of the monarch? Within the government there was a growing tendency in favour of getting rid of the Kaiser in order to facilitate negotiations with Wilson. By abdicating and making one of his grandchildren successor to the throne, Wilhelm II could have markedly improved the monarchy's chances of survival. Yet he refused, saying that he held his office by God's grace and could not resign for that reason. His reluctance became a growing obstacle for the government in Berlin in controlling the political situation in Germany. What was to become of Wilhelm II, who tried everything to remain in power? General Wilhelm Groener, a comfortable, middle-class man from Württemberg, suggested

[55] Balfour, *Der Kaiser*, p. 445.

that a member of the Hohenzollern family could not go into exile. Rather, surrounded by officers from headquarters, he should seek death on the battlefield in a specially staged attack. Indeed, following his almost two million subjects who had died in this war would have allowed him to give his reign, which was coming to an end, the aura of a Wagnerian *Götterdämmerung*.[56] But what general or commander likes to die with his troops? Neither Hannibal nor Napoleon died with their armies, preferring exile or banishment. In addition, Wilhelm II somehow felt that he was not to blame for the war. 'That is not what I wanted!' is the famous sentence that the satirist Karl Kraus bitterly put in the Kaiser's mouth. Wilhelm II felt deeply innocent, he did not want to die, nor to abdicate, rather he wanted to continue to reign. So he refused all too long to step down, demanded of his sons that they promised not to succeed him, and was ultimately forced to leave, rather than do so of his own volition. He fled ingloriously into his Dutch exile and lived in comfort for another twenty-two years. To the end, he hoped to return.[57]

The rest – exile in Amerongen and Doorn – will not be considered here. But it is not unimportant to recognize that Wilhelm spent the last twenty-two years of his life in all comfort, with a small court, with fifty-five railway carriages of personal property, and without any financial problems. And he did not recognize his own failures or try to establish his own shortcomings, but rather lived in the feeling that he had been betrayed by nearly everybody. Only one day after his abdication he talked for hours about the fact that during his reign 'he had always wanted only the best'.[58] And in the following years he accused nearly everybody of being to blame for the fact that he lost his crown, individual political and military leaders, the German people,[59] Jews – but he excepted himself from any criticism. With his insistence on his own person in autumn 1918, but also during the Weimar years, as the only possible candidate for the German throne, he made any attempt of a monarchical restoration in Germany impossible. Wilhelm II was not only the last German Kaiser, but also the grave-digger of the German monarchy.

---

[56] On the topic of the death ride, see also Isabel Hull's contribution in this volume, pp. 235–58.

[57] Cecil, *Emperor and Exile, 1900–1941*; Willibald Gutsche, *Ein Kaiser im Exil, Der letzte deutsche Kaiser Wilhelm II. in Holland. Eine kritische Biographie*, Marburg 1991; Sigurd von Ilsemann, *Der Kaiser in Holland, Aufzeichnungen des letzten Flügeladjutanten Kaiser Wilhelms II.*, edited by Harald von Koenigswald, Munich 1967–8.

[58] Ilsemann, *Der Kaiser in Holland*, p. 46 (diary entry, 10 November 1918).

[59] Ibid., pp. 118f. (diary entry, 29 October 1919).

CONCLUSION

If we return to the question of whether Wilhelm II was a mere 'shadow Kaiser' during the First World War, we must ask whether such an idea does not itself derive from the notion of an imaginary opposite, namely, an omnipotent ruler who holds all the strings in his hands, a fantasy that was perhaps created in part by Wilhelm himself. This idea of a ruler was still very much alive in Imperial Germany, as was the desire for such a monarch. Wilhelm II could not be one. He was no Friedrich II and no Bismarck; he lacked both the understanding and the talent to fulfil such a role. Nor was he a Hitler or a Stalin; for this he lacked the consistency and the ideas. Wilhelm was not as isolated at the heart of the political decision-making process as they were. It is impossible to argue against Lyncker's judgement of 19 May 1917: 'He [Wilhelm II] is very weak and strong only when he fights for his personal interests . . . He is not adequate to his great task, neither with his nerves nor intellectually.' On the other side Wilhelm II managed, with the help of his entourage, to control political and military decision-making, even if it was sometimes only by way of appointments or dismissals.

How can Wilhelm II's influence on the political and military decision-making processes during the First World War be evaluated? He was certainly not in a position to lead operations himself, or to make a substantial personal contribution. He was incapable of developing a consistent strategy, and too passive to provide any real co-ordination in strategic planning between politicians, the army and the navy. However, if these departments could not agree, the role of umpire fell to him. In addition, Wilhelm II possessed the lever of personnel policy which allowed him to appoint to important posts whomever he considered suitable, both in the civilian and military spheres. As a consequence, attitudes towards him were influenced by the fact that this staff depended on him for their future and their career hopes. However, the summer of 1916 was a very clear turning-point for the lever of personnel policy. The appointment of Hindenburg and Ludendorff at the end of August 1916 was forced on Wilhelm by the crisis of that summer, and by the entire imperial entourage. He was naturally influenced by his surroundings, by the chiefs of the cabinets, adjutants, and other advisors. During the period of the Third Army Supreme Command, the Kaiser's influence waned, but did not completely disappear. Instead, the chaos in the German leadership structures further increased.

Last but not least, by way of his right to veto all important decisions Wilhelm II could prevent or delay developments that he opposed, even if this did perhaps not amount to active policy making. What is more, his surroundings often expected or anticipated his veto and decided not to propose solutions with which he might disagree. These factors clearly show that the term 'shadow Kaiser', with its implication that Wilhelm II did not play a significant role during the First World War, is unjustified. On the other hand, this is not to claim that he made a great or positive contribution to his country during the war. The nature of the outbreak of the war, and outcome of this catastrophe categorically prohibit any positive assessment of Wilhelm II's role as supreme warlord of the German Empire.

CHAPTER 9

Germany's 'last card'. Wilhelm II and the decision in favour of unrestricted submarine warfare in January 1917

Matthew Stibbe

Wer die See beherrscht, beherrscht auch den Handel, und wer den Handel beherrscht, dem gehören auch die Schätze der Welt und damit die Welt selbst.

Ernst Bassermann, National Liberal spokesman, during the Reichstag debate on the Second Navy Law in 1900[1]

The decision of the German government to launch a campaign of unrestricted submarine warfare in the waters around the British Isles in January 1917 was arguably the turning point of the First World War and certainly one of the main causes of Germany's collapse and defeat in 1918. It has been described in previous literature as the Reich Chancellor Theobald von Bethmann Hollweg's 'darkest hour' and as a 'literal capitulation of political authority before the military in the most crucial issue of the entire [war]'.[2] Alternatively, it has been portrayed as a desperate gamble determined by the 'exorbitant war aims' of German industry and agriculture;[3] as the last chance to 'repay' London for its 'starvation blockade' of Germany;[4] as a propaganda exercise designed to lift morale and combat 'war weariness'

---

[1] Cited in Baldur Kaulisch, ' "... und bitter not ist uns eine starke deutsche Flotte!" Die Flottenrüstung des deutschen Imperialismus um die Jahrhundertwende', in Willibald Gutsche and Baldur Kaulisch (eds.), *Bilder aus der Kaiserzeit. Historische Streiflichter 1897 bis 1917*, Leipzig, Jena, and East Berlin 1985, pp. 38–9.

[2] Gerhard Ritter, *The Sword and the Scepter. The Problem of Militarism in Germany*, 4 vols., Coral Gables, FL 1968–74, vol. III, p. 315.

[3] Baldur Kaulisch, 'Der "Sprung ins Dunkle". Der Entschluß zum uneingeschränkten U-Boot-Krieg im Januar 1917', in Gutsche and Kaulisch (eds.), *Bilder aus der Kaiserzeit*, pp. 292–9.

[4] Holger Herwig, 'Total Rhetoric, Limited War. Germany's U-boat Campaign, 1917–1918', in Roger Chickering and Stig Förster (eds.), *Great War, Total War. Combat and Mobilization on the Western Front, 1914–1918*, Cambridge 2000, p. 198. On the British blockade of Germany see C. Paul Vincent, *The Politics of Hunger. The Allied Blockade of Germany, 1915–1919*, Athens, GA 1985; Avner Offer, 'The Blockade of Germany and the Strategy of Starvation, 1914–1918', in Chickering and Förster, *Great War, Total War*, pp. 169–88.

during the 'turnip winter' of 1916/17;[5] and even as part of the 'logic of total war . . . in both the material and moral senses'.[6] But what role did Kaiser Wilhelm II play personally in the coming of unrestricted submarine warfare? How far did he share the optimistic assessment of his naval advisers that England would be brought to its knees within six months, as well as the popular desire for revenge against 'Perfidious Albion'? And why did he choose to abandon the moderate stance he had previously adopted on this issue?

Until recently historians have largely ignored such questions. Rather, unrestricted submarine warfare has been interpreted as the product of a power struggle between 'responsible' officials in the Foreign Office and Reich Chancellery on the one hand, and the more extreme anti-English elements within the Admiralty staff and the Reich Naval Office on the other – with the latter receiving support from the supreme military commanders in the East, Hindenburg and Ludendorff, and from a variety of right-wing industrialists and annexationist pressure groups.[7] By contrast, Wilhelm himself is described as having 'increasingly lost control of events' during the last four years of his reign,[8] proving that he was 'not up to the demands of his position as Supreme War Lord'.[9] In particular he is accused of failing to mediate effectively between the two sides in the debate on submarine warfare and related issues such as the war aims question, so that he became, in effect, a peripheral figure in the decision-making process, a mere *Schattenkaiser* without any meaningful influence on the course of the war.[10] These views were also shared by many of Wilhelm's contemporaries,

---

[5] David Welch, *Germany, Propaganda and Total War, 1914–1918. The Sins of Omission*, London 2000, p. 129.

[6] Offer, 'The Blockade of Germany', p. 173.

[7] See e.g. Ritter, *The Sword and the Scepter*, vol. III, *passim*; Hans Gatzke, *Germany's Drive to the West* (Drang nach Westen). *A Study of Western War Aims During the First World War*, Baltimore, and Madison 1950; Fritz Fischer, *Griff nach der Weltmacht. Die Kriegszielpolitik des kaiserlichen Deutschlands, 1914–18*, 2nd edn, Düsseldorf 1962; Fritz Klein *et al.*, *Deutschland im Ersten Weltkrieg*, 3 vols., 2nd edn, East Berlin 1970; Konrad Jarausch, *The Enigmatic Chancellor. Bethmann Hollweg and the Hubris of Imperial Germany*, New Haven and London 1973. Also, the more recent work of Raffael Scheck, 'Der Kampf des Tirpitz-Kreises um den uneingeschränkten U-Boot-Krieg und einen politischen Kurswechsel im deutschen Kaiserreich, 1916–17', *Militärgeschichtliche Mitteilungen (MGM)*, 55 (1996), pp. 69–91; and Raffael Scheck, *Alfred von Tirpitz and German Right-Wing Politics, 1914–1930*, Atlantic Highlands, NJ 1998.

[8] Willibald Gutsche, *Wilhelm II. Der letzte Kaiser des Deutschen Reiches. Eine Biographie*, Berlin 1991, p. 174.

[9] Wilhelm Deist, 'Censorship and Propaganda During the First World War', in Jean-Jacques Becker and Stéphane Audoin-Rouzeau (eds.), *Les sociétés européennes et la guerre de 1914–1918*, Paris and Nanterre 1990, p. 200. See also Deist, 'Kaiser Wilhelm II als Oberster Kriegsherr', in John C. G. Röhl (ed.), *Der Ort Kaiser Wilhelms II. in der deutschen Geschichte*, Munich 1991, pp. 25–42.

[10] Lamar Cecil, *Wilhelm II*, vol. II: *Emperor and Exile, 1900–1941*, Chapel Hill, NC 1996, p. 212.

including those who came into contact with him on a regular basis. Thus Admiral Georg Alexander von Müller, the Chief of the Naval Cabinet, complained repeatedly in his diaries and letters that the Kaiser had chosen to take a 'back seat' during the war and had allowed himself to be displaced by the High Command on all the major strategic and political issues affecting the Empire.[11] Likewise James Gerard, the United States ambassador in Berlin between 1913 and 1917 and thereafter an ardent critic of 'Kaiserism', wrote that there was only 'one force in Germany which ultimately decides every great question, except the fate of its own head . . . [and that] is the Great General Staff'.[12]

The judgements made above are doubtless justified to a point. Nonetheless, as will be argued in more detail below, there are alternative ways of reading the evidence from Müller's diaries and other eye-witness accounts which suggest that in spite of the Kaiser's ill-health and volatile moods, he was able to make a number of indirect and direct contributions on major strategic issues. For instance, although in practice he was largely excluded from operational command of Germany's land forces, he was able to use his position as commander of the navy to block any move towards a premature engagement with the British Royal Navy in the opening weeks of the war. In this he was at one with the views of the Chancellor, Bethmann Hollweg, who wished to keep the German battle fleet intact as a possible bargaining tool at any future peace conference.[13] Furthermore, Wilhelm also retained the right to promote and dismiss all senior military officers and civilian officials within Prussia and the Reich. By the end of 1916 he had already dismissed two of his army chiefs of staff in succession – Helmuth von Moltke and Erich von Falkenhayn – and two chiefs of admiralty staff – Hugo von Pohl and Gustav Bachmann. With the support of Bethmann Hollweg he had also sidelined and then dismissed Admiral von Tirpitz, the Secretary of State at the Reich Naval Office since 1897 and a keen advocate of unrestricted submarine warfare. In this sense, at least, Wilhelm had been able to demonstrate his continued importance as supreme warlord.[14]

[11] Walter Görlitz (ed.), *The Kaiser and His Court. The Diaries, Note Books and Letters of Admiral Georg Alexander von Müller, Chief of the Naval Cabinet, 1914–1918*, London 1961, p. 253 (Müller's diary entry for 3 April 1917).
[12] James W. Gerard, *Face to Face with Kaiserism*, London 1918, p. 21.
[13] Alan Palmer, *The Kaiser. War Lord of the Second Reich*, London 1978, pp. 184–5. Christopher Clark, in his recent study *Kaiser Wilhelm II. Profiles in Power*, London 2000, also notes that Wilhelm exercised 'a more direct, if largely restraining influence, on the wartime operations of the German navy' (p. 227).
[14] Cf. Holger Afflerbach, 'Wilhelm II as Supreme Warlord in the First World War', *War and History*, 5 (1998), pp. 427–49, esp. pp. 440–6. A revised version of this article appears in this volume, pp. 195–216.

The case for a partial reassessment of the Kaiser's role in the First World War has already been made by a number of scholars in recent years. Particularly influential has been John Röhl's notion of a 'kingship mechanism' operating at the heart of the decision-making process in pre-war Wilhelmine Germany, an idea which Holger Afflerbach has now applied, in a more limited sense and with certain modifications, to the years 1914 to 1918.[15] The purpose of this essay is to extend this debate by focusing in particular on the manner in which the decision to announce unrestricted submarine warfare came about. Here, it will be argued, Wilhelm's influence was crucial, if largely negative. His uncertain and wavering support for the more 'moderate' line on submarine warfare until the end of 1916 was combined with a failure to devise any alternative strategy for overcoming the stalemate on the Western Front – including the possibility of sacrificing some of Germany's war aims on the continent in exchange for a negotiated peace settlement with one or more of the Allies. For this, Wilhelm, as supreme co-ordinator of military and civilian affairs, was ultimately responsible. The narrower question of naval strategy against Great Britain also never found a convincing solution, partly because this would have required co-operation between the army, navy, and politicians, and partly because it would have meant overcoming the Kaiser's determination not to hand over command of the navy to a subordinate such as Tirpitz. As we shall see below, the lack of a unified naval command necessarily restricted Germany's ability to wage an effective campaign at sea in the first two years of the war while simultaneously enabling Wilhelm to veto any alternative strategies suggested by his top naval and civilian advisers.[16]

Finally, the U-boat issue also crossed paths with another important development in the last four years of Hohenzollern rule which is frequently alluded to in the Müller diaries: the changes in the popular perception of the monarchy brought about by Wilhelm's increasing withdrawal from the centre stage of public affairs and by the simultaneous rise to prominence of Field Marshal Paul von Hindenburg, military commander in the East and victor over the Russians at the Battle of Tannenberg, as an alternative focus

---

[15] See Röhl's essay, 'Der "Königsmechanismus" im Kaiserreich', *Historische Zeitschrift*, 236 (1983), pp. 539–77. English translation in: Röhl, *The Kaiser and His Court*, pp. 107–30. Cf. Afflerbach's discussion in 'Wilhelm II as Supreme Warlord', *passim*; and my own contribution to the debate, 'Kaiser Wilhelm II. The Hohenzollerns at War', in Matthew Hughes and Matthew Seligmann (eds.), *Leadership in Conflict, 1914–1918*, Barnsley 2000, pp. 265–83.

[16] Cf. Werner Rahn, 'The German Naval War, 1914–1918. Strategy and Experience', in Hugh Cecil and Peter H. Liddle (eds.), *Facing Armageddon. The First World War Experienced*, London 1996, pp. 121–34.

for nationalist loyalties and expectations.[17] The question therefore arises as to how far Wilhelm was aware of these shifts in public opinion and how far they determined the stance he was to take on unrestricted submarine warfare in 1916–17. Before looking at this particular issue in more depth, however, it is first necessary to consider the crisis facing Germany on 4 August 1914 when, contrary to expectations, Britain too joined the Allied coalition against the Central Powers.

THE STRATEGIC DILEMMA

Although from 1897 onwards Wilhelm II had played a decisive role in the emergence of German 'world policy' and the construction of a battle fleet to rival that of the British Royal Navy,[18] there is little evidence to suggest that he had ever considered in detail how he might use it to conduct a naval campaign against Britain in the event of a real war, let alone what he would do if Britain held back its own fleet and instead mounted a distant economic blockade of the German coastline, a possibility raised by August von Heeringen, the then Chief of Admiralty Staff, in a report on the annual naval manoeuvres in 1912.[19] True, at the notorious 'War Council' of 8 December 1912, which Admirals von Heeringen, von Müller, and von Tirpitz all attended, Wilhelm had identified England as a likely enemy in a future conflict and had called upon the navy to prepare itself accordingly. In particular he foresaw a need for 'immediate submarine warfare against English troop transports in the Scheldt or by Dunkirk [and] mine warfare in the Thames' making it an imperative to ensure a 'speedy build up of U-boats etc.'.[20] Nonetheless, the envisaged conference of 'all naval authorities concerned' did not take place after 8 December 1912 and the rate of submarine building also slackened considerably. Consequently Germany entered the war with no coherent strategy for defeating its enemies

---

[17] On this issue see also Bernd Sösemann, 'Der Verfall des Kaisergedankens im Ersten Weltkrieg', in Röhl (ed.), *Der Ort Kaiser Wilhelms II. in der deutschen Geschichte*, pp. 145–70.

[18] Paul Kennedy, 'The Kaiser and German *Weltpolitik*. Reflexions on Wilhelm II's Place in the Making of German Foreign Policy', in John C. G. Röhl and Nicolaus Sombart (eds.), *Kaiser Wilhelm II. New Interpretations*, Cambridge 1982, pp. 143–68. See also the very detailed evidence now presented in John C. G. Röhl, *Wilhelm II. Der Aufbau der Persönlichen Monarchie, 1888–1900*, Munich 2001, esp. pp. 1109–52.

[19] Heeringen's report is referred to in Werner Rahn, 'Strategische Probleme der deutschen Seekriegsführung, 1914–1918', in Wolfgang Michalka (ed.), *Der Erste Weltkrieg. Wirkung, Wahrnehmung, Analyse*, Munich 1994, p. 345.

[20] On the 'War Council' see John C. G. Röhl, *The Kaiser and His Court. Wilhelm II and the Government of Germany*, Cambridge 1994, pp. 162–89.

at sea, and with only twenty U-boats ready for active service.[21] In the intervening eighteen months before July 1914, Wilhelm had fallen back upon the policy preferred by Bethmann Hollweg, which was to concentrate on building up conventional land forces against Russia and France while reducing expenditure on naval armaments in an effort to appease England. In this way Bethmann hoped to ensure British neutrality if and when it came to a clash of arms on the continent.[22]

With the outbreak of war at the beginning of August 1914, and the unwelcome confirmation that Britain would intervene after all to prevent the German army from crushing France and Belgium, an immediate row broke out within the Kaiser's inner circle as to what naval strategy to pursue. The Chancellor, supported by Helmuth von Moltke, the Chief of the General Staff, and Admirals von Müller and von Pohl (Chief of the Naval Cabinet and Chief of the Admiralty Staff respectively) urged the Kaiser to stick to the original cabinet order of 30 July 1914, which had instructed naval commanders to prepare for the possibility of limited guerrilla operations against the Royal Navy only. Admiral von Tirpitz and his officials in the Reich Naval Office, who wished for a strategy of drawing out and engaging the Royal Navy in large-scale battle at the outset of the war, were ardently opposed to this decision. Part of the reason for this, it must be said, was that Tirpitz feared that the German army might conclude the war on the Continent by itself and thus reap all the glory, leaving the navy as a minor and expendable player in subsequent peace negotiations with a Britain undefeated at sea.[23]

The way in which Wilhelm settled this dispute over strategy was to come down unequivocally against Tirpitz and his demand for a decisive naval battle early in the war. On 6 August 1914 he issued new instructions preventing the immediate use of the High Seas Fleet. This in turn was a reflection of confidence that early victories over France and Russia would force the British to come to terms with Germany, or at least ensure its defeat in a 'Second Punic War'. It was also a clear message that Tirpitz, the

---

[21] The figure of twenty U-boats is given in Baldur Kaulisch, 'Die Auseinandersetzung über den uneingeschränkten U-Boot-Krieg innerhalb der herrschenden Klassen im zweiten Halbjahr 1916 und seine Eröffnung im Februar 1917', in Fritz Klein (ed.), *Politik im Krieg, 1914–1918. Studien zur Politik der deutschen herrschenden Klassen im Ersten Weltkrieg*, East Berlin 1964, p. 95, n. 14. According to Wilhelm Deist, only three new submarines were built in Germany between mid-1912 and July 1914, compared to fifteen submarines between November 1910 and mid-1912, a fact which further underlines the lack of adequate preparations for naval warfare against Britain in the aftermath of the December 'War Council'. See Deist, 'Kaiser Wilhelm II. als Oberster Kriegsherr', p. 35.

[22] Fischer, *Griff nach der Weltmacht*, pp. 41–6.

[23] See my discussion of this in Matthew Stibbe, *German Anglophobia and the Great War, 1914–1918*, Cambridge 2001, pp. 82ff.

architect of the German battle fleet, would not be allowed to interfere in strategic decisions, let alone take over command of the fleet from the Kaiser himself. 'I have created and trained the fleet', Wilhelm told the admiral on one occasion later in the war. 'Where, when and how I wish to use it is exclusively the supreme commander's business. Everybody else will have to remain silent on this matter and obey.'[24]

If Tirpitz were to be sidelined from strategic decision-making, however, and if the High Seas Fleet were to remain in port, what other options did Germany have in terms of conducting an effective naval campaign against Britain? In particular, how might the navy be used to support the army's campaign on the Continent? One solution was to allow sporadic raids on the British coast-line, such as the bombardment of eastern towns like Scarborough and Hull in December 1914. However, such actions were nothing but pinpricks to Britain, irritating but hardly threatening to the security of the mainland as a whole. Another was to send out small-scale sorties of battle cruisers into the North Sea to test the water, but after the Dogger Bank incident in January 1915, when the *Blücher* was caught and sunk in an engagement with superior British forces, the Kaiser was reluctant to risk even that.[25] Finally, there were the Zeppelin raids on several British towns from January 1915 onwards, which were highly popular in the German press but caused alarm in Foreign Office circles because of their likely impact on neutral, especially American, opinion. In total fifty-one Zeppelin raids and fifty-seven aeroplane raids had resulted in 1,413 deaths and 3,407 injuries on the British mainland by the end of the war, hardly a large tally but enough to undermine further Germany's image abroad. Indeed, as Gerard De Groot has argued recently, 'the propaganda value to the British [resulting from these raids] heavily outweighed their strategic value to the Germans'.[26]

One option, which could have brought results, had it been tried more systematically in the opening months of the war, was to focus attention on the English Channel as the major transit route of the British Expeditionary Force between Britain and France. A concentrated attack here, while the main part of the British battle fleet remained far away at its bases in Scotland, could well have caused major disruption to the British army's supply lines, even if it did not result in immediate or outright victory.[27] However,

[24] Palmer, *The Kaiser*, p. 186.

[25] After the Dogger Bank incident Wilhelm dismissed the Commander-in-Chief of the Fleet, Admiral von Ingenohl, and replaced him with Admiral von Pohl (who was in turn replaced by Vice Admiral Scheer in January 1916). Cf. Rahn, 'The German Naval War', p. 123.

[26] Gerard J. De Groot, *Blighty. British Society in the Era of the Great War*, London 1996, p. 200.

[27] Scheck, *Alfred von Tirpitz*, p. 24.

as Werner Rahn points out, the implementation of this plan required common strategic planning between the army and the navy, which was only possible through the person of the Kaiser. Here again, Wilhelm's influence was decisive, if only in the negative sense that he failed to seize the initiative or to bring his military and naval advisers together on this issue. As a result, the German navy had to be content with some very minor propaganda successes overseas, such as the breakthrough of the battleships *Goeben* and *Emden* through the Mediterranean to Constantinople and their formal handover to the Turkish authorities at the end of August 1914. According to Rahn, examples like this merely drew attention to the lack of 'strategic interplay between operations overseas and in home waters', increasing discontent in naval circles with the negative consequences of 'personal rule' and lending weight to rumours that Wilhelm had ordered the main part of the fleet to remain in port out of cowardice, incompetence, or a misguided consideration for his royal cousins in England.[28]

In the meantime, the British, through their more favourable geographical position, were able to establish a 'distant' economic blockade of German ports using surface ships, which caused increasing disruption to German trade and imports via neutral countries. In February 1915, under some pressure from Tirpitz and his circle, Wilhelm agreed to retaliate by establishing an exclusion zone around the British Isles and threatening to sink without warning any ship that entered these waters. The key problem, however, was that the more rigorously these blockade measures were applied, the more likely it became that important neutral countries, such as the United States, would be alienated from Germany. The prospect of America entering the war indeed weighed heavily on the Kaiser's mind, as we know from Admiral von Müller's diaries.[29] Already in May 1915, following the sinking of the British passenger liner *Lusitania* with 128 American citizens among the 1,200 dead, he had issued orders to submarine captains to refrain from attacking neutral vessels, and further restrictions introduced at the end of August 1915 meant that U-boat activity virtually ceased along the west coast of England, where most trans-Atlantic vessels arrived and departed.[30] When Tirpitz threatened to resign over this issue for a third time in March 1916, Wilhelm decided to let him go, although not without

---

[28] Rahn, 'The German Naval War', p. 125.
[29] See e.g. Görlitz (ed.), *The Kaiser and his Court*, pp. 131 and 154 (Müller's diary entries for 1 February 1916 and 30 April 1916).
[30] The arguments and U-turns over submarine warfare in 1915–16 are summarized in detail in Ernest R. May, *The World War and American Isolation, 1914–1917*, Cambridge, MA 1959, pp. 197–252. See also Clark, *Kaiser Wilhelm II*, pp. 230–2.

a sense of foreboding, for Tirpitz was by now a popular figure not only within the navy, but also among the public at large.[31]

By this time, indeed, pressure was mounting from other sources to resume unrestricted submarine warfare – that is, the sinking of both armed and unarmed merchant vessels sailing in the 'war zone' around the British Isles without consideration for neutrals. An important convert at the end of 1915 was Falkenhayn, the army Chief of Staff, who now believed that the submarine was 'the only weapon at our disposal which can safely and directly hit England in its vital nerve centre'.[32] Falkenhayn's demands were ruthlessly pursued by Tirpitz and by the new Chief of Admiralty Staff, Admiral von Holtzendorff, who told the Kaiser in January 1916 that the removal of all restrictions on submarine commanders was 'essential' if Germany was to emerge from the war victoriously. Attempts to limit U-boat warfare to enemy shipping alone would not work, Holtzendorff argued, because of Britain's continued 'abuse of [neutral] flags'.[33]

By contrast, Bethmann Hollweg and his supporters within the Kaiser's entourage, most notably the Chief of the Civil Cabinet, Rudolf von Valentini, and the Foreign Office representative, Karl Georg von Treutler, argued repeatedly that the chances of success with the submarine weapon were still too small to justify taking the risk of an American entry into the war. At Bethmann's request, the shipping magnate Albert Ballin also sent a letter to the Kaiser in the middle of January 1916 urging him not to give way to Tirpitz on the submarine question. 'In English ports', Ballin wrote, 'at least 200 overseas cruisers arrive each day and an equal number depart. We would certainly do England some damage if we were to sink 30 or 40 ships a day, but I doubt if we would force her to sue for peace.'[34]

Caught between the conflicting views of his military and civilian advisors, Wilhelm was now faced with 'the most difficult decision of his life'.[35] Another factor in the equation was the growing food shortages at home and the outbreak of bread riots in several cities in the early months of 1916, which gave rise to fears of a possible breakdown of law and order.[36] Something was needed to boost public morale, and if victories on the

---

[31] Cf. Görlitz, *The Kaiser and his Court*, p. 144 (Müller's diary entry for 9 March 1916).

[32] Falkenhayn to Bethmann Hollweg, 13 February 1916. Reproduced in Helmut Otto and Karl Schmiedel (eds.), *Der Erste Weltkrieg. Dokumente*, East Berlin 1977, pp. 162–4.

[33] Görlitz, *The Kaiser and his Court*, p. 129 (Müller's diary entry for 24 January 1916).

[34] Cited in Klein *et al.*, *Deutschland im Ersten Weltkrieg*, vol. II, p. 331.

[35] Görlitz, *The Kaiser and his Court*, p. 126 (Müller's diary entry for 15 January 1916).

[36] On bread riots see Ute Daniel, *The War From Within. German Working-Class Women in the First World War*, Oxford 1997, esp. pp. 246–50 and Belinda Davis, *Home Fires Burning. Food, Politics and Everyday Life in World War I Berlin*, Chapel Hill and London 2000, esp. pp. 76–88.

battlefield could not achieve this, success with the 'miracle' submarine
weapon could.[37] Wilhelm was also under pressure from conservative figures
within the imperial entourage and even from members of his own family,
including the Empress Auguste Viktoria, Crown Prince Wilhelm, and the
Kaiser's second eldest son Eitel Friedrich, all of whom despised Bethmann
Hollweg personally and plotted on Tirpitz's behalf to remove him from
office.[38] In spite of this, Wilhelm decided once again to back 'his' Chancellor
and not to launch unrestricted submarine warfare in the spring of 1916. One
factor was his principled opposition to the notion of killing women and
children. Another was his determination to avoid a war with America, if
at all possible.[39] However, there were also signs that Wilhelm was starting
to waver, and, more crucially, that he was beginning to be influenced by
public opinion on this matter. In this sense the popular outrage in right-
wing circles caused by Tirpitz's dismissal proved to be a significant turning
point.

THE IMPACT OF PUBLIC OPINION

Public criticism of the government's supposedly 'weak-kneed' stance on the
submarine question had been mounting throughout the year 1915; but in
the first months of 1916 it suddenly increased in both volume and intensity.
The first sign of this was a resolution introduced by the Conservatives into
the budget commission of the Prussian House of Deputies on 9 February
1916 condemning the government's policy of yielding to American pressure
on the submarine issue.[40] This was followed by a petition organized by
Professor Dietrich Schäfer of the Independent Committee for a German
Peace in favour of unrestricted submarine warfare which was presented
to the Reich Chancellor's office with over 90,000 signatures on 15 March
1916. Copies of the same petition were also sent by post to every member
of the Reichstag and every member of the Bundesrat, as well as to leading
members of Germany's princely households.[41]

The government's response to such agitation was to make even greater
use of its powers of censorship under the state of siege in order to suppress

---

[37] On the notion of the submarine as a 'miracle weapon' see also Herwig, 'Total Rhetoric, Limited War', p. 198.

[38] See e.g. Görlitz, *The Kaiser and his Court*, pp. 105, 149–50 (Müller's diary entries for 9 and 10 September 1915, 24 March 1916, and 8 April 1916). Another figure in the anti-Bethmann court faction was the influential Minister of the Royal Household, Count August zu Eulenburg. Cf. Scheck, 'Der Kampf des Tirpitz-Kreises', p. 75; and Scheck, *Alfred von Tirpitz*, pp. 48–9.

[39] Görlitz, *The Kaiser and his Court*, pp. 138 and 153–4 (Müller's diary entries for 23 February 1916 and 30 April 1916).

[40] Klein *et al.*, *Deutschland im Ersten Weltkrieg*, vol. II, p. 374.

[41] Copy of petition in Bundesarchiv Berlin, Akten der Reichskanzlei, No. 1422/1.

debate on the submarine issue. It also organized a series of police raids on the offices and private addresses of well-known right-wing extremists (for instance, 268,650 copies of Schäfer's petition were confiscated in raids on several Berlin business premises at the end of March 1916).[42] Later in June 1916 Bethmann Hollweg even used the occasion of a debate in the Reichstag to attack those he called the 'pirates of public opinion', in particular the East Prussian Conservative Wolfgang Kapp, who had become a hero of the German Right after revealing himself as the author of an anti-government pamphlet entitled *Die nationalen Kreise und der Reichskanzler*.[43] According to Kapp, Bethmann had brought disaster for Germany by refusing to make full use of submarine warfare and by allying himself with liberals and socialists against the 'national circles' who represented the most loyal citizens of the Reich. Other secretly produced pamphlets went even further than this, accusing both the Chancellor and the Kaiser of harbouring a secret love affair with England, or, worse still, of having fallen under the influence of 'international Jewry' which was allegedly seeking to destroy Germany from within. One particularly nasty flysheet, which was confiscated by the police in both Berlin and Munich in the summer of 1916, read as follows:

The Kaiser is completely surrounded by Jews. His most powerful advisors are the Israelites Ballin, Rathenau, v. Mendelssohn, Arnold, James, Simon, v. Bleichröder, Goldschmidt-Rothschild, Carow, Koppel and others, who as members of an international plutocracy take full advantage of the fact that their relatives sit in high places in all the governments of foreign lands. Even the Kaiser's Oberhofmeister, Frhr. v. Reischach, is the son of a Frankfurt Jewess, Bertha Bonn. The Kaiser's first Leibarzt, Dr. v. Ilberg, comes from a Jewish family. A pillar of the England-party (*Engländerpartei*) is Countess Maria Esther Waldersee, an American Jewess, née Lee, who works in Waldeck on behalf of the English *Judenmission*. The Kaiser is visibly in close alliance with the Jews, associated with, among others, His Excellency Paul v. Herrmann, the son of a Jewish stock-broker in Berlin. Helfferich, whom the Jews have selected to be the next Reich Chancellor, is himself treated by them as one of their own. The exclusion of Germanic elements is apparent everywhere, and so it is now high time to form a front against the suppression of *Deutschtum* in Germany and against the delivery of the government into the hands of the Jews and the international monetary powers.[44]

How far was the Kaiser aware of the growing hostility towards the Chancellor, and, by extension, towards his own person, as a result of the U-boat

---

[42] Cf. Traugott von Jagow to Wilhelm von Loebell, 23 March 1916, in Geheimes Staatsarchiv Preußischer Kulturbesitz, Berlin-Dahlem, Ministerium des Innern, Rep. 77, Tit. 863a, no. 6.

[43] Copy in ibid., Rep. 92, Nachlaß Wolfgang Kapp, no. 582. On Kapp himself see also Jarausch, *The Enigmatic Chancellor*, pp. 359–62.

[44] Copies of flysheet in Bundesarchiv Berlin, Akten der Reichskanzlei, no. 1418, and Bayerisches Hauptstaatsarchiv IV – Kriegsarchiv, Munich, Akten des stellvertretenden Generalkommandos des I. Bayerischen Armeekorps, no. 1938. See also Stibbe, *German Anglophobia and the Great War*, p. 158.

controversy? Recently discovered documentary evidence suggests that the idea of him being safely cocooned at Headquarters and shielded from bad news is only a partial truth. Bethmann Hollweg and Valentini, for instance, regularly provided Wilhelm with copies of newspaper reports attacking the government in order to arouse the Kaiser's anger against Tirpitz and his circle and to convince him that Tirpitz was seeking to establish an 'alternative government' within the Reich Naval Office by feeding selective information to the press. On one occasion in November 1915 Wilhelm described a pro-submarine speech by the right-wing journalist Count Ernst zu Reventlow as a 'deliberate incitement, with a clear lunge at *My* government' and demanded that strong action be taken against him.[45] Six months later, in a letter to Crown Prince Wilhelm, he called Wolfgang Kapp an 'arch scoundrel and a liar'. He also ordered the dismissal of Jaspar von Maltzahn, the Crown Prince's special advisor, who was known to be a follower of Tirpitz and to have encouraged the Crown Prince in his anti-Bethmann views.[46]

The problem for Wilhelm, however, was that he also remained desperate to identify himself with popular causes, especially those which were patriotic in inspiration and drew support from 'educated' middle-class opinion, as Tirpitz's campaign undoubtedly did. This perhaps explains why he approved an interim order for 'intensified' but not unrestricted submarine warfare in February 1916 and why, during a discussion at Supreme Headquarters on 30 April 1916, he sided with Falkenhayn against the 'moderates' and declared: 'We are now faced with a choice: Verdun or the U-boat war.'[47] In fact, this stage of the submarine crisis lasted until the end of May 1916, when even 'intensified' U-boat war against armed enemy merchantmen was cancelled. This left German submarine commanders operating under a variety of restrictions which remained in force for the remainder of the year.[48]

In the meantime, the 'moderates' were also not especially encouraged by what they saw as the Kaiser's inability to stand up to the extreme advocates of unrestricted submarine warfare. Wilhelm's continued refusal to replace Falkenhayn as Chief of Staff with the more popular Hindenburg was another source of discontent, especially given the repeated failure of

---

[45] Ibid., p. 90.
[46] Scheck, *Alfred von Tirpitz*, p. 50. Cf. Görlitz (ed.), *The Kaiser and his Court*, p. 173 (Müller's diary entry for 20 June 1916).
[47] Görlitz, *The Kaiser and his Court*, p. 153 (Müller's diary entry for 30 April 1916).
[48] May, *The World War and American Isolation*, p. 242. Cf. Ritter, *The Sword and the Scepter*, vol. III, pp. 264–88.

Falkenhayn's strategy of attrition in the West and the virtual collapse of the Verdun offensive by June 1916, which seemed to offer the submarine enthusiasts another excuse to continue their agitation. August Stein, for instance, editor of the left-liberal *Frankfurter Zeitung*, became convinced that continued setbacks on the battlefield coupled with right-wing agitation at home would lead to the collapse of the Hohenzollern monarchy and a 'frightful period of military dictatorship after the war'.[49] Likewise the prominent banker and former Colonial Secretary Bernhard Dernburg wrote to a friend on 15 August 1916 expressing his fears that the Chancellor and the Kaiser were no longer able to maintain effective control over the direction of the German war effort: 'the danger is that we will be led into desperate measures, because nobody knows what to do to achieve victory now that we have been pushed onto the defensive on all fronts'.[50]

Such was the situation inside Germany when Romania entered the war on the Allied side on 23 August 1916, forcing the Reich leadership to rethink its strategy in an effort to regain the initiative from the enemy coalition.

THE SUBMARINE CRISIS INTENSIFIES

In fact, one of the first casualties of Romania's entry into the war was Falkenhayn, who was finally dismissed by the Kaiser on 27 August 1916 and replaced by Hindenburg and Ludendorff. This was a real turning point, because the new supreme army commanders were not merely determined to assert their power in the operational sphere, but also to extend their influence over German naval and diplomatic strategy, and over the German home front as well, thus encroaching directly on Wilhelm's prerogatives as Kaiser. In effect, the army was now in charge of the entire German war effort, and Wilhelm, together with his civilian advisors and officials, was increasingly pushed to the sidelines. An example here would be the preparation of new legislation to increase wartime controls over the civilian work force, a move which was rigorously but unsuccessfully opposed by the Chancellor and the government on the grounds that such legislation could damage morale on the home front and destroy the last vestiges of the wartime political truce or *Burgfrieden*.[51]

---

[49] Stibbe, *German Anglophobia and the Great War*, p. 119.
[50] Dernburg to Adolf von Harnack, 15 August 1916. Cited in Klein *et al.*, *Deutschland im Ersten Weltkrieg*, vol. II, p. 383.
[51] For a good discussion of the auxiliary service law, which finally came into effect at the end of 1916, see Gerald Feldman, *Army, Industry and Labor in Germany, 1914–1918*, Princeton 1966, pp. 149–249.

The late summer and early autumn of 1916 also saw the submarine question reach its crisis point in terms of German domestic politics. On 18 September 1916, for instance, pro-submarine campaigners in Munich announced the formation of a People's Committee for the Rapid Overthrow of England (Volksausschuß für rasche Niederkämpfung Englands), soon to be followed by the appearance of similar committees, composed largely of Pan-Germans and their supporters, throughout Bavaria. The aim of the Pan-Germans was to use these committees as a front to put pressure on the government in Berlin to introduce unrestricted submarine warfare without further delay and to 'enlighten the people about the dangers from an undefeated England', especially with regard to Germany's economic future.[52] The Munich-based Volksausschuß also received strong support from the Conservative, Free Conservative and National Liberal parties, who together formed an unofficial 'U-boat bloc' in the Reichstag in order to oppose the Chancellor's policies. The National Liberal deputy Gustav Stresemann, for instance, described the pro-submarine campaign in a speech on 22 October 1916 as 'the product of a genuine feeling in the soul of the German people' and warned that a failure to overcome the Allied naval blockade would reduce Germany to 'a nation of beggars at England's mercy'.[53]

On 7 October the Chancellor suffered a further blow to his authority when the Catholic Centre Party's chief spokesman in the Main Committee of the Reichstag, Adolf Gröber, put forward a motion on the submarine question calling upon the government to re-align its policies with those of the High Command, whose support for unrestricted U-boat warfare was well known.[54] On top of this, in early November another usually loyal party, the Progressive People's party or left-liberals, also issued a new policy statement which openly criticized the government and drew attention to a possible rift between the political and military leadership of the Reich:

We have – as already mentioned – complete confidence in the leaders of our General Staff and regret only one thing, that these two men were not given the opportunity at an earlier date to establish themselves in their current posts. But we wish that this confidence also be installed to the same degree in our Admiralty Staff, whose views tend to be disregarded in discussions on the U-boat question. We cannot, however, express the same degree of confidence in those offices of the

---

[52] The full text of the Volksausschuß's manifesto is reprinted in *Deutsche Tageszeitung*, no. 474, 20 September 1916. Copy in: Bundesarchiv Berlin, Pressearchiv des Reichslandbundes, no. 8274, fos. 3–4.

[53] Text of Stresemann's speech reprinted in *Deutsche Tageszeitung*, no. 540, 25 October 1916. Copy in ibid., fo. 28. On the agitation of the Volksausschuß für rasche Niederkämpfung Englands in general see also Stibbe, *German Anglophobia and the Great War*, pp. 148–57.

[54] Fischer, *Griff nach der Weltmacht*, pp. 370–1.

Reich who are responsible for the conduct of economic affairs, and, to our regret, we must also say the same with regard to the conduct of foreign policy as well.[55]

Bethmann Hollweg, in other words, now relied, at least in theory, on the moderate wing of the Social Democratic party as the only genuine supporters of his submarine policy against the rival claims of Hindenburg and Ludendorff, an unheard-of and very dangerous position for a Chancellor of the German Reich to be in. By this time, indeed, even the Kaiser was beginning to re-think his attitude on the submarine question, although once again he stopped short of giving in to calls for Bethmann's dismissal, mainly because there was no obvious successor, or at least not one who enjoyed the support of both the monarch and the High Command. (Tirpitz was, of course, out of the question as far as Wilhelm was concerned, as was another potential candidate, the former Chancellor Bernhard von Bülow.)

On 8 December 1916, two days after the fall of Bucharest to German forces which freed up German troops to defend the Dutch and Danish borders from possible attack, Hindenburg demanded the opening of unrestricted submarine warfare by the end of January 1917, and Wilhelm agreed.[56] Bethmann was to be given one last chance, however: with the Kaiser's approval, he was allowed to make a limited peace offer to the Allies at the end of 1916. Accordingly, on 12 December Bethmann informed the Reichstag that Germany was prepared to enter into preliminary peace negotiations with the enemy, but stopped short of setting out any concrete conditions. In fact, neither the Chancellor nor the Kaiser seriously expected that the offer would be accepted; rather, they were simply looking for a way of securing a half-hearted diplomatic victory over the Allies in order to offset the damage that would be done to Germany's image abroad by the launching of unrestricted submarine warfare. This, at any rate, was how Wilhelm himself described the purpose of the peace offer in a conversation with his American dentist Arthur Davis: 'We've got the English and French governments in a nice predicament, trying to explain to their people why they don't make peace. They're wild with rage at us for surprising them in this way.'[57]

When the Allies' negative response to the peace note was published at the end of December, the dice were therefore already cast in favour

---

[55] 'Erklärung über die Stellung der Fortschrittlichen Volkspartei zur auswärtigen Politik', 10 November 1916. Copy in Bundesarchiv Koblenz, Nachlaß Gottfried Traub, no. 44. See also Stibbe, *German Anglophobia and the Great War*, p. 162.

[56] See Martin Kitchen, *The Silent Dictatorship. The Politics of the High Command under Hindenburg and Ludendorff, 1916–1918*, London 1976, pp. 111–17.

[57] Arthur N. Davis, *The Kaiser I Knew*, London 1918, p. 152.

of unrestricted submarine warfare. Hindenburg and Ludendorff had also hinted very strongly that they would resign if a positive decision was not now forthcoming. On 9 January 1917, at a Crown Council held at Schloß Pleß in Silesia, Wilhelm allowed himself to be persuaded by the arguments put forward by his senior military and naval advisors. England, they all agreed, would be defeated within four to six months, rendering any American assistance to the Allies meaningless. If the United States declared war, Wilhelm himself now noted in an apparent reversal of his previous position, then 'so much the better', although something might still be done to avoid this by making concessions to American passenger liners.[58] In fact, no such concessions were made when the commencement of unrestricted submarine warfare was formally announced in a note to Washington on 31 January 1917, in spite of the Chancellor's continued efforts to ensure American neutrality. In the meantime, the United States broke off all diplomatic relations with Germany on 3 February and went on to declare war some eight weeks later, on 6 April. The scene was now set for the final stage in the establishment of a fully fledged army dictatorship in Germany, beginning with the dismissal of Bethmann Hollweg in July 1917 – partly in revenge for his previous stance on the submarine question – and ending only in the autumn of 1918 when Ludendorff advised the Kaiser to introduce significant constitutional reforms at a time when military defeat was already a virtual certainty.[59]

CONCLUSION

Looking back on the decision made at Pleß on 9 January 1917 it is undeniable that the driving force behind this 'leap in the dark' designed to reverse Germany's declining fortunes in the war was the High Command under Hindenburg and Ludendorff.[60] Their combined threat to resign gave the final push necessary to persuade the Kaiser to give his approval to a measure which ultimately, by way of the United States' entry into the war, led to Germany's defeat in the First World War. This is certainly how James

---

[58] Görlitz, *The Kaiser and His Court*, p. 230 (Müller's diary entry for 9 January 1917).

[59] For further details on the establishment of army rule and Ludendorff's role in domestic politics at the end of the war see Martin Kitchen, 'Civil–Military Relations in Germany During the First World War', in R. J. Q. Adams (ed.), *The Great War, 1914–1918. Essays on the Military, Political and Social History of the First World War*, London 1990, pp. 39–68.

[60] The phrase 'leap in the dark' was used by Albert Ballin in a letter to Hellmuth Freiherr Lucius von Ballhausen, German Ambassador in Stockholm, on 10 January 1917. Here Ballin wrote 'Hindenburg will undoubtedly demand a firm decision on the U-boat question in the very near future. This decision will be a leap in the dark.' Quoted in Kaulisch, 'Der "Sprung ins Dunkle"', p. 299.

Gerard, the American ambassador, interpreted events soon after he returned home to the United States in the spring of 1917. In his view:

It was not the Chancellor, notoriously opposed; it was not the Foreign Office, nor the Reichstag, nor the Princes of Germany who decided to brave the consequences of a rupture with the United States on the submarine question. It was not the Emperor, but a personality of great power of persuasion. It was Ludendorff, Quartermaster-General, chief aid and brains to Hindenburg, Chief of the Great General Staff, who decided upon this step.[61]

Nonetheless, the fact remains that the meeting at Pleß would not have taken place if the leading 'moderates', first and foremost the Kaiser and the Chancellor, had not begun to weaken in their opposition to unrestricted submarine warfare in the final months of 1916 and even secretly to sympathize with the views put forward by the military and their supporters. Why was it, then, that Wilhelm gave way on an issue which he had refused to sanction on a number of previous occasions and which carried so many uncertainties and risks, not only to the German war effort, but ultimately to his own person?

Public opinion, as Christopher Clark has recently argued, had some part to play in the Kaiser's change of mind.[62] However, it is important not to exaggerate this. Wilhelm was certainly aware to some extent of the mood at home and of the popularity of the submarine as a 'miracle weapon' capable of bringing down 'Perfidious Albion'. The fact that nearly all members of the Reichstag apart from the SPD supported a more vigorous policy on this issue, even if it meant causing a breach in relations with the United States, cannot have escaped his notice, for instance. Nonetheless, as John Röhl has also pointed out, Imperial Germany was not a parliamentary monarchy ruled by a government dependent on the Reichstag, still less a plebiscitary democracy forced to take note of the views of the masses.[63] Neither the war-aims majority in the Reichstag, nor the pro-Tirpitz press, nor right-wing pressure groups like the Pan-German League could have forced the Kaiser to unleash unrestricted submarine warfare, however much they wanted him to do this.

A more convincing explanation is that Wilhelm, like Bethmann Hollweg, simply gave in to the arguments of his generals and admirals because he had no alternative strategy for winning the war, a huge failing in itself, and because he was not yet prepared to accept defeat or even a compromise

[61] Gerard, *Face to Face with Kaiserism*, p. 23.
[62] Clark, *Kaiser Wilhelm II*, p. 233.   [63] Röhl, *The Kaiser and his Court*, p. 8.

peace. As in July 1914, so again in January 1917, he did not want to appear weak-willed in the face of his military and naval advisors, whose opinions and attitudes he had always valued more highly than those of his civilian ministers and court officials. These same military and naval advisors had of course been calling for unrestricted submarine warfare for at least twelve months before January 1917, and had mobilized a 'seemingly irrefutable' group of industrialists, financial experts, and statisticians to draw up memoranda backing their case.[64] On top of this, Wilhelm may have feared that he would not live up to the glorious precedents set by Friedrich the Great and by his grandfather, Wilhelm I, should he fail to take a tougher line against Germany's enemies. Thus, as Isabel Hull has also argued in relation to the German mobilization of 1914, the Kaiser was ultimately 'shamed' into approving a measure which he had previously shied away from because of the terrible burden of responsibility such a move represented.[65] Indeed, at stake over the weeks and months that followed the meeting at Pleß was not only the future of the German empire, but also of the Hohenzollern monarchy itself.

[64] Cf. Herwig, 'Total Rhetoric, Limited War', pp. 194–8.
[65] Hull, *The Entourage of Kaiser Wilhelm II*, p. 265.

CHAPTER 10

Military culture, Wilhelm II, and the end of the monarchy in the First World War

Isabel V. Hull

The German monarchy ended on 9 November 1918 with a whimper, not a bang. As the royal train slipped over the Dutch border, the public and the new revolutionary government turned their attention to the more pressing matter of survival. At Third Army headquarters and doubtless elsewhere, high-ranking officers discussed counterrevolution, but nothing came of it.[1] Wilhelm II's silent departure to Holland was preceded by years of declining authority. This chapter investigates how that decline actually occurred during the First World War, and examines the unconscious role that monarchists themselves played in undermining both the monarch and the monarchy.

Historians see the decline of monarchical authority in three stages: the rise and fall of 'personal regime', the failure of *Weltpolitik*, and the eclipse of Wilhelm's governing power during the war. The historian this Festschrift honours, John Röhl, has contributed most to illuminating the first problematic, the question of personal regime.[2] The picture that has emerged, and is still emerging in Röhl's monumental multi-volumed biography of the Kaiser, shows an activist but uneven and sporadic monarch, who sought to wield power personally, but in a modern-seeming way. Wilhelm II took advantage of the tremendous power invested in the monarch (especially in foreign policy and military command power) by Chancellor Otto von Bismarck's peculiar constitution, on the one hand, and by the popular hunger for a national representative and embodiment of the modern Germany, on the other. Wilhelm successfully made himself an icon of German industrial and military might. His policies (especially building

---

[1] Karl von Einem, *Ein Armeeführer erlebt den Weltkrieg; persönliche Aufzeichnungen*, edited by Junius Alter, Leipzig 1938, p. 467.

[2] John C. G. Röhl, *Germany Without Bismarck: The Crisis of Government in the Second Reich*, London 1967; John C. G. Röhl, *Young Wilhelm: The Kaiser's Early Life, 1859–1888*, Cambridge 1993 (reprint 1998); John C. G. Röhl, *Wilhelm II.: Der Aufbau der Persönlichen Monarchie 1888–1900*, Munich 2001; Isabel V. Hull, ' "Persönliches Regiment" ', in John C. G. Röhl (ed.), *Der Ort Kaiser Wilhelms II. in der deutschen Geschichte*, Schriften des Historischen Kollegs, no. 17, Munich 1991, pp. 3–23.

the battle fleet) and enthusiasms (for modern technology, industry, and science) alienated the Conservative Party and made other patriots hope he might indeed lead Germany 'to glorious times', in his famous phrase. But Wilhelm's unsteadiness, his gratuitous disruptions of foreign policy, and his numerous political *faux pas* fed criticism and culminated in the *Daily Telegraph* affair of November 1908 – a resounding popular and parliamentary rejection of personal regime. Thereafter, Wilhelm withdrew from the flamboyant public exercise of power. Nonetheless, he had succeeded in personifying Germany and its foreign policy.

Wilhelm's main policy innovation had been *Weltpolitik* (world policy), which aimed at catapulting Germany from a mere European to a world power.[3] Rivalling (or in some scenarios, displacing) Great Britain meant building a battle fleet, which Wilhelmine Germany began in 1898. But already by the 1906 Algeciras Conference, ordinary newspaper readers could see that the fleet brought not greater power, but more enemies. By the Second Moroccan Crisis of 1911 the failure of *Weltpolitik* was undeniable; German resources henceforth poured into the army which would have to defend it against the ring of foes that German foreign policy had created.[4] The unskilled attempt in 1914 to break through this ring consciously risked and ended by precipitating the world war.

The First World War saw the third and final stage of decline in monarchical authority. The constitutionally separated spheres of civil and military policy were united only in the person of the Kaiser, who thus bore the entire responsibility for coordinating the conduct of war. Wilhelm ducked this responsibility, with the result that Germany lacked a genuine strategy.[5] Military, foreign, and domestic policy ran at cross purposes, making Germany incapable of using its strengths optimally or of recognizing when these had been exhausted. Furthermore, Wilhelm did not command militarily, either. He vanished from public view. Some historians see in the Third Supreme Command of Paul von Hindenburg and Erich Ludendorff after August 1916 a real military dictatorship.[6] Everyone agrees that monarchical legitimacy slipped from the monarch and came to rest in Hindenburg,

[3] Paul Kennedy, 'The Kaiser and German Weltpolitik: Reflections on Wilhelm II's Place in the Making of German Foreign Policy', in John C. G. Röhl and Nicolaus Sombart (eds.), *Kaiser Wilhelm II. New Interpretations*, London 1982, pp. 157–64.

[4] Volker R. Berghahn, *Germany and the Approach of War in 1914*, 2nd edn, New York 1993.

[5] Wilhelm Deist, 'Strategy and Unlimited Warfare in Germany: Moltke, Falkenhayn, and Ludendorff', in Roger Chickering and Stig Förster (eds.), *Great War, Total War: Combat and Mobilization on the Western Front, 1914–1918*, Cambridge 2000, pp. 265–79.

[6] Martin Kitchen, *The Silent Dictatorship; The Politics of the German High Command under Hindenburg and Ludendorff, 1916–1918*, New York 1976.

who became a kind of Ersatz Kaiser. Hindenburg embodied the nation as the monarch once had done. The impending defeat consumed whatever legitimacy the monarchy still retained, and when the United States President Woodrow Wilson's notes seemed to demand abdication in return for armistice, there was no way of retaining the Kaiser.

This doubtless too brief synopsis of monarchical legitimacy in the Kaiserreich makes sense as a broad outline, but it raises a number of problems. Four of the most interesting puzzles concern the war in the monarchy's final crisis. First, Kaiser Wilhelm was in fact more active in setting broad wartime policy than it first seems. The view of the passive, indecisive Kaiser was the product of wartime political polemics launched first by Grand Admiral Alfred von Tirpitz, who disagreed with the Kaiser's personnel decisions (his loyalty to Chancellor Theobald von Bethmann Hollweg and to the second Chief of the General Staff, General Erich von Falkenhayn) and his naval strategy (withholding the battle fleet and not immediately launching unrestricted submarine warfare).[7] After the war, Tirpitz's interpretation became common. This view recognized that Wilhelm had not co-ordinated military and civilian policy. But it was at best a personalized criticism of the fundamental constitutional-political problem that had plagued Germany since 1871. More importantly, it conveniently shifted blame for defeat onto a single person and away from the larger institutional system, its assumptions and supporters, and especially from the military. By championing Bethmann and Falkenhayn and keeping them in office despite constant intrigues aimed at unseating them, Wilhelm opted for a more moderate and realistic prosecution of the war than Tirpitz or later Ludendorff and Hindenburg urged.[8] Similarly, even after Wilhelm had been forced to appoint the latter as the Third Supreme Command (OHL), he nevertheless blocked personnel appointments (for example, of Tirpitz) that would have moved policy in still more radical directions.[9] In other words, loss of monarchical legitimacy during the war, especially in 'conservative' circles, may have been due less to the monarch's fabled indecisiveness, than to his actual decisions.

A second curiosity in the monarchy's decline concerns the Third OHL's 'silent dictatorship'. Ludendorff (under Hindenburg's aegis) certainly did

[7] Alfred von Tirpitz, *Erinnerungen*, Leipzig 1919, pp. 431, 435, and *passim*. See also Matthew Stibbe's contribution to this volume, pp. 217–34.

[8] Holger Afflerbach, *Falkenhayn: politisches Denken und Handeln im Kaiserreich*, Munich 1994, and Karl-Heinz Janßen, *Der Kanzler und der General; die Führungskrise um Bethmann Hollweg und Falkenhayn, 1914–1916*, Göttingen 1967.

[9] Bruno Thoß, 'Nationale Rechte, militärische Führung und Diktaturfrage in Deutschland 1913–1923', *Militärgeschichtliche Mitteilungen*, 42 (1987), pp. 27–76, here 47–8; Heinz Hagenlücke, *Deutsche Vaterlandspartei; die nationale Rechte am Ende des Kaiserreichs*, Düsseldorf 1997, p. 280.

make decisions far beyond his professional, military bailiwick. The military was indeed catastrophically predominant. Yet, despite fabulous popular acclaim and numerous, insistent attempts by officers, advisors, and important political actors to get them to institutionalize their power, both Ludendorff and Hindenburg always explicitly declined to inaugurate an actual 'military dictatorship'. Hindenburg made a fetish of his disdain for politics, while Ludendorff claimed he was militarily indispensable. But the fact remains that neither man had consciously abandoned monarchy. In Bruno Thoß's words,

for all its vehemence, the criticism of the ineffective monarchy had never moved beyond the monarchical system as the most appropriate state form for Germans. All the schemes for a military dictatorship stopped before the breaking point and at most proposed a temporary 'vacation' for the monarch or his abdication in favour of the crown prince.[10]

And yet, losing the war discredited only the monarchy, not the military or the officer corps whose doctrines, policies, practices, and leadership were in fact chiefly responsible for that defeat. This is the third oddity. Social Democrats and Communists did pin the blame where it belonged. But among other strata the *Dolchstoßlegende* ('stab-in-the-back' legend) succeeded beautifully in shielding the military from its responsibility.[11] The legend, however, saved only the military and not the monarch, to whom its officers had sworn personal allegiance, nor the state form which the military was supposed to protect and which the constitution had made almost synonymous with military authority.

Finally, when abdication had advanced to the forefront of the political agenda in October and early November 1918, the old Wilhelmine political spectrum no longer predicted how individuals or parties would act. The majority socialist Philipp Scheidemann did more to try to save the monarchy than the 'conservative' rallying movement, the German Fatherland Party. Members of the officer corps behaved inconsistently and bizarrely. Many of the most vehemently self-proclaimed monarchists in fact actively undermined Wilhelm and the monarchy, apparently without realizing or desiring it. Despite such lack of self-reflection, and seemingly in contradiction with

---

[10] Thoß, 'Nationale Rechte', p. 62.
[11] Friedrich Frhr. Hiller von Gaertringen, ' "Dolchstoß-Diskussion" und "Dolchstoß-Legende" im Wandel von vier Jahrzehnten', in *Geschichte und Gegenwartsbewußtsein. Festschrift für Hans Rothfels zum 70. Geburtstag*, Göttingen 1963, pp. 122–60; Wilhelm Deist, 'Der militärische Zusammenbruch des Kaiserreichs; zur Realität der "Dolchstoßlegende"', in Ursula Büttner (ed.), *Das Unrechtsregime; Internationale Forschung über den Nationalsozialismus*, vol. 1: *Ideologie – Herrschaftssystem – Wirkung in Europa*, Hamburg 1986, pp. 101–29; Joachim Petzold, *Die Dolchstoßlegende; eine Geschichtsfälschung im Dienst des deutschen Imperialismus und Militarismus*, Berlin 1963.

their avowed values, their behaviour had system to it. It can be explained by examining the assumptions embedded in Germany's military culture, assumptions which the officer corps to a man thought consistent with or even identical to the 'monarchical persuasion (*monarchische Gesinnung*)', but which in fact deeply contradicted it. The puzzles we have identified reflect the tension between the monarchical persuasion and military culture.

MILITARY CULTURE

'Culture' is an overused term these days. Its elasticity threatens to make it not just protean, but useless as an analytical tool. But if used stringently, 'culture' in an anthropological and organizational-systematic sense accounts very well for seemingly irrational behaviour in institutional settings and for inconsistencies between norms or values and actual practice. Elsewhere I have discussed military culture at some length; here I will summarize those aspects of that discussion that seem most germane to the issue at hand.[12]

The anthropologist Clyde Kluckhohn has called culture 'those historically created designs for living, explicit and implicit, rational, irrational, and nonrational, that exist at any given time as potential guides for the behavior of men'.[13] The 'designs' are both normative/theoretical/explicit and practical/unreflected. By predisposing people to perceive and understand situations in a limited number of ways, culture offers groups short-cuts to decision-making and action, indeed makes action possible at all, since otherwise we would be paralysed by infinite choice.

Organizations develop cultures, too.[14] Organizational culture may be understood similarly as the historical learning of a unit as it operates in its environment. The lessons that have worked for it become systematized. In sociologist Edgar Schein's words, these

solutions eventually come to be assumptions about the nature of reality, truth, time, space, human nature, human activity, and human relationships – they come to be taken for granted and, finally, drop out of awareness. The power of culture is derived from the fact that it operates as a set of assumptions that are unconscious and taken for granted.[15]

---

[12] Isabel V. Hull, *Military Culture and 'Final Solutions' in Imperial Germany* (forthcoming), chs. 4–8.

[13] Clyde Kluckhohn, 'The Concept of Culture', in Richard Kluckhohn (ed.), *Culture and Behavior*, New York 1962, pp. 19–73, here, 54.

[14] James G. March and Herbert Simon, *Organizations*, New York 1958; J. Steven Ott, *The Organizational Culture Perspective*, Chicago 1989; Andrew M. Pettigrew, 'On Studying Organizational Cultures', *Administrative Science Quarterly*, 24, 4 (1979), pp. 570–81.

[15] Edgar H. Schein, 'How Culture Forms, Develops, and Changes', in Ralph H. Kilmann, Mary J. Saxton, and Roy Serpa (eds.), *Gaining Control of Corporate Culture*, San Francisco 1985, pp. 17–43, here, 19–20.

Schein therefore emphasizes the unconscious dimension of culture, which is important for our subject. But organizational culture also operates more explicitly, for example in (military) doctrine, which combines a conscious and codified level visible to the practitioners, together with hidden assumptions and dynamic developmental consequences that remain obscure to them.

Military culture is organizational culture of a specific kind, for militaries typically differ from other organizations because of their unique task of wielding deadly force and their imperative command hierarchy.[16] They are 'strong' organizations. The culture a particular military develops in a given period will depend upon a number of factors: its task (in addition to being the sole legitimate wielder of force, it may have domestic policing tasks, or national-representative ones as well), its relation to state and society (its constitutional place, its social prestige, its openness to fashionable ideologies), its hierarchical structure and procedures, its social basis, its resources (monetary, technological, educational, etc.), its gender constituent, and its past history (particularly the last engagement it fought).[17] As this list makes evident, the Wilhelmine army shared many fundamental characteristics with the armies of its neighbours. In important ways, it was more like contemporary militaries than different from them. But where it was different, this was due primarily to its relation to state and society, to national tasks it had acquired, and to its past history (especially the 'lessons' it had learned in the wars of unification in 1864, 1866, and particularly 1870–1).

The imperial German army was distinguished by its imbrication with the Prussian monarchy, on the one hand, and with the German national state, on the other. The identification of the army as the bulwark of the monarchy had a long history, consolidated and transformed in modern times by the army's role in 'saving' the monarchy from revolution in 1848–9. The monarch and the officer corps remained convinced that each was the guarantor of the other. That is why, when Bismarck engineered the monarchy's survival by creating a federal empire with the Prussian monarchy at its centre, the officer corps swore loyalty to the monarch's person, not to the constitution or nation. And it is why the German constitution shielded the army to a great extent from parliamentary or public interference. At the same time, the wars of national unification had elevated the army to heroic stature as a national, not merely Prussian-particularist, institution. Like the monarch, the army also came to represent the new German nation and

---

[16] Elizabeth L. Kier, *Imagining War: French and British Military Doctrine Between the Wars*, Princeton 1995, chs. 1 and 2.

[17] Hull, *Military Culture*, ch. 4.

its peculiar virtues of disciplined, organized strength and manly valour. National representation enlarged the army's task and made it more burdensome by raising the stakes of every engagement; a potential military loss reverberated far beyond the battlefield. As long as the national state was actually a monarchy, few except socialist critics imagined that the army's dual identification as Prusso-German-monarchical and national could ever become contradictory. During the world war, however, the national and the monarchical drifted further and further apart.

The most important result of the army's monarchical/national stature was its protection from civilian-governmental and parliamentary scrutiny. Command power and officer appointments rested solely with the Kaiser. The chiefs of the general staff and the military cabinet and the sixty-one wartime (deputy) commanders of military districts and fortifications were all directly subordinate to the Kaiser; no Chancellor or minister was empowered to check, or even to know, their plans or actions.[18] In institutional terms this meant that the army lacked critical feedback from outside the organization. The culture that developed inside – the standard operating procedures, the scripts for understanding and solving problems, the training doctrines, the hidden basic assumptions about deadly force and its prerogatives – all these were permitted to grow luxuriously and peculiarly with barely any regular means of correcting or controlling them. It is possible to see this process as a kind of 'professionalization', by which an institution becomes more and more specialized.[19] But professionalization is a misleading term in this context because of its suggestion of greater effectiveness and goal-rationality. Freedom from non-military criticism and oversight created instead a hypertrophied military that became dysfunctional if we measure effectiveness by the military's contribution to national security.

If we regard military culture as a complex of the explicit/doctrinal and the implicit/unreflected/assumed, then it is perhaps convenient to begin describing it at the doctrinal level. The Schlieffen Plan gives a brilliant

[18] Manfred Messerschmidt, *Militär und Politik in der Bismarckzeit und im wilhelminischen Deutschland*, Darmstadt 1975; Wilhelm Deist, 'Armee in Staat und Gesellschaft, 1890–1914', in Wilhelm Deist, *Militär, Staat und Gesellschaft*, Munich, 1991; Wilhelm Deist, 'Zur Institution des Militärbefehlshabers und Obermilitärbefehlshabers im Ersten Weltkrieg', *Jahrbuch der Geschichte Mittel- und Osteuropas*, 13–14 (1965), pp. 222–40.

[19] Michael Geyer, 'Professionals and Junkers: German Rearmament and Politics in the Weimar Republic', in Richard Bessel and E. J. Feuchtwanger (eds.), *Social Change and Political Development in Weimar Germany*, London 1981, pp. 77–133; Morris Janowitz, *The Professional Soldier; A Social and Political Portrait*, New York 1971; Morris Janowitz, 'Professionalization of Military Elites', in Morris Janowitz, *On Social Organization and Social Control*, Chicago 1991, pp. 99–112.

snapshot of German doctrinal thinking.[20] The plan played such a central role in guiding military planning, training, and prosecution of war through to the defeat in 1918 that it has sometimes seemed a 'cause' of Germany's military culture. But it was not. Instead, it distilled, codified, and honed the lessons that Chief of Staff Helmuth von Moltke had developed with such seeming success in 1864, 1866, and especially 1870–1.[21] Alfred von Schlieffen (Chief of Staff from 1891 to 1905) selected aspects of Moltke's legacy, polishing and extending them in the plan designed to solve the problem of 'encirclement' by France and Russia. An entire generation of general staff officers, the elite of the army, were steeped in these principles, which they eagerly internalized. Schlieffen's plan was breathtakingly daring. It envisaged concentrating virtually all of Germany's armed forces in the West where they were to sweep around the French army's left flank, rolling it up and annihilating its entire forces in a single battle. At the conclusion of this immense movement, which Schlieffen calculated would take no more than six weeks, the German army would rush across Europe to meet and similarly annihilate the slower-mobilizing Russian armies.

The Schlieffen Plan makes clear the salient features of Wilhelminian military doctrine. It was (1) purely military. It ignored foreign and domestic political considerations; it was to be used regardless of why the war broke out, or against whom, or what the war's goals were. It aimed at (2) a purely military victory of force, understood in the Clausewitzian sense of the annihilation of the enemy's entire army. Anything short of annihilation was not victory; there was no room in this thinking for 'ordinary' victories, much less a negotiated settlement. Yet, the Plan (3) ignored Germany's actual military-political-industrial strength. Germany lacked the means to defeat France and Russia together, much less if Great Britain fought too. The 'short war illusion' and the lack of careful logistical planning both reflected the temptation simply to overlook Germany's actual strategic shortcomings.[22] Instead, the Plan relied on a series of techniques in order to compensate for Germany's evident numerical inferiority. It

---

[20] Gerhard Ritter, *Der Schlieffenplan; Kritik eines Mythos*, Munich 1956; Jehuda L. Wallach, *The Dogma of the Battle of Annihilation; The Theories of Clausewitz and Schlieffen and Their Impact on the German Conduct of Two World Wars*, Westport, CT 1986; Paul M. Kennedy (ed.), *The War Plans of the Great Powers 1880–1914*, Boston 1979, and Gunther Rothenberg, 'Moltke, Schlieffen, and the Doctrine of Strategic Envelopment', in Peter Paret (ed.), *Makers of Modern Strategy: From Machiavelli to the Nuclear Age*, Princeton 1985, pp. 296–325; Dennis Showalter, 'German Grand Strategy: A Contradiction in Terms?', *Militärgeschichtliche Mitteilungen*, 48, 2 (1990), pp. 65–102.

[21] Hull, *Military Culture*, ch. 7.

[22] Martin van Crefeld, *Supplying War: Logistics from Wallerstein to Patton*, Cambridge 1977; Lothar Burchhardt, *Friedenswirtschaft und Kriegsvorsorge; Deutschlands wirtschaftliche Rüstungsbestrebungen vor 1914*, Boppard am Rhein 1968.

depended on (4) minute, detailed planning (superior organization) and (5) exact discipline of its troops (superior troops). It proposed (6) an offensive of unequalled (7) daring and risk, to be accomplished according to (8) an unrealistically tight schedule. In short, it focused on (9) operative and even tactical techniques to overcome strategic deficits. If all this failed, in the end the Plan rested on (10) certain moral characteristics of its officers: the will to victory and to destruction (*Siegeswille, Vernichtungswille*), reckless daring (*Kühnheit*), self-sacrifice, and exemplary disdain of death (*Todesverachtung*). The system of 'mission tactics' (*Auftragssystem*), whereby German officers received general orders and were left to carry them out as they saw fit, greatly increased effective leadership, but also encouraged officers to go beyond the book and fulfil the task at whatever cost.

With the moral characteristics expected of officers, we have already begun to cross the line from the doctrinal into the realm of hidden, basic assumptions and unintended dynamics. In fact, the border separating the two is fluid. The military culture behind Schlieffen's doctrine contained many elements driving it toward *irreality* and *extremes*. The lack of external feedback encouraged solipsism (some authors have called this 'autism'), meaning a self-replicating tendency to see the world only self-referentially, within one's narrow frame.[23] Breaking out of this vicious circle was made more difficult by the assumption of one's own (organizational, technical, moral/emotional) superiority, which prevented learning from failure. So, for example, when the Schlieffen Plan failed in September 1914, the new Chief of Staff, Erich von Falkenhayn, supported by virtually every army commander, simply applied its precepts again and again (until the disaster at Ypres in November 1914), in the hope that technical virtuosity and willpower would finally make it work. The reaction of officers to the defeat at the Marne in 1914 shows clearly their difficulty in recognizing, assessing, or admitting defeat. In the absence of realistic assessment, German military culture was primed to increase the spiral of force. The crushing pressure to overcome material deficiencies by élan, daring, *Siegeswille*, and voluntaristic actionism added more fuel to the vicious circle. The expectations generated by military culture labelled as dereliction of duty anything short of an all-out effort to the bitter end. On this analogy, 'whole decisions' (*ein ganzer Entschluß*), as they were called, were the measure of correct military decision-making.[24] 'Whole decisions' committed one entirely, without

---

[23] Dieter Senghaas, *Rüstung und Militarismus*, Frankfurt 1972, pp. 46–61.

[24] Wilhelm Groener, citing Schlieffen, in *Lebenserinnerungen; Jugend, Generalstab, Weltkrieg*, edited by Friedrich Frhr. Hiller von Gaertringen, Göttingen 1957, p. 179.

reserve, to a given action. Decisions taking account of ambiguity or limits were easily dismissed as incompatible with correct military leadership.

Rejection of reality (especially concerning objective limits or failure) and going to extremes were thus likely, but unintended, potentials of German military culture. They were supported by further assumptions concerning the *nature of war and victory*. The war of 1870–1 had indeed been 'existential' – it had brought Germany into existence. Afterwards, German officers took it to be paradigmatic for war in general; all war, every war, was a life-and-death struggle. Social Darwinism, fashionable in non-military circles, encouraged this conviction. So did the Clausewitzian understanding of victory as annihilation of the opposing military force. The doctrine that arose from this constellation of ideas was 'military necessity', which Germany used from 1871 until the First World War to argue against constraining military action by international law.[25] International law recognized that armies needed to be able to pursue military action against enemy troops, on the analogy of self-defence. From the beginning of the Kaiserreich the German view differed by construing military necessity as that which was needed 'to lead the battle to victory', as General Julius von Hartmann succinctly put it in 1877.[26] Victory, not defence, and not 'peace' was the goal of war. This higher standard meant that 'military necessity' was almost infinitely expandable.

'Military necessity' in the Wilhelmine usage had two further consequences for military practical assumptions. First, it *eviscerated legal restraints* to military action. During the war, debate and propaganda focused attention on international law, but the evisceration applied equally to domestic law, visible for example in the sway of the deputy commanding generals, or in the demands of the Third OHL in the original version of the 'Hindenburg Programme'.[27] But military necessity could equally trump that other beneficiary of legal order – the monarchy. Wilhelm's boast that he had never read the constitution cloaked the fact that the German monarchy was a creation of that constitution. As a legal institution, it too could be threatened by the supra-legal claims of imperative military necessity.

---

[25] Manfred Messerschmidt, 'Völkerrecht und "Kriegsnotwendigkeit" in der Deutschen Militärischen Tradition', in Manfred Messerschmidt, *Was Damals Recht War. NS-Militär- und Strafjustiz im Vernichtungskrieg*, Essen 1996, pp. 191–230; Geoffrey Best, 'How Right is Might? Some Aspects of the International Debate about How to Fight Wars and How to Win Them, 1870–1918', in Geoffrey Best and Andrew Wheatcroft (eds.), *War Economy and the Military Mind*, London 1976, pp. 120–35; Julius von Hartmann, 'Militärische Nothwendigkeit und Humanität; ein kritischer Versuch', *Deutsche Rundschau*, 13–14 (1877–8), vol. XIII, pp. 111–28 and 450–71; vol. XIV: pp. 71–91.

[26] Hartmann, 'Militärische Nothwendigkeit', p. 116.

[27] Lothar Dessauer, *Der Militärbefehlshaber und seine Verordnungsgewalt in der Praxis der Weltkrieges*, Berlin 1918.

Lack of accepted legal restraints further encouraged the drift toward *instrumentalization* already inherent in any military organization. Officers must have found it easy to extend the expectation of exemplary self-sacrifice they held for themselves first to their troops, and from there to civilians (occupied and German). This tendency was widely visible in Germany's conflicts in the colonies and was ubiquitous during the war.[28] Military necessity as a principle weakened or destroyed whatever limits hedged *actionism*. It is not surprising that the Kaiser himself should ultimately have fallen victim to this same process.

UNDERMINING THE MONARCHY

The advance guard in the triumph of military-cultural actionism over the monarchy were men like Tirpitz or Ludendorff, whom historian Bruno Thoß calls men of a 'new type'. Their 'loyalty was more strongly attached to the national state than to the legitimate crown and the social order it represented', he writes. 'They approached problems and crises no longer according to social [i.e., political] considerations, but instead according to a vision developed from their military professionality of what was necessary for leadership in this war of a new type.'[29] It would be more accurate to say that their loyalty was attached not to the national state, but to the armed forces which they claimed embodied and were synonymous with it. The distinction is important because the former position could conceive of sacrificing, for example, 'military honour' in the interests of saving the nation state, as Prince Max von Baden's cabinet reasoned while it debated accepting the armistice in late October/early November 1918.[30] Neither Tirpitz nor Ludendorff could even understand that logic. Both were prepared to fight a hopeless 'last battle', if necessary on German soil with the terrific destruction that promised, in order to uphold military honour, without which a nation would be 'ruined', as Ludendorff and many officers claimed at the end of October 1918.[31]

---

[28] Hull, *Military Culture.*   [29] Thoß, 'Nationale Rechte', p. 39, also p. 37.

[30] Erich Matthias and Rudolf Morsey (eds.), *Die Regierung des Prinzen Max von Baden*, vol. II of *Quellen zur Geschichte des Parlamentarismus und der politischen Parteien*, Erste Reihe, Düsseldorf 1962, *passim*, but especially p. 339 (24 October 1918) and pp. 406–7 (28 October 1918).

[31] Ludendorff note of 31 October 1918, cited in Bernhard von Schwertfeger's report in Eugen Fischer, Walther Bloch, and Albrecht Philipp (eds.), *Die Ursachen des Deutschen Zusammenbruches im Jahre 1918*, Vierte Reihe im Werk des Untersuchungsausschusses der Verfassunggebenden Deutschen Nationalversammlung und des Deutschen Reichstages 1919–28, Verhandlungen/Gutachten/Urkunden, Berlin 1928, vol. II, p. 367; Tirpitz to Max von Baden, 17 October 1918, Alfred von Tirpitz, *Deutsche Ohnmachtspolitik im Weltkriege*, Hamburg and Berlin 1926, pp. 617–18.

Putting the accent on men of the 'new type' suggests that younger officers were more likely to sacrifice the monarchy to seemingly military-professional values.[32] Former Secretary of Foreign Affairs Admiral Paul von Hintze observed from general headquarters in late October 1918 that younger officers were beginning to favour abdication and were even turning against the Ersatz Kaiser, Hindenburg, whereas 'people of older [higher] rank are decidedly for both'.[33] At almost the same time Philipp Scheidemann told his fellow cabinet members in Berlin that 'a large number' of younger officers (to the rank of colonel) had told him they supported abdication.[34] It seems clear that the war had opened a rift between the generations inside the officer corps. Younger officers, exposed to the realities of industrial warfare, found the transition to a non-monarchical government easier, so long as the army's position was saved. But high-ranking officers rejected abdication because they had two more radical alternatives in mind, solutions that developed logically from the tenets of Wilhelmine military culture: the 'final battle' (*Endkampf*), which they believed could not be fought without the Kaiser remaining in office, and/or the exemplary death of the Kaiser in battle (*Königstodesritt*) (to both of which we shall return). Older officers understood themselves as monarchists to the end (which encouraged contemporaries and historians to see them the same way), without seeing the implications of their actions. Let us look at the odyssey of Karl von Einem as an example of the unintended drift of a model monarchist and officer.

Generaloberst von Einem had fought as a young man in the Franco-Prussian War. After service in the general staff and the war ministry, Einem became Prussian War Minister from 1903 to 1909 where he enjoyed close contact with the Kaiser. As War Minister Einem distinguished himself by supporting technical improvements while vehemently opposing army expansion, lest inclusion of 'unreliable' social elements dull its sharpness as a domestic weapon for the monarch against social democracy and liberalism. In September 1914 Einem became commander of the Third Army, which he successfully guided in difficult defensive operations throughout the entire war on the Western Front. Einem's letters and diary entries bespeak a genuine emotional attachment to the monarch and the institution of monarchy. Like most high-ranking officers, Einem attached great importance to his

---

[32] Thoß, 'Nationale Rechte', p. 48.
[33] Hintze to Wilhelm Solf, 29 October 1918, in Alfred Niemann, *Revolution von oben, Umsturz von unten; Entwicklung und Verlauf der Staatsumwälzung in Deutschland 1914–1918*, Berlin 1927, p. 242.
[34] Prince Max von Baden, *Erinnerungen und Dokumente*, Berlin and Leipzig 1927, p. 540, 31 October 1918.

personal relation to the Kaiser (and the Crown Prince).[35] After the Kaiser's abdication, the Crown Prince fled to Einem's headquarters where Einem promised to protect him and, despite the revolution, bring him safely back to Germany. Instead, on 12 November, the Crown Prince followed his father to Holland. As the Crown Prince left, Einem declared that 'we [the officers] would be loyal to the house of Hohenzollern for all time'.[36] Einem kept his pledge; he was one of the few officers who called for restoring the monarchy during the Weimar Republic.[37]

Nonetheless, the war had changed Einem's standard of judgement; measured against its imperative demands the Kaiser was wanting. Einem repeatedly calls Wilhelm a 'peacetime Kaiser.' 'The poor Kaiser!', he wrote in 1916:

He is not made for such a test [as the war]. It is a shame that God should have burdened with a world war the heart and shoulders of a man who loved peace so much. Simple bourgeois morality will always gratefully acknowledge that he did not want war and that his whole striving was directed toward peace. History won't remember him so happily, because a monarch must know that war is an element in God's order [a famous phrase of Moltke the elder's], which is needed and must be risked for honour but also under certain conditions for the interests of the nation.[38]

It is noteworthy that Einem listed (military) honour before national interest.

The precepts of war as military culture interpreted them placed Einem close to Tirpitz, though Einem opposed Tirpitz's constant calls for military dictatorship, 'since we have a monarchy'.[39] Like Tirpitz, Einem utterly rejected the three men who were Wilhelm's closest wartime advisors: Chancellor Bethmann Hollweg, Chief of Staff Falkenhayn, and Civil Cabinet Chief Rudolf von Valentini. They all sinned against the 'whole decision'.[40] The Chancellor, Einem complained, 'doesn't know what he wants'.[41] In Einem's judgement Falkenhayn was similarly indecisive. After the Marne he shrank from Schlieffen's lesson to risk everything at a single point (in the West in the autumn of 1914). And he continued to split Germany's strength instead of concentrating it in the East (late autumn 1914 / spring 1915), where

---

[35] Einem, *Armeeführer*, letter, 15 August 1916, p. 249.

[36] Ibid., (diary entry), 12 November 1918, p. 469.

[37] Gotthard Breit, *Das Staats- und Gesellschaftsbild deutscher Generale beider Weltkriege im Spiegel ihrer Memoiren*, Boppard am Rhein 1973, p. 123, n. 63.

[38] Einem, *Armeeführer*, letter, 15 August 1916, p. 249.   [39] Ibid., letter, 22 March 1915, p. 113.

[40] Tirpitz typically referred to Valentini and Georg von Treutler as 'weak, half people' for opposing unrestricted submarine warfare. Tirpitz to his wife, Charleville, 26 November 1914, Tirpitz, *Erinnerungen*, p. 431. (On the question of unrestricted submarine warfare, see also Matthew Stibbe's chapter, pp. 217–34 in this volume.)

[41] Einem, *Armeeführer*, letter, 26 July 1915, p. 130.

Einem and many commanders judged Ludendorff and Hindenburg to be more daring and consequent. Einem summed up Falkenhayn's failings: 'he lacked intuitive leadership ability'.[42] By 'intuitive', Einem meant the constellation of emotional/characterological virtues that strove unswervingly toward the single goal of victory.

The real problem with Bethmann and Falkenhayn was that they saw a much more complicated and dour reality than military culture recognized. Both came to doubt Germany could win a pure *Siegfrieden* on both fronts, and both consequently reduced their military and foreign-political plans.[43] Their moderation made it difficult to recognize them as leaders.[44] Contemporaries typically labelled them as the antithesis of the traits cultivated by military culture: 'indecisive', 'nervous', 'pessimistic', and 'weak'.

Einem was jubilant when Ludendorff and Hindenburg replaced Falkenhayn in August 1916 and when they toppled Bethmann the following year. In January 1918 Ludendorff and Hindenburg drove out the last holdout, Civil Cabinet Chief von Valentini. Einem crowed: 'the chief of the nervous nellies (*Angstmeier*) and Beth-men is thus removed. Thank God, a victory!'[45] Einem was utterly oblivious to the damage these personnel changes did to the monarch's power. Wilhelm was not. He clung to Bethmann and Falkenhayn because they enjoyed his personal trust, because they stuck to the boundaries of their respective offices and never tried to elevate themselves above the Kaiser, and because, for all his explosive rhetoric and momentary bombast, the Kaiser was open to a much more sober and realistic view of Germany's limited wartime prospects than the military (and civilian) 'optimists'.[46] That openness caused Wilhelm to make cautious decisions. It was thus Wilhelm's decision *not* to risk unrestricted submarine warfare in early 1915 that caused Tirpitz to claim that 'it is characteristic of the Kaiser that he does not want to reach a decision or accept responsibility'.[47] Wilhelm

---

[42] Ibid., diary, 29 August 1916, p. 253, also pp. 70, 73.

[43] Afflerbach, *Falkenhayn*, pp. 259–60, 294–5, 300–7.

[44] Ibid., pp. 442–5.   [45] Einem, *Armeeführer*, letter, 18 January 1918, p. 361.

[46] Wilhelm had said in March 1916 that 'One must never utter it nor shall I admit it to Falkenhayn, but this war will not end with a great victory.' Holger Herwig, *The First World War: Germany and Austria Hungary 1914–1918*, London 1997, p. 194. See also Alfred Niemann, *Kaiser und Revolution; die entscheidenden Ereignisse im Großen Hauptquartier*, Berlin 1922, p. 32; Niemann, *Revolution von oben*, p. 400.

[47] Tirpitz to his wife, 2 January 1915, Tirpitz, *Erinnerungen*, p. 435. Similarly, Colonel Bauer calling for a Ludendorff dictatorship to replace the 'indecisive' Kaiser in January 1918, ibid., p. 29. On Wilhelm's more active and more sober decision-making during the war see Gerhard Ritter, *Staatskunst und Kriegshandwerk; Das Problem des 'Militarismus' in Deutschland*, 4 vols., vol. III: *Die Tragödie der Staatskunst, Bethmann Hollweg als Kriegskanzler (1914–1917)*, Munich 1964, pp. 22, 33; Alfred Niemann, *Kaiser und Heer; Das Wesen der Kommandogewalt und ihre Ausübung durch Kaiser Wilhelm II.*, Berlin 1929, pp. 364–5.

also recognized where the personnel changes led; he had already remarked in July 1916 that he had no intention of 'abdicating in favour of the people's tribune, Hindenburg'.[48] But that is exactly what happened with the full approval of the Einems of the officer corps, guided by their unreflective understanding of military leadership and necessity. Oblivious to the consequences of his own opinions, Einem was outraged at the October Reforms which the government of Prince Max hurried to put in place in order to get the armistice that Ludendorff and Hindenburg had demanded. The October Reforms were the first institutional results of the failure of war *à outrance* and the rest of the military certainties that the OHL had pressed to the end. Einem wrote: 'Ruling by the grace of God is gone just like the power of command – given to the Chancellor with his galoshes and umbrella. Everything is simply given away as if it were nothing, as if one were changing a coat. Who would want to serve as officer under this system?'[49] Just as it did not take responsibility for losing the war, the upper-level officer corps felt guiltless about its role in losing the monarchy.[50]

By October and November 1918 the predominance of military necessity had even advanced into the Kaiser's entourage. Nothing illustrates this more clearly than Ludendorff's dismissal on 26 October.[51] Ludendorff and Hindenburg had come to the palace threatening to resign in order to force the Kaiser to endorse the hopeless final battle. They had in the past successfully undermined the Kaiser's authority using this method. This time, however, Wilhelm stood his ground; he accepted Ludendorff's resignation as quartermaster general, but asked him to continue to serve in a command position. Incredibly, Ludendorff brushed this request aside and brusquely, dropping all accepted forms of deferential discourse, insisted on going. Wilhelm had to remind him to whom he was speaking. But most incredible of all was the reaction of the Kaiser's oldest serving adjutant general, General and Chief of the Maison Militaire Hans von Plessen. For twenty-six years Plessen had served the Kaiser personally as adjutant.[52] He had been at Wilhelm's side during the entire war and he was there during the scene with Ludendorff. But Plessen, whose 'optimism' in the military sense was legendary, wholly supported Ludendorff's demand for *Endkampf*. Plessen overlooked Ludendorff's harsh, disrespectful style, which was consonant with the single-minded military leader focused entirely on battle,

[48] Thoß, 'Nationale Rechte', p. 43.   [49] Einem, *Armeeführer*, letter of 27 October 1918, pp. 455–6.
[50] Breit, *Staats- und Gesellschaftsbild*, pp. 122–3.
[51] This account follows Siegfried A. Kaehler, 'Vier quellenkritische Untersuchungen zum Kriegsende 1918', *Nachrichten der Akademie der Wissenschaften in Göttingen I. Philologisch-Historische Klasse*, no. 8, Göttingen 1960, pp. 439–46.
[52] Isabel V. Hull, *The Entourage of Kaiser Wilhelm II, 1888–1918*, Cambridge 1982, pp. 185–6.

and instead remarked unfavourably upon the Kaiser's 'passivity' during the
meeting and condemned Wilhelm's decision: 'I am deeply shocked by this
entirely un-Prussian decision of His Majesty', he wrote just afterwards.[53]
The essence of 'Prussian' was now summed up for Plessen in Ludendorff
and his ruthless demand to continue the lost war, not in the monarch,
whose decision to save Germany from destruction followed the political
line of the new government. Like Einem, Plessen did not understand that
he had shifted from a monarchical to a military-instrumental position. He
thought he was being consistent by following the values of military culture
to their logical conclusion.

INSTRUMENTALIZING THE KAISER

In mid-nineteenth-century conservative Prussian thinking and in rhetoric
throughout the war, the military was supposed to be the tool of the monarch,
who commanded it to keep order at home and security (or glory) abroad.
But in the course of the war, this relation reversed itself. By the autumn
of 1918 the monarch was being instrumentalized for military purposes.
Civilian leaders in the reform cabinet and Reichstag often tended to equate
military interest with the national good.[54] High-ranking officers followed
a different agenda which considered military interests ends in themselves.
But both subordinated the Kaiser to these.

The idea of a final battle developed seamlessly from the prosecution of
the war. Neither Falkenhayn nor Ludendorff and Hindenburg had ever
given up the hope of winning a purely military victory of force in the West.
After the Bolshevik Revolution took Russia out of the war, Ludendorff
deployed the entire arsenal of standard German military virtues to win a
Siegfrieden. Spurning political tools (for example, a pre-attack peace initiative), Ludendorff defined the task as strictly military and furthermore as a
purely tactical (not even operative, much less strategic) problem of breaking through the enemy's trenchlines. He concentrated all resources on this
task. He retrained officers and selected troops for it and developed clever
(and for a while successful) techniques that made the most of Germany's
limited strength. When the great offensive failed to annihilate the French
and British armies, Ludendorff repeated bloody, costly offensives four more
times at different locations. And he would have gone on repeating offensives had the allies not finally learned how to adapt to German techniques,

[53] Kaehler, 'Untersuchungen', pp. 439, 441.
[54] See e.g. Haußmann (16 October) and Friedberg (24 October), in Matthias and Morsey, *Die Regierung*,
pp. 211, 340.

and had the advent of fresh American troops not permanently pushed Germany onto the defensive. But even now, in late July/early August 1918, the OHL refused to admit defeat. Instead of preparing and falling back to defensive lines while attempting a negotiated settlement, Ludendorff and Hindenburg ordered Germany's dwindling, exhausted, and increasingly in-disciplined troops to hold on to every inch. Only on 28 September 1919, when he believed that the Allies were days, perhaps only hours away from a final breakthrough, did Ludendorff demand that the civilian government offer an immediate armistice. He did so to save the army from 'catastrophe', that is, from the battle of annihilation that remained the dominant vision of military outcomes.

Germany's war conduct in 1918 shows that both the doctrines and the hidden assumptions of its military culture were still hegemonic after four years of war. There was growing criticism of Ludendorff's leadership among some army and army-group commanders and mid-level staff officers, but it was exceedingly rare for this criticism to break out of the military-cultural mould.[55]

Endkampf was simply another step along this same path.[56] For Luden-dorff and the many officers who championed it, the final battle was to occur after an armistice had bought German troops a few weeks' rest. Then a scorched-earth retreat destroying what was left of Northern France and Belgium would usher in bloody, ruthless defensive fighting that might wash up against Germany's Rhine defences and (who knew?) farther into Germany itself. The wishful thinking behind this scenario was identical to the fallback argument concerning the March Offensive (and to Falkenhayn's thinking at Verdun): if Germany could not 'force' a *Siegfrieden*, then it could annihilate its foes by exhaustion and force them to acquiesce to an 'hon-ourable peace', meaning one that left Germany its military power, its huge gains in eastern Europe, and its pre-war territory in the West, and perhaps more than this (border rectifications with France, veiled dominance over Belgium), which would improve its strategic position in the next war. Even if the army went down to defeat, which Ludendorff acknowledged was possible, that would still be an 'honourable' end, instead of surrendering

---

[55] Hull, *Military Culture*, ch. 11.

[56] Michael Geyer, 'Insurrectionary Warfare: The German Debate About a *Levée en Masse* in October 1918', *Journal of Modern History*, 73 (September 2001), pp. 459–527; Friederike Krüger and Michael Salewski, 'Die Verantwortung der militärischen Führung deutscher Streitkräfte in den Jahren 1918 und 1945', in Jörg Duppler and Gerhard P. Groß (eds.), *Kriegsende 1918; Ereignis, Wirkung, Nach-wirkung*, Munich 1999, pp. 377–98; Michael Epkenhans, 'Die Politik der militärischen Führung 1918: "Kontinuität der Illusionen und das Dilemma der Wahrheit" ', in *Kriegsende 1918*, pp. 217–33; Hull, *Military Culture*, ch. 11.

without having gone to the last extreme.[57] According to the army view, the enormous loss of life and destruction was worth it for keeping military honour.

But civilians hatched *Endkampf* schemes of their own. One early version was Foreign Minister (and Admiral) Paul von Hintze's. He hoped that merely bluffing determination to fight to the end would be sufficient to pry an honourable peace from the exhausted French and British. Hintze's plan thus continued the long line of Wilhelmine foreign-political bluffs that had been at the heart of *Weltpolitik*.

The civilians of Prince Max von Baden's reform cabinet, which included parliamentary leaders, were made of sterner stuff. They seemed truly determined to fight. The war had militarized them as it had many civilians, and they therefore embraced military force as a means and did not shrink from destructive costs for troops and civilians alike. Their plan differed from the officers' in two ways, however. First, the cabinet was not going to engage in a quixotic fight for military honour. *Endkampf* was merely a method of achieving better armistice or peace conditions; the cabinet had to be convinced that fighting had a real chance of success before it would agree to scrap armistice negotiations.[58] Second, *Endkampf* was meant not to continue the war in the same old way, but to inaugurate a new phase in which a representative government waged war backed by broad national support. Of course, the officer supporters of *Endkampf* recognized, too, that the war could not continue without popular support, but their conception of a public appeal remained of the manipulative sort typical of Wilhelminian policy; they simply wanted more reserves to keep on keeping on. The cabinet members wanted more, and this is where the Kaiser came in.

Prince Max, heir to the throne of Baden and thus a monarchist in flesh and blood, tried to save the German monarchy right down to 9 November. Max was an equally strong proponent of *Endkampf*. President Wilson's Third Note (22 October) forced him to choose, at least between the current monarch himself and the final battle. He chose the latter. Whatever Wilson may actually have intended, his note was popularly interpreted as a demand to remove the Kaiser and possibly to end the monarchy in return for an armistice and fair peace conditions. Two things seemed clear to Max: the allies would interpret further fighting under the Kaiser as a

---

[57] Officers generally mentioned 'honour', even when they were trying to argue for more practical reasons: Payer, *Von Bethmann Hollweg*, pp. 140–2; Generals Max von Gallwitz and Bruno von Mudra to the cabinet on 28 October 1918, in Matthias and Morsey, *Die Regierung*, pp. 399–400, 405.

[58] Matthias and Morsey, *Die Regierung*, pp. 217, 243, 339, 400, 406–7.

continuation of the 'militarism' they were sworn to root out and therefore would renege on both an armistice and latitudinarian peace terms, and the German public would refuse the call to further sacrifice as long as they held the Kaiser responsible for standing in the way of peace. Therefore, Max's plan was to manoeuvre the Kaiser into 'voluntarily' abdicating for himself and the Crown Prince, who was equally tainted by the old system. The Kaiser's farewell message would be a call to arms if the armistice or peace terms were unacceptably harsh. The Prince complained on 31 October that, if the Kaiser had abdicated two weeks earlier, 'we could be fighting now'.[59]

One of the most surprising aspects of these twilight government delibera-tions was that avowed monarchists and upper-level civil servants were more enthusiastic about instrumentalizing the Kaiser in this fashion than were the party representatives. Max's position was shared by the conservative diplomat Ulrich von Brockdorff-Rantzau, Foreign Minister Wilhelm Solf, and Prussian Interior Minister Bill Drews. Aside from the south German Progressive Party leader Conrad Haußmann, the rest of the cabinet in the last days of October shrank from pressing the monarch to resign.[60] War Minister Heinrich von Scheüch was only opposed because he believed that without the Kaiser the officers would refuse to fight.[61]

Prince Max stuck to his position, which he summed up as: 'either the Kaiser goes or we give up national defence'.[62] On 1 November he began clearing a 'voluntary' abdication with the Bundesrat while an aide drafted the public appeals to fight on that Wilhelm was to deliver as his political legacy. But neither the Kaiser nor the people played along. Despite repeated pleas, the Kaiser refused to abdicate. Finally on 4 November the cabinet buried its hopes of *Endkampf* as Scheidemann flatly declared that the people would not fight further, and as news of the mutiny in Kiel, confirming his views, reached Berlin.[63]

Like the *Endkampf*, the idea for the Kaiser's orchestrated, heroic sui-cide emerged spontaneously in several different places at the end of Octo-ber/beginning of November 1918. Ludendorff's successor General Groener revealed the idea to the public in early 1919: 'I tried several times to bring the Kaiser where in my view he belonged, in battle on the battle field

---

[59] Max von Baden, *Erinnerungen*, p. 545.   [60] Ibid., pp. 532, 534, 541, 546.
[61] Ibid., pp. 547, 550.   [62] Ibid., p. 550.
[63] Ibid., p. 571. According to Geyer, *Endkampf* was already impossible on 24 October, but the cabinet continued serious deliberations on the subject until the 4th, and the new Chief of Staff Wilhelm Groener mentioned it again to the cabinet the following day. Geyer, 'Insurrectionary Warfare', p. 507; Matthias and Morsey, *Die Regierung*, p. 530.

as his great ancestor [Friedrich the Great] used to do in such situations.'
Groener explained why. 'If the Kaiser had been killed, then it would have
been an heroic end; if he had been wounded, then there would have been
a possibility to change public opinion in his favour.'[64] In 1925 Groener
offered other explanations. He said that by the beginning of November
1918 he felt that the Kaiser's position could not be saved, but that abdication would have dreadful psychological consequences for the army.[65] On
5 November 1918 Groener told the cabinet that abdication would cause
the army to disintegrate into chaos, sending marauding soldiers pouring
back into Germany.[66] It is unclear how Groener believed abdication would
trigger chaos, but most other high-ranking officers were convinced that it
would do so by releasing officers from their personal oath to the Kaiser
and cause them to stop serving.[67] That is the reason why, when Wilhelm
actually did abdicate, he made the Ersatz-Kaiser Hindenburg his successor
as Commander-in-Chief of the army and appealed to officers to transfer
their loyalty to him.

Wilhelm's former personal adjutant, Admiral von Hintze, who had left
the post of Foreign Minister and returned to the OHL in October 1918 as the
Foreign Office's representative, also pressed for the Kaiser's heroic suicide.
During the first two days of November, 'the more I thought the matter
over, the more I became convinced that the Kaiser had to go to the front,
the fighting front. Nothing better could happen for him, the monarchy,
or the dynasty, than if he had been, for example, wounded at the fighting
front.' Later in the same memorandum Hintze would say 'killed'.[68] When
Hintze broached the idea to the Kaiser on 3 November, he explained it as
an alternative to abdication. He argued that 'abdication would result in
the dissolution of the army and the destruction of our ability to defend
ourselves and therefore the defeat of Germany'.[69] Hintze thus presented
abdication in the same way Wilhelm repeatedly described it in these days,
as imperial dereliction of duty, as treason to the military tradition of the

---

[64] Groener on 2 February 1919, cited in Kuno Graf von Westarp, *Das Ende der Monarchie am 9. November 1918; abschließender Bericht nach den Aussagen der Beteiligten*, Stollhamm (Oldenburg) 1952, p. 146.
[65] Groener at the 1925 'Dolchstoß' trial in Munich, cited in Westarp, *Das Ende der Monarchie*, p. 153.
[66] Matthias and Morsey, *Die Regierung*, p. 532; Max von Baden, *Erinnerungen*, p. 581.
[67] In a heated altercation with General Friedrich von der Schulenburg on 9 November, Groener blurted out that the oath was a meaningless 'phrase'. Most other officers took it very seriously. Niemann, *Kaiser und Revolution*, p. 135; Werner Conze in Westarp, *Das Ende der Monarchie*, p. 198. General Loßberg thought only left-leaning officers would use the oath as an excuse to quit their posts: Fritz von Loßberg, *Meine Tätigkeit im Weltkriege 1914–1918*, Berlin 1939, p. 361.
[68] Paul von Hintze, 'Aufzeichnung des Staatssekretärs v. Hintze (Anfang des Jahres 1919 dem Minister des Königlichen Hauses vorgelegt)', in Niemann, *Revolution von Oben*, pp. 366–83, here 367.
[69] Ibid.

Prussian monarchy which, as historian Gerhard Ritter put it, 'was based entirely on authority and soldierly obedience'.[70]

Hintze's account conflates Wilhelm with the monarchy, the dynasty, the army, *Endkampf* ('our ability to defend ourselves'), and (undefeated) Germany. Hintze makes clear how much the king's heroic suicide was simply a personalized version of *Endkampf*. The identity of the two is also clear in former Chancellor Georg Michaelis's plea to the Kaiserin on 28 October that Wilhelm, together with the government, must set out for the front, 'calling on his people to join the last battle and declaring that he personally was drawing his dagger'.[71] The Vice-President of the Prussian Ministry of State Robert Friedberg told the cabinet virtually the same thing on 31 October: that the government should wait for the allies to reveal their perfidious armistice demands, and 'then there would still be a good finish, if the Kaiser went to the front and personally led the fight against the conditions'.[72] The acerbic and clear-sighted south German liberal leader, Friedrich Payer, who served as Vice-Chancellor, remarked afterwards that Wilhelm had done a good deed to the German people 'by dropping the death ride and the useless further bloodshed connected with it, which even greater romantics than he had expected of him'.[73]

For Payer, the 'death ride' was a 'useless' escapade dreamed up by 'romantics'. The irrationality of the whole thing is also what most struck Siegfried Kaehler, the historian to whom we owe the clearest account of these half-hidden and in the end fruitless machinations. Kaehler describes the plan as 'strange', 'illusionist thinking', 'astonishing', 'astonishingly anachronistic', and 'emotionally determined, rationally difficult to understand'.[74] Yet it was championed by a wide spectrum of high-ranking officers and officials including many who are hardly remembered today as romantics or illusionaries. For example, Hintze's stint in the diplomatic corps had exposed him to wider sources of information; his assessment of Germany's parlous military condition in August and September 1918 was much more accurate and realistic than OHL's. Groener, a Württemberger whose staff duties on the eastern front had kept him out of the hot-house atmosphere around Ludendorff and Hindenburg until he was called to be Ludendorff's successor, was constantly under attack as too democratic and progressive (read: politically modern). Two of the main younger conspirators at the OHL were Colonel Wilhelm Heye and Major Joachim von Stülpnagel,

[70] Ritter, *Staatskunst*, vol. IV, p. 459.
[71] Cited in Kaehler, 'Untersuchungen', p. 471.   [72] Max von Baden, *Erinnerungen*, p. 541.
[73] Friedrich Payer, *Von Bethmann Hollweg bis Ebert: Erinnerungen und Bilder*, Frankfurt 1923, p. 182.
[74] Kaehler, 'Untersuchungen', pp. 471, 473–4.

who had both been called to the OHL in September 1918 in order to replace Ludendorff's too 'optimistic' staff officers. It was they who apparently
moved Ludendorff and Hindenburg (briefly) to admit defeat at the end
of September.[75] Another was Colonel Albrecht von Thaer, a soldier with
immense front experience, who, again, had been only briefly at the OHL
(since June 1918) and whose independence of mind and judgement had
led him to tell Ludendorff and Hindenburg as early as May 1918 that the
troops' condition would not permit a continuation of their Schlieffenesque,
offensive warfare.[76] In addition to these younger men, Thaer believed that
the circle of officers willing to give their lives to accompany Wilhelm on
his death ride included 'most of the older officers' at headquarters.[77]

The death ride thus had wide support at the OHL (and elsewhere, as we
have seen with Michaelis). It was not just talk, either. The riders had signed
on and the decisive meeting was set for 8 November. At that afternoon
meeting, less than a day before Wilhelm's abdication, Hindenburg and
Plessen called the death ride off for reasons that remain unclear.[78]

Despite the widespread support and the earnest planning, Kaehler (and
Payer) were quite right: the king's death ride was entirely illusory. Given the
immensity and anonymity of the First World War battle-field, the gesture
would not have been heroic (the likeliest death would have been by artillery
shell or machine-gun fire from a hidden nest) and would have been seen, if
at all, by only a handful of soldier-witnesses. It could hardly have inspired
the *Endkampf* or saved the monarchy. At the same time it instrumentalized
the Kaiser in a more shocking way than had ever before been suggested,
since its goal was nothing less than his exemplary death. As Kaehler writes,
'without being conscious of it, the loyal servants of the monarch, whether
they were ministers or soldiers, were in the process of mediatizing their
king in a different, but much more effective way than had just happened
via the parliamentarizing of the constitution'.[79]

Kaehler outlined the two chief puzzles the death ride poses for historians:
its senselessness and its unconscious instrumentalization of the Kaiser. He

---

[75] Wolfgang Foerster, *Der Feldherr Ludendorff im Unglück: eine Studie über seine seelische Haltung in der Endphase des ersten Weltkrieges*, Wiesbaden 1952, pp. 68, 85–9. Albrecht v. Thaer (see below) called Heye 'a very cautious, thoughtful man'. Albrecht von Thaer, *Generalstabsdienst an der Front und in der O.H.L.*, Abhandlungen der Akademie der Wissenschaften in Göttingen, philologisch-historische Klasse, Dritte Folge, no. 40, edited by Siegfried Kaehler, Göttingen 1958, p. 225.

[76] Thaer, *Generalstabsdienst*, pp. 194–9, 252.

[77] Cited in Kaehler, 'Untersuchungen', p. 462. Breit believes that 'most officers' would have welcomed the death ride; Breit, *Staats- und Gesellschaftsbild*, p. 120, n. 52.

[78] Westarp, *Das Ende der Monarchie*, pp. 147–8; Niemann, *Kaiser und Revolution*, p. 142.

[79] Kaehler, 'Untersuchungen', p. 476.

entertained a number of possible explanations, most of which he seemed rightly to think were unconvincing.[80] The explanation he most favoured makes a great deal of sense. Slightly reformulated, it claimed that Wilhelm had successfully made the monarchy charismatic, which ironically made it more vulnerable to losing legitimacy when it was defeated in the war. The death ride was thus a desperate effort to regain legitimacy through an exemplary gesture.[81] This is a sensible, abstract way of categorizing what happened. But it still does not explain how the actors arrived at such an outlandish idea or why they seemed so unconscious of the implications of their plan. Addressing this problem means taking more seriously than Kaehler does his observation that even the civilian officials who favoured the death ride were overwhelmingly reserve officers.[82]

The death ride was a military fantasm. It did not represent, as Kaehler writes, 'a transvaluation of old values'.[83] On the contrary, it developed seamlessly (and therefore seemingly spontaneously) out of the overt values and hidden assumptions of Wilhelmine military culture. It was of a piece with the practices that had guided the prosecution of the war. That is why it did not seem to the officers who supported it at all outlandish or incredible, or to clash with tradition – that is, with the officers' tradition, not with the monarchy's, which contained no precedent for such an orchestrated suicide. The death ride was a final repetition of the way Wilhelmine military culture perceived and went about solving problems. Rather than acquiescing to defeat, which abdication would have done, military culture predisposed its charges flatly to deny it. One instead applied force to the problem. One attacked it offensively, by actionism. The action was a 'whole decision'. It held nothing back, it threw the most precious elite (the officers of the OHL) and the Kaiser himself into the last single battle of (self-)annihilation. The moral virtues of the officer-leader were rehearsed one last time – if not *Siegeswille*, then at least *Wille*, disdain of death, reckless daring, and exemplary self-sacrifice. The uselessness of the action was immaterial. Throughout the war officers had been calculating success by the fearless and clever way combats had been carried out, not by their effectiveness in achieving a larger goal.[84] As General Einem lamented in a letter from

---

[80] Among those were: a kind of internalization of the allies' charge that Germany was guilty of beginning the war, the shock of defeat, a personalistic understanding of authority which was based on emotion, Caesarism, and possible influence of the samurai suicide cult (on Michaelis, who had studied in Japan!). Ibid., pp. 467, 469, 474–7.

[81] Ibid., pp. 469, 476; Max Weber, *On Charisma and Institution Building; Selected Papers* (transl. by S. N. Eisenstadt), Chicago 1968, pp. 3–77.

[82] Kaehler, 'Untersuchungen', p. 475.   [83] Ibid., p. 476.

[84] Breit, *Staats- und Gesellschaftsbild*, pp. 20, 62.

7 November 1918, 'the German people will never forgive the army for not remaining the victor. No one will remember that the army fought against a world of enemies; its thousands of victories will be forgotten.'[85] The unrealism of the whole venture was therefore not 'romanticism', as Payer thought, but reckoning according to a different scale.[86] Besides, the death ride was no more unrealistic than the Schlieffen Plan had been, or the navy's pre-war plan for the single battle of annihilation against the world's greatest naval power, or the March Offensive, or the ensuing offensives. It was no more self-destructive than the navy's final battle (prevented only by the sailor's revolt), or than the more extreme versions of *Endkampf*.[87] The words of Naval Captain William Michaelis concerning the navy's plans for a final battle with Great Britain in October/November 1918 apply equally to the death ride, and indeed, to Imperial Germany's entire military enterprise in the world war as the officers saw it: 'I know it is a pure risk. But if there is no other possibility, then the risk is justified. If it succeeds, everything is won; it if fails, nothing more is lost than if it were not attempted.'[88] In the end what counted was that the redemptive gesture of self-sacrifice would recoup the honour of the army and of the monarchy and demonstrate that they were as harmonious as the officers and their monarch wanted them to be.

But in fact the monarchy and the military had drifted far apart. The war released the dynamics of extremism inherent in military culture, while the monarchy seemed to stand still. Military actionism conforming to the expectations of military culture and increasingly formalistic and non-goal-oriented, chased the spiral of force and thereby inexorably undermined the limited (in Einem's word, 'peaceful') foundations of monarchism. When forced to choose, many, perhaps most monarchists in the officer corps and upper officialdom found military-cultural tenets more real-seeming and compelling than the paler 'traditions' of the young monarchy.

---

[85] Einem, *Armeeführer*, p. 464.

[86] On the growing unrealism and wishful thinking in the last year of war see Michael Epkenhans, 'Die Politik der militärischen Führung 1918: "Kontinuität der Illusionen und das Dilemma der Wahrheit"', in *Kriegsende 1918*, pp. 217–33; and Hull, *Military Culture*.

[87] Geyer, 'Insurrectionary Warfare', p. 499.

[88] Kapt. z. See William Michaelis to Admiral v. Levetzow, Berlin, 5 October 1918, Bundesarchiv-Militärarchiv Freiburg, NL Levetzow, N 239/95, fos. 11–16, cited in Gerhard P. Groß, 'Eine Frage der Ehre? Die Marineführung und der letzte Flottenvorstoß 1918', in *Kriegsende 1918*, pp. 349–65, here 355, n. 32.

CHAPTER 11

Rathenau, Wilhelm II, and the perception of Wilhelminismus

Hartmut Pogge von Strandmann

Walther Rathenau, one of Germany's leading industrialists, bankers, and widely read authors, has often been regarded as a critic of his time in general, and of Wilhelmine Germany in particular. However, his vigour of criticism with regard to the latter was not in the same league as that of his one-time friend, Maximilian Harden, the editor of the influential paper, *Die Zukunft,* or that of the political left. In the field of politics, Rathenau restricted himself to complaints about some constitutional deficits and about the Prussian state's treatment of the Jewish minority in Germany. Despite these criticisms he identified strongly with the pre-war political system and Wilhelmine Germany in general. He did not want to overthrow anything. His liberal reformist aims were to strengthen Wilhelmine Germany abroad and to integrate the entirety of the German population more strongly with the state. This dialectic approach to politics and to affairs of society in general raises the question as to whether the label *Wilhelminist* is an appropriate one to describe his position.

Given his close identification with the Wilhelmine epoch, it was not surprising that Rathenau was deeply shocked by the military and political collapse of Imperial Germany in November 1918. One of his reactions to the newly developing political and social circumstances was the publication, among many articles and booklets, of a tract in March 1919 with the title *Der Kaiser.*[1] In the first parts of this book he analysed the monarchy under Wilhelm II in Germany. He discussed the Kaiser's popularity, his similarity to other European monarchs, and his relationship with various social groups in German society. He then went on to characterize the monarch in some

---

[1] By 1923, 57,000 copies of the booklet had been printed. There were translations into French, Dutch, and Swedish, but interestingly not into English. See for this and the subsequent information E. Gottlieb, *Walther-Rathenau-Bibliographie,* Berlin 1929. Rathenau's *Der Kaiser* was based on an earlier unfinished manuscript written after the *Daily Telegraph* affair. This particular version was published posthumously as an article in 1928 under the title 'Zur Psychologie der Dynasten' ('On the Psychology of Dynasts') and is not identical with *Der Kaiser.* W. Rathenau, *Nachgelassene Schriften,* vol. 1, Berlin 1928, pp. 31–51.

detail, but skirted the issue of the Kaiser's role in the decision-making process which had led to the war in 1914. Although Rathenau knew better, he nevertheless argued that the poisoned and war-like situation in Europe which had been in existence for some decades had been a cause of the First World War. He also discussed the Peace Treaty of Versailles, the American intention to create a new European order and Germany's punishment at the hands of the peacemakers. But all this was to Rathenau a consequence of the previous era which was typified by the Kaiser and the political regime of his time. In the future a different political set-up would be concentrating on social concerns in the widest sense. As the book was Rathenau's farewell to his own past, his treatment of the Kaiser was relatively generous. He directed most of his criticism at the upper classes.

Like others Rathenau had been surprised by the military defeat and the subsequent revolutionary events. He had tried to prevent a collapse by appealing days before for a last stand, a *levée en masse*. His aim was to obtain better peace conditions from the Allies and to avoid a revolution. His initiative failed, but this did not lead to his withdrawal from public life nor did he abandon his ultimate ambition, namely to play a major role in politics. He tried to found a democratic league and was very much involved in setting up the Stinnes–Legien Agreement and the subsequent Zentralarbeitsgemeinschaft (Central Working Association). These were the first moves made by Rathenau to demonstrate his willingness to accept the new transitory political conditions without becoming a convinced demo-crat or republican. As a realist who was accustomed to bankruptcies and subsequent fresh starts in the business world, he was able to adapt quickly to the newly emerging situation. However, he hoped to be given a more prominent role in politics as a result of his writings, such as his book *Of Things to Come* in which he adopted the role of a futurologist, newspaper articles, and other publications. Despite his efforts, he was to be disap-pointed in 1918/19, because he was regarded as being too closely associated with the old regime. He tried to meet this criticism with a feverish cam-paign of publishing seven booklets and articles in which he explained his political positions, including his critique of some political institutions of the past, his beliefs and future expectations.[2] But defending his reputation under changed political circumstances was not his only concern. He was also worried about political threats. Thus the first fear he had was that he would be extradited to face charges for having recommended to Erich

---

[2] H. Pogge von Strandmann (ed.), *Walther Rathenau. Industrialist, Banker, Intellectual, and Politician. Notes and Diaries 1907–1922*, Oxford, repr. 1988, pp. 24–5.

Ludendorff the deportation of Belgian workers to Germany in 1916 and for having requisitioned raw materials in France and Belgium. He also feared the charge by the political left that he had prolonged the war by founding the War Raw Materials Department in the Prussian Ministry of War in 1914, and by advocating a *levée en masse* against the emerging Allied conditions for an armistice. Rathenau was also unpopular on the Right as he was accused of having advocated a kind of state socialism as the dominant economic order in Germany for the post-war years. To regain political credibility in the post-war world he tried to distance himself from the previous political system with which he had been largely identified, and to throw in his political lot with those democratic and bourgeois forces which were going to shape the republic.

As it was known that he had belonged to a circle of people close to the Imperial Court and that he had met the Kaiser on several occasions, he was anxious not to be viewed as a 'friend' of the monarch. His identification with Wilhelmine Germany before the war had led him to make only modest criticisms of the political system and to recommend only moderate reforms. Now there was an opportunity to apprise the public of his role as an observer of the political system and to place his criticism of the monarch into a wider political and social context. However, after the publication of *Der Kaiser*, Rathenau was charged with hypocrisy for his attacks on the *haute bourgeoisie* in general and his fellow industrialists in particular, because he had behaved exactly as they had. He had worked hard to obtain imperial decorations and was proud of his contacts with Wilhelm II. Like other business men, Rathenau had publicized his contacts with the Kaiser and had used them commercially as far as he had been able to. Gustav Stresemann took Rathenau to task over the critical stance in his book in the obituary he wrote about him. Stresemann felt that Rathenau 'should never have written the book *Der Kaiser*. When he reproached the old bourgeoisie for basking in imperial glory and for being deeply engrossed in pomp and circumstance he should have admitted that he had acted like those he characterized.'[3]

According to Rathenau, Wilhelm shared typical attributes of other European monarchs, in that he was superficial and fearful of democratic pressures. Their reigns tended to be made up of a sequence of spectacular events produced for the people whom they pretended to love. They regarded their people as subjects and not as citizens, and whatever their belief in divine right, religion and the church played a central role in their lives.

[3] H. Pogge von Strandmann, 'Der Kaiser und die Industriellen. Vom Primat der Rüstung', in J. C. G. Röhl (ed.), *Der Ort Wilhelms II. in der deutschen Geschichte*, Munich 1991, p. 119.

In Rathenau's interpretation, Wilhelm II's policy of preserving the political and social *status quo* was willed by God and thus represented a godly order. So it made sense to Rathenau that the Kaiser regarded the 'feudals', who were mainly interested in preserving their positions, as his most important prop, with the *haute bourgeoisie* as the next group near the throne to support him, longing for influence, honours, and medals. Yet without the support of the people, even in Germany the monarchy would not have been able to survive. Rathenau maintained that whatever group the Kaiser was in touch with he always experienced approval and virtually no criticism. Thus successive Chancellors never attempted to reduce the Kaiser's powers. To Rathenau's mind they and the leading ministers distrusted the common people more than the monarchical system they served. Rathenau pointed out that not one of the first seven of the Chancellors had resigned because of any objection to the monarchical system. Even general constitutional issues had never been at stake – obviously Rathenau had overlooked the actual reason for Bismarck's dismissal. He pointed out that Chancellors and ministers had given the Kaiser the impression that he decided matters, a position which was supported by the court and his close advisors.

Rathenau's reflections on Wilhelm II and the relationship between them inspired two well-known authors to make a comparison between the Kaiser and the industrialist-cum-banker. One of these authors was Rathenau's biographer, Count Kessler. He believed that both men were not entirely dissimilar: 'For the Kaiser was also timid at heart and governed principally by the impulse to mask his weakness by brilliant talk and assumed leadership; the difference was that he was more of an actor than Rathenau and entirely lacked his gift of intuition.'[4] Golo Mann also commented on their tangible similarities and compared the lifestyle of both men and their 'courts':

Both are dilettanti, one absolutely so and the other in many areas which are not his special subject. Both are born speakers. Both are brilliant, captivating, fascinating. Both startle through the gift of accumulating knowledge fast and understanding quickly. Both need and use men in great numbers, both long for friendship without ever being fully satisfied. Both suffer despite being fortunate; Wilhelm because of his well-known burdens; Rathenau because of being Jewish and because of his envy of those with fair hair. Both are full of unrest, always on journeys . . . Both courts . . . have in common that in their openness to the world and in their colourful manifoldness they are not quite true to style, however much Rathenau tries to create a style.[5]

[4] H. Kessler, *Walther Rathenau. His Life and Work*, London 1929, p. 50.
[5] G. Mann, 'Am Hofe Walther Rathenaus', in *Die Zeit*, 23 February 1968.

Of course there were fundamental differences between the two which could be outlined as well, but Rathenau's official biographer, Kessler, and Golo Mann who retained a life-long interest in Rathenau, wanted to make the point that the two were representative of an era and so it was worth making comparisons. One of the fundamental differences between them is that the Kaiser was born into his position whereas Rathenau had to work hard to achieve his wealth and his position in society. In contrast to the Kaiser, Rathenau was immensely creative and productive, while the Kaiser's mental abilities were never really tested.

According to Kessler, whenever Rathenau met the Kaiser he 'felt his way into the monarch's mind and veiled whatever criticism he had to offer in the semblance of heartfelt sympathy'. Rathenau did not want to blame Wilhelm II for his 'Byzantine emperordom', but rather held members of his entourage, the establishment, leading business circles, and the National Liberals, largely responsible for the type of monarchical reality Germany had to endure. For him it was no accident that an era in Germany bore the name of its monarch, and he added: 'The Wilhelmine epoch has done more harm to its monarch than the monarch to it.'[6] Nevertheless he realized that the upper echelons of society were interlinked with their monarch. The downfall of one would have meant the collapse of the other. Therefore the Revolution of November 1918 started with the end of the monarchy in Germany. But Rathenau's judgement did not only apply to the interdependence of society and monarchy, but affected political decisions as well. Thus for Rathenau the causes of the First World War lay in Berlin, but he did not want to blame the Kaiser for them. That would have been too simple. To him Wilhelm II was only one link in the chain of the decision-making process. Thus when Rathenau was critical of the Kaiser in his booklet, he applied this more to the general conditions and less to the personality of Wilhelm II himself. Whatever his criticisms, he also admired the Kaiser, and this general attitude colours his publication.

In his tract Rathenau accused his own class – the *haute bourgeoisie* – of political indolence, over-zealous collaboration with, and even servility towards, the monarchy, but did not make any reference to his own life or apply the criticism to himself. He took shelter behind his role as a writer, outsider, and observer. He illustrated his accusations against the *haute bourgeoisie* by describing a journey he had made with a group of fellow industrialists in the Rhineland. When they made embittered remarks about the Kaiser, he asked them whether they would sign a petition to the Kaiser and Reichstag

[6] W. Richter (ed.), 'Der Kaiser', in *Walther Rathenau. Schriften und Reden*, Frankfurt 1964, p. 261.

asking for a reduction of the monarch's powers. Apparently they agreed, but then Rathenau told them they were deceiving themselves: 'None of you would sign. The prospect of becoming a member of the [Prussian] Upper House and the nobility would be at an end. Your son's career would be finished. No further invitations would come from the court and its dignitaries would cut you.'[7] He concluded his post-war reminiscences by underlining that 'not one of them contradicted me. The upper middle classes knew it to be true, wanted it like that, and confined themselves to verbal criticism.' In writing this anecdote he made it clear that he did not share their attitude and implied that he followed a more critical line. But nothing could be further from the truth. He pursued an active social diplomacy, was proud of his meetings with the Kaiser, flattered him as much as others and cherished his connections with the court. The meetings between the Kaiser and Rathenau were in a way characteristic of the era. Both were conscious of the worlds they stood for. Rathenau represented banking, industry, and technology and acted as a grandmaster of Capitalism. Wilhelm II, on the other hand, was, unlike his grandfather and father, the first modern German Emperor who managed to leave the constraints of the Prussian monarchy firmly behind. The Kaiser had stamped the period with his name and stood as a striking symbol of an ambitious state, while Rathenau, as a representative of the most dynamic European electro-concern, embodied an industry which was the pacemaker of the age of the 'second wind' in the industrialization process.

Rathenau managed to see the Kaiser 'about twenty times between 1901 and 1914, on an average once or twice a year, sometimes for several hours at a time; this was enough to observe the monarch closely'.[8] When they first met, the Kaiser was different from what he had expected. 'I was familiar', Rathenau went on,

with pictures of a dashing young man with wide cheeks, a bristling moustache and menacing eyes; the dangerous telegrams and the vigorous speeches and maxims . . . And now there sat before me a youngish man in a bright uniform covered with exotic-looking medals. His hands were very white and decked with many coloured rings, and on his wrists he wore bracelets. His skin was delicate, his hair soft, his teeth small and white; a veritable prince; intent on the impression he was making; for ever struggling with himself, and tyrannizing his nature in an attempt to win from it mastery, dignity and strength. He had scarcely an unconscious moment; he was unconscious only – and this was the pathetic thing – of the struggle within himself. He was a nature unwittingly directed against itself.

[7] Ibid., p. 247; H. Burte, *Mit Rathenau am Oberrhein*, Heidelberg, repr. 1948, p. 21.
[8] Richter, *Rathenau Schriften*, pp. 247–9.

And later Rathenau was asked his impression. 'He is an enchanter and a man marked by fate', he replied. 'Torn by inner strife, yet does not feel the division. He is on the road to disaster.' Kessler tried to defend Rathenau against the criticism that he had written down these observations with hindsight after the war, by pointing out that Rathenau had used the same words when he talked to him about the Kaiser back in 1906.[9]

At their first meeting, which had probably been arranged at Rathenau's request by Victor von Podbielski, Secretary of State of the Post Office, the industrialist had to repeat to the Kaiser a scientific lecture which he had already delivered in front of a larger audience two days before he repeated it to the Kaiser.[10] Both lectures dealt with the use of electrical power in the new electro-chemical works in Rheinfelden which Rathenau had established in 1897–8. After the lecture he demonstrated some experiments, the Kaiser thanked him and a dialogue developed in which the usefulness of acetylene lamps was discussed. Wilhelm II seemed to prefer them to those fuelled by paraffin: 'Away with paraffin! Foreign product, continues to get expensive. And such paraffin lamps spoil the air in small flats. Well, we must extend the use of hydropower! In Silesia. Think of those waterfalls.' The Kaiser also referred to Cecil Rhodes's admiration for the factories of the AEG (Allgemeine Elektrizitäts-Gesellschaft) he had seen in Berlin. Rathenau replied: 'Your Majesty, the English can learn something from our German factories. They put their installations together in a piecemeal fashion. We plan and project the whole thing uniformly. And then, modestly and conscientiously, the German bureaucrat always steps back and gets on with his task.' The Kaiser agreed: 'Yes, we have got the material.' Rathenau referred to the emphasis on organization, and made the flattering remark, 'We look at the Prussian state and try to copy it in our small world.' Although he held the view that it was really industry which provided the model for state bureaucracy, the Kaiser accepted his flattery: 'Organization

[9] Kessler, *Rathenau,* p. 51.
[10] The first lecture was delivered on 8 February, the second on the 10th. Both occasions took place at the Postal Museum. Walther Rathenau, *Briefe,* vol. I, Dresden 1927, p. 37, Rathenau to Puche, 13 January 1900. H. D. Hellige (ed.), *Walther Rathenau. Maximilian Harden. Briefwechsel 1897–1920,* Munich and Heidelberg 1983, pp. 327–8, 8 March 1900; see also p. 886, excerpt from Harden's article published in *Die Zukunft* on 1 July 1922. The lecture was circulated as a private print shortly afterwards and also published posthumously in W. Rathenau, *Nachgelassene Schriften,* vol. II, Berlin 1928, pp. 385–403. The conversation between Rathenau and Wihelm II was first published by H. D. Hellige, 'Wilhelm II. und Walther Rathenau', in *Geschichte in Wissenschaft und Unterricht,* 19 (1968), pp. 542–4. See also E. Schulin (ed.), *Walther Rathenau. Hauptwerke und Gespräche,* Munich and Heidelberg 1977, pp, 621–4, and E. Schulin (ed.), *Gespräche mit Rathenau,* Munich 1980, pp. 35–9. A reference to the Nernst lamp and the Kaiser can be found in E. Schulin (ed.), *Hauptwerke und Gespräche,* p. 665.

is the main thing, be guided there by the state.' Then they talked briefly about the use of wireless connections in the navy. Rathenau was convinced that the experiments in the German navy were not inferior to the English ones: 'Now Marconi is supposed to come to Berlin. But what the Italians can do, our men can do here as well.' The Kaiser agreed emphatically and then commented on the experiments Count Arco had carried out during the talk: 'If only our sixth-formers could see a table like this and could make the experiments! But they have not got a clue.' Rathenau replied, 'No, but the Greek poets and the dialects, these things we still carry round in our heads.' The Kaiser lamented, 'and what about the Landrat or Councillor! Now there's a man who has to decide about the electric power stations. He hasn't a clue about them. And even if he did want to learn about them him-self, he would not be able to understand.' Rathenau pointed out that 'they throw their factory doors wide open and say: come and see for yourself. And people come from America and Australia. But from here?' The Kaiser's classic remark to that was 'Well, there you are. The prophet has no honour in his fatherland.' Finally the Kaiser asked Rathenau whether he was afraid of the Americans. Rathenau denied that he was, at least for the time being, but warned the Kaiser that 'the Germans could not fend off American over-production without protective tariffs if there should be a slump one day'. 'Well', the Kaiser replied, 'then we must do something about that. Besides, you could simply invent an installation like this one here [referring to the use of sodium] and throw those lads back over the water.'

The meeting between the two was not only a social event. The Kaiser's interest in modern developments in science and technology is well known. Obviously he was also keen as supreme warlord to know the firms which supplied the army and the navy with armament material. However, Ra-thenau's intentions may have gone further. He would probably have wanted to gain the Kaiser's approval for AEG products and to use his name in some way when the AEG bid for navy contracts. Thus the talk Rathenau gave to Wilhelm II was perhaps designed to win over the monarch for the wire-less communication system developed by the AEG. The Kaiser had visited the AEG factories in 1900 and is supposed to have been very impressed by their size, their exactly thought-out organization and the model-like discipline of the workforce.[11] He may have been won over by the AEG system of telegraphic communications and have added his voice to those who favoured the AEG system. In the event the naval telegraphic stations on land and in the Baltic and North Seas were built and equipped by the

---

[11] *50 Jahre AEG*, Berlin 1956, p. 128.

AEG.[12] However, the army operated a different system developed by Braun and Siemens. When Marconi threatened to make it difficult for the two German companies to make use of his system for further improvements, the Kaiser intervened in 1902 and supported a merger between the branches of the two German companies.[13] Consequently in 1903 the AEG and Siemens set up a new company called the 'Company for Wireless Telegraphy – System Telefunken', of which the AEG and Siemens owned equal shares.

The Kaiser intervened a second time in the business affairs of the AEG when the company was intending to set up a new turbine company combining its own Riedler-Stumpf patents with those of General Electric's Curtis plants and with the technical expertise of Brown & Boveri. Riedler and Stumpf objected until the Kaiser intervened in December 1903.[14] The result was the foundation of a turbine company which sold its new turbines successfully to the navy. The AEG's supply of electrical equipment to nine out of thirty-six battleships built between 1900 and 1914, to five out of thirty-seven light cruisers, and to ships of the Russian navy gives an indication of the firm's involvement in the armaments industry.[15] AEG turbines and electric motors were delivered to ten out of thirty U-boats and to twenty-eight out of seventy-two torpedo boats. In addition the AEG had a monopoly on small turbines which were used on board for specific functions such as pumps, etc. It is also noteworthy that the Navy Office intervened several times over the years to make sure that the AEG was given contracts and that the companies of the Siemens concern were not favoured any more.

Between 1899 and 1902 Rathenau belonged to the executive board of the AEG and thus the contact with Wilhelm II may have been important for the future as well, as the navy began to use more and more electrical equipment. Obviously the Kaiser must have realised how important the growth of the electro-technical industry had become. At this stage, as the British historian John Clapham noted, no other industry combined a similarly high level of technical, scientific, and economic advance: 'Beyond question, the creation of this industry was the greatest single industrial achievement of modern Germany.'[16]

---

[12] M. Pohl, *Emil Rathenau und die AEG*, Berlin and Frankfurt 1988, p. 184.

[13] H. Wessel, *Die Entwicklung des elektrischen Nachrichtenwesens in Deutschland und die rheinische Industrie. Von den Anfängen bis zum Ausbruch des Ersten Weltkrieges*, Wiesbaden 1983, pp. 506–9; G. Hecker, *Walther Rathenau und sein Verhältnis zu Militär und Krieg*, Boppard 1983, pp. 105–6; H. Pogge von Strandmann, 'Der Kaiser und die Industriellen', p. 126.

[14] Ibid. See also *50 Jahre AEG*, pp. 159, 422.   [15] Hecker, *Walther Rathenau*, pp. 97–104, 119–20.

[16] J. H. Clapham, *The Economic Development of France and Germany, 1815–1914*, Cambridge 1921, p. 308.

Shortly after the meeting with the Kaiser, Rathenau published an article in *Die Zukunft* (under a pseudonym) about the 'Physiology of Businesses' (*Physiologie der Geschäfte*), which was reviewed critically by Theodor Herzl.[17] Rathenau lifted his pseudonym in their subsequent correspondence and Herzl admitted that for a short time he had suspected Harden, with whom he had many disagreements, to be the author of that article. He then went on to mention one particular disagreement. Unlike Harden he was a great admirer of Wilhelm II whom he knew personally. In his reply Rathenau insisted that he shared Herzl's sympathies for the Kaiser, the more so as he also knew him personally: 'And may I add I know him well.' Herzl, who then realized that Rathenau and the editor of *Die Zukunft*, Maximilian Harden, were friends, suggested to Rathenau that he would be willing to ask the Kaiser to pardon Harden, who at this stage was in prison because of lese-majesty. But nothing came of it.[18]

Unlike Harden, who was very critical of Wilhelm II, Rathenau basked in his acquaintance with the monarch. Several social occasions followed: parties in Berlin, sailing weeks in Kiel and Hamburg, ship launches, investiture ceremonies and rides in the Berlin Tiergarten, all of which Rathenau seems to have savoured. In short, Rathenau enjoyed being *persona grata* with Wilhelm II, but he was not in the same league as the shipping magnate Albert Ballin, who was even invited to dinners at court. The Kaiser was very ready to meet Walther Rathenau unofficially, but when it came to court functions Rathenau may not have ranked highly enough in Wilhelmine society to be included in the official invitation list. Nevertheless, Rathenau enjoyed a privileged position compared to Gustav Stresemann and Ernst Bassermann, two leading National Liberals, neither of whom managed to be presented to the Kaiser at the Kiel regatta in June 1914. Stresemann was terribly upset by what he regarded as an affront.[19]

There may also have been occasions when Rathenau accompanied his father Emil to the latter's meetings with the Kaiser, but no source has come to light so far to provide any details.[20] Walther kept a record of some of his own meetings, but none was as detailed as the stenographic account

[17] 'Physiologie der Geschäfte', in *Die Zukunft*, 35 (1901), pp. 495–514; Hellige, *Briefwechsel*, p. 351.

[18] Hellige, *Briefwechsel*, p. 352. See also R. Kallner, *Herzl und Rathenau. Wege jüdischer Existenz an der Wende des 20. Jahrhunderts*, Stutgart 1976, pp. 290–4.

[19] W. Stresemann, *Mein Vater Gustav Stresemann*, Munich 1979, p. 87; J. Wright, *Gustav Stresemann. Weimar's Greatest Statesman*, Oxford 2002, p. 63.

[20] Pohl, *Emil Rathenau und die AEG*, pp. 203–4. On 12 July 1900 Wilhelm signed the document in Norwegian waters which made Emil Rathenau a *Geheimer Baurat*. W. Mosse, *Jews in the German Economy. The German-Jewish Economic Elite 1820–1935*, Oxford 1987, p. 78.

of the conversation with the Kaiser after Rathenau's lecture in the Postal Museum.

No transcript seems to have survived of the meeting between Wilhelm, Chancellor von Bülow, and Rathenau on the occasion of the reconciliation dinner between the monarch and his Chancellor in March 1909.[21] It is unlikely that Rathenau's efforts at mediation in the Eulenburg-Affair in 1907 would have been referred to at this meeting with Bülow, but Rathenau could probably have watched how the master courtier Bülow treated the Kaiser. It may be that Rathenau asked Bülow on a different occasion how he managed to keep the Emperor in such a good temper, to which Bülow replied: 'His Majesty delights in explaining mechanical contrivances like a clock, or a compass, or a barometer. I keep a special barometer, and whenever the Emperor comes I ask him to explain how it works, saying that I have forgotten what he told me last time. He gives an admirable and lengthy exposition, but it puts him in an excellent temper, and he signs my Decrees.'[22] Rathenau may have learnt something from the master courtier during this dinner.

Shortly after the reconciliation dinner Rathenau bought Schloss Freienwalde from the Prussian crown for 262,000 marks. He was allowed to keep the title Royal for the Schloss which had been built in 1795 with the aid of architect David Gilly. The Schloss had been the country seat of the Prussian Princess Wilhelmine, the daughter of Friedrich Wilhelm II and later wife of King William I of the Netherlands.[23] Rathenau then set to work to restore the house as far as possible to its original form and style. He dedicated time and money to this venture which resulted in a home not far from Berlin where he could indulge his admiration of late eighteenth- and early nineteenth-century Prussia.[24] The Kaiser never visited Rathenau in Freienwalde, but had he done so he would not have admired it. His taste was very different, as can be gauged from the architecture of the Berlin Dome whose construction he influenced. Rathenau's criticism of Berlin as a 'Parvunopolis', and his dislike of what was called Berlin-baroque was well expressed in his correspondence with Harden. The two agreed that the Kaiser's influence on art and architecture was not beneficial to the image

[21] Hellige, *Briefwechsel*, p. 581.
[22] House of Lords Records, Lloyd George Papers, F/54/2, D'Abernon to Hankey, 7 March 1922. In the published version of this report it was not mentioned that it was a letter to Hankey and that the name of Bülow was omitted.
[23] Pogge von Strandmann, *Rathenau*, pp. 91, 97.
[24] H. Fürstenberg, *Carl Fürstenberg. Die Lebensgeschichte eines deutschen Bankiers*, Wiesbaden 1961, pp. 477–9.

of the capital. So in that sense Rathenau's restoration of Freienwalde could be seen to represent a critique of the Kaiser's vulgar and monumental metropolis.[25] However Rathenau's disdain for some features of Berlin and for the Kaiser's influence on some of the building projects did not lead to a deterioration in their relationship, although it did show that Rathenau was not completely taken in by the Kaiser. Nevertheless he appreciated the Kaiser's friendly attitude towards him, as became clear again in 1911.

In that year Rathenau was invited to become a National Liberal candidate for the forthcoming Reichstag elections. Eventually nothing came of it, but he must have felt appreciated when he heard through Ballin that the 'Kaiser [was] very pleased about my candidature; regards it as a great sacrifice, etc.'[26] However, in his obituary of Rathenau, Gustav Stresemann published another version according to which the Kaiser appeared to be offended by Rathenau's willingness to stand for the Reichstag. And when the Kaiser next met Rathenau, he is supposed to have withdrawn his hand with the words: 'Then you do not want to remain my friend.'[27] In fact, however, it is very unlikely that the Kaiser said anything like that. Although he was not in favour of the Reichstag, he did not oppose industrialists being elected as deputies, as is demonstrated by the case of Friedrich Alfred Krupp, who was elected in 1893.

At this stage the Kaiser had a positive opinion of Rathenau. When the Kaiser went to London for the funeral of Edward VII, he talked to the French Foreign Minister, Stéphan Pichon, about Moroccan politics and German interests there. According to French sources, the Kaiser mentioned Rathenau as a possible official mediator between the clashing industrial claims of the Union des Mines and the brothers Mannesmann, and recommended Rathenau to the French side as a man who had his confidence.[28] Over the next few years the Kaiser seems to have been positively inclined towards Rathenau, who recorded every meeting he had with his monarch in his diaries. At their first encounter in 1911 at Admiral von Hollmann's place the Kaiser talked to Rathenau about a number of issues, such as the

---

[25] See for Rathenau's earlier view of Berlin his article 'Die schönste Stadt der Welt', which was published in *Die Zukunft* on 7 January 1899 and republished in Rathenau, *Nachgelassene Schriften*, vol. II, pp. 259–80.

[26] Pogge von Strandmann, *Rathenau*, p. 130, 26 June 1911. For the reasons why Rathenau eventually refused to take up the candidature see Pogge von Strandmann, 'Hochmeister des Kapitalismus. Walther Rathenau als Industrieorganisator, Politiker und Schriftsteller', in H. Wilderotter (ed.), *Die Extreme berühren sich. Walther Rathenau 1867–1922*, Berlin 1994, p. 36.

[27] Pogge von Strandmann, 'Der Kaiser und die Industriellen', pp. 119–20.

[28] Pogge von Strandmann, 'Rathenau, die Gebrüder Mannesmann und die Vorgeschichte der Zweiten Marokkokrise', in I. Geiss and B. J. Wendt (eds.), *Deutschland in der Weltpolitik des 19. und 20. Jahrhunderts*, Düsseldorf 1974, p. 255. See also Hellige, *Briefwechsel*, pp. 605–14.

Mannesmann affair and thus probably also about Rathenau's mediation efforts, about Schloss Freienwalde, about the success Rathenau had with the production of synthetic rubies at the Electro-Chemical Works at Bitterfeld, and about the Kaiser's dislike of the architectural style of Karl Schinkel.[29] They then did not see each other until nearly a year later when they met again at the Hollmanns'.[30] On this occasion, shortly after the Haldane mission, Rathenau had a long political conversation with Wilhelm II which he judged to be a 'clear, pointed presentation throughout'. The Kaiser talked about the Haldane Mission, his unwillingness to reduce the German fleet-building programme, about the French role as 'disturber of the peace' during the Second Moroccan Crisis of 1911, his distrust of the British Foreign Secretary, Sir Edward Grey, and Kiderlen-Wächter's mistake about England. He ended his monologue about England with a reference to his usual belief in the success of his own personal diplomacy: He 'only wanted to go to Cowes again, then he would settle everything. The King [George V] trusted him.' The Kaiser also referred to Alfred de Rothschild, whom he had decorated a number of years before and who had trust 'in the Kaiser's love of peace'. He alleged that the London banker 'has gone to Grey on behalf of the City and has told him that he would not get any money for the war (?!)'. The Kaiser then spoke of his future plan, namely to set up a 'United States of Europe against America. The English are not unsympathetic to this. Five states (incl. France) could do something.'[31] A few weeks later Rathenau published an article entitled 'England and Us' in which he believed, like the Kaiser, that Britain had to make the first step in order to preserve peace by offering neutrality if she wanted to maintain the entente with France.[32]

A few months passed before Rathenau met the Kaiser again, this time to celebrate the two-hundredth anniversary of the foundation of the Berlin merchant bank of Schickler.[33] This time Rathenau was not brow-beaten by the Kaiser and gave Wilhelm II a detailed and lengthy account of how he had brought about the merger of the two private banks Delbrück and Schickler 'which had been concealed from him [the Kaiser]'. This must have surprised Rathenau, as Ludwig Delbrück was the Keeper of the Privy Purse

[29] Pogge von Strandmann, *Walther Rathenau*, p. 114, 16 March 1911. All entries in the published version of the diaries about the meetings with the Kaiser have been checked against the handwritten originals discovered in the Special Archives in Moscow ten years ago. No discrepancies were found. See also Hellige, *Briefwechsel*, p. 603.

[30] Pogge von Strandmann, *Walther Rathenau*, pp. 146–8, 13 February 1912.

[31] Ibid., pp. 153–4.

[32] The article 'England und Wir' appeared in the Vienna *Neue Freie Presse* on 6 April 1912.

[33] Pogge von Strandmann, *Walther Rathenau*, p. 160, 6 June 1912.

to Wilhelm II. The Kaiser then went on to tell Rathenau about the new German Ambassador in London, Freiherr von Marschall, who apparently had published notes in the press 'on the Franco-English alliance, the origins of which the English presume to be Paris'. Apart from this indiscretion, they talked about Rathenau's father, who had been seriously ill, about Rathenau's article 'England and Us', and Rathenau's ideas for the plan to build a Bismarck memorial at Bingen on the Rhine. They also talked at length about the planned new opera house in Berlin, about which Rathenau and the Kaiser disagreed. The diaries do not contain any details about the disagreement and whether it was voiced or papered over.[34] In any case they had another brief encounter a few days later before dinner after the Elbe Regatta in Hamburg, but nothing is recorded of this meeting.[35]

When the Kaiser and Rathenau met again it was during the maiden voyage of the liner *Imperator* in 1913.[36] This time politics do not seem to have figured prominently. Instead Rathenau noted down some of the jokes the Kaiser told and one example may suffice to indicate their character. The Kaiser mentioned a Swedish Countess who had produced twins several times. When she was asked 'whether she had them every time?', her reply was: 'No, hundreds of times . . . , nay thousands of times nothing happens at all.' This time there is no indication that Rathenau was favourably impressed with the Kaiser. His critical attitude seems to have grown by the time they talked to each other in March 1914.[37] Wilhelm II was still preoccupied with of the Zabern Crisis, used stereotypes to describe the *Wackes*, a disparaging word for the inhabitants of the Alsace, and recommended that a wall be built between France and Germany. Rathenau noted in his diaries that he 'tried to object, stating that only an upper-class group of a thousand people in Strasbourg and Mulhouse had disturbed the peace', but his objection had had no effect. It was 'in vain' to raise objections against some of this silly talk. On the same day he wrote to his father about the meeting with the Kaiser, but did not mention anything about the Zabern Crisis or the Kaiser's remarks.[38] Instead he referred to a 'boring lecture' about safety measures on the railway system. He suspected that the lecture was only a pretext and that he had, in fact, been invited at the Kaiser's suggestion, because most of the afternoon the Kaiser only talked with him and Breitenbach, the Prussian Minister for Public Works. On this occasion Rathenau was also

---

[34] Hellige, *Briefwechsel*, p. 648. On 19 March 1912 Rathenau had criticized the plans for a new opera house, which were based on the demolition of the old one built by Knobelsdorff, in the *Berliner Tageblatt*. The new plans had been influenced by the Kaiser.

[35] Pogge von Strandmann, *Rathenau*, p. 161, 18 June 1912.

[36] Ibid., pp. 179–80, 8 July 1913.   [37] Ibid., pp. 182–3, 12 March 1914.

[38] Special Archive Moscow, 634/1/263, Rathenau to his father, 12 March 1914.

able to lay his plans open for a fast electric railway system in Bitterfeld in co-operation with the state. He was convinced that this had made a good impression upon the Kaiser.

Rathenau was so fascinated by the Kaiser that the latter figured prominently in his life. Not only was he proud of meeting the Kaiser, but he also talked about him to a number of other people. The left liberal politician, Hermann Pachnicke, reported that Rathenau thought Wilhelm II was good-willed, but had never learnt to work properly. 'He knew something about everything, but only in the most superficial way. Of a machine one had to tell him that it is the biggest in the world. Of a Nernst lamp that nobody else would be able to do that.'[39] Only if one talked in such an exaggerated way would one find that he had listened. Pachnicke also referred to an incident which Rathenau was to mention several times. When Wilhelm and Rathenau rode together on one occasion towards the Brandenburg Gate in Berlin, the Kaiser explained the defence strategy of the German colony Kiaochow in China. The Kaiser's line was that Kiaochow would never be attacked and would hold out in war. Rathenau later told the British Ambassador, Lord D'Abernon, that he was impressed by the Kaiser's powers of persuasion, but that he remained unconvinced. In fact Kiaochow fell within weeks after the outbreak of war.[40]

Two German authors have given accounts of meetings between Rathenau and the Kaiser. Fritz von Unruh recalled that the Kaiser had recommended conversion to Christianity to Rathenau, so that he could make him a reserve officer in a guard regiment. This is highly unlikely given that, as far as is known, the Kaiser and Rathenau had never discussed the fact that Rathenau was a Jew.[41] What is much more likely is that Chancellor von Bülow decided not to offer Rathenau a ministerial post primarily because he was a Jew, and Rathenau may have mentioned this to Fritz von Unruh. However, there is no direct evidence even for this.[42] The other author who recorded an account of a conversation with Rathenau was Hermann Burte. Rathenau's supposed remarks about the Kaiser read as follows: 'the Kaiser is of a tragic nature always has a tear in his eye; he means well but fails in everything [he does]'.[43] The reference to a tragic nature could have been genuine, but in *Der Kaiser* Rathenau wrote that the monarch lacked sufficient insight to be tragic and 'did not even have any unconscious feeling of the problem'.[44]

---

[39] Schulin, *Hauptwerke und Gespräche*, p. 665.
[40] House of Lords Records, Lloyd George Papers, F/54/2, D'Abernon to Hankey, 7 March 1922.
[41] Schulin, *Hauptwerke und Gespräche*, p. 681.
[42] Pogge von Strandmann, *Walther Rathenau*, p. 29; Hellige, *Briefwechsel*, p. 489.
[43] Schulin, *Hauptwerke und Gespräche*, p. 693.   [44] Richter, *Rathenau Schriften*, p. 261.

The roles were changed when Rathenau met Prince Bülow in Rome in June 1911, and the latter talked about the Kaiser. It was now Rathenau's turn to listen and make notes. According to Rathenau, Bülow did not characterize Wilhelm II, but mentioned three of his reactions to the Kaiser: 'First admiration, then disappointment and finally pity.'[45] He also told Rathenau how the Prussian Minister of Finance, Johannes von Miquel, and the Councillor in the German Foreign Office, Friedrich von Holstein, had summed up the Kaiser. The former had said that the Kaiser was politically colour-blind and the latter had said in English: 'He lives in a fool's paradise.' In explaining the Kaiser's political style, Bülow outlined that the Kaiser's parents' and grandmother's dislike of Bismarck had strengthened Wilhelm's wish not to be dependent on one minister. All this was building material for Rathenau's judgement of the Kaiser and his post-war book on him.

When the British Ambassador, Lord D'Abernon, asked Rathenau about his opinion of the Kaiser in 1922, the then German Foreign Minister summed up his judgement of the Kaiser:

One of the Kaiser's misfortunes was his real superiority to his entourage both in memory, and in argumentative ability. He had an incorrect instinct, his judgement was usually wrong, but he could put his case admirably and overwhelm his antagonists by feats of memory. The latter was exercised in the main on insignificant detail, but it served its controversial purpose.[46]

Obviously Rathenau had no high opinion of the circle around the Kaiser, but seems to have given the monarch some credit for his argumentative powers.

Generally speaking Rathenau was aware that the Kaiser, along with most other German monarchs, was inadequate to meet the needs of a modernizing society, and therefore in Rathenau's eyes the final revolution had been inevitable. And revolutions never occur, so he thought, without the guilt of those in power. This was in Rathenau's eyes a damning judgement, although there were others who felt that in his account he let the Kaiser off lightly. Rathenau seems to have retained some sympathy for a somewhat reduced monarchy, but would have been prudent enough not to advocate such thoughts after 1918. For the most ardent followers of Wilhelm II Rathenau's tract may have been treasonable, but others went so far as to misinterpret it as a defence of the monarch. It has to be added that some in the military circles had become totally disillusioned with the Hohenzollerns. They accused Wilhelm II of having deserted the army and Germany when

---

[45] Pogge von Strandmann, *Walther Rathenau*, 2 June 1911, p. 127.
[46] House of Lords Records, Lloyd George Papers, F/54/2, D'Abernon to Hankey, 7 March 1922.

he had fled to Holland in 1918. They certainly did not envisage a restoration of a Hohenzollern monarchy during the days of the Kapp Putsch in 1920.

Rathenau's critical interpretations, couched in a complex language and avoiding an outright attack on the Kaiser, did not go down well with some conservatives and anti-republicans. To them the pamphlet *Der Kaiser* appeared to be a general attack on the politics of pre-war and wartime Germany. But there was another reason why a man like Ludendorff was to turn against Rathenau, with whom he had had good contacts during the war. Earlier in 1919 Rathenau had defended the general when the latter was blamed for having lost the war.[47] At that time, Ludendorff was still grateful to Rathenau. The break came when the latter reproached Ludendorff for having been indecisive in the summer of 1918. First the general had demanded an end to the fighting, but then ten days later had changed his mind and believed that the front would be able to hold. According to Rathenau the general should then have stood by his new intention and should have continued to fight. Ludendorff never forgave Rathenau for accusing him of having been undecided and lacking courage.[48] It was therefore not surprising that Ludendorff, at the hearing of the Reichstag Committee in the autumn of 1919, which had been set up to investigate the causes of Germany's defeat, quoted a passage out of Rathenau's booklet in order to attack him. Ludendorff tried to fend off any responsibility for the loss of the war and told the deputies on 18 November 1919:

I regret that I am compelled to repeat a remark of Walther Rathenau's to the effect that on the day that the Kaiser and his paladins on their white chargers ride victorious through the Brandenburg Gate, history will have lost all meaning. Thus there were currents of opinion in the nation which did not subscribe to the view of the Supreme Command that we must fight to a victorious conclusion, and these currents of opinion must be taken into account.[49]

He blamed Rathenau and others for undermining morale at home, and took this as evidence for the 'stab-in-the-back legend'. Rathenau immediately realised the danger emanating from his declaration and published a lengthy article in the *Berliner Tageblatt* a few days later in which he refuted Ludendorff: 'Had Ludendorff taken the trouble to read this [pamphlet], he would have understood its sense: Under the leadership of those men under whom Germany had then gone into war (the remark was made in

---

[47] Hecker, *Walther Rathenau*, p. 473.   [48] Ibid., pp. 474–7.
[49] E. Ludendorff (ed.), *Urkunden der Obersten Heeresleitung über ihre Tätigkeit 1916–18*, Berlin 1922, p. 581. Kessler, *Rathenau*, pp. 279–80. In the English edition Ludendorff's presentation was wrongly dated to November 1920.

September 1914) we could not win.'[50] In the poisoned atmosphere of the immediate post-war years, Rathenau's self-defence was to no avail. In the eyes of the nationalist circles Ludendorff's character-assassination stamped Rathenau as a traitor and 'from then on he was', according to Kessler, 'a marked man'. In his defence Rathenau did not mention that the former Chancellor von Bethmann Hollweg had used a similar sentence in his statement to the Committee of Enquiry: 'A people that were under such leadership could not win.'[51] Some people did not believe that Rathenau had made such a remark as early as 1914 particularly as he did not identify the witness he had quoted. But several years later Prince von Bülow came to his aid. In his memoirs he wrote that Rathenau had reminded him in 1922 of a meeting in the autumn of 1914 when Rathenau had pointed out to him the incompatibility of a victorious Kaiser, riding together with Bethmann and Falkenhayn through the Brandenburg Gate, and the political system prevailing in Germany at the time.[52] There may have been other witnesses, but only one came to Rathenau's rescue, Heinrich Spiero, one of Rathenau's closest colleagues in the War Raw Materials Department in the Prussian Ministry of War. He offered to make a declaration under oath that Rathenau's remark 'had a different meaning to the one assumed [by Ludendorff]'.[53]

Whatever tribulations Rathenau may have suffered at the hands of Ludendorff, the Kaiser's immediate reaction to *Der Kaiser* and to Ludendorff's attack remains so far unknown. Even if he had not read Rathenau's booklet he must have become aware of it through reviews, newspaper articles, occasional visitors, and comments made by his entourage in Amerongen and Doorn. It could be assumed that during his increasingly anti-Semitic years in exile he must have resented Rathenau's booklet, his increased role in the public sphere and later his two ministerial appointments in 1921 and 1922. But the little evidence we have points to a much more mixed reaction. First of all in 1926 he judged Rathenau to have been a 'mean, deceiving, rascally traitor'.[54] And he added that 'there is nothing

[50] Kessler, *Rathenau*. Rathenau's article was headed 'Schicksalsspiel' and was re-published in 1920 in a pamphlet *Was wird werden?* (What is to become?). In his article he referred to his meetings with Ludendorff and what they had discussed. This was to prove that Rathenau was not a defeatist.

[51] Bethmann's pleading took place on 30 October 1919 and was published in *Vossische Zeitung* on 3 November 1919. Hellige, *Briefwechsel*, p. 757.

[52] B. Fürst von Bülow, *Denkwürdigkeiten*, vol. III, Berlin 1931, p. 42.

[53] Hecker, *Walther Rathenau*, p. 475. There was also a quarrel between Rathenau and Harden about whose idea it had been to refer to the image of the Brandenburg Gate and who had used it first. Hellige, *Briefwechsel*, pp. 757–8.

[54] L. Cecil, 'Wilhelm II. und die Juden', in W. E. Mosse and A. Paucker (eds.), *Juden im Wilhelminischen Deutschland 1890–1914*, Tübingen 1976, p. 344, Wilhelm II to G. S. Viereck, 29 January 1926. Viereck's

of "great importance" about him at all'. But then in the same letter he changed his tack. He wrote that according to some accounts, Rathenau's boast about the Kaiser riding through the Brandenburg Gate as a victor was 'genuine'. But he did not refer to the second part of the passage, which implied that under such conditions history would have lost its meaning. By 1926 he may have forgotten that part of the passage, and he was in any case mistaken about the date the booklet was published. However, he misrepresented Rathenau's intentions completely when he mentioned in his letter that 'he [Rathenau] wrote about me during the first part of the war lauding me up to the skies'.

The Kaiser made another mistake in the letter when he referred to Rathenau belonging 'to the 200 of the "Inner Circle" of the International Rulers of Jewish descent'. In fact, Rathenau had published an article in the Vienna *Neue Freie Presse* in 1909 in which he wrote that 'three hundred men all acquainted with each other control the economic destiny of the Continent'.[55] Rathenau's mention of such a group has often been misunderstood, especially by anti-Semitic authors who took it as a proof of the existence of a worldwide Jewish plot. What this letter demonstrates is that at least in 1926 the Kaiser's judgement of Rathenau himself was more negative than his judgement of Rathenau's pamphlet. The letter also raises the question as to whether his dislike of Rathenau was the result of his growing post-war anti-Semitism, or whether he had turned against Rathenau because he had become a public figure in the new republic. The question cannot easily be answered because of lack of evidence. But one point is clear. The Kaiser seems to have lowered the threshold for his anti-Semitic outbursts with the result that Jews he tolerated or even liked before the war now attracted his invective. In 1928 the Rathenaubund (Rathenau League) offered to work for the Kaiser's return to Germany so that he could take up residence in Bavaria. His response was: 'The Rathenau League should lick my . . .! See Götz von Berlichingen!'[56]

Taking this post-war attitude to Rathenau into account, the Kaiser's alleged comment on Rathenau's assassination in 1922 does not offer any more surprises: 'It serves him quite right.'[57] Whatever he may have felt about Rathenau before the war changed once he was in exile. During his years in

private papers are kept in the Houghton Library, Harvard University, Cambridge, MA. I am very grateful to John Röhl for having supplied me with a full version of this letter. See also J. C. G. Röhl, *Kaiser, Hof und Staat. Wilhelm II, und die deutsche Politik*, 4th edn, Munich 1995, p. 95.

[55] W. Rathenau, 'Unser Nachwuchs', in *Neue Freie Presse*, Vienna, 25 December 1909. The article is reprinted in Rathenau, *Nachgelassene Schriften*, vol. II, p. 350. See also Kessler, *Rathenau*, p. 121.

[56] W. Gutsche, *Wilhelm II. Der letzte Kaiser des Deutschen Reiches*, Berlin 1991, p. 207.

[57] W. Pfeiffer-Belli (ed.), *Harry Graf Kessler. Tagebücher 1918–1937*, Frankfurt 1961, p. 386, 3 April 1923.

Holland the Kaiser turned into a virulent anti-Semite, a tendency which had always been latent before the war but was tamed to some extent by political considerations, his admiration for the wealth of some Jews, the financial advice he received, the general knowledge and worldliness they offered him in their conversations, as well as the relief from the boredom of talking to some members of his entourage. Among the Jews who were singled out by the Kaiser, the so-called *Kaiserjuden*, were Ballin – the Kaiser later claimed not to have known about him being a Jew – Simon, Warburg, Fürstenberg, and the two Rathenaus, to name but a few. The Kaiser continued to meet Ballin during the war, but so far no evidence has come to light to suggest that Rathenau had the opportunity to meet his monarch during those years. It may be that social occasions of the pre-war type no longer took place. In addition, different attitudes towards the purpose of the war may have stood in the way of another meeting. Politically the Kaiser was bound by the military belief in an outright German victory, whereas Rathenau vacillated between scepticism and even pessimism towards a German victory and hoped merely for a good end to Germany's struggle. Despite his conviction that Germany was in some ways the wrong country to win the war, he had worked for a German victory and hoped for an improvement in the political system. But he realized rather late that the two aims might be incompatible. Nevertheless he had ruled out any simple return to the political *status quo* of 1914. A joke circulated in Berlin represented two different political positions for which the Kaiser and Rathenau stood: 'Above the war when it was won there would gleam a symbol – a huge W.R. – which some would take to mean Wilhelm Rex and others Walther Rathenau . . .'[58]

Rathenau had become well known both to political insiders and even to others outside the political club *Deutsche Gesellschaft*. Despite his criticisms and his self-assumed role as an observer, he identified fully with Wilhelmine Germany and supported many of its institutions. His political criticisms were only concerned with partial reforms, such as the Prussian franchise and the re-drawing of the constituency-boundaries for the Reichstag elections. In this way he wanted to modernize the Second Empire and strengthen its political, economic and social fabric by also giving more power to industry and its representatives. Thus he wanted to improve, not to overthrow; and it is this which justifies the labelling of him as a *Wilhelminist*. This term could be interpreted in another way. It could describe those who helped to free Wilhelm II from Bismarck's tutelage and assisted the young Kaiser

[58] F. von Rabenau (ed.), *Seeckt. Aus meinem Leben 1918–1936*, Leipzig 1940, p. 325; H. Pogge von Strandmann, *Rathenau*, p. 237.

to establish a hold over political affairs. This group tried to steer Imperial Germany clear of the Scylla of parliamentarianism and the Charybdis of military dictatorship.[59] But if interpreted in this way, the term would become too narrowly focused and would lose any dialectic dimension and thus any aspect of reformist identification. Rathenau, for one, wanted to reform the political system rather than to change it radically. The aim was a strengthened Germany abroad and a stable political condition at home. His proposals for reform were directed against a conservative predominance and were designed to take the steam out of more radical proposals for reform. Like most other industrialists he was not convinced that Germany was faced by a political crisis, but he could foresee mounting difficulties which should be met by reforms. Although German industrialists tended at the time to be supporters of the political *status quo*, Rathenau went a step further and by forward planning tried to anticipate future situations which might endanger the further expansion of large concerns. Rathenau's ideas on reform were not all that dissimilar to those of Friedrich Naumann, as described in *Demokratie und Kaisertum*. However, Rathenau was not as keen to work with the existing party system. During the war he seized the opportunity of explaining the need to widen the basis of the monarchy to a staunch conservative, Elard von Oldenburg-Januschau, when they met accidentally in Freienwalde.[60] 'Les extrêmes se touchent', were apparently the words Rathenau used when meeting Oldenburg, but the latter stuck to his political line and no further progress was made.

Rathenau, as a *Wilhelminist*, did not spare his criticism of the Kaiser and the Prussian nobility. In fact, he blamed the nobility for politically mismanaging the empire and for blocking a more modern selection system for high office, although he found its attitude 'excusable because it defended old privileges'.[61] For him the defeat of Imperial Germany was the result of a faulty political system under the Kaiser, and of an *haute bourgeoisie* too willing to accept and tolerate this system.

Rathenau believed that his success in life justified his reformist stance. As his economic success was inevitably linked to the existing socio-economic order, any radical changes might have endangered the prosperity of his businesses. Reforms were in the same range of aims as gains in productivity. Therefore to ensure continuous success he wanted to open the selection process for political, administrative, and business careers. He was very keen

[59] J. C. G. Röhl (ed.), *Philipp Eulenburgs Politische Korrespondenz*, vol. 1, Boppard am Rhein 1976, p. 9.
[60] E. von Oldenburg-Januschau, *Erinnerungen*, Leipzig 1936, pp. 180–1.
[61] Richter, *Rathenau Schriften*, p. 247.

on the idea that the most able men should run industry and eventually the country as a whole. To make his elitism work he rejected the idea of a formal democracy and open decision-making. Rathenau had hoped to achieve some of his aims under the aegis of the Second Empire, ideally in co-operation with the traditional orders. However, before the war most conservatives had not felt sufficiently threatened to embrace reforms. Rathenau realized that the war would lead to fundamental changes in society and politics and thus he began gradually to lose his particular stance as a *Wilhelminist*. After the war had ended he stopped worshipping the gods of the pre-war era and adapted to the new circumstances without, however, identifying with the new political system.

CHAPTER 12

Structure and agency in Wilhelmine Germany: the history of the German Empire – past, present, and future

Volker R. Berghahn

Through his research and teaching, John Röhl has made a major contribution to our knowledge and understanding of the Wilhelmine period and his achievements are rightly being honoured with this collection of essays by his friends and students. However, the sixty-fifth birthday of an eminent scholar who has tilled the field of the history of the German Empire for some forty years, beginning with his Cambridge doctoral thesis and reaching its latest, though by no means final culmination point in 2001 with the publication of the second volume of his biography of Wilhelm II, covering the years 1888 to 1900, is also a good moment to take stock again of where we are in this field.[1]

This is the purpose of this chapter which, I hope, will also resolve a confusion that may have arisen in the minds of some readers with regard to its subtitle. To be sure, the history of Wilhelmine Germany *as history* does not have a present and future, only a past. But the history of that period *as historiography* does have a present and future. Even if historians do not like to look ahead, preferring to leave prediction to the social scientists, I will pluck up all my courage to offer at least a few speculations and hopes about where the field might be going, especially with respect to the decade before 1914 which will be at the centre of Röhl's volume III.

However, there is the constraint of a strict word limit. Space therefore will not allow me to trace the historiography of the Wilhelmine period from its end in 1918 through the first sixty or so years until 1980. Fortunately, this period has been well covered by other scholars. Thus we know quite a lot about what historians wrote about the German Empire during the Weimar

---

[1] John C. G. Röhl, *Germany without Bismarck*, London 1967; John C. G. Röhl, *Kaiser Wilhelm II.*, Munich 1989; John C. G. Röhl, *Wilhelm II. Die Jugend des Kaisers, 1859–1888*, Munich 1993; John C. G. Röhl, *Kaiser, Hof und Staat. Wilhelm II. und die deutsche Politik*, Munich 1995; John C. G. Röhl, *Wilhelm II. Der Aufbau der Persönlichen Monarchie, 1888–1900*, Munich 2001; John C. G. Röhl (ed.), *Der Ort Kaiser Wilhelms II. in der deutschen Geschichte*, Munich 1991; John C. G. Röhl and Nicolaus Sombart (eds.), *Kaiser Wilhelm II. New Interpretations*, Cambridge 1982.

Republic.[2] Considerable progress has recently also been made in analysing the historical profession and its writings during the Third Reich and the early post-war years.[3] Nor is there any need for me to retrace the Fischer Debate of the 1960s and 1970s that also shaped John Röhl's scholarship so profoundly.[4] Instead I propose to undertake a twenty-year retrospective by going back to a long two-part review article which Richard Evans published in *The Historical Journal* in 1983 under the intriguing title 'From Hitler To Bismarck: "Third Reich" and Kaiserreich in Recent Historiography'.[5]

Having critically evaluated a total of nineteen books, some generously and others more severely, the author ultimately tries to draw a balance sheet and arrives at three conclusions:

1. The biographical approach has, he believes, 'reached the limits of its usefulness', at least in 'its present form'. Taking as an example Margaret Anderson's biography of Windhorst, the questions to which she addressed herself, he continued, 'might arguably have been better answered by focusing more sharply' on the context 'than on the life of one individual'. In other words, according to Evans she should have written 'a monograph on the Catholic Centre Party'. In his view, 'more traditional "Great Man" biographies have little to offer'. Singling out the weaknesses of recent biographies of Hitler and having knocked psychohistory particularly hard, Evans feels that the points he has made with respect to Anderson are no less 'relevant to an understanding of Kaiser Wilhelm'. Indeed, 'if biography is to have a future, it needs to incorporate not an historiographically unattainable psychoanalytic understanding, but a sociological or anthropological concept of the individual'.

2. The 'structuralist' approach, Evans asserts, is 'also coming up against the limits of its explanatory power'. Well aware of how much this kind of criticism had already rattled the 'structuralists' when it was first advanced in his *Society and Politics in Wilhelmine Germany* and later in even more pointed form in *Mythen deutscher Geschichtsschreibung*, written by his friends Geoff Eley and David Blackbourn, he does not omit to mention that much of the work conceived in a structuralist vein is 'undoubtedly of

---

[2] See e.g. Wolfgang Jäger, *Historische Forschung und politische Kultur*, Göttingen, 1984; Ulrich Heinemann, *Die verdrängte Niederlage*, Göttingen 1983.

[3] See e.g. Winfried Schulze and Otto G. Oexle (eds.), *Deutsche Historiker im Nationalsozialismus*, Frankfurt 1999; Ernst Schulin (ed.), *Deutsche Geschichtswissenschaft nach den Zweiten Weltkrieg*, Munich 1989; Stefan Berger, *The Search for Normality*, New York 1997.

[4] See e.g. John W. Langdon, *July 1914: The Long Debate*, New York, 1991; Annika Mombauer, *The Origins of the First World War. Controversies and Consensus*, London 2002.

[5] Richard J. Evans, 'From Hitler to Bismarck: 'Third Reich" and Kaiserreich in Recent Historiography: Part I', *Historical Journal*, 26, 2 (1983), pp. 485–97; Richard J. Evans, 'Part II', *Historical Journal*, 26, 4 (1983), pp. 999–1020. The following quotations are from his conclusions in Part II, pp. 1018ff.

the highest quality'.[6] In dispensing this praise, he must have thought of the sharp pen of the fearful Hans-Ulrich Wehler and his colleagues in Bielefeld. And yet he insists that 'Marxist and neo-Marxist approaches (particularly of a Gramscian rather than an Althusserian variety)', as espoused, for example, by Tim Mason and Eley, 'clearly have much more value and originality to offer'.[7] Nor, in light of this verdict, can he resist adding the rhetorical question of 'how far can the study of decision-making processes, of bureaucratic instances, legislative chambers, government ministers, economic and ideological pressure groups and political parties take us towards an understanding of the major questions of modern German history?' Even studies 'like Eley's, which make reference to local and regional socio-economic structures, suffer from the lack of available research monographs in this area'.

3. This leads Evans to his preferred approach: a local and regional history that is not antiquarian and moves away from 'mainstream history' with its 'unmistakably centralising tendency, even to the extent of ignoring most of Germany other than Prussia'. Evans thus arrives at the very happy conclusion that 'historians are now beginning to be aware that the regional and local diversity of German society holds the key to a number of important general questions about the development of modern Germany'. By this he means 'more than simply saying that things were more complicated than was previously supposed, or that there were regional variations on national themes'. Germany, he reminds us, 'was politically united only late in the day, and German society remained highly localized throughout the nineteenth century'. No less importantly, 'the development of the German economy was uneven, and political groupings such as the liberals had their roots above all in local social structures'. All in all therefore, 'the meaning and role of politics in everyday life and its relations to economic and social structures can really only be studied at a local and regional level, where the evidence is sufficiently thickly textured to facilitate a thorough exploration of these problems'.

Looking at these statements some twenty years later, there can be little doubt that Evans's 1983 predictions have been accurate. Although biographies and structural analyses did not disappear, the great expansion in the field of German history occurred in the areas that he so explicitly favoured in

---

[6] Richard J. Evans (ed.), *Society and Politics in Wilhelmine Germany*, London 1978; Geoff Eley and David Blackbourn, *Mythen deutscher Geschichtsschreibung*, Frankfurt, 1980, subsequently also in English as *The Peculiarities of German History*, Oxford 1984.

[7] Tim Mason, *Social Policy in the Third Reich*, Oxford 1993; Tim Mason, *Nazism, Fascism, and the Working Class*, New York 1995.

his review article. This is particularly true of scholarship on the Wilhelmine period. A younger generation – perhaps because it saw a chance to escape from the alleged 'orthodoxies' of the 'Bielefelders' – shifted its research interests very firmly away from the 'Prussian' centre toward the peripheries of the German Empire. Grass-roots history and 'thick description' inspired by anthropology became *en vogue*.[8]

The fruits of some twenty years of this type of work in the Wilhelmine field have been impressive, even if we cannot possibly discuss or mention the many publications in all the proliferating new genres of historical writing.[9] It is also important to emphasize that the new work developed not just in opposition to the structuralist 'orthodoxies' of the 1970s that Evans was so keen to leave behind. Notwithstanding the occasional claims that something quite different had been developed, there was research that expanded and built on earlier work rather than refuting it. A good example of this evolutionary development would seem to be the *Bürgertumsforschung* project that Jürgen Kocka and others developed in Bielefeld.[10] This project may originally still have been conceived in more 'orthodox' terms, but it changed over time and did so because the contributions of scholars who came from other disciplines and had worked on the middle classes in other European societies were taken on board. Perhaps the most intriguing and remarkable case in point is how gender history came to be integrated into this ambitious comparative project. Initially unconvinced, the project leaders were slowly won over to the view that this was an important and indeed crucial aspect of their entire enterprise.

Since then women's and later gender history did become a major field of historical writing on the evolution of the German Empire.[11] If the initial quest was to make women visible as historical subjects in the first place and thereby to give a voice to one half of the population that previous generations of historians had ignored, the emergence of gender history has raised further major questions of the kind that Evans proposed to focus on. Accordingly we certainly know more today on how different regions of

---

[8] See e.g. the long review article by Thomas Kühne, 'Das Deutsche Kaiserreich, 1871–1918, und seine politische Kultur: Demokratisierung, Segmentierung, Militarisierung', *Neue Politische Literatur*, 2 (1998), pp. 206–63.

[9] For a good survey see e.g. James Retallack, *Germany in the Age of Kaiser Wilhelm II*, New York 1996.

[10] Jürgen Kocka (ed.), *Bürger und Bürgerlichkeit im 19. Jahrhundert. Deutschland im europäischen Vergleich*, 3 vols., Munich 1988.

[11] See e.g. Ute Frevert, *Women in German History*, Oxford 1989; Jean H. Quataert, 'Writing the History of Women and Gender in Imperial Germany', in Geoff Eley (ed.), *Society, Culture, and the State in Germany, 1870–1930*, Ann Arbor 1996, pp. 43–65.

Germany 'ticked' at grass-roots level, be it in the villages of Upper Bavaria or in the workers' colonies in the Ruhr mining districts.[12]

Another example showing that the new directions in historical writing on the Wilhelmine Empire did not merely arise in opposition to the structuralists is the effective undermining of the feudalization thesis, as undertaken by Dolores Augustine in her *Patricians and Parvenus*.[13] This book emerged from work on social mobility, originally done in macroscopic and primarily quantitative perspective by Hartmut Kaelble, her thesis supervisor. Other cases in point may be found in the research of British and American historians in the field of regional and local history.

Some publications, it is true, were written in an explicitly contrarian vein. In the Federal Republic *Alltagsgeschichte*, as advocated by a group of then younger historians at the Göttingen Max-Planck-Institut für Geschichte, while stimulating fresh research on a social and socio-cultural history that was deliberately decentred, had little appeal to the Bielefelders.[14] In the United States it was prominently Blackbourn, one of the original critics of the structuralists, who led the way into the study of popular piety and of *Marpingen* in a remote part of South-West Germany.[15]

There was also the discovery of *Heimat* and the important work that this concept has spawned.[16] Mention must finally be made of the research done by James Retallack in Canada and a cluster of scholars in Germany devoted to the history of Saxony as a possible 'third Germany', next to the Prussian and southern German one at the centre of the work by Blackbourn and others.[17] Consequently, there is now a large body of research on the non-Prussian parts of Germany of the kind that Evans had encouraged some two decades ago, and whatever gaps may be left are quickly being filled by doctoral dissertations and monographs produced on both sides of the Atlantic.

And yet, looking back over the period since Evans's review article, the question must be asked how accurate he was when he argued that biography

[12] Martin Broszat, Elke Fröhlich, and Falk Wiesemann, *Bayern in der NS-Zeit*, 4 vols., Munich 1977–83; Franz J. Brüggemeier and Lutz Niethammer, 'Lodgers, Schnapps-Casinos and Working-Class Colonies in a Heavy-Industrial Region', in Georg G. Iggers (ed.), *The Social History of Politics*, Leamington Spa 1985, pp. 217–58.
[13] Dolores L. Augustine, *Patricians and Parvenus. Wealth and High Society in Wilhelmine Germany*, Oxford 1994.
[14] See Alf Lüdtke, *Alltagsgeschichte*, Frankfurt 1989.
[15] David Blackbourn, *Marpingen*, New York 1994.
[16] Celia Applegate, *A Nation of Provincials. The German Idea of Heimat*, Berkeley 1990; Alon Confino, *The Nation as a Local Metaphor*, Chapel Hill 1997.
[17] See e.g. James Retallack (ed.), *Saxony in Germany History*, Ann Arbor 2000; David Blackbourn, *Class, Religion, and Local Politics in Wilhelmine Germany*, New Haven 1980.

and structuralism had had their day and that the hour of socio-cultural and regional history had come. At the root of the debates that he and others triggered when they criticized received interpretations of the German Empire was another 'rebellion' against the structuralists. It was the quest to reclaim human agency and to reintroduce the role of the subject into historiography against various varieties of determinism. Seen in this light, it is first of all no accident that 'Marxists and neo-Marxists' (Evans) should engage in this debate that had divided them since the days of the first appearance of the *Communist Manifesto*. This key document had left open the question whether a deterministic structuralism or agency had pride of place in the Marxian vision of history. After all, the first part of the *Manifesto* presented a condensed version of the unfolding of the allegedly scientific laws of history as it passed from feudalism to capitalism and ultimately to communism. The second part then contains an account of the world-historical and activist role that the proletariat is to play in moving the historical process toward the final stage of a classless society.[18]

Marx having left this tension unresolved, the issue gave ample scope for vigorous disputes among his followers after his death in 1883. Thus the debate between Rosa Luxemburg and Karl Kautsky generated plenty of heat before 1914 in the German Social Democratic Party.[19] It re-emerged in the internal ideological struggles within Bolshevik Russia. After 1945 it reappeared most prominently in the arguments between cultural Marxists in Britain and the unrepentant structuralism of Marxists on the European Continent, particularly in France and West Germany.

On the British side, Edward Thompson was possibly the most influential advocate of a position that insisted on the centrality of human agency. This position is encapsulated in his title of his book *The Making of the English Working Class* that he believed best reflected the notion that his was 'a study in an active process that owes as much to agency as to conditioning'.[20] For 'the working class did not rise like the sun at an appointed time. It was present at its own making.' And further: 'I do not see class as a "structure", nor even as a "category", but as something which in fact happens (and can be shown to have happened) in human relationships.'

Like their predecessors, Thompson and his followers subsequently became embroiled in a controversy with fellow-Marxists writing in a

---

[18] Karl Marx and Friedrich Engels, *Manifesto of the Communist Party*, Moscow n.d. The crucial sentence (ibid., p. 53) reads: 'But not only has the bourgeoisie forged the weapons that bring death to itself; it has also called into existence the men who are to wield those weapons – the modern working class – the proletarians.'

[19] See e.g. Erich Matthias, *Kautsky und der Kautskyanismus*, Tübingen 1957.

[20] Edward P. Thompson, *The Making of the English Working Class*, London 1968, p. 9.

Continental-European philosophical mode and in particular with Louis Althusser whom, in his review article, Evans had juxtaposed to the cultural Marxism of Antonio Gramsci.[21] However, the problem of agency versus structure also preoccupied non-Marxist scholars and conservative social thinkers, as they grappled with the manifest forces of mass politics, modern bureaucracy, and the role of technology in advanced industrial societies. Weberians as well as *Annalistes* started off as structuralists, but in the long run they, too, did not escape the magnetic force of a culturalism that insisted on the relevance of the human subject in History.[22]

It is probably fair to say that in Britain the Thompsonites won out among historians at an early stage. Thenceforth, *The Making of the English Working Class* unleashed a wave of epigonic research that aimed to retrieve and demonstrate more unambiguously than Thompson had done the agency of the working class. Soon larger numbers of young historians, in the wake of the expansion of the British system of higher education in the 1960s and 1970s, were beginning to leave their mark in Europe and the United States upon the 'new labour history'. In due course this work, as the most fashionable genre of historical writing, turned from the activities of organized labour to the daily-life experiences and perceptions of 'ordinary' workers.

This trend that became more and more microscopic and local was accelerated when women's history made its appearance, soon to be expanded by questions of gender history. What moved into the centre of interest were the experiences of 'ordinary' women, first at their places of work and eventually also of their activities inside and outside the home and their families. A renewed interest in popular culture, first of the working class, which soon proliferated to the study of the lives of other social groups – peasants, land labourers, artisans, shopkeepers – complemented and completed the turn to a new socio-cultural history. It was a historiography that Thompson had initiated – if not exclusively, certainly importantly – through his quest to overcome the 'enormous condescension of posterity' shown by previous generations of historians toward the lower classes and those who did not have a voice in history. The task was to examine their lives, their perceptions of the world, their *Eigen-Sinn*.[23]

Considering that the basic assumption underlying all this rich research was that all these groups had had agency and that it was time for the

[21] See e.g. Edward P. Thompson, *The Poverty of Theory*, London 1978; James Joll, *Gramsci*, London 1976.
[22] Most striking if Fernand Braudel's work is compared with that of Alain Corbin.
[23] Alf Lüdtke, *Eigen-Sinn. Fabrikalltag, Arbeitererfahrungen und Politik vom Kaiserreich bis zum Faschismus*, Hamburg 1993.

historian to stop seeing them merely as passive objects and victims of an overwhelming capitalist system and its powerful and highly organized structures, Thompson offered an approach that also appealed to many liberal historians. Unlike the Marxists and neo-Marxists of the time, they remained, it is true, unconvinced that societies required radical and, indeed, revolutionary collective action on the part of 'the wretched of this earth'.[24] Instead they advocated gradual reformist change that avoided revolution. Still, for our purposes, the crucial point is that non-Marxists, like the Thompsonites, started from a sense that groups and even individuals still mattered.

If the structures of the modern world had put humankind into an 'iron cage of serfdom',[25] with no hope of changing the predicament of the millions, the time had come to counter the allegedly inexorable bureaucratizing trend through action at the grass-roots level. The erstwhile despair in the face of the modern world that had haunted Max Weber began to fade. The subject returned and one studied his/her activities as responsible and concerned members of a civil society. Thus, liberal economic historians advocated, if not the reassertion of the entrepreneurial individual *vis-à-vis* the powerful encasing structures of the modern welfare state, the significance of pluralistic or liberal-corporatist coalition, conflict, and eventual consensus. Meanwhile their counterparts who were interested in society and politics searched for the conditions under which free citizens and their elected representatives had forged solutions to local, national, and international problems in opposition to anonymous bureaucracies that were simply grinding on, embodying a 'rationality without reason'.[26]

I hope that, however brief this exposition has been, sufficient evidence and argument have been provided of what I would see as the larger trends and at times unspoken assumptions about the world in the social sciences in general and historical writing in particular. And this is also the context in which the arguments presented in Evans's article must be seen. If his review was primarily an attack on structuralism, his advocacy of the local and regional was, on closer inspection, a plea to retrieve the agency of the 'common people' in contradistinction to the view that the evolution of modern history is best understood in terms of socio-economic and political structures, of the *forces profondes* that were so central to the work of other scholars, Marxist as well as non-Marxist.

---

[24] Frantz Fanon, *The Wretched of the Earth*, New York 1963.
[25] See e.g. Wolfgang J. Mommsen, *The Age of Bureaucracy*, Oxford 1974.
[26] Term by C. Wright Mills. See also Robert Dahl, *Pluralist Democracy in the United States*, Chicago 1967.

How are these broader currents in historical writing in the past four decades or so related to today's historiography on Wilhelmine Germany? The first point to emerge from this analysis is that much of the local and regional history that Evans had encouraged in 1983 is in fact devoted to establishing agency at the periphery of the Kaiserreich against the view from Berlin and its centralizing bureaucracies. Much of the work on *Heimat* and on many other topics that deliberately decentred historical questions (some of which have been mentioned above) revolved around this basic theme.

However, partly because historians of Germany took the path that Thompson had mapped out relatively late, they were able to avoid a trap that much of British social and working-class history fell into: by concentrating on the agency and socio-cultural activities, experiences, and mentalities of ever smaller groups; by writing – to take a made-up example – about pub-life in a Yorkshire mining village, their writings became not only decentred, but also 'depoliticized' in the sense that questions of power moved out of focus. The fact that this mining village was still part of a larger political complex and that power and class relations were important frequently eluded researchers, the more so since many of them were trained in a firmly empirical tradition. Taking on board this criticism, advanced by Geoff Eley and others, historians of the Wilhelmine period remained acutely conscious of the power-political dimensions of their topics. For most of them the periphery was not isolated from the centre; central state-bureaucratic structures and agency at the local level could not be compartmentalized. David Blackbourn's *Marpingen*, however caringly it describes village life and popular piety, nevertheless upholds this crucial point.

Margaret Anderson's *Practicing Democracy* is a more recent example, a fine analysis of the interrelationship and interaction between authoritarian political structures and the agency of voters protesting electoral abuse at the grass-roots level.[27] Even if her counterfactuals at the end of the book may be slightly far-fetched, she provides plenty of evidence for this constant interaction. The deeper underlying problem is, of course, one of the imbalance of sources. Central records tend to be plentiful; evidence on the actions and views of 'ordinary people' is still much more difficult to come by. Sources not generated at the time but based on memory pose other methodological obstacles. One way out of this dilemma in recent years has been to rely on a discourse analysis of relevant journals and newspapers. Yet, however careful this analysis of the contemporary voices of intellectuals

---

[27] Margaret L. Anderson, *Practicing Democracy*, Princeton 2000.

and writers (many of whom did not even come from the region concerned) may be, it was prone to suffer from one unfortunate weakness: it was never clear or certain how much these discourses actually related to and reflected the lives and opinions of those whom the historian claimed these writers spoke for. Consequently, it has remained one of the great challenges of this type of historical writing to demonstrate a link between ideas and ideologies that they analyse and the reader at whom they were aimed.

Put differently, the research agenda that Evans outlined some twenty years ago as the most promising one of the future may have succeeded in undermining the predominance of the structuralists and in refocusing scholarly attention upon the question of agency in history. But the focus has been on the actions of collectives whose agency has frequently remained intangible.

It is at this point that we come back to John Röhl's *Lebenswerk*. He began to write about Wilhelm II when the structuralists ruled the field of Wilhelmine history. They did not react kindly to his central quest, that is, to establish the agency, not of some larger collective, but of an individual and of a small and clearly identifiable clique around the monarch. The charge was that he had lapsed into a 'personalistischer Forschungsansatè' (Dirk Stegmann), a charge that, I am sure, still rings in his ears. However, the criticisms of Evans and Eley were no kinder. Two years after Evans's article, the latter followed suit with a review of Röhl's edition of the Eulenburg Correspondence in which he doubted the centrality of Wilhelm II as the director of policy in the late 1890s and beyond.[28] He thought that Röhl's 'exaggerated enthusiasm' for 'the importance of personalities and the ramifications of sexual scandals in the entourage' was 'somewhat misplaced. Symptomatically this can tell us much about the official culture and dominant morality of the period. But its political relevance is anything but clear.' In the end, Eley continued, it would be better to 'abandon the chimera of personal rule and concentrate more systematically on the broader ideological front – on representations of the *Kaiser* and of *Kaisertum* in the official ideologies and popular cultures of the time'.

Eley did not change his mind. Only last year the Michigan historian spoke of Röhl's 'gargantuan Young Wilhelm', the first volume of his biography of the *Kaiser*, published in 1993.[29] The tome was followed seven years later by another 1,400-page volume, dealing with the first twelve years of Wilhelm II's rule and selling some 7,000 copies in the first two months.

---

[28] Geoff Eley, 'The View from the Throne: The Personal Rule of Kaiser Wilhelm II', *Historical Journal*, 28, 2 (1985), p. 485.

[29] See his review in *German History*, 20, 2 (2002), p. 251.

More importantly, the author has never wavered from his key argument that his study was about a man who very clearly had agency and who therefore decisively influenced the course of German history, indeed world history. It may be that Röhl felt compelled to make that point over so many pages because he was beleaguered by both structuralists and his younger British-American colleagues. As he put it in volume II: 'The last Kaiser, the Right and the Left maintained, was a mere shadow emperor, too impulsive to be able to intervene effectively into policy-making, too ridiculous to be taken seriously by historians.'[30] 'For many years', he added, 'I was virtually on my own with my views on the constitutional realities of the monarchy that Bismarck had created . . . and on the outstanding decision-making powers of Wilhelm II.' True, some English-language studies had come to similar conclusions. Yet 'a general revision of the historical image of that era that ought to have followed from those insights never happened'.

However, there is a shift in this volume that indicates that this solitary fighter has not been impervious to more than two decades of criticism. In his Preface, he sets out to examine 'the construction of the personal power position of Emperor Wilhelm II within the monarchical-militaristic structures that were enshrined in the Bismarckian constitution of the Reich, and . . . to identify the consequences to be drawn from this'. He thinks it obvious that, given this set of questions, his book amounts to 'more than person history'. He believes that German policies would have taken a different turn, 'if the power struggle between the *Kaiser* and the leading statesmen that forms the main theme of this biography had had a different outcome'. Consequently, his study 'is not just about Wilhelm II, but also about who controlled the German state apparatus in the heart of Europe and how the broad lines of domestic and foreign policy were determined'. At the centre of his book, he concludes, 'are the survival chances of the monarchical constitutional form in the twentieth century' and there is also the question of 'the continuity, resp. inexorability of German history in its evolution from the founding of the Reich to the Third Reich'.

Now, with Röhl using his archival sources to the full, it may not be entirely easy for the reader, overwhelmed by the biography's richness, to discover this line of argument in the chapters that follow the Preface. But on closer inspection there are two temporal phases that structure his book. The first phase, running from 1889 to 1896, traces the Kaiser's gradual and by no means inevitable 'taking [of] the reins of power'.[31] It was a struggle

---

[30] John C. G. Röhl, *Wilhelm II. Der Aufbau der Persönlichen Monarchie, 1888–1900*, Munich 2001, pp. 16f., also for the following citations.
[31] Ibid., p. 17.

in which there were – as the author notes – many warning voices against the reintroduction 'of a half-absolutist personal monarchy in a federalized empire in the age of industrialized mass society with its unrestricted freedom of thought and publicity'. Some opponents even thought of forcing the monarch to abdicate. But he stayed in power at the head of a government machinery that was now effectively run by trusted advisors who agreed with the monarch's political ambitions.

The second phase began in mid-1896 'when the dramatic power struggle behind the scenes was virtually over'. Thereafter, the Kaiser's decision-making powers in domestic and foreign policy were 'at most still restricted by the two Berlin parliaments – the Reichstag and the Prussian Diet – whose influence in the field of diplomatic and military policy was in turn delimited by the Bismarckian Constitution'. In fact, both fields were the exclusive preserve of the monarch. Röhl marshals plenty of evidence in support of his two-phase model and it is therefore quite plausible that by 1900 Wilhelm II had succeeded in establishing a 'Personal Monarchy'.

The crucial question is how his analysis will proceed from the turn of the century in the next volume. At the end of volume II the author gives a few hints about the thrust of the third volume, but then, instead of elaborating them, ends, somewhat surprisingly, with a description of the Kaiser's probable mental illness and of a hereditary disease, porphyria, which, he believes, afflicted the monarch. Other passages speak of the monarch's mental illness and his 'weak nerves'.

It is worth relating Röhl's work to that of other scholars who have introduced the question of the group subject and of agency into the debate on the basic character and the evolution of the Wilhelmine Empire prior to the First World War. It appears that they have gone too far when they treat the years 1900 to 1914 as a unit, juxtaposed to the 1890s. It may be more fruitful to divide this period into two phases. The first phase saw the disintegration of the position that Wilhelm had built up by 1900. This process reached its nadir by 1906–7 and is reflected in the repeated breakdowns of the monarch. However, what followed in the next seven years up to 1914 was not a 'polycratic, but uncoordinated authoritarianism'.[32] Rather it was in this period that various, by then highly organized, socio-political forces that had slowly filled the parliamentary and extra-parliamentary space began to block one another, producing general political paralysis. These forces all moved rather frantically in this space, trying to assert their own group as a subject of history without, however, being able to gain the edge over their

---

[32] Thus Hans-Ulrich Wehler, *The German Empire, 1871–1918*, Leamington Spa 1985, p. 62.

competitors. In other words, just as Wilhelm II had become paralysed as an individual actor, the group subjects suffered a similar fate.[33]

In pointing to this demise, I do not wish to stop research on, for example, the power of the big cities and their mayors in shaping local affairs. Nor do I want to discard investigations of *Heimat*. But I do postulate that no single local or regional power, however articulated and organized it may have been, was able to assert itself durably at the national level. By the end of the second phase in 1914, this self-blockage of the political parties and extra-parliamentary interest groups was virtually total. It was into this situation that – as Isabel Hull has shown – the *maison militaire* increasingly inserted itself, seizing the reins of power from the monarch in the only sphere in which the Constitution gave him a supreme privilege, that is, to conduct the foreign policy of the Reich and to decide whether to stay at peace or to go to war.[34]

If Röhl's third volume takes up and integrates the three themes of the dissolution of monarchical power, increasingly paralysed peripheral power, and the rise of the military, he will have an analytical framework that does not ignore the weight of structures and is able to handle both collective and individual agency. The task is to explain why German society ended up, not in the Third Reich, but in a catastrophic First World War. Twenty years after Evans rejected structuralism and biography in favour of the study of the group subject and its agency, the time may have come to reintegrate his own perspectives with the other two and to focus on the most crucial period of Wilhelmine history, that is, the years 1907 to 1914. It is a period about which we continue to know much less than about the 1890s. If approached from the angle of structure and agency, as outlined in this chapter, we are likely to come closer to an understanding of why Germany unleashed a catastrophic war in 1914.

---

[33] Gustav Schmidt, 'Innenpolitische Blockbildungen in Deutschland am Vorabend des Ersten Weltkrieges', *Das Parlament (Beilage)*, 13 May 1972, pp. 2ff.
[34] Isabel V. Hull, *The Entourage of Kaiser Wilhelm II, 1888–1918*, New York 1982.

Index

Wilhelm II has not been included in this index.